INDIA IN BONDAGE

INDIA IN BONDAGE

HER RIGHT TO FREEDOM

By

JABEZ T. SUNDERLAND, M.A., D.D.

GYAN

Published by

Gyan Publishing House
5, Ansari Road
Daryaganj, New Delhi-110002
Phone: 011-47034999, 9811692060
E-mail: books@gyanbooks.com

Distribution Network
gyanbooks.com
India, USA, Canada, UK, Australia, France

ISBN : 978-81-212-6761-8 (PB)
First Published, 1928

2nd Impression 2022

Printed at: Gyan Press, Delhi.

INDIA IN BONDAGE HER RIGHT TO FREEDOM
Author: JABEZ T. SUNDERLAND

INDIA IN BONDAGE

HER RIGHT TO FREEDOM

BY

JABEZ T. SUNDERLAND, M.A., D.D.

Former President of the India Information Bureau of America and Editor of "Young India" (New York). Twice Special Commissioner and Lecturer to India. Author of "India, America and World Brotherhood," "Causes of Famine in India," "Rising Japan," etc., etc.

"No nation is good enough to rule another nation."

---ABRAHAM LINCOLN.

1928.

DEDICATION

This Book is affectionately dedicated to two persons, very dear to me, who were deeply interested in India.

One, my beloved **Sister, Harriet Sunderland Clough,** who for many years was a Teacher and Missionary in India, and who at her death was loved and mourned by hundreds whom she had taught and to whom she had ministered.

The other, my beloved **Daughter, Florence Sunderland,** who travelled with me widely in India, who had many dear friends there, and whose earnest desire for India's Freedom has been a constant inspiration to me in writing these chapters.

"He who ruleth high and wise,
Nor falters in his plan,
Will take the stars out of the skies
Ere Freedom out of Man."

—EMERSON.

CONTENTS

THE ARGUMENT OF THE BOOK

The central contentions of the following pages are:

1. That no nation has a right to rule another; therefore Great Britain has no right to rule India.

2. That British rule in India is unjust, tyrannical and highly evil in its effects on the Indian people (as that of any foreign Government must be).

3. That for a great civilized nation, anywhere in the world, to be held in forced bondage by another nation, as India is held in forced bondage by Britain, is a crime against humanity and a menace to the world's freedom and peace, and therefore should be condemned by all nations.

4. That the Indian people, who ruled themselves for 3,000 years, making their nation one of the greatest and most influential in the world, are abundantly competent to rule themselves to-day.

5. That if in any respect they are incompetent to rule themselves now, the British are responsible,—it is the result of Britain's crime of conquering them and holding them in bondage; therefore the remedy is the cessation of the bondage and their restoration to freedom.

6. That the Indian people can rule themselves far better than the British (or any other transient foreigners) can; and for the following four reasons:

(1) The Indian people are the equals in natural intellectual ability and in moral character of the British or any European nation.

(2) They are possessors of a civilization and of a culture far older and in some respects higher

than that of Great Britain or any other Western nation.

(3) India is the own country of the Indian people, in which they have always lived, therefore their knowledge of India—its civilizations, its institutions, and its needs—is incomparably greater than that possessed by the British or any other foreign transients; which means that they can rule India with vastly greater intelligence than the British or any other foreigners can possibly do it.

(4) The fact that India is the own country of the Indian people makes it inevitable that, if they ruled the country, they would do it primarily in the interest of India, primarily for the benefit of India, as every country in the world ought to be ruled in the interest of its own people and not that of foreigners; whereas, the British, because they are foreign and their interests are foreign, in the very nature of things have always ruled India, are ruling it to-day, and so long as they hold it in forced bondage always must rule it, primarily for the benefit, not of India, but of their own foreign nation, Great Britain; which has always been, and as long as it lasts must continue to be, an unparalleled wrong and disaster to the Indian people.

The grounds for these contentions are stated in the following pages.

FOREWORD

In this Twentieth Century after Christ, ought any nation in the world to be held in subjection by foreign bayonets? Then ought great historic India to be so held?

Just what is India?

Is it a nation of barbarians, or semi-barbarians, as many seem to think? Is it a nation of little importance? Has it ever been anything or done anything of sufficient interest to mankind so that anybody need care whether it is free or slave? Let us see.

India is the second largest nation in the world, containing a population of three hundred and twenty millions, more than one-sixth of the entire human race.

India is the oldest nation in the world, going back for its origin more than three thousand years.

India is a highly civilized nation,—a nation which developed a high culture much earlier than any nation of Europe, and has never lost it.

India is a nation a large part of whose people are Aryans, that is, belong to the same great race with the Greeks, the Romans, the Germans, the English and ourselves.

India contributed enormously to the advancement of civilization by giving to the world its immensely important decimal system, or so-called Arabic notation, which is the foundation of modern mathematics and much modern science.

India early created the beginnings of nearly all of the sciences, some of which she carried forward to remarkable degrees of developments, thus leading the world. To-day, notwithstanding her subject condition, she possesses scientists of eminence.

India has created, and to-day possesses, architecture equal to the finest produced by Greece,—as witness the Pearl Mosque, the Kutab Minar and the Royal Palace of Delhi and the Taj Mahal of Agra, the Jain Temples at Abu, the rock-cut Temples at Ellora, the Palace at Deeg in Rajputana, the Great Vishnu Temple at Srirangam and the great Pagoda at Tanjore.

If we may credit the judgment of Mr. H. G. Wells, India has given the world two of its six greatest men of all time—Buddha and the Emperor Asoka the Great. If we may trust the judgment widely held in America and Europe, the two most eminent men in the world to-day, the two men most widely known and honored among all civilized nations at the present time, are sons of India, namely, Rabindranath Tagore and "Mahatma" Gandhi.

India has produced great literature, great arts, great philosophical systems, great religions, and great men in every department of life,—rulers, statesmen, financiers, scholars, poets, generals, colonizers, ship-builders, skilled artisans, and craftsmen of every kind, agriculturists, industrial organizers and leaders in far-reaching trade and commerce by land and sea.

For 2,500 years India has been pre-eminently the intellectual and spiritual teacher of Asia, which means of half the human race.

For 2,500 years before the British came on the scene and robbed her of her freedom, India was self-ruling, and one of the most influential and illustrious nations of the world.

Such a nation is India. Should such a nation

be held in bondage by the sword of foreigners? Has not such a nation a right to liberty, to self-government, to a place among the great nations of mankind?

I very much desire not to be misunderstood as to my motive in writing this book. Let no one say, or for a moment believe, that the book means enmity to Great Britain. It means nothing of the kind, any more than pleas for freedom of the slave in the old days of American slavery meant enmity to the American nation which permitted slavery. I speak very plainly; but in everything I endeavor to be candid and fair, and to treat with respect and courtesy those who hold views different from my own. I say some things which sympathizers with British rule in India will doubtless deem severe, and perhaps even resent. But I do not think them severe in any other sense than that in which a surgeon is severe who probes a wound with a view to its cure. I am in no sense whatever England's foe or ill-wisher. What I advocate for India I believe to be for England's good as well as for India's. I want no wrong done to England, in connection with India or anywhere else. But I also want England to do no wrong to India, or through India to the world.

I would like also to make clear, at the outset, that I am far from condemning all Englishmen, or Englishmen indiscriminately, on account of England's great wrong of holding India in bondage. While I believe that many Englishmen are seriously blameworthy, I gladly recognise that many are not.

The plain fact is, there are two Englands, just as there are two Americas. One of the Englands—that which I like to think of as the *true* one—believes in justice and freedom, not only at home but everywhere else. This is the England of Magna Charta; of Milton and Pym and Hampden; of

Pitt and Fox and Burke in 1776 when they demanded justice for the American Colonies; of Burke and Sheridan in connection with the trial of Warren Hastings, when they demanded justice for India; the England that abolished its slave trade in 1807 and slavery in all British dominions in 1833; the England of the Reform Bills; the England of such friends of India as Cobden and Bright, Lord Ripon, Mary Carpenter, Professor Fawcett, Charles Bradlaugh, A. O. Hume, Sir William Wedderburn, Sir Henry Cotton, and many others in the past; and many to-day, both inside and outside of Parliament (and particularly the Labor Party).

This England I honor and love. This is the England that the world honors, and that has made the name of Britain great. If this England had been in power, India would never have been conquered and reduced to bondage; but would have been dealt with justly, befriended, and helped to rise in freedom to an influential place in the world like that of Japan. I have written every word of this book in earnest sympathy with what I believe the principles of this true and nobler England.

There is much reason to believe that this England, if in power to-day, by offering to the Indian people promptly, generously, courageously, honestly, in absolute good faith, freedom and self-government under "Dominion Status" like that of Canada and Australia, could retain India as a contented (and, of course, immensely important) member of the British Empire.

Unfortunately, there is another England. Unwilling as one may be to confess it, or to have it so, there is an England whose ideals and political principles are almost the exact opposite of those just described. It is the England which fought against Magna Charta ; which refused to give justice and freedom to the American Colonies in 1776 ; which has constantly allied itself with militarism and imperialism ; which fought two wars to force opium on China ; which long held Ireland in bondage ; which opposed all efforts to abolish the slave trade and slavery ; which has opposed practically all political and social reforms in England, and which to-day, while giving profuse promises to India of pots of gold at the end of a rainbow, thrusts into prison without trial Indian leaders who agitate for freedom, and gives no assurance of any real intention of ever loosening its iron grip upon what King George calls "My Indian Empire."

This England I do not love or honor. It is solely against this evil, and as I believe dangerous England, that any hostility or criticism found in the following pages is directed.

In my judgment, this England, unless held in check, will create irreparable hostility between the Indian people and Great Britain, and thus make India a smouldering volcano of unrest, certain in no distant day to burst into an eruption of the most dangerous possible character.

In other words, I believe that this imperialistic, might-makes-right England, if kept in power, will as certainly lose India to Britain, as the rising of the sun. The men at this England's head are the Lord Norths of our time, who are driving India to revolution, just as Lord North and George III in 1776 drove the American Colonies to Revolution. And India's revolution, if it comes, will be sympathized with by all Asia and by all intelligent lovers of liberty in the entire world. And there will be no possibility of its being put down. India will emerge a free, independent and great nation, wholly independent of Britain.

Something ought to be said here regarding my qualifications for writing about India. Have I sufficient knowledge of the subject to make my book worthy of the attention of intelligent readers? As a partial answer, I venture to submit the following personal statements.

I have been deeply interested in India during all my adult life. That interest began in my boyhood, as the result of reading and hearing much about Indian Missions and becoming acquainted with two returned missionaries. Early the dream took possession of my mind of becoming a missionary myself. This dream was constantly with me in college and theological seminary, and my studies, and reading were shaped largely with a view to a life in India. My sister, next in age to myself, went there as a missionary; so did my college-mate and dearest friend.

As for myself, my thought changed and I chose a different calling. But my deep interest in India did not wane and has never waned. For more than forty years I have been a constant student of India's great religions, her extensive literature, her philosophies, her remarkable art, her long history and, above all, her pressing and vital present-day social and political problems.

On account of my known long-time interest in Indian matters, in 1895-96 I was sent by the British National Unitarian Association on a special commission to India to study the religious, social, educational and other conditions of the Indian people, and make an extended report upon the same in London on my return. In 1913-14, I was sent again, on a similar commission, by the joint appointment of the British Unitarian Association and the American Unitarian Association.

In prosecuting the inquiries and performing the duties of those two commissions, I travelled in

India more than 13,000 miles, visiting missionaries, government officials, English business men and prominent Indians, speaking in nearly all the more important cities, and holding conferences with Indian leaders of all religious and political parties.

Nor were my investigations confined to cities. On the contrary, I took pains to prosecute my inquiries in many smaller towns and villages, spending weeks travelling on horseback from village to village in remote country places where no American had ever before been seen. By these means I was able, as few foreigners have been, to come into direct contact with all classes, and study India's problems from the side of the people themselves, as well as from the side of Great Britain, and thus find out first hand, the actual conditions existing in the land.

I was fortunate in being able to attend two annual sessions of the Indian National Congress, the Indian National Social Conference, and the All-India Theistic Conference,—speaking at the first two named, and speaking and presiding at the last; and, what was very important, forming acquaintances at these great gatherings with political leaders, leaders of social reform, and Brahmo and Arya Samaj and other Theistic leaders, from all parts of India.

While in India, I became deeply interested in the important periodical press which I found there—dailies, weeklies, and monthlies—some of which quite surprised me by their great excellence. These periodicals I read extensively during both my visits; and ever since returning home from my first visit in 1896, I have been a regular subscriber to, and reader of, never fewer than seven of these, published in Calcutta, Bombay, Madras, Poona, Lahore and Allahabad. Thus during all these years I have been able to keep in almost as close touch with the affairs of India as with those of my own country.

Nor has my reading about India been confined to these constantly arriving and important periodicals; there have been few books of importance upon Indian matters (particularly books dealing with political affairs and social questions) published in England, India or America within the past thirty years, that I have not imposed upon myself the duty, and given myself the pleasure, of reading.

And possibly most important of all, during the entire five years of the stay of Mr. Lajpat Rai in America (from 1914 to 1919), I had the privilege and honor of being intimately associated with that distinguished Indian leader in active work for India, reading the proofs of the three books written and published by him in this country, writing the extended "Foreword" of the first, and assisting him in other ways; and when he returned to India, becoming editor of the monthly, *Young India*, which he had established in New York.

In conclusion, it may not be out of place to add that I have lectured somewhat extensively in this country and Canada on India, its Religions, Art, Literature, Social Problems and Struggle for Self-Rule. Also I have written much for Indian periodicals; and two books from my pen have been published in India.

Rev. J. T. Sunderland

INDIA IN BONDAGE: HER RIGHT TO FREEDOM

CHAPTER I

A VISIT TO INDIA: WHAT BRITISH RULE MEANS

INTRODUCTORY

The impression is widespread in America that British rule in India has been, and is, a great and almost unqualified good. The British themselves never tire of "pointing with pride" to what they claim to have done and to be doing for the benefit of the Indian people. What knowledge we have in America regarding the matter, comes almost wholly from British sources, and hence the majority of us do not suspect that there is another side to the story. But the Indian people claim, very earnestly claim, that there is another side, which cannot fail to prove a disillusionment to all who learn the truth about it.

During the days of chattel-slavery in the Southern States of the American Union, so long as the world knew of slavery only through the representations of it given by the slave-holders, the impression was common that slavery was a beneficent institution. It was not until the slaves themselves began to find a voice and the "sacred institution" came to be described from the standpoint of the bondman, that its real character began to be understood.

I

What, in reality, does British rule in India mean,—not from the standpoint of the British Government, which gets such great political prestige from the holding of this vast Asiatic dependency; not as it is seen by the army of British officials in India who derive their living and their wealth from British economic domination there; but what does it mean as experienced by the 320 millions of Indian people, who are not barbarians or "half civilized" as many seem to suppose, but people who represent an ancient and high civilization, who as a nation have had a long and proud past, but who more than a century and a half ago were conquered by force of arms and by commercial and diplomatic duplicity, and have been held in subjection ever since by a foreign power?

Ever since Edmund Burke's famous impeachment of Warren Hastings for his misdeeds in India, there have not been wanting Englishmen, both in India and at home, who have seen and deplored, and to some extent pointed out, what they have believed very serious wrongs connected with the British rule of the Indian people. Naturally such utterances have been unpopular in England, and have been "hushed up" as much as possible. It has not been uncommon to denounce such plain speaking as unpatriotic and traitorous. However, free speech has not been wholly suppressed. A great body of testimony has been accumulated, both in England and India, showing that the results of foreign conquest and foreign rule in this instance have not been essentially different from results of such conquest and rule everywhere else. This or that foreign domination may be a little more or a little less intelligent here or cruel there, but in every case and in every country and age its essential nature is the same. It is founded on force and not on justice. Its result is certain to be deep and widespread injury to those robbed of their freedom and their rights, and in the end to those who do the robbing, as well. The rule of any people by the sword of a foreign conqueror is always a bitter thing to those who feel the sword's pitiless edge, whatever it may be to those who hold the hilt of the sword. But it is worse than bitter; it is demoralizing, degenerating, destructive to the character of those held in subjection. It tends to destroy their self-respect, their power of initiative, their power of self-direction, to create a slave-psychology and rob them of all hope and incentive in life. Injury of this kind is the deepest that can be inflicted upon humanity.

II

To understand fully the great problem confronting the people of India to-day, we must have clearly in mind the exact relation between India and England. India is a "dependency," not a colony. Great Britain has both colonies and dependencies, and many persons suppose them to be identical. But they are not necessarily so. Colonies may be self-ruling—six of those connected with the British Empire are, namely, Canada, Australia, New Zealand, South Africa, Newfoundland, and the Irish Free State. But other British colonies are not self-ruling. These are dependencies. As already said, India is a dependency.

As the result of a pretty wide acquaintance in England and a residence of some years in Canada, I am disposed to believe that nowhere in the world can be found governments that are more free, that more fully embody the intelligent will of their people, or that better serve their people's many-sided interests and wants, than those of the self-ruling colonies or "dominions" of Great Britain. I do not see but that these are in every essential way as free as if they were full republics. Probably they are not any more free than the people of the United States, but it is no exaggeration to say that they are essentially as free. The connection of most of them with England, their mother-country, is not one of coercion but of choice; it is one of reverence and affection. That the British Government assures such liberty in even a part of its colonies is a matter for congratulation and honorable pride. To this extent it stands on a moral elevation equal, if not superior, to that of any government in the world.

But turn now from Britain's free colonies to her dependencies. Here we find something for which there does not seem to be any natural place among British political institutions. Britons call their flag the flag of freedom. They speak of the British Constitution, largely unwritten though it is, as a constitution that guarantees freedom to every British subject in the world. *Magna Charta* meant self-government for the English people. Cromwell wrote on the statute books of the English Parliament: "All just powers under God are derived from the consent of the people." Since Cromwell's day, this principle has been fundamental, central, undisputed, in British home politics. It took a little longer to get it recognized in colonial matters. The American colonies in 1776 took their stand upon it. "Just government must be based upon the consent of the governed." "There should be no taxation without representation." These were their affirmations. Burke and Pit and Fox and the broader-minded leaders of public opinion in England were in sympathy with their American brethren. If Britain had been true to her principle of freedom and self-rule she would have kept all her American Colonies in 1776. But she was not true to it and so she lost them. Later she came very near losing Canada in the same way. But her eyes were opened in time and she gave Canada freedom and self-government. This prevented revolt and fastened Canada to her with hooks of steel. Since this experiment with Canada, it has been a settled principle in connection with Britain's free colonies or dominions, as well as with her home politics, that there is no just power except that which is based upon the consent of the governed.

But what are we to do with this principle when we come to the dependencies? Is another and different principle to be adopted here? Are there indeed peoples whom it is just to rule without their consent? Is justice one thing in England and Canada and another thing in India? It is the belief and conviction that what is justice in England and Canada is justice everywhere, that made Froude declare, "Free nations cannot govern subject provinces."

III

Why is England in India at all? Why did she go there at first and why does she remain? If India had been a comparatively empty land as America was when it was discovered, so that Englishmen had wanted to settle there and make homes, the reason would have been plain. But it was a land already full, and as a matter of fact practically no Englishmen have ever gone to India to settle or make homes. If the Indian people had been savages or barbarians, there might have seemed on the surface of the question, some reason for England's conquering and ruling them.

But they were a people with a highly organized government far older than that of Great Britain, and with a civilization that had risen to a splendid development before England's was born.

Lord Curzon, while Viceroy of India, said in his address at the Great Delhi Durbar in 1901:

> "Powerful Empires existed and flourished here (in India) while Englishmen were still wandering painted in the woods, and while the British Colonies were still a wilderness and a jungle. India has left a deeper mark upon the history, the philosophy, and the religion of mankind, than any other terrestrial unit in the universe."

It is such a land that England has conquered and is ruling as a dependency. It is such a people that she is holding without giving them any voice whatever in their own destiny. The honored Canadian Premier, Sir Wilfred Laurier, at the Colonial Conference held in London in connection with the coronation of King Edward, declared: "The Empire of Rome was composed of slave states; the British Empire is a Galaxy of Free Nations." But is Great India a free nation? In a speech made at the League of Nations in Geneva, in September, 1927, Sir Austin Chamberlain described the British Empire as "a Great Commonwealth of Free and Equal Peoples." Why do these statesmen use such language when they know how contrary to the facts it is? India, which constitutes more than four-fifths of the Empire, is not free; it is in bondage. Its people are not allowed "equality" with the free minority, the free one-fifth, but are ruled without their consent. Thus we see that in truth the British Empire is to a four or five times larger extent a "Slave Empire," than it is a "Galaxy of Free Nations" or a "Great Commonwealth of Free and Equal Peoples."

Perhaps there is nothing so dangerous or so evil in its effects, as irresponsible power. That is what Great Britain exercises in connection with

India—absolute power, with no one to call her to account. I do not think any nation is able to endure such an ordeal any better than is Britain, but it is an ordeal to which neither rulers of nations nor individuals in private life should ever be subjected. The risks are too great. The wrongs and tyrannies inseparable from it are too serious. England avoids it in connection with her own rulers, by making them strictly responsible to the English people. The rulers of Canada are strictly responsible to the Canadian people. Every free nation safeguards alike its people and its rulers by making its rulers answerable in everything to those whom they govern. But here is the anomaly of British rule in India—Britain rules India but does not acknowledge any degree whatever of political responsibility to the people of India. Whatever freedom or political privileges they enjoy are purely "favors" which she in her "kindness" "graciously grants" to them ; she does not for a moment admit that any political freedom or political power belongs to them of right—is their just possession, which they may rightly demand of Great Britain and which she has no right to withhold. Her will is the supreme law ; and India must submit in everything.

What is the result ? Are the interests and rights of India protected ? Is it possible for the rights of any people to be protected without self-rule ? I invite Americans to come with me to India and see. What we find there will go far towards furnishing a key to the meaning of India's struggle for freedom and self-government.

IV

Crossing over from America to London, we sail from there to India on a magnificent steamer. On board is a most interesting company of people, made up of merchants, travellers, and especially

Englishmen who are either officials connected with the Indian Government or officers in the Indian army, who have been home on furlough with their families and are now returning. We land in Bombay, a city that reminds us of Paris or London, or New York or Washington. Our hotel is conducted in English style. We go to the railway station, one of the most magnificent buildings of the kind in the world, to take the train for Calcutta, formerly the capital, some fifteen hundred miles away. Arrived in Calcutta, we hear it called the City of Palaces, nor do we wonder at the name.

Who owns the steamship line by which we came to India? The British. Who built that splendid railway station in Bombay? The British. Who built the railway on which we travelled to Calcutta? The British. To whom do these palatial buildings in Calcutta belong? Mainly to the British. We find that both Calcutta and Bombay have a large commerce. To whom does the overwhelming bulk of this commerce belong? To the British. We find that the Indian Government, that is, the British Government in India, has directly or indirectly built some 40,000 miles of railway in India; has created good postal and telegraph systems reaching practically throughout the country; has founded law-courts after the English pattern, and has done much else to bring India in line with the civilization of Europe. It is not strange that visitors begin to exclaim, "How much the British are doing for India!" "How great a benefit to the people of India British rule is!"

But have we seen all? Is there no other side? Have we probed to the underlying facts, the foundations upon which all this material acquisition is based? Are these signs of prosperity which we have noticed, signs of the prosperity of the Indian people, or only of their English masters?

If the English are living in ease and luxury, how are the people of the land living? Who pays for those fine buildings that the British rulers of the land occupy and take the credit for? And the railways, the telegraphs and the rest? Do the British? Or are they paid for out of the taxes of a nation which is perhaps the most poverty-stricken in the world? Have we been away at all from the beaten track of tourist travel? Have we been out among the Indian people themselves, in the country as well as in the cities? Nearly eight-tenths of the people of India are "ryots" small farmers who derive their sustenance directly from the land. Have we taken the trouble to find out how they live, whether they are growing better off or poorer year by year?

Especially, have we looked into the causes of those famines, the most terrible known to the modern world, which have long swept like a besom of death over India, with their black shadows, plague and pestilence, following in their wake? Here is a side of India with which we must become acquainted, before we can understand the true situation. The great disturbing, portentous, all-overshadowing fact connected with the history of India in recent years has been the succession of these famines, and the consequent plague epidemics.

V

What do these famines mean? Here is a picture from a recent book written by a distinguished British civilian who has had long service in India and knows the Indian situation from the inside. Since he is an Englishman, we may safely count upon his prejudices, if he has any, being upon the side of his own countrymen.

Mr. W. S. Lilly, in his "India and Its Problems," writes as follows:

"During the first eighty years of the nineteenth century, 18,000,000 of the Indian people perished of famine. In one year alone—the year when Her Majesty, Queen Victoria, assumed the title of Empress,—5,000,000 of the people of Southern India were starved to death. In the District of Bellary, with which I am personally acquainted,—a region twice the size of Wales—one-fourth of the whole population perished in the famine of 1876-77. I shall never forget my own famine experience: how, as I rode out on horseback, morning after morning, I passed crowds of wandering skeletons, and saw human corpses by the roadside, unburied, uncared for, half devoured by dogs and vultures; and how—still sadder sight—children, 'the joy of the world' as the old Greeks deemed them, had become its ineffable sorrow there, forsaken even by their mothers, their feverish eyes shining from hollow sockets, their flesh utterly wasted away, only gristle and sinew and cold shivering skin remaining, their heads mere skulls, their puny frames full of loathsome diseases engendered by the starvation in which they had been conceived and born and nurtured—the sight, the thought of them haunts me still."

Every one who has been in India in famine times, and has left the beaten track of western-made prosperity, knows how true a picture this is.

Mr. Lilly estimates the number of famine-deaths in the first eight decades of the last century at 18,000,000. Think what this means—within a little more than two generations as many people died from lack of food as the whole population of Canada, New England, and the City and State of New York; nearly half as many as the whole population of France! But the most startling aspect of the case appears in the fact that the famines increased in number and severity as the century went on. Suppose we divide the last century into quarters, periods of twenty-five years each. In the first quarter there were five famines, with an estimated loss of 1,000,000 lives. During the second quarter of the century there were two famines with an estimated mortality of 400,000. During the third quarter there were six famines, with a recorded loss of life of 5,000,000. And during the last quarter of the century—what do we find? Eighteen famines, with an estimated mortality reaching the awful total of from 15,000,000 to 26,000,000. And this does not include the many more millions (over 6,000,000 in a single year) kept alive by government doles.

As a matter of fact, virtual famines are really perpetual in India. They exist when they are not reported by the Government at all, and when the world knows nothing of their existence. Even when the rains are plentiful and crops are good, there is always famine, that is, starvation on a wide scale, somewhere in the land, taking its toll of thousands and even millions of human lives, of which we read nothing in any Government statement, and of which we know only when we see it with our own eyes. Millions of the people of India who are reported by the British Government as dying of fever, dysentery and other similar diseases, really perish as the result of emaciation from this long and terrible lack of food, this endless starvation. When epidemics appear, such as plague and influenza, depletion from life-long starvation is the main cause of the terrible mortality.

VI

What is the explanation of all this terrible and persistent famine, seen and unseen,—this famine, part of it reported under its true name, part under some other name, but most of it not reported at all ?

The common answer is, the failure of the rains. But there seems to be no evidence that the rains fail now any oftener or in greater extent than they did a hundred years ago. Moreover, why should failure of rains bring famine? It is a matter of indisputable fact that the rains have never failed in India over areas so extensive as to prevent the production of ample food for the entire population. Why, then, have the people starved? Never because there was any real lack of food. Never because there was any lack of food even in the famine areas, brought by railways or otherwise within easy reach of all. There has always been plenty of food raised in India, even in the worst famine years, for those who had money to buy it with. And until during the World War, the price of food in India has been quite moderate. This is the report of two different British Commissions that have carefully investigated the matter. Why, then, have all these millions of people died for want of food?

Because they were so indescribably poor. All candid and thorough investigation into the causes of the famines of India has shown that the chief and fundamental cause has been, and is, the poverty of the people—a poverty so severe and terrible that it keeps the entire population on the very verge of starvation even in the years of greatest plenty, prevents them from laying up anything against times of extremity, and hence leaves them, when their crops fail, absolutely undone—with nothing between them and death unless some form of charity comes to their aid. Says Sir Charles Elliott, long the Chief Commissioner of Assam, "Half the agricultural population do not know from one half-year's end to another what it is to have a full meal." Said the honorable G. K. Gokhale, one of the Viceroy's Council, "From 60,000,000 to 70,000,000 of the people in India do not know what it is to have their hunger satisfied even once in a year."

Nor does there seem to be any improvement.

Indeed, Mahatma Gandhi and the Rev. C. F. Andrews, witnesses of the most competent and trustworthy character, have both recently given it as their judgment that to-day the people of India are growing steadily poorer.

VII

Here we get a glimpse of the real India. It is not the India which the usual traveller sees, following the common routes of travel, stopping at the leading hotels conducted after the manner of London or Paris, and mingling with the English lords of the country. It is not the India to which the British "point with pride" and tell us about in their books of description and their commercial reports. But this is India from the inside, it is the India of the Indian people, of the men, women, and children to whom the country of right belongs, who pay the taxes and bear the burdens, and support the costly government carried on by foreigners. It is the India of the men, women, and children who do the starving when the famine comes. It is the India of the men and women who are now struggling for their independence, as their only hope of ever getting rid of the exploitation of their country, and therefore of their poverty and misery.

What causes this awful and growing poverty of the Indian people? Said John Bright:

> "If a country be found possessing a most fertile soil and capable of bearing every variety of production, yet notwithstanding, the people are in a state of extreme destitution and suffering, the chances are there is some fundamental error in the government of that country."

VIII.

One cause of India's impoverishment is heavy taxation. Taxation in England and Scotland is high, so high that Englishmen and Scotchmen complain bitterly even in normal times, times of peace. But the people of India are taxed more than twice as heavily as the people of England and more than three times as heavily as Scotland. Mr. Cathcart Watson, M. P., said in the British House of Commons, "We know that the percentage of the taxes in India, as related to the gross product, is more than double that of any other country." But high taxation in such countries as Scotland and England and America does not cause a tithe of the suffering that it does in India, because the incomes of the people in these countries are so very much greater than are the incomes of the Indian people. Herbert Spencer in his day protested indignantly against "the pitiless taxation which wrings from the poor Indian ryots nearly half the product of their soil." Yet the taxation now is higher than in Spencer's day. No matter how great the distress, taxes go up and up.

Notice a single item, the tax on salt. All civilized nations recognize that salt is one of the last things in the world that should be taxed in any country, for two reasons: first, because it is everywhere a "necessity of life" and therefore nothing should be done to deprive the people of a proper quantity of it; and second, because in the very nature of the case a tax on it falls most heavily on the very poor. Bnt it is a tax which is easily collected, and which, if fixed high, is sure to produce a large revenue, because everybody must have salt or die. And so it has been the fixed policy of Government to impose a heavy salt tax upon the Indian people. During much of the past, this tax has been so high as actually to compel the reduction of the quantity of salt consumed by the impoverished millions of the country to less than one-half the amount declared by the medical authorities to be absolutely necessary for health, if not for life itself.

IX

Another cause of India's impoverishment is the destruction of her manufactures as a result of British rule. When the British first appeared on the scene, India was one of the richest countries of the world ; indeed, it was her great riches that attracted the British to her shores. The source of her wealth was largely her splendid manufactures. Her cotton goods, silk goods, shawls, muslins of Dacca, brocades of Ahmedabad, rugs, pottery of Sindh, jewelry, metal work, and lapidary work, were famed not only all over Asia, but in all the leading markets of North Africa and Europe. What has become of those manufactures? For the most part, they are utterly gone, destroyed. Hundreds of villages and towns of India in which these industries were carried on are now wholly depopulated, and millions of the people who were supported by this work have been scattered and driven back on the land, to share the already too scanty living of the poor ryot. What is the explanation? Great Britain wanted India's markets. She could not find much entrance for British manufactures so long as India was supplied with manufactures of her own. So those of India must be sacrificed. England had all power in her hands, and so she proceeded to pass tariff and excise laws that ruined the manufactures of India and secured this market for the manufactures of Manchester and Birmingham. India could not retaliate with counter tariff laws, because she was at the mercy of the conqueror. It is true that India is getting back manufactures in some degree. Cotton mills, jute mills, woolen mills and others, in considerable numbers, are being built and operated in several of her large cities. But their value to India is questionable. The wealth they produce does not reach and benefit the Indian people at all to the extent which that produced by India's former manufactures did; it enriches practically nobody except the mill-owners and a few capitalists, a majority of whom are British. Of course, these mills give employment to quite large numbers of Indian workers: but for the most part it is under conditions of low wages, long hours, insanitation, and wretched housing which are hardly less than inhuman.

X

A third cause of India's impoverishment is the enormous and wholly unnecessary cost of her government. Writers in discussing the financial situation in India have often pointed out the fact that her Government is the most expensive in the world. Of course, the reason is plain: it is because it is a government carried on by men from a distant country, not by the people of the soil. These foreigners, having all power in their own hands, including power to create such offices as they choose and to attach to them such salaries as they please, naturally do not err on the side of making the offices too few, or the salaries and pensions too small. Nearly all the higher officials throughout India are British. To be sure, the Civil Service is nominally open to Indians. But it is hedged about with so many restrictions that Indians are able for the most part to secure only the lowest and poorest places. The amount of money which the Indian people are required to pay as salaries to this great army of foreign civil servants and appointed higher officials, and then, later, as pensions for the same after they have served a given number of years in India, is very large. That in three-fourths, if not in nine-tenths of the positions, quite as good service, and often much better, could be obtained for the government at a fraction of the present cost, by employing educated and competent Indians, who much better understand the wants of the country, is demonstrably and incontrovertibly true. But that would not serve the purpose of England, who wants these lucrative offices for her sons. Hence poor Indian ryots must sweat and starve by the million, that an ever-growing army of foreign officials may have large salaries and fat pensions. And, of course, much of the money paid for these salaries and practically all paid for the pensions, goes permanently out of India.

XI

Another burden on the people of India which they ought not to be compelled to bear, and which does much to increase their poverty, is the enormously heavy military expense of the Government. I am not complaining of the maintenance of such an army as may be necessary for the defence of the country. But the Indian army is kept at a strength much beyond what any possible defence of the country requires. India is made a sort of general rendezvous and training camp for the Empire, from which soldiers may at any time be drawn for service in distant lands—in many parts of Asia, in Africa, in the islands of the sea and even in Europe. Numerous wars and campaigns are carried on outside of India, expense for the conduct of which, wholly or in large part, India is compelled to bear. For such foreign wars and campaigns in which India and the Indian people of India had no concern, from which they derived no benefit, the aim of which was solely conquest and extension of British power—India was required to pay during the last century the enormous total of more than $450,000,000. This does not include her expenditures in connection with the war in Europe in 1914-18. Toward the maintennce of that war India contributed 1,401,350 men—combatants and non-combatants. (These are official figures). She also paid—was compelled to pay despite her awful poverty—the terrible sum of £100,000,000 ($500,000,000). This was announced to the world as a "gift," but it was a gift only in name. As a matter of fact, it was forced, coerced, wrung from the Indian people, as all India knows to its sorrow. Nor was this sum all, as the world generally supposes. Other sums were contributed from India (under pressure, virtual compulsion) in different forms, under different names, all taken together totalling—it is claimed—almost another $500,000,000. How many such burdens as these can the people of India bear, without being destroyed?

XII

England claims that India pays her no "tribute." Technically this is true; but in reality it is very far from true. In the form of salaries spent largely in England, and pensions spent wholly there, interest drawn in England from Indian investments, "profits" made in India and sent "Home," and various forms of "exploitation" carried on in India for the benefit of Englishmen and England, a vast stream of wealth (whether it is called tribute or not) has been pouring into England from India ever since the East India Company landed there some three hundred years ago, and is going on still with steadily increasing volume.* Says Mr. R. C. Dutt, author of the "Economic History of India" (than whom there is no higher authority):

"A sum reckoned at twenty millions of English money or a hundred millions of American money—some authorities put it much higher—is remitted annually from India to England without any direct equivalent. It should be borne in mind that this sum is equal to half the net revenues of India. Note this carefully—one-half of what we here in India pay every year in taxes goes out of the country and is of no further service to those who have paid this tax. No other country on earth suffers like this at the present day. No country on earth could bear such an annual drain without increasing impoverishment and repeated famines."

We denounce ancient Rome for impoverishing Gaul and Egypt, Sicily and Palestine, to enrich herself. We denounce Spain for robbing the

---

* Major Wingate, in his book, "A Few Words on our Financial Relations with India," (pages 2 and 3) says:

"The British Indian empire has been acquired, extended and consolidated, by means of its own resources, and up to this present hour the British treasury has never contributed a shilling in aid of any Indian object whatever...Not only is it a fact that India has been acquired without the expenditure of a single shilling on the part of this country (Britain), but it is actually a fact that India has regularly paid to Great Britain a heavy tribute ..Tribute is a transference of a portion of the annual revenue of a subject country to the ruling country, without any material equivalent being given in exchange...Its effect is, of course, to impoverish the one country and to enrich the other...The exaction of a tribute from India, as a conquered country, would sound harsh and tyrannical in English ears; so the real nature of the Indian contribution (tribute) has been carefully concealed from the British public, under the less offensive appellation of 'Home Charges of the Indian Government'."

(Major Wingate was Revenue Survey Commissioner for the Bombay Presidency. His book was published in 1859 by William Blackwood and Sons, London, and republished in 1926 by Major B. D. Basu, I. M. S., in Allahabad.)

New World and the Netherlands to amass wealth. England is following exactly the same practice in India. Is it strange that under her rule she has made India a land of widespread and continuous starvation?

XIII

But India's poverty, terrible as it is, is only a part of the wrong done to her by England. The greatest injustice of all is the loss of her liberty—the fact that she is allowed little or no part in shaping her own destiny. As we have seen, Canada, Australia, and other British colonies are free and self-governing. India is kept in absolute subjection. Yet her people are largely of Aryan blood, the finest race in Asia. There are not wanting men among them, men in great numbers, who are the equals of their British masters in knowledge, ability, trustworthiness, in every high quality. Not only is such treatment of such a people tyranny in its worst form (as many Englishmen themselves realize) but it is a direct and complete violation of all those ideals of freedom and justice of which England boasts and in which Englishmen profess to believe. It is also really a most short-sighted policy as regards England's own interests. It is the kind of policy which cost her the American colonies, and later came near to costing her Canada, as well. If persisted in, it must cost her India also.

XIV

What is the remedy for the evils and burdens under which India suffers? How may the Indian people be relieved from their abject and growing poverty? How can they be given prosperity, happiness and content?

Many answers are suggested. One is—lighter taxes. This, of course, is, indeed, vital. But how can it be brought about so long as the people have no power to change in the slightest degree the cruel tax laws from which they suffer? The Government wants these heavy taxes for its own uses, and is constantly increasing the rates. The protests of the people fall on deaf ears. Taxes were never so high as they are now. Under the Government's boasted "New Reforms Scheme" of 1919, they were not lowered, but actually increased.

Another remedy suggested for India's suffering is that of enacting such legislation and inaugurating such measures as may be found necessary to restore as far as possible the native industries which have been destroyed. This is exactly what India would like, and would bring about if she had power—if she had self-rule; but will an alien government, one which has itself destroyed these industries for its own advantage, ever do this?

Another remedy proposed is to reduce the unnecessary and illegitimate military expenses. This is easy to say, and, of course, is most reasonable. But how can it be brought about so long as the Government insists on such expenditures, and the people have no power to order the contrary?

Another thing urged is to stop the drain of wealth by England. But how can a single step be taken in this direction of stopping it, so long as absolutely all power is in the hands of the very men who created the drain, who are enriched by it, and who are determined to continue it?

It all comes back to this: The fundamental difficulty, the fundamental evil, the fundamental wrong, lies in the fact that India is a subject land, politically a slave land, ruled by foreigners. It is for this reason that she is unable to guard her own interests, unable to protect herself against unjust laws, unable to inaugurate those measures for her own advancement which must always come from those immediately concerned.

XV

In other words, the only remedy for India's wrongs, her economic ills and her political degradation, is that which in all ages of the world and in all lands has been found to be the only possible remedy for the evils of foreign rule, and that is, the self-rule which India is demanding. England knows this, and would perish before she would permit any foreign nation to rule her. Every nation in Europe knows it and hence every one would fight to the death before it would surrender its freedom and independence. Canada, Australia, New Zealand, and South Africa know it; therefore, although they are all children of Great Britain, not one of them would consent to remain in the British Empire unless permitted absolute freedom to make and administer its own laws, and therefore to protect itself and shape its own destiny.

Here lies India's only hope. She must become an absolutely independent nation with no connection with Great Britain, or else, remaining in the Empire, she must be given the place of a real partner (not that of a subordinate under a partner's name), a place of as true freedom and of as perfect equality with the other partners in the Empire, as that of Australia, or New Zealand, or South Africa, or Canada.

We have now before us the data for understanding, in a measure at least, the meaning of India's struggle for freedom. That struggle means the normal, necessary and just awakening and protest of a great people long held in subjection. It is the effort of a nation, once illustrious and still conscious of its inherent superiority, to rise from the dust, to stand once more upon its feet, to shake off fetters that have become unendurable. It is the endeavor of the Indian people to get for themselves again a country that in a true sense will be their own, instead of remaining—as for more than a century and a half it has been, a mere preserve of a foreign power—in John Stuart Mill's words, England's "cattle farm."

CHAPTER II

AMERICA'S INTEREST IN INDIA

The claim is not infrequently made that India's affairs are solely "domestic concerns of Great Britain;" therefore, they should be left to Britain alone; and any suggestions concerning them, or criticism of the manner in which they are managed is "meddling," is an impertinence and a wrong. In other words, with regard to everything that pertains to India, Britain has a right to say to the world, "Hands off! It is none of your business."

Is this claim valid? After Poland had been seized by Russia, Germany, and Austria and divided up among them, was then Poland's right to liberty a mere domestic question of her captors? And had other nations no right to object? If so, why at the close of the Great War did the Allies set her free, and restore her to her old place among the nations?

If to-day China were grabbed by Great Britain or Japan or France, would the question whether that great country ought to be held in subjection by a foreign power, be merely a domestic affair of the nation that had done the grabbing? If so, why did our own and other nations object to Japan's keeping Shantung?

On its very face, is not the idea either the extremest folly or sheer insanity, that the political freedom or slavery of a great nation like India, of 320,000,000 of people—more than one-sixth of the population of the entire world—can in any true sense whatever be called a domestic affair of a little nation of 45,000,000—one-eighth of its numbers wholly unrelated to it, and located at a distance of one-third the circumference of the globe? The plain truth is, there is no great question now before the world which has less right to be considered a domestic matter or which more justly demands to be recognized as a world concern, than that of the freedom or the enslavement of India. And for three reasons:

1. Great Britain demands to have the largest navy in the world and to control the seas. Why? Primarily in order that she may be able to keep India. No one can deny that the possession of such a navy and of such sea control is a world concern of the first magnitude.

2. Nearly all the wars of Great Britain for a hundred years and more, in all parts of the world (and she has fought far more than any other nation), have been caused directly or indirectly by her possession of India. These wars have all been matters of world concern.

3. The greatest danger now threatening the future of mankind is a conflict between Asia and Europe—the yellow and brown races with the white. What makes that danger imminent is Europe's treatment of China, Persia, Turkey, Syria, Arabia, Egypt; and, above all, Britain's possession of India. If here we have not a matter of world concern, then nothing can be such.

To say that England's right to control India is a domestic question, which no other nation has a right to deny and with which none may interfere, is virtually to declare any nation has a right to rule any other nation, if it has the force; which is to give up the whole principle that nations have a right to freedom and self-determination, and that just government rests on the consent of the governed.

If and when any of us in America protest against Britain's tyranny in India, the reply is sometimes made by Englishmen, and not without reason: "Physician, heal thyself." "Men living in glass-houses should not throw stones." Sometimes the reply takes the form of a question: "Would you Americans like it if we Englishmen protested against your negro lynchings and your holding of the Philippines against the will of their people ?" I think the answer we ought to make is: "Whether we like your question or not, it is just, and entirely proper on your part; and even if for the time being it makes us mad, as it will be likely to, in the end it will do us good." If such questions were asked Americans oftener than they are, they would set us wondering whether it would not be wise for us to substitute for our glass-houses other houses less fragile. The fact is, observation by nations of other nations—observation of their superiorities and their defects; outspoken recognition, on the part of nations, of the excellencies of other nations and also criticisms of their short-comings and wrong deeds, if made in the right spirit, if made not cynically or bitterly, or to set one's self up above others, but courteously, constructively, and with the purpose of helping to bring about better conditions for mankind—these are among the most valuable things in the world.

The truth is, the world is one in all its deeper and real interests. Every nation is related to every other, and all are related to the whole. No nation can do another wrong without all suffering. None can be injured without all the rest to a greater or less extent being injured. None can prosper without the rest being benefited. In the very nature of things, political freedom—freedom of nations and peoples—is a matter of world concern. Every nation held in bondage just so far limits the world's freedom, and thus makes the world a less desirable place for all the other nations to live in. On the other hand, every nation that is free adds just so much to the general freedom of the world, and thus makes world conditions better for all other nations. Therefore, when any civilized people which is held in subjection by another enters upon a struggle to gain its freedom, every other civilized people has a just and necessary interest in the struggle, and ought, for its own sake and for the sake of the cause of freedom in the world, to extend to the struggling people its sympathy, and moral support.

Even Mr. Ramsay Muir, the British imperialist, declares in his "Expansion of Europe" (p. 99): "No free nation can afford to be indifferent to the fate of liberty anywhere on the earth."

We cannot assert too emphatically the broad truth, important to all humanity, that freedom for nations and peoples is not, and in its very nature cannot be, a mere domestic question of the nation holding the struggling people in bondage; it is a matter which the whole world should and must interest itself in, if freedom is to make progress among mankind. So long as there is one important nation or people in the world held in bondage by another, the peace of the world is imperilled. That oppressed and wronged nation or people is a volcano which at any moment may burst into an eruption of revolution and war, and the war may spread, no one knows how far.

Says Bishop Charles H. Brent:

"Moral questions have no boundaries. The world of to-day is steadily revealing itself to be a world of identical moral interests. If we exploit abroad, the downfall of the exploited will eventually become our own downfall."

Gandhi is right when he says that

"India's present condition of bondage and helplessness hurts not only India, not only England, but the whole world."

India held in subjection by Great Britain works much injustice to the United States of America. It ought not to be overlooked that India is a great and important nation with which the United States has a right to have, and would be much advantaged by having, free and unobstructed political, commercial, industrial, cultural, and other intercourse. This we could have if India were free; but we cannot have it with her controlled by any foreign power. For England to hold her in subjection, to carry on her government and manage her affairs with British interests supremely in view, and to prevent her from having commercial and other relations with us and other nations except under conditions which are fixed by England and which give Englishmen advantages over all others, is unjust. It is unjust to us and to every other nation in the world.*

---

* To prevent misunderstanding, it should be said that technically Britain offers in India an "open door" to all nations. But this is only technical. Actually she controls all the avenues of commerce as well as those of political government. Through various kinds of seen and unseen preferences and privileges enjoyed by Britishers in every sphere of business and life, Britishers control India, to the very serious disadvantage of both Indians and foreign competitors. As a single conspicuous example, it will be remembered that at one time when an Indian shipping concern (mainly Indian but representing several outside interests) was started to compete with the British P. and O. Steamship Company, notoriously and persistently unfair competition was initiated and maintained by government-favored British merchants and by the government itself, until the Indian shipping concern was broken down and put entirely out

Consider the single fact that the United States is not permitted by Britain to have ambassadorial or consular relations and mutual service between this country and a country so important as India. India is not only a civilized nation, but it is as populous as all Europe outside of Russia; and yet India's foreign masters do not allow us to have among us a single representative of that great country, of any kind, to look after the mutual relations and mutual interests of the two nations; not an Ambassador or Minister in Washington, such as every independent nation, even the small republics of South and Central America, have, and not a single Indian Consul in any one of our cities to give information to or otherwise assist Americans who desire to do business with India. When our Government desires to communicate upon any matter officially with India, it must be done round about by way of the British Ambassador, the official not

---

of business. (For particulars, see the life of J. N. Tata, by F. R. Harris, Oxford University Press.)

Mr. S. R. Wagel, the eminent Indian economist, says in a letter to the New York Times, of October 30, 1915: "The control of trade and railways is in the hands of Englishmen who viciously discriminate against Indians. Mr. Tata had to bring in Japanese companies to fight the British shipping companies who would have killed the Indian yarn trade with China. In the railways, an Indian has not a ghost of a chance of getting his cargo to the port in time and competing with the English merchant."

Says the Englishwoman, Mrs. Barbara Wingfield Stratford, in her book on India, published in 1922: "There is crying need for the furtherance of Indian trade; every one allows that the country might be greatly enriched and benefited, and the general poverty of the lower classes alleviated by the development of India's rich natural resources. Yet England deliberately cripples any trade venture that seems likely to enter into competition with her own."

of India, but of the nation that is holding India in bondage. And when our American business men want any consular service in connection with India, they are compelled to go to British consuls, most of whom are ignorant of Indian affairs, and all of whom are representatives not of India but of her foreign rulers and oppressors.

How long should the United States government consent to this humiliation? And how long should our business men be willing to submit to these business inconveniences and injustices?

I repeat, India is a vast land—almost a continent—rich in resources of every kind—agricultural products, forests, fisheries, minerals. In the nature of things, we and all the rest of the world have an interest in these. Why should they be controlled by a single power, in the interest of a single power, and that power not India? India is a great market; why should that market be controlled by a single nation, instead of being open to all nations on an equality? India has a great foreign commerce; why should that commerce be managed and shaped to the disadvantage not only of India but of all other nations except Great Britain, and to the primary advantage of Britain alone?

What would Americans say if we were obliged to transact all our business with Japan or China or Russia or Germany or France under conditions fixed by Great Britain and shaped for the benefit of Great Britain? Would we endure such injustice? Yet the wrong done us would be no worse than that to which we are subjected now in relation to the great and important nation of India. Britain has no more right to control our business with India, and herself monopolize the trade and commerce of that vast country, than she has to control our business with Japan or France, or monopolize the commerce of those nations. Thus we see that Britain's robbing India of her freedom and holding her in political bondage, is by no means a British domestic matter. Besides being an immeasurable wrong to India, it is a great injustice to this country and to every other nation in the world, an injustice to which neither the United States nor any other nation should submit.

A very serious wrong has been done to us as a nation, and to the world, by the fact that India, contrary to her will, has been arrayed against America in the fight which for many years we have been waging to rid ourselves and the world of the terrible curse of opium. It was the United States that called the first International Opium Conference ever convened in the world—that held in Shanghai in 1909, the object of which was to devise means for controlling and eventually abolishing this world-wide evil. It was the United States that was chiefly instrumental in creating the Opium Conference at the Hague in 1912, and (indirectly) that in Geneva in 1924. So deep was the interest of this country in that matter that in 1923 both houses of Congress passed a joint resolution urging international action, and pointing out a practical plan by which the opium menace could be overcome, namely, by limiting the opium allowed to be produced in the world to the amount required for strictly medicinal and scientific purposes ; and the next year (in 1924) our Government sent to the Geneva Conference a strong delegation of distinguished Americans, headed by Hon. Stephen G. Porter, Chairman of the Committee on Foreign Relations of the House of Representatives, to urge the adoption of the plan suggested in the Congressional Resolution. There is every reason to believe that the Conference would have taken the action desired by America, thus insuring the early safeguarding of the world against the opium curse, had it not been for the fact that India, the greatest producer of opium in the world, was made by her British masters to throw her great influence against the American plan,—and indeed against any plan that would limit the revenue derived by Great Britain from her opium traffic. The people of India were earnestly in sympathy with the American plan, and sent to the Geneva Conference a great petition signed by many thousands of her most influential men, urging its adoption. But the petitioners were thwarted (and at the same time the world was deceived) by the unjust action of Great Britain in not allowing India, although ostensibly a member of the League of Nations, to send representatives to the Conference held under the auspices of the League ; but foisting on the Conference, as so-called representatives of India, men appointed not by the Indian people at all but by Britain, who really represented at the Conference British interests and not the interests or will of the people of India. All this occurred because India is a subject nation—the political slave of Great Britain. If she had been free, she would have had representatives of her own at the Conference who would have stood earnestly with America throughout the Geneva fight, and the battle against opium would have been won. In view of these facts, who may say that America has no interest in the question of India's freedom or bondage ; and that the matter is simply Great Britain's affair ?

(The general subject of India and Opium is discussed in full in another chapter of this book, to which readers are referred. But the particular facts bearing on it which are stated above, have a fitting place here.)

In 1922 the United States Government called an International Conference in Washington to consider reduction of armaments and also certain other important matters regarding the Pacific Ocean and the Orient. It was essential that India, the second largest nation in the Orient, should be represented. Was she represented? No. Our Government was mocked by having sent to us, by India's foreign masters, so-called representatives of India who did not represent India at all, who were not chosen by India. True, they were Indian by birth, but they were selected under the authority of Great Britain to *represent British interests* and *not the interest of India.* If this was a wrong to India, it was also a wrong to the *United States* and to all the nations represented in that Conference.

The possession and forcible rule of India by Great Britain, has probably been the most powerful single influence in the modern world, against democracy, against just government based on the will of the peoples governed, and in support of autocracy, imperialism, government by force. It has been so because it is by far the most imposing and conspicuous example in modern times of a great nation conquered, ruled, and exploited by and for the benefit of another nation. We may almost say that it is the *mother-example* of the kind in the modern world. India is so great, both in area and in population; its place in the history of mankind has been so prominent; its wealth and its resources in the past have been so vast; and the wealth that it has yielded to the nation which has ruled and despoiled it has been so immense, that its domination for nearly two centuries by a foreign power takes its place not only as an event of first magnitude in modern history, but as the greatest political crime of modern times, because it affects more people, is more wide-reaching in its influence, and has been more disastrous to the progress of political liberty and justice among modern peoples, than any other political crime of the modern world.

I have called Britain's conquest and domination of India a "mother-example" of its kind. And a terrible *brood* it has brought forth. For, it has set a precedent so conspicuous that all the world has had its attention drawn to it, and so dazzling, so attractive and so appealing to the lower passions and ambitions of nations that it has been irresistible, it has caught and spread like wild fire, until all the leading nations of Europe have felt its influence, and have had aroused in them ambitions to follow, to conquer for themselves dependencies, in Asia, in Africa, in the islands of the sea (and in America except for the Monroe Doctrine), and thus gain for themselves wealth and prestige and power as Britain has done in India.

Even our own nation has felt it. Except for Britain's Indian career, the United States would never have gone away to the coast of distant Asia and seized the Philippines. Everybody, who remembers those days, knows that our militarists and imperialists held up what Great Britain had done in India as their strongest argument and justification. And even more than that. It is well-known that some of our most prominent leaders, not only military men but political leaders, at that time contemplated and actually advocated in high government circles the "appropriating" for ourselves of a "good fat slice of China," urging as justification for so doing the example of the European nations in Asia, and especially that of Britain in India. And there seem to be reasons of considerable strength for believing that had it not been for the honorable and inflexible opposition of John Hay, at that time our Secretary of State, we actually would have proceeded to capture and take permanent possession of a section of China.

No other event in modern history has kindled so much envy and jealousy in other nations as Great Britain's creation for itself of a vast empire in Asia ; and therefore, no other has had so powerful and wide-spread an influence in causing other nations to say, "We too! Why should we not do what England has done ? If she may capture and rule and despoil great India, why may we not conquer and exploit any land in Asia or elsewhere that is not strong enough to resist us ? And if Britain claims that her motive is India's benefit, of course, we will proclaim just as loudly that our motive is the same."

This subject need not be pursued further. It is enough simply to emphasize our contention that England's domination of India has been in the past, and continues to be still, the greatest of all destroyers of the spirit of democracy in the world. If in the future the spirit of freedom is to make any headway among the nations, by far the most important single thing to be done is the creation of a world-wide public opinion which will condemn and drive out of existence the shocking spectacle of the oldest and second largest civilized nation in the world held in subjection by a foreign sword.

Many Americans are troubled by what seems to them the marked growth in this country within recent years of an imperialistic spirit. Such a spirit is manifesting itself as appears to them, in many insidious, unexpected, largely unnoticed but real and threatening ways. Some of these ways are—the increase in the number of persons among us who speak lightly of democracy, and wonder if a more aristocratic and autocratic form of government is not better ; who look with more or less favour upon Mussolini and the Fascisti movement in Italy, and the rise of dictators in several other nations ; who scout the ideas of the human equality found in our Declaration of Independence ; who boast of "ancestry" and aristocratic or distinguished "blood" wherever they can find the slightest peg to hang such boasting on ; whose highest ambition is to get admission to British aristocratic society or to be invited to a function at Buckingham Palace, or above all to marry a daughter to an English lord or other foreign titled person ; who regard the world as having been made for the white race and especially for Nordics, and look down on all the other races ; and who would like to have Britain and America unite against the so-called "yellow peril" and "brown peril", that is, unite to dominate Asia and as far as possible the rest of the world. I say this imperialistic spirit, this anti-democratic spirit, this aristocratic and arrogant spirit (which nearly everywhere allies itself with militarism and largely with capitalism) seems to many thoughtful persons to have been insidiously but steadily growing in this country for some years past.

From what source does it come ? It is believed that it comes largely, indeed, mainly from England. Not, of course, from the nobler, truer England, the England which in the days of our American revolutionary struggle pleaded for justice and freedom for America, and which to-day would give justice and self-rule to India ; but from that England which in 1776 sided with George III and Lord North against the rights of the American Colonies, and which to-day is determined to retain India in its grip, as then it was determined to retain America.

Every student of English history knows that this undemocratic spirit, this aristocratic, autocratic, imperialistic, "nabob" spirit, is not indigenous to England. England got it from outside and within the last two centuries. From what source? It is more and more believed by those who look into the matter, that the true answer is, she got it mainly from her conquest and rule of India. The evil spirit of arrogance, domination, pride of class, indifference to the rights of others, imperialism which the men who have gone to India and spent half their lives in autocratic rule there have instinctively imbibed there, has been brought back by them to England, on their return from their place of autocratic rule abroad, to poison the ideals and the political and social life of England.

Nor could this evil spirit—this poison—be confined to England. It was inevitable that it should spread, especially that it should come across the sea to us, because of our close relations with England. It has done so, and it will continue to do so, to poison our ideals and our life, as long as England continues to dominate India by force, and therefore, as long as that unjust domination continues to poison England's own ideals and life.

This is one of the reasons why India is America's concern, and why American public opinion ought strongly to demand India's freedom. We should demand it in self-defense, and so should every nation in the world.

CHAPTER III

WHAT EMINENT AMERICANS SAY ABOUT SUBJECT INDIA

This chapter consists of two parts.

In part one I cite utterances of honored Americans about *all national bondage, all* forced rule of one nation by another,—which, of course, *includes India,* although India is *not mentioned by name.*

In part two I quote things said by distinguished Americans about *India itself,* as held in subjection by Great Britain.

PART I

What have honored Americans said, and what are they saying, about the *right* of *all* nations and peoples to *freedom* and *self-determination* ?

1. *The American Declaration of Independence.*

This most conspicuous utterance of this country to the world affirms :

"We hold these truths to be self-evident, that all men are endowed by their Creator with certain inalienable rights; that among these are life, liberty and the pursuit of happiness. That to secure these rights, governments are instituted among men, deriving their just powers from the consent of the governed; that, whenever any form of government becomes destructive of these ends, it is the right of the people to alter or to abolish it, and to institute a new government, laying its foundations on such principles, and organizing its powers in such form, as to them shall seem most likely to effect their safety and happiness."

If words mean anything, the principles here set forth apply to India to-day as directly, as exactly and as fully as they did to the American Colonies in 1776; with these differences, however, that: (1) the people who suffered oppression in the Colonies numbered only three millions, whereas those who suffer in India number three hundred millions; (2) the oppressions and wrongs of the Colonists were very much lighter as well as of shorter duration than are those of the Indian people; (3) the British had much more right to rule over the Colonists than they have over the people of India, because they (the British) had largely *created* the Colonies, and the inhabitants were largely British in blood and civilization; whereas the British did not in any sense create India; none of the people of India except a bare handful are British or even descendants of the British, and the civilization of India is far removed from that of Great Britain.

2. *Abraham Lincoln.*

The word of no American carries more weight in his own country, or among all nations, than that of this great statesman and emancipator. Here are some of Lincoln's utterances, which, while not mentioning India, are unanswerable arguments in support of the right of the Indian people to freedom and self-government.

"No man is good enough to rule another man, and no nation is good enough to rule another nation. For a man to rule himself is liberty; for a nation to rule itself is liberty. But for either to rule another is tyranny. If a nation robs another of its freedom, it does not deserve freedom for itself, and under a just God it will not long retain it."

Again:

"In all ages of the world tyrants have justified themselves in conquering and enslaving peoples by declaring that they were doing it for their benefit.

Turn it whatever way you will, whether it comes from the mouth of a king, or from the mouth of men of one race as a reason for their enslaving the men of some other race, it is the same old serpent. They all say that they bestride the necks of the people not because they want to do this but because the people are so much better off for being ridden. You work and I eat. You toil and I will enjoy the fruit of your toil. The argument is the same and the bondage is the same."

Still further :

"Any people anywhere, being inclined and having the power, have the right to rise up and shake off an existing government which they deem unjust and tyrannical, and form a new one that suits them better. This is a most valuable, a most sacred, right, a right which we hope and believe is to liberate the world."

If Lincoln had had India directly in mind, he could not possibly have covered her case more perfectly.

3. *Woodrow Wilson.*

No man ever uttered nobler words in advocacy of the right of all nations to be free and to govern themselves, than this great American. Although he suffered partial defeat in his efforts to get them carried into immediate practical realization (a defeat which cost him his life), some of his utterances are immortal, and will hearten fighters for liberty in every coming age.

Said President Wilson in an Address to the United States Senate (April 2, 1917):

"We fight for the liberation of all the world's peoples . . . for the rights of nations, great and small, and the privilege of men everywhere to choose their way of life and of obedience."

If this means anything, it applies to India.

In an Address to Congress (February 11, 1918):

"National aspirations must be respected. Peoples may be dominated and governed only by their own consent. Self-determination is not a mere phrase. It is an imperative principle of action, which statesmen will henceforth ignore at their peril."

This applies exactly to India.

In a Message to Russia (May 26, 1917):

"We are fighting for the liberty, the self-government and the undictated development of all peoples. . . No people must be forced under sovereignty under which it does not wish to live."

Again this applies to India.

In an Address to the Senate (January 22, 1917):

"No peace can last or ought to last, which does not recognize and accept the principle that governments derive their just powers from the consent of the governed.... I am proposing that every people shall be left free to determine its own policy, its own way of development, unhindered, unthreatened, unafraid: the little along with the great and powerful.... These are American principles. We can stand for no others. They are principles of mankind, and must prevail."

Although these great utterances do not mention India by name, if they do not apply perfectly and unequivocally to the case of India, then words have no meaning.

PART II.

I come now to declarations of honored Americans *directly about India.*

William T. Harris, United States Commissioner of Education:

"England's educational policy in India is a blight on civilization. I have studied the problem pretty closely. In the latter part of the eighteenth century, Wilberforce, the English philanthropist, proposed to send school teachers to India, but a Director of the East India Company objected, saying: 'We have just lost America from our folly in allowing the establishment of schools and colleges, and it would not do for us to repeat the same act of folly in regard to India.'

"There are no free public schools in India (in British India), and no compulsory system of even primary education. Young Indians are hungry for education; and it is England's duty to do whatever she can to help the spread of education in that great country of ancient culture and wonderful philosophy,"

These words are part of an address delivered by Dr. Harris before the American National Council of Education at its meeting in Cleveland, in 1908. The British Government has made very little advance in popular education in India since these statements were made.

2. *Charles Cuthbert Hall,* President of Union Theological Seminary, New York.

On returning from his second tour through India as "Barrows Lecturer", Dr. Hall gave an address in the New York Bar Association Club Rooms (January, 1908) in which he said :

"There is no denying the fact that England is administering India for England's benefit and not for India's. It is hard for me to say this, because until I went to India my sympathies were all on the English side. My early education was much in England, and I have many dear personal friends there. But it is the truth and the truth must be told.

"Mr. Morley made a speech in which he said that he 'hoped he would not be blamed for the Indian famine; he did not suppose even Indians will demand of the Secretary of State that he plays the part of Elijah on Mount Carmel,' implying that the only difficulty is the failure of rains. But this is not true, and it seems incredible that any intelligent, adequately informed man could so mistake the situation. There are factors in this terrible problem which I would not care to discuss in this room. But the obvious fact remains that there is at no time, in no year, any shortage of food-substance in India, if all produce were allowed to remain where it was produced. The trouble is that the taxes imposed by the English government being 50 per cent of the values produced, the Indian starves that England's annual revenue may not be diminished by a dollar. Eighty-five per cent. of the whole population has been thrown back upon the soil, because England's discriminating duties have ruined practically every branch of native manufacture; and these tillers of the soil, when they have over and over again mortgaged their crops and their bit of land, when they have sold themselves for the last time to the money-lender, are 'sold out' by the tax collector, to wander about until they drop by starvation.

"Once when I was in Rugah, just after a terrible famine, I saw several small children viciously hitting another, a little girl, and trying to take something away from her. It proved to be a lump of mud mixed with a little wheat chaff she had found in a shed. She was carrying it away to eat, and the others, brutal from hunger, were trying to get it from her. We send ship loads of grain to India, but there is plenty of grain in India. The trouble is, the people are too poor to buy it. Famine is chronic there now, though the same shipments of food-stuffs are made annually to England, the same drainage of millions of dollars goes on every year."

3. *Henry George.*

In his well-known book, "Progress and Poverty" we find the following passage (p. 17), which gives the result of Henry George's study of the Indian situation.

"The millions of India have bowed their necks beneath the yoke of many conquerors, but worst of all is the steady grinding weight of the English domination—a weight which is literally crushing millions out of existence, and, as shown by English writers themselves, is tending inevitably to a wide catastrophe. Other conquerors have lived in the land, and though bad and tyrannous in their rule, have understood, and been understood by the people. But India now is like a great estate *owned by an absentee and alien landlord.*"

4. *Andrew Carnegie.*

Mr. Carnegie made a visit to India, and after his return, contributed several articles to periodicals giving his impressions. From one published in *The Nineteenth Century and After*, of August, 1908, and a second, in *Der Morgen*, a German paper (January 17, 1908, republished in English in *The Mahratta* of Poona, India, February, 1908), I take the following brief passages:

"I have travelled through India and been introduced to leading natives as well as to British officials. To the Briton, his master, the Indian is naturally reserved; but to the American he is drawn by sympathetic bonds; thus I believe I obtained an insight into the situation in India which few Britons can secure. There is a strong desire on the part of the educated Indians to govern their own country. Education makes rebels against invaders and conquerors. Young Indians know the long and glorious struggle of the English people against absolute monarchy; they also know the story of Washington and the American Revolution. These histories cannot be read by men whose country is under a foreign yoke without inspiring in them an invincible resolve to free and govern their own country... It is not Russia or any foreign attack that the British military officials dread. It is the strong home rule sentiment. It is not against the foreigners, but against the Indian people, that the legions are to be moved.... It seems the fashion to speak of India as the brightest jewel in "the British Crown." God grant that this gem may not one day glow blood-red! If a native of India lives in contentment while his country is ruled by foreigners, we despise him....I do not believe God ever made any man or any nation good enough to rule another man or another nation."

5. *William Jennings Bryan.*

This eminent American, who was Secretary of State and three times a candidate for the National Presidency, made a trip around the world, stopping for a somewhat extended visit in India, and on his return published a pamphlet on "British Rule in India" which had a large circulation in this country and England. In the pamphlet he says:

"I have met in India some of the leading English officers (the Viceroy and the chief executives of the province of Bengal, the United Provinces of Agra and Oude, and the President of Bombay, the three largest Indian States) and a number of officials in subordinate positions; I have talked with educated Indians—Hindus, Mohammedans and Parsis; have seen the people, rich and poor, in the cities and in the country, and have examined statistics and read speeches, reports, petitions and other literature that does not find its way to the United States; and British rule in India is far worse, far more burdensome to the people and far more unjust than I had supposed. The trouble is that England acquired India for England's advantage, not for India's: she holds India for England's benefit, not for India's; and she administers India with an eye to England's interest, not to India's."

6. *Charles Edward Russell.*

This diplomat and author of many books says (in an article in *Young India*, New York, August, 1920):

"I know of nothing more extraordinary than that any American could think or speak favourably or even tolerantly of political absolutism, political despotism, that which exists in India to-day, or any other. If America does not stand for free government everywhere, will some one kindly tell me what it does stand for? The idea that we are to applaud political autocracy because it is British is somewhat refreshing. Does wearing the British name change its character? We are not called upon to admire absolutism because it is Russian or Turkish, or was at one time Prussian. There is no more reason why we should admire or tolerate it because it is British. The subjugation and rule of one nation by another, wherever it may be found, is loathsome, hateful, poisonous to the people who are compelled to live under it. Yet this is what we have in India,—a foreign rule forced on a great civilized people by the power of the bayonet, and the bomb-bearing aeroplane."

7. *Professor Edward E. Ross*, University of Wisconsin.

In an address delivered in New York in January, 1926, on his return from an extended visit to India, Professor Ross gave the following interesting testimony as to the intellectual ability of the Indian people, and therefore their fitness to govern themselves:

"I was greatly impressed with the physical beauty

of the people of India, and still more with their intellectual ability. Being myself a University professor, I was particularly interested in the students there, of whom I met a large number. The students of India struck me as much more studious and much more serious in their attitude towards life than the students of America. They seemed conscious of the great part they were destined to play in life. I met with universal testimony to the intellectual keenness of the students. Once I asked an American missionary, "What do you think of the intellectual capacity of the Indian people as a whole ?" He answered ; 'There is no question that it is equal to that of the American people.' I think it is even greater."

Should such a people be held in bondage by a foreign power ?

8. *Professor Robert Morse Lovett,* University of Chicago.

In his Introduction to "India in World Politics" (by Dr. Taraknath Das), Professor Lovett says :

"It is only because of the myopic vision with which we tend to view the ethics of nations, that the holding in political subjection and social inferiority of three hundred millions of human beings by forty millions, who are for the most part entirely ignorant and uninterested in their wards, does not appear as a *hideous abnormality.*

9. *Professor William James,* Harvard University.

This great thinker regarded the struggles of subject peoples everywhere to gain their freedom as in the highest degree praiseworthy and noble, and the efforts of tyrant powers to crush such struggles, as a crime of the darkest dye. He said:

"In undertaking to crush out the attempt of a long enslaved nation [like India] to obtain possession of itself, to organize its own laws and government, and to be free to follow its own internal destinies according to its own ideals, *we are crushing out the grandest thing in this human world...and we are helping to destroy faith in God and man."*

10. *United States Senator, George W. Norris,* Nebraska.

Much has been said at one time and another in both Houses of the United States Congress, condemning the forced rule of one nation by another, especially the most conspicuous case of such rule now existing in the world, that of great historic, civilized India by Britain.

In a speech delivered in the Senate in February 1920, Senator Norris defended the right of the people of India to freedom, and especially condemned the conduct of Great Britain in refusing to give India self-government after she had sent more than a million men into the Great War of 1914-18 to fight on Britain's side.

"The fact that England treats Canada well," declared Senator Norris, "is no defense or justification of her when she abuses India. *No nation on earth should be ruled without its consent.*"

11. *Senator Joseph I. France.*

On the 14th of October, 1919, Senator France, of Maryland, delivered a speech in the United States Senate, on the ratification of the Versailles Treaty. He opposed the ratification on several grounds, one of which was that the treaty practically guaranteed the perpetuity of British rule in India, a rule which, he contended, had reduced the Indian people from a great, rich and influential nation, to a condition of helplessness and abject poverty. He summed up by saying:

"Gentlemen of the Senate, we, the United States of America, *cannot justify ourselves* in signing and sealing an international agreement which thus sanctions and aims to make permanent the *practical enslavement of a great nation,* and which, making the situation still worse, also gives and guarantees to Great Britain nearly 931,000 additional square miles of territory, to rule and exploit for British benefit, as India has been ruled and exploited."

12. *Congressman William E. Mason.*

On March 2, 1920, Congressman Mason, of Illinois, carried the cause of India into the United States House of Representatives, delivering an address on the *crime of Great Britain in holding a great civilized nation,* such as India is, *in forced subjection,* and the *duty* of *this country to sympathize* with the Indian people in their struggle for freedom, and to *extend to them such moral support* as may lie in our power. At the close of his address, he introduced into the House the following Concurrent Resolution, which was referred to the Committee on Foreign Affairs, and ordered to be printed, with the expectation that later it would come before both Houses of Congress.

CONCURRENT RESOLUTION

"Whereas all just powers of government are derived from the consent of the governed ; and

Whereas it has been the policy of the Republic of the United States to give recognition without intervention to the struggling peoples who seek self-determination; and

Whereas the atrocities committed in India by British soldiers and officers, which have met the approval of the British officials, has shocked the sense of justice of the American people ; and

Whereas as a result of the great war many of the heretofore oppressed peoples of the world are being recognized by the United States as they seek to govern themselves ; and

Whereas the American people believe the same rules of self-determination should apply to peoples who are subjected by force to the government of Great Britain that is applied to the other nations that have sought self-determination and are encouraged by the United States ; and

Whereas the Government of Great Britain, which now controls India and governs it by force without the consent of its people, has tried to make it appear by its propaganda that it has given, or is giving, so-called 'home rule' to India, which is substantially the same brand of home rule which has always been given by the master nation to the slave nation:

Therefore be it

Resolved by the House of Representatives (the Senate concurring). That it is the duty of the Government of the United States to carry out the will of the people to *give such recognition* without intervention to the people of India who are struggling for self-determination, as *will assist them in their efforts for self-government*."

CHAPTER IV

IF OTHER NATIONS SHOULD BE FREE, WHY NOT INDIA ?

If freedom and nationhood are the acknowledged right of all civilized nations in the world, why are they denied to India ?

It was declared throughout all the Great War in Europe that one of the chief objects of that war was to give freedom to oppressed peoples. This more than any other was the slogan which took America into the conflict. Said President Wilson : "We are fighting for the liberty and self-government of all peoples." The Treaty of Versailles proposed to carry out that idea. This was why Poland was restored to her old freedom and nationhood. This was why Czecho-Slovakia, Jugo-Slavia and other much smaller new nations were created.

Then why was not India, by far the greatest of all the subject nations of the world, given her freedom ? Why did not age-long subjection, not to mention her contribution of vast sums of money and more than a million men to help the allies to win the war, win for her some consideration at Versailles ?

In justice India should have been the first of the subject peoples to be set free. The nations in Europe that were given their freedom, all combined, had a population which was only a fraction of that of India. All were very young compared with her. None of them had occupied anything like so important a place in the world's history as she. None of them had been deprived of their liberties so completely, or reduced to such dire poverty, as had India. Yet so shamefully unjust was the Versailles Treaty that it did not give a word of consideration to this great suffering nation, but left her as absolutely under the heel of foreigners as if the war had never been fought.

It will help us to understand whether India has a right to freedom, and whether she possesses a just claim to the sympathy of mankind in her struggle to obtain it, if we make some comparisons.

Beginning at home, we in America may very fittingly consider first the case of the American Colonies of 1776. Was their right to freedom greater than is that of India to-day ? We well know that those Colonies had many sympathizers even in England. Their cause was defended over and over in the British Parliament in great speeches by eminent public leaders. Pitt "rejoiced that America had resisted." Horace Walpole "thanked God" for the news of Burgoyne's surrender at Saratoga. Fox went so far as to declare that the British ministers for waging war against us ought to be sent to the scaffold. Great numbers of the common people of England took our side.

France not only sympathized with us, but furnished us with indispensable financial and military help. She loaned us money. She sent a strong fleet to aid us by sea. Lafayette came with his great influence and ability and threw himself with all his soul into our cause.

From Germany came Baron von Steuben, bringing his important military assistance.

Was the cause of our Colonies, which thus found so much sympathy abroad, even in England itself, any more just than is that of India to-day? Had they suffered any deeper wrongs than India has suffered? Were they any more worthy of sympathy than is India? On the score of population and importance in the world, how do the two compare? The number of the people of India to-day is almost exactly a hundred times as great as was that of the revolting American Colonies. Has a very great people less right to freedom and nationhood than a very small one? Furthermore, Great Britain had herself actually created most of those Colonies, populating them with her own sons and daughters, transporting them to their new homes in her own ships, and giving them their language, their religion, their whole civilization. Therefore, was it strange if she felt she had a right to rule them? But as for India, she had nothing to do with creating it. She did not give it any part of its permanent population, or any of its languages, or its religions, or any part of its real civilization—the civilization which it had enjoyed for 3,000 years. She was and is simply a conqueror and intruder camping as it were on a foreign soil.

Moreover, wrongs and oppressions inflicted on the American Colonists, as enumerated by Jefferson in our Declaration of Independence, are far, far exceeded in number and in the seriousness of their injustice, by any true list of the wrongs and oppressions inflicted on the people of India, as abundantly shown in any true history of India. If, then, our forefathers were justified in throwing off the yoke of England, even at the cost of war, why are not the people of India justified in their struggle by peaceful means to free themselves from the far, far heavier yoke of their foreign rulers?

In any attempt to make comparisons between

India and other subject peoples, a case that comes naturally to mind is that of Italy, last century, in her long and finally victorious struggle to free herself from the domination of Austria. Probably there is not a lover of liberty in the world who does not regard that struggle on the part of Italy as just and noble. Yet her domination by Austria was very limited as to both the extent of territory and the population involved, as compared with Great Britain's domination of India. Nor were the Italian people domineered over or humiliated to anything like the degree that was and is true of the people of India ; nor were they compelled to witness anything like such contempt for their institutions, their ideals and their whole civilization, or to submit to any such ruthless and persistent exploitation of their country, as has been and still is the case in India.

Still further, in the very nature of the case, the Austrians were far better fit to rule the Italian people than the British are to rule the people of India, and this for clear reasons. The two nations were neighbors, and of course, had always been, and therefore to a considerable degree were acquainted, and knew each other's needs ; whereas Great Britain and India are separated by more than a quarter of the circumference of the globe and have never known anything of one another until very recent times when the British went to India as traders and conquerors. Also, what is highly important, the religion of Austria and that of Italy is the same, as also is the whole civilization of the two nations ; whereas the religions and the civilization of Great Britain and India are well nigh or quite as different from one another as any historic religions or any advanced civilizations in the entire world. If, therefore,

Austria was not fit to rule Italy, is Britain fit to rule India ? And if Italy was justified in driving out the invader and gaining her freedom why is not India justified in her struggle to be free ?

Let us compare India with China, although China is not in the full sense a subject nation. All the better public opinion of the world is recognizing that great wrongs have been inflicted by other nations on China, and that the time has come when these wrongs should be righted. But are the wrongs of China greater than those of India ? Let us see. Great Britain, in connection with her opium wars, seized a number of China's most important commercial cities as "treaty ports," and holds and controls them to-day as virtually her own. Public opinion in America condemns this, and the better public sentiment of all nations is more and more doing the same. How about India ? When Britain went there, did she stop with seizing half a dozen Indian cities ? She seized every Indian city and all the country besides, and still holds and controls all.

Half a dozen European nations by the use of pressure and force of one kind and another, have secured "spheres of influence" in China, by means of which they get various unjust railroad, mining, manufacturing, shipping and other concessions and monopolies, which are a form of tyranny over the land and an insidious means of robbing it of its resources and wealth. Impartial judges in all nations recognize this as wrong. How about Britain in India ? Did she stop with obtaining by forceful means mere local spheres of influence here and there ? She seized by force the whole country, over all of which she exercises to-day unhindered monopolistic and exploitatory control.

European nations have insisted on extra-territorial

courts and legal regulations in China, by means of which they free all persons of their own nationalities in the country, whether residents, or transients, from control of the Chinese government and from submission to Chinese law. The public opinion of the world is demanding the abolition of this injustice. But in India a very much worse form of virtual extra-territoriality exists, and on a vastly larger scale. There, not only are all Europeans in the land free from control by laws made by the Indian people, but all the Indian people themselves are compelled to submit to a legal system imposed upon them by foreigners.

Foreign nations have forced unjust tariff regulations on China and so manipulated and controlled her customs as to rob her of more than half her revenue. But Britain controls all of India's revenue. Not a rupee of it can the Indian people expend without the consent of their foreign masters. True, these foreign masters use part of it for India's benefit ; but how small a part ! They consume more than half in carrying out their own imperialistic and militaristic ends.

For years we in America made a great ado over Japan's having taken possession of Shantung, a province or part of a province, of China. Yet Shantung is very small and relatively unimportant compared with Great India. Nor did the Japanese rule the Chinese in anything like the way in which the British rule the Indian people. Why did we lift up our voices against Japan's wrong, when at the same time we said not a word about Britain's far greater wrong ? Indeed, our Government was so much concerned about Shantung that our President called a great International "Disarmament Conference" in Washington, one of the principal parts of whose business was to insure the return of Shantung to China and to arrange conditions for effecting the same.

Let us suggest one more comparison. It is not unnatural to think of the case of Ireland, in connection with that of India. If freedom in a large measure has been given at last to Ireland, why has it not to India? It is true, that England's tyrannies and wrongs against Ireland were of longer standing than British rule in India, but British rule in Ireland was in no sense worse than British rule in India. The wars she fought to conquer and hold Ireland were bloody: but the Irish blood shed in all the 700 years of England's dominance was as rills to rivers compared with the blood of India's sons shed by Britain in the long wars required to conquer the country and in the sanguinary war of the mutiny (of 1857) required to hold it. Ireland is located close to England, and many Englishmen have always claimed, and with some degree of plausibility, that England's safety demanded that both countries should be under one government. But India is located on the opposite side of the globe from England, and nobody could ever without absolute lunacy claim that holding such a land in subjection was necessary for England's safety. If then England ought to have given Ireland freedom, why should she not give freedom to India?

From the above facts, it will be seen that nothing can be more inconsistent, more unfair, or more unjust than for Americans, after having extended their sympathies freely and nobly, as they have done, to all the oppressed nations which have been named above (and others which might be mentioned), *to refuse to do the same to Great India*, the most conspicuous example in the entire world of a civilized, historic and honoured nation conquered by foreign force; robbed without cause of its nationhood, disarmed so that no citizen without special permission from his foreign masters may even possess a rifle with which to shoot a tiger attacking his home from the jungles; exploited in order to enrich its conquerors; and in face of its constant protest, held in subjection by battleships in its harbors capable of levelling its cities to the ground; by cannon, forts and armed forces at every strategic centre in the land watching with eagle eyes for disaffection; and by bombing æroplanes ready in a good many places to drop death and destruction on its villages at the first sign of revolt. For Americans not to sympathize with such a nation struggling for freedom, can mean only one of two things: either that we are amazingly ignorant of the facts as they exist, or else that we are unworthy of the freedom which we ourselves enjoy.

CHAPTER V.

IS BRITAIN RULING INDIA "FOR INDIA'S GOOD"?

Are the British in India primarily for India's benefit, or for their own? This question is one which occupies so prominent a place in nearly all books and discussions about British rule in India that it deserves a careful and somewhat full answer.

Wrote John Morley: "The usual excuse of those who do evil to others is, that their object is to 'do them good.' "

This has been especially true of military conquerors and rulers of subject peoples. It is interesting to see from the newly discovered records of ancient Egypt, Babylonia and Assyria how unselfish were the founders of those early empires and kingdoms—how careful they all were to send proclamations ahead of their invading armies to inform the nations which they were proposing to conquer and reduce to slavery, that they were coming as their "friends", to rule them "for their good." Alexander the Great carried on his conquests always for the "good" of the nations that he subdued. Rome did the same. The Spaniards made loud professions that their conquests of Mexico, Peru and other parts of the New World, were for the benefit of the peoples of those lands; the particular benefit they wished to confer on them being the highest possible, namely, that of bringing to them the Christian religion, so that their souls might be saved even if their cities and homes were devastated and they themselves were killed. Napoleon's conquests were always preceded by eloquent announcements to the nations about to be invaded, that he was coming to liberate them and give them better governments. Thus for a score of years half the countries of Europe ran red with blood "for their good."

I regret to say that the United States has engaged to a degree in the same kind of "beneficence." We have invaded (really invaded, though there has been no declaration of war) the island of Haiti, overturned its government, forced upon its people an alien constitution, taken possession of its customs and shot without warrant some hundreds of its citizens; but we have claimed that it has all been done for Haiti's good. We have also trampled upon the rights of Salvador, Nicaragua and Panama in various ways, but always with the profession of benevolence.

The most conspicuous illustration of our unselfish imperialism in recent time has been our conquest of the Philippines. Many of us remember in connection with that conquest how widespread was the talk of our military men, our imperialists, many of our politicians and even some of our religious leaders, about the "white man's burden" which we were so nobly taking up, about our "sacred responsibility" to "inferior peoples," and what a high and important place "benevolent despotism" fills in the world. Thus we eased our conscience by persuading, or half persuading, ourselves that we were doing it all "for their good" when we waged a war of conquest against a people who had never harmed us, killed thousands of them, burned hundreds of their villages, overturned the Republic which they had set up and compelled them to submit to our rule.

Great Britain has extended her conquests more widely over the earth than any other nation, her soldiers fighting and dying everywhere, until all lands and shores, as Kipling puts it, are "blue with their bones." Why? Always professedly for the "good" of the peoples thus conquered and compelled to submit to British rule,—India being the most conspicuous of the lands thus brought under the yoke.

About the year 1900, when our own American Government was waging its unselfish war in the Philippines; when the Powers of the West were carrying on their Christian punitive movements in China for China's good, and doing it with armies most of which (I believe the Japanese and American armies were exceptions) widely pillaged and looted the Chinese people; when Great Britain was fighting the Boers in South Africa, for their good, and shutting them up, men, women and children, in pens and stockades where they died by the hundred; and when Great Britain was also holding down by military force the uneasy people of India for their good,—at that time Mr. Bertrand Shadwell wrote a very striking poem (widely read and famous for several years) which made perfectly clear how justifiable and even how noble are all wars of conquest waged against weaker peoples, and all cases of ruling them without their consent, and all exploiting them and all robbing them, if only done as part of the "white man's burden," with "benevolent intentions," "for the good" of the peoples conquered and despoiled. When Mark Twain read Mr. Shadwell's lines, he wrote him, saying: "I thank you for your poem. It is what I would have written myself, but for lack of the poetical faculty." Many will remember the poem.

"If you see an island shore
Which has not been grabbed before,
Lying in the track of trade, as islands should,
With the simple native quite
Unprepared to make a fight,
Oh, you just drop in and take it for his good,
Not for love of money, be it understood.

But you row yourself to the land,
With a Bible in your hand.
And you pray for him and rob him, for his good:
If he hollers, then you shoot him for his good.
Or this lesson I can shape
To campaigning at the Cape,
Where the Boer is being hunted for his good;
He would welcome British rule
If he weren't a blooming fool:
Thus you see it's only for his good.
So they're burning houses for his good,
Making helpless women homeless for their good,
Leaving little children orphans for their good.
In India there are bloody sights
Blotting out the Hindu's rights
Where we've slaughtered many millions for their good,
And, with bullet and with brand,
Desolated all the land,
But you know we did it only for their good.
Yes, and still more far away,
Down in China, let us say,
Where the "Christian" robs the "heathen" for his good,
You may burn and you may shoot,
You may fill your sack with loot,
But be sure you do it only for his good.

MORAL

If you dare commit a wrong
On the weak because you're strong,
You may do it if you do it for his good!
You may rob him if you do it for his good;
You may kill him if you do it for his good."

There is nothing that we hear oftener, or that is more constantly declared to the whole world, than the claim of Great Britain that she is in India for purely unselfish reasons, for "India's good;" that she regards herself as a "trustee" of the Indian people, "responsible" for them (but not *to* them!); that "providence" has placed them "in her care" and "under her protection," and therefore it is her "duty" to hold them and rule them, even without their consent and against their protest; that she is trying conscientiously to bear the "white man's burden ;" that she sincerely approves their aspiration to be free and rule themselves ; but they are inferior people, ignorant, only partly civilized, children as it were, who do not know what is good for them, as their superior British masters do, and therefore who have to be dealt with as children ; in fact, because of her sympathy with them and unselfish desire for their freedom she is actually educating them for self-government, but, of course, she has to do it very slowly and with great caution ; for if she allowed them to rule themselves too soon, the results would be terrible.

I say such things as these we are hearing and the world is hearing all the while.

But are they anything else under heaven except either self-delusion or pretense? Is there anywhere, from any source or in any form, any real evidence that Great Britain is ruling India primarily for India's good, or that any person with intelligence on the subject really believes she is ?

Of course, there are many individual Englishmen in India who personally are large-minded, unselfish men, who feel sympathetic towards the Indian people, and are trying, so long as they remain in the country, to be kind to them and to benefit them in any way they can. But this is not the question. Do these very men themselves believe that Britain conquered India, and is holding her in subjection by means of a large army, and is ruling her against her constant protest, wholly or primarily from benevolent motives, and not from political motives such as desire for imperial prestige and power, and commercial and financial motives such as markets, trade, cheap raw material, fine positions with fat salaries for young Englishmen, and so on?

A no less impartial student of world affairs than

the American scholar and historian, Dr. Herbert Adams Gibbons, gives his judgment of the motive of British rule in India as follows:

"The reading of books like Captain Trotter's 'History of India' and Lovat Fraser's 'India Under Curzon and After' causes one to realize the perverted or rather unawakened moral sense of intelligent and high-minded Englishmen, when it is a question of India. Some of the finest men I have known have served Great Britain in India in a civil or military capacity. It never occurred to them to question their right to draw large salaries from a starving people against their will, to raid and shoot frontier tribes, to flog and condemn to death Indians for acting precisely as they themselves would have acted under similar circumstances. Inability to see any wrong in Great Britain's actions toward India is an inherited quirk of the Britishers. The Britisher is sincere in his patriotism. He believes he is serving his country, if not humanity. But if he will analyze the motives behind British rule in India, and his presence there, he could not escape the conclusion that 'bearing the white men's burden' means (1) selling goods in a market where others do not enjoy an equal opportunity; (2) preference in investment and concession privileges; and (3) getting on the payroll. If it be objected that orderly government is sufficient compensation to India for commercial exploitation, the ready reply is forthcoming that the administration is paid for separately in hard Indian cash; and far from being a philanthropic service, it provides congenial and remunerative employment for a large number of Englishmen who could not have found the same opportunity elsewhere." *

But we do not need to rely upon the judgments of Americans; we have sufficient testimonies from Englishmen themselves to make it entirely clear whether or not the British are in India for unselfish reasons—for "India's good."

As long ago as 1864 Sir G. O. Trevelyan, in

* "The New Map of Asia," (Century Co.) pp. 43,44, and Ibid. footnote p. 44. Also Richard Jebb, "Studies in Colonial Nationalism," (London) p. 322.

his at the time famous book, "Letters from a Competitionwallah," said:

"There is not a single person in India who would not consider the sentiment that we hold India for the benefit of the inhabitants of India a loathsome un-English piece of cant." *

In 1899, Mr. J. A. Hobson published an article in *The Ethical World* (February 18), in which, while praising the British Civil Service officials in India, he declares that to affirm that these men are impelled to spend twenty years in governing India from the philanthropic desire to take up the "white man's burden," or that any such desire is any substantial part of their inducement to service, "would be too gross a piece of Bunkum for the platform of a Primrose League."

In an article in the *Empire Review* of February, 1919, Mr. Justice Beaman of the Bombay High Court declares:

We did not take India, nor do we keep India, for the Indians. Only those claims can be allowed to be legitimate which can be granted compatibly with maintaining in the full efficiency the supremacy of England in India... If, as I think, we took India solely in the interests of England and hold India in the interests of England, it follows that the interests of England not only in fact are, but ought to be, avowed to be the guiding principle of our Indian policy. Every reform, every large measure, all important administrative changes should be referred to one standard and *one standard only*, the *interests of England*."

Sir William Joyson-Hicks, Home Secretary in Mr. Baldwin's Cabinet, has recently declared the same, and in quite as strong words. He says:

"We did not conquer India for the benefit of the Indians. I know it is said at missionary meetings that

---

* "Rise of the Christian Power in India," Major B. D. Basu, Vol. 1. Preface XXVI.

we conquered India to raise the level of the Indians. That is cant. We conquered India as an outlet for the goods of Great Britain. We conquered India by the sword, and by the sword we should hold it...We hold it as the finest outlet for British goods in general, and for Lancashire cotton goods in particular." *

During the spring and early summer of 1920, an extensive discussion was carried on in the English periodical press on the questions, Why is Britain in India? What is the value of India to the British Empire? Why should India continue to be held? In the many articles brought out by the discussion, there was here and there a reference to England's "responsibility," to her "beneficent purpose," to the claim that she is there and must stay for "India's good." But all these considerations were quickly passed by for others of more importance, the writers giving plain evidence that they had put them forward merely because they were expected to do so, or to ease the British conscience, knowing all the while how hollow they were. The real and all over-shadowing reasons given why England is in India and why she intends to stay there, were that India is of great value to the British Empire; that she is a great asset financially, industrially, commercially, politically and militarily. Some of the writers laid stress upon her great area and vast population, which would render her, if she should be lost to Britain and become hostile "almost as formidable as China," or "as Russia and Germany combined." Others emphasized her very great and as yet undeveloped material resources, which England could not afford to lose.

The Lord Chancellor of England took a hand, and urged that India is indispensable and must be

* See report in *Navavidhan* (The Brahma Somaj weekly of Calcutta), April 7, 1927.

kept because she contributes so greatly on the one hand to Britain's trade and wealth and on the other to her prestige and power. He declared:

"India is an incalculable asset to the Mother Country. [As if England were India's "mother" country in any possible sense.] Great Britain has always drawn from India large quantities of foodstuffs and raw materials essential to her industries. Out of the total exports of India, which before the Great War were roughly worth £ 50,000,000 ($700,000,000), more than 25 per cent were sent to the United Kingdom, and over 40 per cent. to the whole Empire. But it is on the other side of the trade account that the value of India to Great Britain is most evident; for India is the greatest outside market for British manufactures. Before the War no less than 63 per cent. of the total imports of India came from Great Britain, and 70 per cent. from the British Empire."

Continues the Lord Chancellor:

"In the fabric of the British Empire India is a vital part. Unless, indeed, we are content to abandon the great heritage of the past, and sink into political and commercial insignificance, the surrender of India would be an act not only of folly but of degenerate poltroonery. To make such a surrender would be to remove the keystone of the arch. The loss of India would be the first step in the disintegration of the Empire."

The discussion spread into Parliament, where the prevailing sentiment expressed was in substantial harmony with that of the Lord Chancellor.

Here we have the whole story,—from the London press and from leading officials of the British Government. The Indian people—more than one-sixth of the population of the earth—must be held in subjection (1) because India is the keystone of Britain's power and greatness as a world-wide Empire based on conquest and force; and (2), because from India is drawn a large part of Britain's material wealth.

It all seemed like an echo (only somewhat softened) of what Sir Edward Dicey wrote many years ago in the *Nineteenth Century* (September, 1899):—

"In every part of the world, where British interests are at stake, I am in favor of advancing and upholding these interests, even at the cost of annexation and at the risk of war. The only qualification I admit is that the country we desire to annex, or take under our protection, the claims we choose to assert, and the cause we desire to espouse, should be calculated to confer a tangible advantage upon the British Empire."

In contrast with all these sordid views, it is heartening to cite the brave and honorable words of a writer in the *New Statesman* (November 7, 1919):

"We went to India to exploit her wealth. We succeeded to the extent of impoverishing her—making her starved, unhappy, uneducated. We have sucked the blood from her veins and scored the flesh from her bones, and having done this, in our comfortable jargon we allude to our 'Indian problem.' The state of India is a crime, and the only problem worth considering is how long we are going to allow this crime to remain on the conscience of Great Britain."

Practically nobody of any intelligence in India, I mean of the Indian people, believes that Britain is ruling India for benevolent ends. In answer to the claim of benefit from British rule, I found many persons in India saying: "If our rulers have wiped away our tears, as they claim, they have torn out our eyes in doing it."

Says *the Modern Review* of Calcutta (February, 1924):

"The assumption that the British ever were or now are in India on a philanthropic mission is pure self-deception or hypocrisy. They came to India for money, and at present are here to make money and to gratify their lust of power. That is the general proposition. Individual Englishmen there were and are who are exceptions, but they are few. Such words from British lips or pens as 'Our responsibility for India cannot be abandoned,' stink in our nostrils. They are nothing but hypocrisy."

Says *The Democrat* of Allahabad:

"No British official in India will ever for a moment consent to anything which will injure the interests of the mercantile community in England. Not one will yield an inch where the trade of England is in the least affected."

This is universally understood in India.

Mr. Alfred Webb, M. P., who spent many years in India and had a chance to learn all about the "white man's burden", wrote in July, 1908:

"The white man's burden is sanctimonious twaddle, to justify the white man in exploiting the colored man for his own advantage."

Probably no living Englishman knows India or the British Government of India or England better, or loves England, the true England, more sincerely than Rev. C. F. Andrews, the eminent Church of England missionary, professor and publicist. Says Mr. Andrews:

"Our whole British talk about being 'trustees of India' and coming out to 'serve' her, about bearing the 'white man's burden,' about ruling India 'for her good,' and all the rest, is the biggest hypocrisy on God's earth."

When George I was brought over from Hanover in Germany to be made King of England, he could speak English only very imperfectly. There is a story told that, as the royal procession passed through the streets of London, the King, overjoyed at the shouts of welcome he received and desiring to assure the people of his beneficent intentions, called out to the enthusiastic crowd: "We have come for your goods." Some one in the crowd called back in reply:

"Yes, and for our chattels too."

England loudly claims that she has come to India for her good. India's bitter answer is: "Alas, long, long ago we found out that you have come not for our good, but for our *goods*, and *chattels too*."

Even if we were to admit that England is in India not for her own advantage, not to gain for herself financial benefit, or increase of political power or prestige in the world, but for purely unselfish ends,—how would that justify England? Are persons or nations justified in committing the greatest of known crimes if only they have a benevolent end in view? What right has England to conquer and rule India "for her good" any more than for any other reason? Does India *want* to be held and ruled by England for her good? Has she *invited* England to rule her for her good? Where did England *get* the right? Does England have a right to rule *Japan* for her good? Has *America* a right to rule *China* for her good? Has *France* or *Germany*, or *Russia* a right to rule *England* for her good? Is there any more justification for a nation to rob another nation of its freedom and its nationhood and rule it for its good, than for a man to rob another man of his liberty and his manhood and rule him for his good?

Nothing that has been said in the foregoing pages is meant to deny that benefits have come to the Indian people during British rule. But in order to understand what those benefits are and what they are not, whether they have come on account of British rule or in spite of it, and what they are worth, two things need to be borne in mind, namely: (1) Whatever benefits India has received during British rule, or from it, have been *paid for wholly by India*; Britain has *not paid one penny.* India paid all the expense even of the *wars by which she was conquered*; and ever since her conquest she has paid all the expense of *maintaining the armies which have held her in subjection*, and all the expense of the *foreign government that has ruled her*,—a government far *more costly* than one of her *own, equally efficient* and *far more beneficial* to her, would have been. So that whatever good India may have received from her British rulers, she has paid *fully* and *dearly* for it. (2) Whatever benefits may have come to the Indian people from British rule, if any such there really have been or are, have been *far more than counter-balanced by injuries, serious and terrible injuries.* The destruction of India's extensive manufactures and commerce, the draining away of its wealth to England, and thus the reduction of its people to their present awful poverty,—this alone is a wrong and an injury which is not compensated for by anything that Britain has done for India.

But this injury is not the worst. India has been robbed of something more precious than money, or even bread for her children. She has been robbed of *freedom and nationhood. This injury outweighs ten-fold all Britain's benefits.* For what is there on earth that can compensate any nation for the *degradation of subjection to a foreign power?*

In view of England's rule of India by the power of the sword, Sir K. G. Gupta writes (in the *Indian Messenger*, of Calcutta):

"We can only pity the nation that is willing to hold another nation in subjection by force; and we pray that the grace of God may descend on it to free it from the bondage of selfishness begotten by self-interest and racial pride, and to lift it from the *moral degradation* which is the punishment of *such a sin.* Rome, the conqueror and ruler of the Mediterranean world, had her fall. May the British people not be blind to the supreme fact that freedom's cause in India, or everywhere else is *the cause of God,* and cannot be trodden under foot with impunity."

CHAPTER VI.

BRITISH ARROGANCE AND INDIA'S HUMILIATION

Some years ago Dr. Charles Cuthbert Hall, President of the Union Theological Seminary, New York, went twice as "Barrows Lecturer" to India, making extended lecturing and preaching tours among all the larger cities and all the principal Christian missions. One of the things that impressed him most deeply in both his visits was the evil effect which living in India as masters and rulers of the land, was having upon the moral character of the British there. Over and over, in many private and public utterances, he expressed the pain it gave him to witness the change of character, the obvious and startling transformation for the worse, which was apparent in English officials (not in all but in a very large number of cases) as the result of their years of dominance over a subject people. He found that their business of ruling others without their consent had the effect to transform them (the rulers), gradually and to a considerable degree unconsciously but almost certainly, into tyrants, into men less refined, less truly gentlemen, less sympathetic with suffering, more tolerant of injustice and wrong, distinctly coarser and harder in their moral nature, than when they left England, and willing habitually to treat the people of the land in ways that they would have scorned when they first reached India.

In an address delivered in the Bar Association

Club House, New York, in January, 1908, Dr. Hall said:

"In connection with British rule in India a most peculiar complication appears in the fact that while the English officials for the most part are fine men, maintaining an honorable and clean public service, many of them men of high breeding and character at home, in England, and in not a few cases truly friends of India in theory, yet as active officials in India, as rulers of a subject people, their whole nature seems to change; their official conscience and their official sentiments become exactly the reverse of what they formerly were. Gentlemen before they came to India, in India they degenerate and in great numbers of cases can no longer be called gentlemen. I have seen Indians of the highest intelligence and character, esteemed personal friends of mine, treated in India with positive discourtesy by Englishmen. These same Englishmen would have cut off their right hands before they would have treated a European so; but they will go out of their way to insult an Indian."

The evidences that these statements of Dr. Hall are true and in no way exaggerated are overwhelming. It is the more important that the facts regarding this whole matter should be clearly made known, because the world does not understand them; America does not, they are not known even to a large part of the people of England. Once clearly understood, they are seen to afford one of the strongest of reasons why British rule in India should not continue. What are the facts, both as obtained from my own observation, and as declared by unimpeachable witnesses, both Indian and English?

In my own extensive travels in India I found it common for Englishmen in all parts (there were of course honorable exceptions) to speak of and to treat the people of the country, no matter how intelligent or well educated or of how high character they might be, distinctly as inferiors. In travelling on the railways they were compelled to occupy inferior cars by themselves. At the stations they must either remain out of doors or crowd into little rooms frequently hardly fit for cattle. I often heard them called "niggers." Not unfrequently I witnessed positively brutal treatment of them. In a large Bombay hotel I saw an English official belabor his servant unmercifully with his thick walking-stick, for some trivial offence,—his servant, a fine looking, educated native, seemingly quite the equal of his master in intellectual ability and infinitely his superior in all the qualities of a gentleman. I saw English merchants and bankers and English Government officials, who had treated me with the utmost courtesy, turn from me to treat their Indian servants and subordinates with harshness that was shocking. Dealing with me they were gentlemen; dealing with Indians they were anything but gentlemen. I was constantly reminded of the way in which, in the days of American slavery, masters in the South (some masters) treated their slaves. Nor is all this strange; the spirit which holds a nation in subjection against its will, is the same spirit as that which holds individuals in bondage.

Says Mr. G. F. Abbott (in his book, "Through India with the Prince," London, 1906):

"I have seen young men (young government officials in India), who have sprung from London suburbs, treating in public aged Indian noblemen in a manner which a gentleman would not have adopted toward his valet. In any other country these things would have begotten sedition long ago. In India they beget a bitterness which is none the less harmful because it is rarely expressed in action."

Says Mr. H. W. Nevinson ("The New Spirit in India," p. 117):

"On almost every railway journey in India one sees instances of ill-manners that would appear too outrageous for belief at home, but it is the same throughout, in hotels, clubs, bungalows and official chambers. The people of the country and especially the educated classes, are treated with an habitual contumely more exasperating than savage persecution. I gladly admit that in every part of India I found Englishmen who still retained the courtsey and sensitiveness of ordinary good manners; but one's delight in finding them proves their rarity."

Says Sir Henry Cotton in his book "New India" (pp. 69, 70):

"There are innumerable instances in which pedestrians have been abused and struck because they have not lowered their umbrellas at the sight of an Englishman on the highway. It is a common outrage to assault respectable residents of the country because when passing on the road they have not dismounted from their horses in token of inferiority. There are few Indian gentlemen, even of the highest rank, who have not had experiences of gross insult when travelling by railway, because Englishmen object to sit in the same carriage with a native. This form of insolence generally takes the shape of a forcible ejection of the Indian, together with all his goods and chattels. Here are two actual occurences which are typical. (1) A petty military officer entered a railway carriage, where to his disgust he found a couple of Hindu gentlemen. He quietly waited until the train was in motion and then "fired them," that is, tumbled them out of the door. (2) A rajah going on an official visit of state to the city of Agra, took his seat, as was his right, in a first class compartment, with a first class send-off by his loyal and enthusiastic subjects. In the compartment were two Englishmen, muddy from snipe-shooting, who made him unloose their hunting boots and shampoo their legs."

Says *The Bengalee*, of Calcutta :*

"Any dispassionate inquirer will find the source of India's unrest to lie far deeper than any of the shallow so-called 'Reforms' with which an alien government foolishly hopes to satisfy a nation that has had a great and proud past. That unrest means the profound protest, the profound mental revolt of the Indian people against the galling fact that they have been robbed of a place

* Quoted in *The Mahratta* (Poona), Nov. 21, 1910.

among the nations, that they have no country which they can call their own—the land of their fathers being a possession of a foreign power: that they must bear the stigma of subjects ruled without their consent, of political slavery, of inferiority. All this they are made to feel by numberless neglects and by positive insults wherever they go or turn in the country of their birth. There are hundreds of illustrations. Notice an Indian desiring to speak to an Englishman or to transact some matter of important business with him. He must not presume to approach the august presence—unless and until the Englishman gives him permission so to do; and also he must not leave the Englishman's presence until permission to retire has been granted him. And this all the same no matter how inferior a person the Englishman is, or how low his office, or, on the other hand, how intelligent or cultured or important the Indian is. Watch an Indian walking along a street in any Indian city. He asks a policeman the way to his destination. In any other land he would be answered promptly, and politely. Not so here. Here he is a serf, a nobody, because he belongs to the subject race. The policeman, the guardian of the street, because he represents the government considers himself the master of the public (the Indian public), not its servant. Therefore, what obligation is he under to help this man? If he is an exceptionally civil policeman he simply ignores the question, giving him no answer. But if he is one of the too common haughtier kind, or if the inquiry is repeated, what happens? Our pedestrian questioner is probably greeted with a shower of abuse that makes his ears tingle and his cheeks burn. And it is no matter who the pedestrian is, whether he is a university professor or a judge of the High Court; if his identity is undisclosed, he is likely to get exactly such treatment as has been described. If, as he proceeds on his way, he chances to meet an Englishman where the side-walk is not very wide and he does not step entirely off the walk to let his Britannic lordship pass, then what happens? The outraged representative of the Imperial race is likely to turn upon him with rage, and he is fortunate if by a profuse and humble apology he is able to save himself from a savage blow. Or if this particular Indian pedestrian happens to be imbued with a spirit of somewhat unusual self-respect and daring, and refrains from apologising to the superior being whom he has so deeply insulted, what follows then? The affronted immortal probably proceeds, then and there, without further ado, to chastise the insolent native: and should the latter have the temerity to stand his ground and in any way defend himself, the watch-dogs of the street appear at once on the scene at the beck of the Englishman, and the Indian offender is put into custody, tried in court, found guilty, and sent to prison; for what weight has his plea of self-defense against the word of a European?

"It is the same story everywhere. An Indian wants to see a representative of the ruling bureaucracy on some important matter. Going to his office, he is kept waiting outside a quarter of an hour, half an hour, an hour—any length of time—while the great man inside smokes a cigar or two, finishes reading his morning papers, or discusses with two or three friends through the telephone the last polo game. It is nothing but a 'native' that he is keeping waiting; why should he hurry? Besides, making the fellow wait will be good for him, it will help him to know his place and to understand that the time of a government official is too important to be thrown away on the affairs of mere Indians. Chagrined and hurt by this treatment, our Indian friend, on his way home, turns aside into a public park to quiet his feelings, and there he finds the most attractive part reserved 'for Europeans only.' With a lump in his throat, he asks himself, where can an Indian go without bearing the hall-mark of inferiority and helplessness? Where can he come in contact with members of the ruling race or with representatives of its government without being stung with reminders of a hundred kinds that he has been robbed of his country, his freedom, his manhood?"

I find in another Calcutta paper the following incident,—a small affair but typical. A group of boys were playing football upon an open space in the suburbs of the city, when one of the number gave the ball an uncommonly vigorous kick, which landed it in the road along which an Englishman was riding, causing his horse to shy. The boys were very sorry and apologized; but the angry Englishman was not to be appeased; getting possession of the ball, he angrily cut it open with his knife, thus destroying it before he would let them have it. Would he have done such a brutal thing if he had not belonged to a nation which was lording it over the land? Would those boys ever afterward cease to associate British rule with that tyrant?

Scenes like the following are common in every Indian city: An Englishman hurrying along a railway platform, collides with another Englishman, and politely apologizes; but this same Englishman makes no apology whatever when, the next moment, he collides with an Indian seller of sweets, half knocking him down and scattering on the ground the whole basketful of wares which he was carrying on his head, on the sale of which his whole living depends.

Writes Mrs. Annie Besant in *The Mahratta* (February 20, 1910):

"On the 19th and 20th of January, just past, the Central Hindu College held its Anniversary, and the 'Old Boys' came from many parts of the country to renew the friendships of their college days and to show their love for their Alma Mater. One of those, with a brilliant record behind him, having bought his ticket, entered, as was his right, a railway carriage for Benares. An Englishman was already in it, and as the young Indian gentleman (for a gentleman he was) was entering, the Englishman roared at him, 'Get out, you Indian dog.' The young man was small in stature and could not fight the bully, and there was nothing for him to do except to go to another carriage. But of course his blood was aflame at the insult he had received. A little while ago an Englishman kicked an Indian to death who had fallen at his feet praying for mercy for some small offense. The Englishman escaped with a fine. Am I asked, why do not the Indians appeal to the law when they are outraged? Alas, it is because they do not believe that the law will protect them."

Kier Hardie, on his return from India, told us of an Indian gentleman, a recipient of high courtesies from the British government in London, a convert to Christianity and well-known for his activity in missionary work, who one day in India went to meet one of his sons returning from a college career in England. In the railway compartment were two British officers, and when his son just from England entered it, the two officers, although it was not a car reserved for Europeans, objected to what they called "another black dog" coming in.*

Professor Edward A. Ross of the University of Wisconsin visited India in 1925. On his return he published an article in the December *Century*, in which he cites many incidents similar to the foregoing, and adds: "You come upon no end of such cases."

Several years ago the wife of the Mayor of the City of Bombay was about to make a railway journey. Her husband accompanied her to the Church Gate station and assisted her in entering a first class carriage or coach reserved for ladies, the proper place for her. In the carriage there was already the wife of an English army officer. Seeing the mayor putting his wife, a lady of culture and refinement, into the carriage, the army officer tried to prevent it and struck the mayor a severe blow. For once he had to pay dearly for his brutality, by a jail sentence from the Bombay High Court. But if his assault had been against an Indian not in high authority, he would have gone scot-free.

Mr. W. W. Pearson, an Englishman who for some years was a teacher in India and who accompanied Dr. Rabindranath Tagore on one of the visits of the latter to this country (America), published a small book entitled "For India" in which he gives many facts of a similar nature to those mentioned above. Among them are the following. He says:

---

* Speech in House of Commons, December 7, 1908.

"I travelled from England to India first-class in one of the largest boats, together with three prominent Indian gentlemen, one a Mahomedan Judge, one a Christian Principal of an important college, and the third a Hindu who was one of the leading citizens of the city of Delhi. From the commencement of the voyage these gentlemen were practically boycotted by the rest of the passengers. At the dinner table the two Englishmen sitting next to two of these Indian gentlemen for ten days addressed not a word to them and even made contemptuous remarks to each other about them. This experience is not exceptional. It is usual on almost all the steamers that carry English and Indians to and from India; and if an Englishman protests or himself shows courtesy toward an Indian, he is compelled to share the boycott."

"If this feeling is found to exist on board steamers from England to India, it is not surprising to find it nearly everywhere in India itself. In writing about it the difficulty is not that of finding material but that of selecting. The whole atmosphere of the official life of India is saturated with the conception that the best way of maintaining the prestige of British rule is to make all Indians, no matter how high their station, feel that they are by nature inferior to their English rulers. To uphold the dignity of British rule, the British official often thinks it necessary to forego all considerations of courtesy and impress upon the 'native' that he must keep his proper place of suppliant for favors from his august rulers."

Recently taking up a chance number of *Glasgow Herald*, I found there a letter from a gentleman (Mr. I. H. MacLean) who had been to India and who told some of the things which he had seen and heard among the British there and on the steamers.

"I was deeply distressed", he says, "by two things. The first of these was the prevalence of the idea that India is to be regarded simply from the point of view of its usefulness to us. With considerable numbers of the people no other view seemed possible. We (the British) must hold India because we require it to provide suitable investments for our capital and good appointments for our sons. We must accordingly see that the Indian people are kept in their place, and not allowed to obtain such an education as will enable them to do without us.

"The second thing that distressed me was the actual

rudeness of a number of the British passengers toward the Indians on the boat going to India. These were for the most part Indian young men returning to their own country after distinguished academic careers in the universities of England and Scotland. In culture and refinement they were far superior to many of the British. Yet throughout the voyage they were made to feel uncomfortable by people who made no secret of the fact that they objected to sitting beside them at table or sleeping near them on the deck. When these educated, well-dressed, gentlemanly young men overheard disparaging remarks about 'black fellows' and 'natives,' and found themselves assigned to inferior quarters, we cannot wonder that their minds should be filled with resentment."

In an Indian weekly that lies before me as I write, of a date just before Lord Reading retired from the Viceroyalty, the editor writes :

"Let Lord Reading travel in India under the guise of an Indian, and he will then get a vision of the galling intolerance and arrogance of his British countrymen. He will then have a chance to witness with his own eyes the vulgar and often brutal manners of the British in dealing with the Indians, their open contempt for the people of the land, and the special rights and privileges which they demand and possess in restaurants and reading rooms. In the professedly 'public' library in the city of Mussoorie no Indian is allowed to enter. The same is true of many other places. British journalism in India is full of race conceit. Let any one read the *Englishman* or the *Pioneer*, and if he has any sense at all of human justice or fairness, he cannot fail to be disgusted and indignant."

Mr. William Archer, in an article in the July, 1914, *Fortnightly Review*, describes the famous Yacht Club of Bombay, the social centre of official European life in that city, and says :

"No one of Indian birth, except servants, not even the Rajput prince or the Parsee millionaire, may set foot across its threshold. It is the same with the Byculla Club ; indeed, every club in India practically follows this model and makes itself a little England, representing exactly the interests, the comforts and the vulgarities of an English Club."

Mr. Archer comments:

"Such a drawing of the color line is of course inexpressibly galling to a proud and sensitive people, who see their rulers, when the business of 'running the country' is over, withdraw into impregnable caste-strongholds."

The following is declared an actual occurrence: An Indian Prince, the ruler of a Native State in India, visits England and by invitation dines with the King in Buckingham Palace. He returns to India and finds himself not allowed to enter any English Club in Calcutta, Bombay, or any other leading city.

Says the editor of an Indian religious weekly:

"Aside from the missionaries and the army the one meeting place of the British in this country, is the European Club of the neighborhood, the members of which form the most arrogant and exclusive body to be found. Those who know at first hand the types of people who constitute the members of these arrogant associations are tempted to say that with them an unblushing assumption of race-superiority takes the place of religion, club life is with them a substitute for church life, and their one aim is exploitation of the country and enrichment of themselves. The European clubs with this smart set are the most anti-Indian and reactionary bodies in the whole of India. These Britishers live apart from the people in the midst of whom they are, and they grow away from the better ideals of their own people in England. They are aliens in India, and a misfit both at home and abroad."*

Says Mr. Eardley Norton, an eminent English man, than whom no one knows India better:

"I have lived in India for forty years; my profession has brought me into touch with the Indian people certainly more close and confidential than that accorded to official Englishmen. The old feeling of personal regard for Englishmen is dead. The arrogance of assumed 'racial superiority', as the years have rolled on, has more and more embittered social and other relations.

---

* *The World and the New Dispensation* (Calcutta), Nov. 16, 1922.

This growing ill-will was bound to come with the recognition on the part of the Indian that he was rapidly establishing his claim to individual equality, man for man, with the Englishman; but it would not have developed so rapidly if the Englishman in India had been less reluctant to admit, that, if the teaching of his professed Christianity is true, the same Divine hand has fashioned the colored man and the white. To-day not a few Indians not merely resent, but are beginning openly to strike back at assertions by the British of individual or national superiority. In private life such claims of superiority ought to be censured as unpardonably discourteous; in public affairs they are politically dangerous.

"I need not travel far for illustrations. In the Bar Library of Calcutta there sit daily about 170 barristers, the enormous majority of whom are Indians. All of them have been in England—many of them have been educated in the public schools there, still more in the Oxford and Cambridge Universities. They belong to a profession which in England holds a high social rank, and which wields an enormous political power. They contrast their courteous treatment in England with their treatment by the British in India. In India a few are superficially patronized in private; but the great majority are socially ostracised. Politically their treatment is even worse. Through the power of the British rulers of the land, the Bench and its honors are almost wholly shut against them. They see the highest prizes handed over to strangers from a foreign land. The discontent of these men is justified. Its existence is the severest condemnation of British statesmanship in India."*

The subject of British prestige in India has been mentioned. Says an influential Indian weekly on the subject (March 9, 1924):

"The average British official in India is always thinking of his 'prestige'. His 'prestige' must be maintained whatever else happens. His idea of prestige is, that he must lord it over the people, treat them as "inferiors, never descend to their level." He must never allow himself to be criticised; nor must he ever welcome a suggestion from them, for does he not know better about every-

---

* "Reminiscences" in *The Looker-On.* Quoted in the London weekly *India*, July 25, 1919.

thing than they do? He must show a 'strong hand' in government. He must seldom, if ever, manifest a kind heart, lest it be taken for weakness. He must let everybody see that he will 'stand no nonsense'. In his conceit and ignorance he really thinks that this attitude of mind and this kind of conduct give him prestige. He may be known to drink whiskey and brandy in his club, and his general character may be shady. He may be known to be biased in his judgment, and to hold the 'native' in contempt. In Simla, the fashionable summer capital, he may allow his wife and daughter to play in dramas and engage in a perpetual whirl of dances that amaze and shock the Indian people. But apparently it never enters his head that these are the things that undermine his influence. One cannot but wish that all officials of this kind, for their own good, could know what the people think about their questionable personal habits, their 'meaningful' plays and dances, their Simla festivities, their luxuries and extravagances, their liquor drinking, their exclusive gymkhanas and clubs, their eagerness for hunting, 'pig-sticking' and killing of animals for the brutal fun of killing, their cynical disregard for the feelings of the people, their haughty and arrogant spirit manifested in everything. One wonders why they cannot see that these things, instead of giving them prestige, are all the while operating powerfully and irresistibly to destroy their prestige, and to make the Indian people hate everything British."

Who are the men whom we see in the streets of all the large cities of India, dressed in spotless linen, wearing cork helmets, riding in limousines, looking down with hauteur upon everybody except persons of their class? They are British officials. Who are the people whom we see in the streets everywhere, dressed in home-spun and walking,—having no money to buy automobiles or any clothes but the very simplest and least expensive? They are the men *who pay the bills* of the *luxurious* and *haughty officials*, the men who out of their poverty and want *furnish the money to buy* the limousines and the fashionable clothes, together with fine houses to match, and rich furnishings and the service of an army of servants.

Are none of these men with scant and often very poor clothing, worthy of the notice of these lordly Englishmen ? The answer is not far to seek. Many of them are members of families with the culture and refinement of centuries in their very blood. Among them are principals of schools, professors in colleges and universities, scholars known in Europe for their learning, lawyers, physicians, editors of periodicals, writers of books, and men carrying on all kinds of honorable business. It is only the simplest truth which nobody can deny, that, as to many of them, they are in no way inferior to their foreign masters except in the dire poverty to which they have been reduced by the tryannical government and exploitation of those masters. Indeed, in intelligence, in ability, in character, and certainly in the qualities which constitute gentlemen, not a few of them are distinctly superior to many of the men who ride in the limousines and draw the big salaries. But alas ! they are members of a conquered and subject nation, and they are not recognized as "white" (though as a fact many of them belong to the Aryan or white race and are actually whiter in color than some of their alien rulers), and therefore they are regarded as inferior, looked down upon, and treated virtually as slaves.

The fitness of the British to rule India seems actually to grow less. The reason is the growing arrogance of the British, their growing indifference to the interests, the rights and the feelings of the Indian people. This is noticed and commented on by the better English themselves. Says Mr. Stephen Graham :*

---

* *The World and the New Dispensation* (Calcutta), March 15, 1923.

"A blatant anti-nigger tendency is increasing throughout the British Empire, and it is very vulgar, very undignified, and at the same time disgraceful. It applies not only to India, but also to Egypt and to the British Colonies in Africa. It is partly due to the long-continued practice of ruling people arbitrarily, without their consent. It is perhaps due partly also to a general deterioration in the education and training of Englishmen to-day. The type of English gentlemen seen in the past is disappearing. It is amazing to think that the race of Livingstone and Stanley and Mungo Park and Harry Johnston should be looking down upon men with darker skins than their own, as if God had not made them aright! In the Victorian age the Englishman could treat his Indian servant as if he were a gentleman, never doubting that an equal dignity invested both master and man. Read memoirs and letters of colonial people in times past and then compare them with the current arrogant, noisy, vulgar prejudice which we see to-day manifested toward the native peoples in India and Africa. To-day we hear young British officers calling not only negroes but Syrians, Arabs and Hindus, 'niggers.' One thing is certain and that is that the British Empire cannot hold together long unless the whites maintain standards of courtesy and justice at least up to the level which formerly existed."

As long ago as 1908 Dr. Joshua Oldfield pointed out, in the London *New Age* (March, 1908), this widening gulf between the English and the Indian people:—

"In the time of the old East India Company India was more harshly though more happily governed. The British nabobs settled down in India and married and became overlords of the people. India was their home and to the people of the land they became attached; but to-day the English are a temporary and alien class. Their home is England. Their hearts are in England. They are always looking for a furlough or a retirement to England; and steamboats and cheap postage have brought India so close to England that there is no need for English officials to be dependent on India for anything,—except sport and salary! The English officials are, therefore, autocratic without being sympathetic; supercilious without being wise; authoritative before becoming experienced; and take no pains to conceal their view that they are *in* India but not *of* India, and that Indians are their inferiors socially, intellectually and morally."

Dr. Rutherford is reported to have declared in a speech in the British House of Commons that Englishmen were in the habit of imagining that they were made first of all the peoples of the world, and that the powers of the Creator were almost entirely exhausted in the effort.

Says Mr. H. G. Wells:

"There is no more evil thing in this present world than race prejudice. It justifies and holds together more baseness, cruelty and abomination than any other sort of error in the world."

Have the British rulers of India no troubled consciences and no uneasy sleep in view of their arrogancies and injustices toward the Indian people? In their dreams does no vision rise before them to smite their souls with terrible words like those of Shylock?—

"Hath not an Indian eyes? Hath not an Indian hands, organs, dimensions, senses, affections, passions? fed with the same food, hurt with the same weapons, subject to the same diseases, healed by the same means, warmed and cooled by the same winter and summer, as an Englishman is? If you prick us do we not bleed? if you tickle us do we not laugh? If you poison us do we not die? And if you wrong us, shall we not *revenge?*"

Fortunately, the Indian people, 320 millions in number, have not yet retaliated upon their arrogant British rulers with *revenge.* Will they always refrain?

What is the explanation of this moral degeneration, this spirit of arrogance, tyranny and disregard of the rights of others, seen so widely among the British rulers of India? The answer is entirely plain, and has already been suggested. It is an effect, a necessary effect of a cause.

The cause is not the natural tyranny or cruelty or injustice of Englishmen. At home, or under normal and right conditions, Englishmen are not tyrannical or cruel or unjust ; they hate these things. The cause is England's great national crime of robbing another nation of its freedom, and holding its people in subjection by force. It is simply inevitable that men to-day associating themselves with that crime, assisting in perpetuating it, should experience the evil contamination of it, should get the intellectual and moral poison of it into their blood. Men cannot long engage in doing wrong deeds without suffering moral degradation.

Says Senator Borah :

"You may take the most humane people in the world and set them to the task, and keep them at it, of holding another people in subjection against their will, and it will make brutes of them."

The situation in India is essentially the same as that which existed in our own Southern States in the former days of American slavery. Many of the slave masters and owners were naturally kind and just men. But the evil institution which they had inherited, which was sanctioned by all around them, and from which they derived large financial profits, blinded their eyes, warped their judgments, seared their consciences, and made them, contrary to their better nature, perpetrators of great cruelities and wrongs.

Many Englishmen, both at home and in India, realize how bad this arrogant spirit, this spirit of domineering, is ; how it coarsens and brutalizes those that manifest it, as well as cruelly injuring those toward whom it is manifested. Many Englishmen have warned against it, as something evil in itself, because it degrades those in whom it appears, and also as something that imperils British rule in India. Many years ago the Marquis of Salisbury, addressing young Englishmen going out to India to be the rulers there, warned them in the strongest terms against this arrogant spirit, declaring that they were "the only enemies England had to fear": that if they manifested this spirit in their dealings with the Indian people, they would "deal a blow of the deadliest character at the future rule of England." John Morley, while Secretary of State for India, repeatedly gave the same warning.

Supplement

This spirit of arrogance, of race and color prejudice, of white-man insolence, is not confined to India. Unfortunately, it manifests itself more or less in each of the British Dominions, in all the British Crown Colonies where there are Indians, and in peculiarly offensive and even brutal forms in East and South Africa. Every person who has read any part of the story of Gandhi's remarkable work in the latter country has been made painfully aware of its presence there. The following instance of it, witnessed by a distinguished and highly honored American woman, illustrates what I mean.

In 1911, Mrs. Carrie Chapman Catt made a visit to South Africa, and admiring the work Mr. Gandhi had done, desired to meet him. In the *Woman Citizen* of March, 1922, she gives the following account of her effort to do so. She writes:

"An English lady gave me a letter to Mr. Gandhi in Johannesburg, assuring me that I would not regret any trouble taken to make his acquaintance. On arriving in that city I sent my letter to him at the address given me, requesting him to call on me at my hotel if convenient at a stated time. At the hour appointed an intelligent and pretty young Jewess called and explained that she was Mr. Gandhi's secretary and that no *Indian* was permitted to enter the hotel and call upon a guest. A prominent lawyer to whom I told the story offered his office for the purpose of an interview; so again I wrote Mr. Gandhi, stating the time and place when I would be glad to see him. Again the pretty little Jewess came—this time to the lawyer's office, to say that Mr. Gandhi had arrived, but the elevator operator refused to take him up, because he was an *Indian*."

This is an illustration of the way in which Indians are treated by the British in South Africa. Of course, Mrs. Catt was indignant that any man, especially any man of the culture, intelligence and high character of Mr. Gandhi, should be thus humiliated and insulted on account of his color.

Mrs. Catt is not the only witness to the way in which Indians are made to suffer in that part of the British Empire. There are scores of others. In the summer of 1925, Bishop F. B. Fisher, of Calcutta, made a visit of investigation to South Africa. On his return home in October, the *Indian Daily Mail* published an interview with him, in which he described the conditions which he had found there, declaring that while the Indians formed an industrious, law-abiding and valuable part of the population, the treatment of them by the British was humiliating, unjust and inhuman to a degree almost unbelievable. He said:—

"In the Transvaal no Indian can board a train without a special licence. The white man can order any Indian to close his shop in one street and move to another. The Indians have no permanent tenure of property and cannot buy even a home. They are segregated in one particular plot in the slums of the cities, and can live nowhere else. Even in that section they have no permanent rights. In tram cars the Indians can occupy only the three rear seats upstairs. All Indians, even the most highly educated, are called 'coolies:' even the text-books in the schools state that 'all Indians are coolies.' No Indians can attend the theaters or use the public libraries. In the schools the children of Indians are allowed to go only as far as the fourth standard. No Indian can enter a hotel except as a waiter."*

Bishop Fisher was not allowed to see any Indians, even graduates of the English Universities of Oxford and Cambridge, inside the hotels where he stayed : he had to go outdoors or to the paths in front of the hotels to greet them.

This inhuman treatment of the Indians in South Africa, reported by Bishop Fisher and known all over India through him and numberless other sources, of course adds greatly to the bitterness existing there toward the British, and makes the Indian people feel more and more that they can never have justice or endurable conditions of life, anywhere, under British rule.

For some years the prevailing demand in India has been (or was), not for entire independence, or complete separation from the British Empire, but for a "Dominion Status" (like that of Canada, Australia and South Africa) within the British Empire or "Common-wealth," in which the Indian people would have complete management of their own internal affairs—complete Home Government,—with their foreign affairs perhaps remaining for a time in charge of Great Britain. But the outrageous treatment which Indians are receiving in South Africa (and their treatment in Canada and elsewhere has not been much better) is causing a strongly growing doubt in India whether, after all, "dominion status" is

---

* Published also in *The People* (of Lahore), November 8, 1925.

practicable, whether it would be anything but a farce, whether it would be endurable, so long as the British everywhere outside of England itself are so deeply obsessed with race arrogance and are so willing to trample on the rights of peoples not of their color. In other words, the feeling is growing that there is no hope for India or for the Indian people anywhere, no probability or even possibility of a future for them that will be anything but one of unbearable humiliation and virtual slavery, except in an Independent India, not only ruled by and in the interest of its own people at home, but strong and able to secure the protection of its people abroad wherever they may be.

CHAPTER VII.

"BABU ENGLISH." RUDYARD KIPLING. INSULTS.

Among the ways in which it is common for many of the British in India to humiliate and insult the Indian people, one of the most unwarranted and galling is that of criticising their use of the English language and laughing at their mistakes. "Babu English" is a phrase of ridicule heard wherever Englishmen (not all, but certain large classes) speak of India or Indians. And singularly enough, it is applied oftenest to the Bengalis, who intellectually, and especially in linguistic attainments and ability, are not second to any Indian people, if to any people in the world. "Bengali Babu" is applied as a phrase of peculiar contempt. Is there any ground for this ridicule? What is the real situation?

The British rulers of the land insist on Indians everywhere addressing them, conversing and doing business with them, in a foreign language—the English. Suppose the tables were turned, and these same rulers were compelled to converse and write and do all their business in the Bengali, the Hindustani, the Tamil or some other of the languages of India. Would they make fewer mistakes? Everybody knows that they would make far more and worse. In the relatively few cases where they attempt to use an Indian tongue the inferiority of their performance is marked. Why, then, do not the Indians ridicule them as they habitually ridicule the Indians? Is it not because the

Indians are the superiors of the English as gentlemen?

There are no classes of Indians that the English so much dislike and take so much pains to insult as the educated classes. The uneducated they despise, neglect and treat almost as slaves; but they do not take the studied pains to humiliate and insult them as they do those whom they recognize as their equals in intelligence. As Sir Henry Cotton says:

"The very thought of equality rankles in the Englishmen's minds; the more intelligent, cultured or intellectual the Indians are the more they are disliked. The sense of jealousy becomes greater. Englishmen are actually ready to encourage the natives who speak broken English more than those who speak good English. They are more pleased with the backward Hindu than with his advanced compatriot, because the former has made no attempt to attain equality with themselves."

The reason why the Bengalis are more disliked by the English than any other race in India is because they are peculiary intellectual, and, taken as a whole, are farther advanced in education than any others; and, of course, for these reasons they have furnished a greater number of leaders in India's struggle for freedom and justice. We have the following remarkable tribute to these despised and insulted Bengalis from Hon. G. K. Gokhale of the Viceroy's Council (himself not a Bengali):

"The Bengalis are in many respects a most remarkable people. It is easy to speak of their faults; they lie on the surface. But they have great qualities which are sometimes lost sight of. In almost all the walks of life open to Indians the Bengalis are the most distinguished. Some of the greatest social and religious reformers of recent times, have come from their ranks. Of orators, journalists, politicians, Bengal possesses some of the most brilliant.........Take law, science and literature: where will you find another scientist in all India to place beside Dr. (now 'Sir') J. C. Bose, or Dr. (now 'Sir')

P. C. Ray, or a jurist like Dr. Ghose, or a poet like Rabindranath Tagore? These men are not freaks of nature. They are the highest products of which the race is regularly capable."*

Such is the race and such are the individual men whom the British take particular pains to ridicule, and to taunt as "Bengali Babus" and utterers of "Babu English."

Lord Curzon was the last man to over-praise Indians, but the following is what his experience as Viceroy and his sense of justice compelled him to declare regarding the high linguistic ability and attainments of the Indian people, which are most conspicuous among the Bengalis. Speaking at the annual dinner of the Incorporated Society of Authors in London, early in 1906, he is reported as saying, that

"While he was in India he was always struck, not by the absurdity and mistakes made by the Indian students and speakers of English there, but by the brilliancy of the success which they attained. He could hardly explain the facility and ability with which the educated people of India acquired the mastery of a foreign tongue. They had a facility in language incomparably greater than that possessed, so far as he knew, by any branch of the Anglo-Saxon race. He knew Indian speakers in India who could address meetings with an ability which might well be the envy of many members of Parliament."†

The Englishman who has been the worst offender against the Indian people in the ways mentioned above, or at least the one whose insults have been most galling because his writings have been so widely read, is Rudyard Kipling. The fact that Kipling was born in India and spent his earlier years there, very

* Speech in Simla, November 1, 1907. This speech, as is evident, was made before other Indian scientists and others had distinguished themselves.

† *Unity and the Minister*, Calcutta, June 10, 1906.

naturally causes his readers to take for granted that his representations are true. But are they true? They are as true as (and they are no more true than) would be a German or a Russian writer's representations of the English people, if Germany or Russia had conquered and was ruling England and if the German or Russian writer was in sympathy with that rule and *wished to convince the world that the English are an inferior people and not capable of ruling themselves.*

Seemingly Kipling's association in India with the English must have been almost exclusively with the military men and with the most imperialistic and domineering of the civil officials. As to India itself, the real India, the great India of the past and the present, with its history and its civilization, he seems to have cared nothing for this, and to have taken no pains to inform himself about it. As to the Indian people, he seems never to have cared to associate or to become acquainted with any but the lowest. Unless we make these assumptions, it seems impossible to account for the facts that in his writings he gives almost no portrayal of, or allusion to, anything of real importance in Indian history, culture or life; and that he seems to take pleasure in heaping ridicule upon the educated classes and in describing the Indian people generally by the use of such contemptuous expressions as "a lesser breed without the law," and "new-caught sullen peoples half devil and half child."

Such of Kipling's writings as are connected with India (and most of those that have attracted greatest attention are thus connected) have always stung the Indian people to the quick. Their popularity in England and the wide acceptance of their misrepresentations as true, have done more than almost any other cause to exasperate leading Indians, and create estrangement between them and the British. The Indian Government has seized, imprisoned and deported many Indians for the alleged crime of stirring up enmity toward Britain, disaffection with British rule, and sedition. Many Indians have told me that if there is sedition in India, Rudyard Kipling more than anyone else is responsible for it; and therefore that if any persons should be deported, the first of the number ought to be this British imperialist and traducer of the Indian people.

Some of the better Englishmen feel deeply the wrong and meanness of all this insulting treatment of the educated and intellectual classes, this girding at the "Bengali Babus," this constant effort to humiliate every Indian who ranks higher than a coolie. A few Englishmen have had the courage and the justice to condemn Kipling for his conspicuous sins of this kind. One of these, some years ago, was Professor Gilbert Murray of Oxford University, who did not hesitate to use a lash that drew blood. Said Professor Murray:

"If ever it were my fate to put men in prison for the books they write, I should not like it, but I should know where to begin. I should first of all look up my old friend, Rudyard Kipling, because in several stories he has used his great powers to stir up in the minds of hundreds of thousands of Englishmen a blind and savage contempt for the Bengali. And many Bengalis naturally have read these stories. You cannot cherish a savage contempt for any one without its being quickly reciprocated. And when both sides regard each other with the same savage contempt, it is not likely that they can dwell together in peace. And in case Mr. Kipling should feel lonely in his cell, I would send him a delightful companion, Mr. Anstey of *Punch*. Year after year, clever natives of India come over to England at great sacrifice of money and trouble, to study in our universities and satisfy the tests for obtaining positions in their own country. They compete with us well, even if all the odds are against them. And year after year they have found in our newspapers caricatures of themselves—representing them as ridiculous Babus, cowardly, vain, untruthful, in every way absurd, talking bad and bombastic English (not nearly so correct, I suppose, as Mr. Anstey's Hindustani), held up for the amusement of the public. Now this is not fair play, and it is not decent. If you must insult somebody, insult some one who is free and can hit you back. If you want to govern a man and to have him a loyal and friendly citizen, well, you must give up the luxury of insulting him. This incessant girding at the Bengalis, the most intellectual and progressive of the peoples of India, has an ugly look. It goes along with irritating hostility to the Indian National Congress, to Indian students, to almost every Indian society or association that professes high aims—such, for instance, as the Arya Somaj. There is in such sneers something piteously like jealousy. And if ever in a ruling race there creeps in a tendency to be jealous of those ruled, to hate them for their good qualities rather than for their bad, to keep them out of power, not because they are unfit for power but because they are too obviously fit, such a tendency is disastrous to any government."*

If Great Britain is to maintain peaceful relations with India, she must breed fewer Kiplings and more Gilbert Murrays.

But Kipling is not the only offender. It is hardly possible to conceive anything more galling to the Indian people than the tone of condescension with which they are nearly everywhere and always spoken of and referred to by the British, in their books about India, in their writings of every kind, their public addresses and their conversation whenever India is mentioned. It is always the same; they, the British, are in India because they are "superior" (of course, they are because they are "white"). They are

* Inaugural Address at the "Conference on Nationalities and Subject Races," 1910. Report in *The Mahratta*, August 7, 1910.

there on a high and noble mission,—the mission of the superior to the inferior; they are there to "bear the white man's burden;" they are there because India so much needs them: they know so much better than she does what is good for her—what kind of laws and institutions she ought to have; they are "lifting her up"; they are "educating" her, slowly, carefully, in the direction of a little greater freedom and a somewhat greater share in her own government. It is a difficult task, and not very safe, but in their kindness and their sympathetic regard for the poor wards whom they have so unselfishly taken under their protection and tuition, they are venturing it. Of course, the fact does not count, that for more than three thousand years, before they, the British, came, India ruled herself wholly, and was one of the leading nations of the world. Such a trifling matter as that need not be considered. The only thing to be borne in mind now is that to-day (after more than a century and a half of British rule) she is so inferior as to be entirely unfit for self-government; and must have long training (nobody can tell how long), before it will be safe for the superior nation to withdraw its wise guidance and steadying hand.

How would England like it if France, in all her literature, all her writing, all her talk about England, habitually mentioned the English people with similar condescension and sneers, as unfit to rule themselves, and as inferior in everything to Frenchmen? In the past we of the United States at times have thought that we have detected in some Englishmen such an air of condescension toward us, such slighting references to our literature, our art, our speech, our institutions and much else (Sydney Smith's "Who reads an American book?" for instance). We have not liked it; indeed, we have resented it keenly. Do we think Indians like the same kind of thing coming to them from Englishmen, and in ten times more exaggerated and more humiliating forms than we have ever experienced? I say, this is the kind of representation that breathes through nearly every book that Englishmen write and nearly everything that they say about India, this arrogant and egotistical assumption of their own superiority and this ignorant and insulting claim that the Indian people are not able to govern themselves. Is it any wonder that India feels and resents the humiliation of it?

Says *The Democrat* of Allahabad (June 5, 1921):

> "Kipling writes of the 'white man's burden.' He has numerous admirers and imitators in England. But we in India find the white man full of arrogance and race conceit. With their egotistical idea of 'racial superiority' the British talk of 'educating Indians in the art of self-government,' as though this ancient nation of ours, which for milleniums and milleniums has been self-governing, is to sit like children at the feet of self-appointed foreign masters to learn our first lessons!"

Late in the year 1923, the British Government sent to India a commission, called a "Royal Commission on Public Service," to examine the work of the Civil Service officials there, ostensibly with the object of insuring a just division of the offices between Englishmen and Indians and proper pay to all, but really to find reasons for keeping as many of the offices as possible filled with Englishmen and increasing their already high pay. Of course, the Commission was made up mainly of Englishmen and, of course, therefore, its spirit was the usual arrogant and condescending one; its avowal being that while Britain wanted to be generous to the "inferior natives" of India and give them as many offices as she could, of course, it would be perilous to grant too many: most of the offices, and especially the more important ones, must be reserved for Englishmen (or other Europeans) in order "to insure the efficiency of the service and the security of the Government." In this spirit the Commission carried on its investigations. To a prominent Association of Indian officials it addressed, among others, this humiliating question:

"To what extent do you consider that the European personnel in the Indian Civil Service must be retained in order to insure the efficiency of the Service and the safety of India."

To this really insulting question, this important Association of Indian officials presented a carefully written, courteous but unflinching, self-respecting and manful reply, to the effect that they saw no need for any European personnel whatever to be retained in the Civil Service in order to insure either the efficiency of the Service or the safety of India.

"No self-respecting Indian," they declared, "can agree to these humiliating suggestions. We deny that, from the standpoint of efficiency, a European element is necessary in any part of the service. Knowing as we do the work of the European officials at close quarters, and possessing exceptional opportunities for comparing their work with our own, it has been a matter of painful surprise to us that it should be taken for granted by Englishmen (and Englishmen in whom we have a right to expect better knowledge) that we lack certain qualities, administrative and other, which Europeans are supposed to possess. We do not wish to sing our own praises; we only desire to call attention to the fact that the people who assert this inferiority on our part, are those and only those who, setting themselves up as a superior race, are unwilling to admit us to any position of equality whatever with themselves. Certainly the verdict of such men should be submitted to independent and strict examination. While we welcome Europeans as our colleagues in the various departments of the Service, we most emphatically repudiate any claim that the European as such is superior to the Indian, either in efficiency or character."

This manly answer made by these Indians to the humiliating question of the British Royal Commission, represents the new spirit which is beginning to appear everywhere in India. The Indian people are rising to their feet. They are daring to look their foreign masters in the face and tell them that they resent their haughty and unfounded assumption of superiority; they resent the claim which Englishmen are all the while making in India, in England, and before the whole world, that Indians are not able to manage their own affairs better than any foreigners can manage them.

The situation in India which I am trying to describe in this chapter and the preceding, namely, the arrogance of a ruling class and the humiliation and consequent resentment of the ruled, is well-explained by the honored Englishman, Mr. H. W. Nevinson, in his "The New Spirit in India" (page 158):

"A race not very sensitive, not very imaginative or sympathetic, trained from boyhood to think little of other people's feelings; take such a race and set a few thousands of its most characteristic members, with the help of rifles and batteries, to dominate an entirely different people, among whom reverential manners are ingrained by birth, and see what evil effects for both races will result! Watch the growing arrogance of the dominant people; watch their demand for deference, their lust for flattery, their irritation at the least sign of independence; their contempt for the race whose obeisance they delight in, their rudeness of manner increasing until it becomes incredible to the relatives they left at home, and would once have been incredible to themselves. Then turn to the subordinate race, and watch the growing temptation to cringe and flatter, the loss of self-respect, the increasing cowardice, the daily humiliation. In that hideous process—that degeneration in the manners of two great races, each of which has high qualities of its own, we recognize the peril which has been advancing upon Indians and Englishmen for the last fifty years of Indian history. But, fortunately, throughout India, of late we are witnessing the birth of a new national consciousness, and with it comes a revival of dignity on the part of the Indian people, and a resolve no longer to take insults lying down, not to lick the hand that strikes, or rub the forehead in the dust before a human being simply because he wears a white helmet and is called white."

In his work on "Representative Government" (Chapter XVIII) John Stuart Mill points out the demoralizing and brutalizing influence of irresponsible power exercised by the strong over the weak, in India and elsewhere. He says:

"If there is a fact to which all experience testifies, it is that when a country holds another in subjection, the individuals of the ruling people who go to the foreign country to make their fortunes, are, of all others, those who most need to be held under proper restraint. Armed with prestige and filled with the scornful overbearingness of the conquering nation, they have the feeling inspired by absolute power without its sense of responsibility. Among a people like that of India, the utmost efforts of the public authorities are not enough for the effectual protection of the weak against the strong. Wherever the demoralizing effect of the situation is not in a most remarkable degree corrected by the personal character of the individual, the foreign intruders think the people of the country mere dirt under their feet; it seems to them monstrous that any rights of the 'natives' should stand in the way of their (the foreign masters') smallest pretensions."

This exactly describes the situation in India to-day.

Is it too much to claim that even if there were no other reasons why British rule in India should cease, one that is sufficient and more than sufficient exists in the facts which have been presented in these chapters,—facts showing the unbridgeable gulf which the British have created between themselves and their Indian subjects by their arrogance, their insufferable airs of superiority, their color—and race—prejudice, their want of sympathy with the people and therefore their inability to understand them, and their brutal treatment of them as underlings and slaves. Even if the Indian people were barbarians or only half-civilized, such an attitude on the part of their rulers would be cruel and seriously evil; but with a civilized people, having a great and proud past and possessing a culture in some of its aspects higher and richer than that of their haughty and egotistical rulers, it is simply unendurable.

In conclusion. For the sake of avoiding misunderstanding, let me say again and with the greatest possible clearness, what has already been said in this and the preceding chapter, that these facts and comments regarding the unjust, humiliating and often insulting treatment meted out to the Indian people by their English masters, do not apply to all Englishmen. As already pointed out and emphasized, there are in India some British officials, and some men not officials (business men) who were gentlemen when they came to India and who, in spite of the influences which tend to the contrary, remain always gentlemen, and who therefore continue always to treat the Indian people as courteously and justly as is possible under such political conditions as exist, that is, under conditions of political slavery, where foreign masters hold all power in their hands and the people have no alternative but to submit and obey. But these courteous gentlemen, who never lose their courtesy, whose manners and actions are never debased by the debasing influence of autocratic rule and irresponsible powers, are the exception. The great majority of Englishmen in India, both officials and business men (the latter following the fashion set by the former), become sooner or later of the overbearing, slave-master type described above. Such is one of the penalties which Great Britain pays, and must pay, for possessing an empire part free and part slave.

CHAPTER VIII

THE KIND OF "JUSTICE" BRITAIN GIVES INDIA

One of the claims oftenest made by Great Britain, is, that she has given to the Indian people better laws and a better judicial system than they ever had before or could create for themselves, and that this service rendered to them, alone, if there were no other, fully justifies her in retaining possession of the land.

Says Sir Robert Fulton, an eminent British official in India:

"The foundation of our empire in India rests on the principle of justice, and England retains its supremacy in India mainly by justice. Without justice we could not hold India for a moment, for it is that which inspires the people of India with a confidence in us and with a belief that in all our dealings with them we will never act otherwise than fairly and justly, and which renders them on the whole satisfied and contented with our rule."

This is what the British are constantly saying to the world in justification of their holding India in subjection. Is it true?

In large part it is untrue. The Indian people are not content with British rule; they want to rule themselves. They do not submit to British rule voluntarily, because they like it, and believe that it insures them greater justice than they could have if they governed themselves. They submit to it because and only because they must; because and only because they have been disarmed and British battleships are in all their harbors ready to bombard their cities; British cannon and machine guns are ready to mow down their men, women and children ; and British bombing air planes are ready to blow up their villages, if they attempt to throw off the yoke of their foreign masters.

As to justice, the Indian people recognize that their rulers are just in many if not in most things which do not affect their own British interests ; indeed, that they are probably as just in everything as it is possible for them to be and commit all the while the supreme, the infinite, injustice of robbing the country of its freedom, with all that that necessarily involves. But to say that the Indian people as a whole, or anything like a majority of them, are contented with British rule and desire that rule to continue because of its administration of justice, is false. Nobody can show that it is true ; there is overwhelming evidence that it is not.

What has Great Britain done for India in the way of promoting and ensuring justice ? What kind of laws has she given to the Indian people ?

Granting that the judicial system of India when the British went there needed improvement (as what legal system in the world at that time did not ?), how did the British set about improving it ? In a careful and constructive way ? In a way which the people of India could understand ? In a way to conserve and utilize and build upon all that was good in the preceding legal system or systems of the land ? That is the way in which we in this country improve our laws. That is the way the British themselves at home improve theirs. They advance slowly and cautiously "from precedent to precedent," avoiding sudden breaks or violent changes, building on what has been, making the whole a growth, a normal evolution, easily understood, easily and safely workable. Did they proceed in that way in India?

They proceeded in a way almost the exact opposite, and why not? Why should they build on anything that was Indian? Were not the Indians barbarians, or at least semi-barbarians? To be sure, they had possessed elaborate codes of laws of their own for centuries and centuries. But why should the British, with their vastly superior wisdom, need to know or care? So they proceeded to frame and to impose on the Indian people without in any way asking assent, a wholly new and strange legal system, patterned after that of England; virtually it was the British system transplanted to the far-off foreign soil of India.

Who was the man in whose hands was placed the chief responsibility in thus fashioning the laws and the courts which were so profoundly to affect the lives and fortunes of the Indian people?

It was Thomas Babington Macaulay.

Who was Macaulay? And what were his qualifications for the task assigned him? Later in life than his Indian career, through his essays, his history of England and other literary works, Macaulay obtained a somewhat high literary fame, and therefore we are naturally disposed to look favorably upon whatever he did in India. This disposition on our part is strengthened by the fact that we have two Essays from him in which he expresses friendly feelings toward the Indian people.* But in the light of a full study of his Indian career, and the results which have flowed from it, it is coming to be more and more the judgment of leading Indians and of intelligent students everywhere, that his work in India was fundamentally bad,—that it was one of the most potent of the many influences which have operated to de-Indianize India, to flout its civilization,

* Essays on Lord Clive and Warren Hastings.

to make its people weak imitators of England, instead of encouraging them to develop their own institutions, their own ideals and their own genius.

This was true in connection with the educational system which Macaulay had the chief part in framing for India, and it was equally true of the legal system, of which he was the prime creator.

It seems amazing that the difficult task (if adequately done, the *stupendous* task) of framing a code of laws for the vast and diverse populations of so great a country as India should have been entrusted to an almost unknown young man in far-off England, who had never been to India, who knew no Indian language, who was almost wholly unacquainted with the history, the customs the institutions and the civilization of the peoples for whom he was to legislate. And yet, after all, it was in line with a large part of England's management of India. Most of the men whom she has sent there, even as Governor-Generals, to rule the land, have been persons who had never set foot on Indian soil and could speak no Indian tongue.

What kind of a Law System did Macaulay frame for India? Was it one suited to her needs? How could it be? He knew next to nothing about her needs, and there is strong evidence that he cared little. Ignorant of India's law codes and of nearly everything else Indian, and knowing no law but that of England, what could he do but plan a legal system similar to that of England, really based on it, and thrust it on the Indian people? This was what was done,

Major Basu, author of *The Rise of the Christian Power in India*, expresses what is the general judgment of Indian scholars, when he says (volume v, p. 21):

"Macaulay came out to this country to shake the pagoda tree, and become rich at the expense of the children of the soil."

He was poor, and was having a hard struggle to make a living as a writer. On August 17, 1833, the year before he went to India, he wrote in a letter to his sister: "I have never made more than two hundred pounds a year by my pen, and I cannot support myself in comfort on less than five hundred." Under such conditions it is little wonder that he thought of India, where many of his friends were making great fortunes. Through the influence of some of these a place was found, or made, for him.

It happened that the Directors of the British East India Company, who at that time controlled Indian affairs, were desirous of giving India a new Legal System, one which would be more satisfactory to them, if not to the Indian people, and one which they could administer with less difficulty than they had experienced in the past. Accordingly they created a new office, that of Law Member of the Government, and assigned it to Macaulay. The position was one of high dignity, and the salary attached to it was enormous, princely—10,000 pounds (50,000 dollars) a year (quite an advance over the 200 pounds which he had earned by his pen before!). He wrote to his sister: "I am assured by persons who know Calcutta intimately and who have mixed in the highest circles and held the highest offices, that I may live in splendor there for five thousand a year, and may save the rest of my salary with the accruing interest. I may, therefore, return to England at only thirty-nine years of age, in full vigor of life, with a fortune of thirty thousand pounds" ($150,000), which for that day was great wealth.

But even this was not all in the salary line. Besides his position as Law Member of the Government, he was also appointed Law

Commissioner, for which he received an additional five thousand pounds, making a total of fifteen thousand pounds ($75,000) a year;—this in a country where the people were among the poorest in the world! And this amazing, this utterly unwarranted and wicked salary, wrung by an alien Government from a nation always upon the verge of famine, was only one of the many such, lavished upon favored Englishmen. This shows how India's money went. Is it any wonder that from the richest of countries it has become the poorest?

How has this Code of Laws which Macaulay was the chief agent in framing, worked? Has it benefited India? Major Basu unhesitatingly answers, No. He declares that it was of a nature to "degrade the Indian people. It gave insecurity to life and property and encouraged corruption and litigation...It showed its framer to have been swayed by no consideration or motive of philanthropy or altruism toward the people of India but solely by regard for the interests of England... In no other civilized country are offenders so severely punished as they are in India under this Code. The principle underlying the law is—once a jail-bird, always a jail-bird. There is an attempt to outcast the criminal from society, and no idea of reclaiming him as a citizen. The Code is like an iron machine whose business is to forge fetters for the Indian. It tends to depress him in spirit, and make him less than a man." And what wonder? framed as it was by a stranger, who knew almost nothing of India, and who looked down with ill-concealed contempt upon its civilization and its people!

Mr. John Dickinson, in his book, "Government of India Under a Bureaucracy," describes the kind of legal system set up by the British and the results which it produced. He says:

"We, the English, ignorantly assumed that the ancient, long-civilized people of India were a race of barbarians who had never known what justice was until we came among them, and that the best thing we could do for them was to upset all their institutions as fast as we could, and among others their judicial system, and give them instead a copy of our legal models at home (in England)·········Even if the technical system of English law had worked well at home (as in many respects it did not), it would have been the grossest political empiricism to force it on a people so different from ourselves as every Oriental people are; and the reader may conceive the irreparable mischief it has done in India. ·········Long before we knew anything of India, native society there had been characterized by some peculiar and excellent institutions, prominent among them a municipal organization, providing a most efficient police for the administration of criminal law, while the civil law was worked by a simple process of arbitration, which either prevented litigation, or else insured prompt and substantial justice to the litigants···Instead of their own simple and rational mode of dispensing justice, we have given the Indian people an obscure, complicated, pedantic system of English law, full of artificial technicalities, which disable the candidates for justice from any longer pleading their own cause, and force them to have recourse to a swarm of attorneys and special pleaders, by means of which their expenses are greatly increased and the ends of justice are defeated."*

Since Macaulay's day there have been some changes in the code which he framed, though they have not been great. Let us examine with some care the law and law practice of India as they exist to-day, to see whether they promote justice to the extent claimed by the friends of British rule,—to such an extent as justifies that rule.

1. A very serious evil which confronts us at the very outset—one which is recognized by the

---

* "Government of India under a Bureaucracy," by John Dickinson, M. R. A. S., F. R. G. S., pp. 41 to 47. London, 1853. Allahabad, India, 1925;

entire Indian people and by many Englishmen—is the union of executive and judicial functions in the same official. In all the lower Indian courts we find this unreasonable, this uncivilized union existing. The Indian people have protested against it from the beginning, as a source of inevitable and perpetual injustices. But it still continues. Think of a legal system being maintained in any civilized country, in which the judge and the prosecutor are the same man! Englishmen look back with shame upon the infamous "Star Chamber" Court of Charles I. In what did the infamy of that court consist? Primarily in the same practice which England maintains in India of uniting the accuser and the judge in the same person.

2. It is claimed, and seemingly on good ground, that a serious cause of injustice in connection with Indian law practice, is the fact that so many of the judges are foreigners (generally Englishmen), who have so little acquaintance with the Indian people. It is true that the Government has the wisdom and fairness to appoint some Indian judges; but not enough. Indeed, it is a question whether *all* judges who *try Indian cases* should not be Indians. The reason why is plain. In the very nature of things Indian judges have an enormous advantage in such cases over Englishmen or any other foreigners, because they know the vernaculars, the habits, the customs, the psychology, of the people, which foreigners and strangers do not and cannot. This knowledge saves them from numerous blunders and injustices which foreign judges cannot avoid falling into. And yet the Government insists in filling a large proportion of the judicial positions of most importance with Englishmen.

Nor is this all. Englishmen are often appointed judges actually who have no knowledge of law, *any* law,—who had not studied law in England before they left there, and who have received no legal training in India. To this ignorance of law, add their too common ignorance of the customs, the habits and the very languages of the people, and it is easy to see how well qualified they are to be administators of justice.

Nor are these ignorant Englishmen appointed because there are no better men, no legally trained Indians, available. Usually there is no lack of Indians, of quite as much ability as the Englishmen,—Indians who have regularly studied law, taking university degrees either in England or India, and who, also, in many cases, have actually had years of active legal practice. But no! the positions must be given to Englishmen because they are Englishmen.

3. One of the confessedly grave evils of Indian law is its cost to the people. The Indian people are so poor that they ought to have the simplest and least expensive possible method of settling their difficulties and obtaining legal justice. This, to a considerable degree, they had in the old days before the British obtained mastery of the country. India is a land of villages. Before the British appeared on the scene, in every village there existed a *Panchayat* or Village Council., usually consisting of five of the leading and most trusted men, who managed the public affairs of the community, legal and other. These village *Panchayats*, existing in all parts of the land, served as courts, always close at hand, available to everybody, in which nearly all the legal difficulties of the people were settled, settled quickly, with a high degree of justice, and with the very minimum of expense. It seems hardly possible to conceive of a legal system more simple, more practical or in any way

better than this. But the British, when they came, in their contempt for everything Indian, and their arrogant assumption of the superiority of everything English, and with their determination to get all power into their own hands, even in the management of the small affairs of the villages destroyed these time-honored *Panchayats*, and set up, to take their place in legal matters, as we have seen, an elaborate, cumbrous, foreign system of laws, courts, judges, lawyers (solicitors, barristers pleaders, attorneys and the rest) which the people could understand only with the greatest difficulty which has led to endless delays and needless litigations, which has failed in justice far oftener than did the simple *Panchayat* system, and which has involved expenses so great as to be ruinous to thousands.

Mr. W. M. Torrens, M. P., in his book, "Empire in Asia" (pp. 100-103), says:

"In most parts of India the village community, from time out of mind, has been the unity of social, industrial and political existence. The village and its common interests and affairs have been ruled over by a council of Elders, always representative in character, who, when any dispute arose, declared what was the customary law. . . . . . In all Indian villages there was a regularly constituted municipality, by which its affairs, both of revenue and police, were administered, and which exercised magisterial and judicial authority. . . . Subordination to authority, the security of property, the maintenance of local order, the vindication of character, the safety of life, all depended on the action of these nerves and sinews of the judiciary system. To maim or paralyze such a system, reticulated minutely through the whole frame of society, and working silently and effectively everywhere, as the British have done, may well be deemed a policy which nothing but the arrogance of conquest could have dictated. Yet these municipal institutions were rudely disregarded or uprooted by the new system of a foreign administration. Instead of the native *Panchayat*, there was established the foreign arbitrary judge ; instead of men being tried, when accused, by an elective jury of their fellow-citizens, they must go before a stranger, who could not, if he would, know half what every judge should know of the men and things to be dealt with. Instead of confidence, there was distrust; instead of calm, popular, unquestioned justice, there was substituted necessarily imperfect inquiry, hopelessly puzzled intelligence, the arbitration of foreign officials guessing at the facts through interpreters, and stumbling over habits and usage which it must take a life-time to learn, but which every native juryman or elder could recall without hesitation. No wise or just historian can note these things without wonder and condemnation."

Sir Henry Cotton in his book "New India," p. 170 (see also pp. 141-143), says:

"The people of India possess an instinctive capacity for local self-government. In the past (before the British came) the inhabitants of an Indian village under their own leaders formed a sort of petty republic, the affairs of which were managed by hereditary officers, any unfit person being set aside by popular judgment in favor of a more acceptable member of his family. It is by reason of the British administration, only, that the popular authority of the village headman has been sapped, and the judicial power of the *Panchayat*, or Committee of Five, has been subverted. A costly and mechanical centralization has taken the place of the former system of local self-government and local arbitration."

Within the past few years, not a few Englishmen themselves have come to realize how great a blunder on the part of the Government and how great a loss to India, the destruction of the *Panchayats* has been, and have done so far as to discuss the question of their restoration. But there does not seem much prospect of anything being achieved, for no one seems able to point out how they can be adapted to, or made to fit in with, the established alien British legal system, which, with its complicated procedures, its delays and its autocratic spirit, is so far removed from the simplicity, the quick efficiency and the democratic spirit of the *Panchayats*.

4. The gravest charge of all against the British legal system in India, remains yet to be mentioned. It is that of partiality, favoritism, toward Europeans, especially Englishmen, resulting in serious and widespread injustice to the Indian people. In other words, the charge is widely made that while the courts are conceded to render, as a rule, satisfactory justice, as between Europeans and Europeans, and generally a considerable degree of justice between Indians and Indians, the case is wholly different between Englishmen and Indians. Here, it is averred, there is no certainty, and seldom even probability, of justice; indeed, here it is declared there is almost absolute certainty of injustice.

This charge is denied by many Englishmen, if not by most. But by some it is admitted; and it is so generally and so strongly affirmed by Indians that it cannot be ignored.

The truth is, the evidences are simply numberless, coming from sources many of which are the most reliable possible, that injustices on this score are occurring constantly and practically everywhere in India, that often they are cruel and bitter in the extreme, and that no Indian anywhere is secure from them. Crimes committed by Indians against Europeans are always punished with great severity, often with penalties far, far beyond those inflicted upon Europeans under like conditions. On the other hand, crimes committed by Europeans against Indians are always punished in the lightest manner possible, often so inadequately as to attract public attention and constitute a scandal. The testimony of one European is often given more weight in a court than that allowed to any number of Indians—Indians of the most unimpeachable character. In cases of dispute or doubt between an Englishman and an Indian the

Englishman practically always gets the benefit of the doubt. Trials by jury are denied to Indians under conditions in which they are allowed in cases of gravity to Europeans.* Great numbers of cases are reported of torture inflicted upon Indians by police to compel them to testify as the British desire. Numerous Indians, including the most eminent and honored in the land, are arrested without warrant, and even without being informed for what they are arrested, and are imprisoned without trial, or with only a scant trial in which they are not allowed to have witnesses or counsel.

Regarding these matters I cite a few testimonies; space does not allow me to give more.

Says a prominent Calcutta daily:

"No man in this country can knock an Englishman down without promptly being arrested and sent to jail. But an Englishman may knock a dozen Indians down and go scot-free. If the Indian attempts to defend himself against his British assailant, the officer is on him in no time, and he goes to jail for a heavy sentence."

Says a Bombay daily:

"A European kicks his servant to death. The local magistrate finds him guilty of simple assault and fines him one pound, six shillings and eight pence. An appeal to the Bombay High Court increases the sentence to nine months' imprisonment."

As I write there lies before me an Indian paper from one of the large interior cities, containing an article entitled, "How Justice is

---

* The Indian Criminal Code makes many invidious discriminations against the native Indian and in favor of the European. One is, it refuses to Indians the right of appeal in summary convictions where it is allowed to Europeans.

Administered in Indian Law Courts," which gives a list of a dozen or so specific cases of crimes committed by Englishmen against Indians, most of them crimes against life, in which no adequate or just punishment is meted out to the perpetrators. I cite three or four as illustrations. In one case, the editor of a government periodical in the Punjab shoots his servant for some alleged offence, and is sentenced to six months' imprisonment and a fine of 200 rupees ($67). In another case a European overseer in a jute mill assaults a worker, causing his death, and is ordered by the Court to pay a fine of the sum just mentioned, and undergo one month's imprisonment. In another, an Englishman kicks a sweeper, rupturing his spleen, which results in his death, and is ordered to pay a fine of 50 rupees ($17), with no imprisonment. In still another case, an Indian is sentenced to twenty years' imprisonment for attempting to rape an Englishwoman, while in the same province an Englishman who gags and rapes a Hindu girl of eighteen, is acquitted, with no punishment at all. The writer of the article emphatically affirms that always, if the criminal is an Englishman, excuses are found for acquittal or making the penalty light. Even in cases of taking of life, palliating circumstances are found which prevent the crime from being called murder, and therefore which save the Englishman from hanging, or from any punishment such as would be meted out if the crime had been committed by an Indian against a European.

In November, 1923, some British soldiers who had been out fox-hunting near the village of Lohagaon, in the vicinity of Poona, fell into an altercation with the villagers, when one of the villagers was shot dead by a soldier named Walker. The soldier was tried by the Sessions

Court before European jurors and British judges, and acquitted. Mr. N. C. Kelkar, President of the Poona City Municipality and Editor of the weekly *Kesari*, commented editorially in his paper as follows:

"Such farces of trials of Europeans accused of crimes against Indians are not new among us. They date back to the times of Warren Hastings. The thing to be most regretted is that with such things taking place before their very eyes there are persons who keep singing the praise of British justice. By good rights a pillar ought to be erected at Lohagaon having engraved on it the full details of this case, as a memorial showing what value is attached to the lives of Indians under British rule."

Mr. A. C. Mozumdar, in an article in the *Indian World* of February-March, 1909 (pp. 183-4), gives the view of this whole matter which he declares almost universally prevails in India. He says in substance (I condense): British justice is asserted as the strongest justification for British rule in India. But this claim of justice receives repeated shocks from the numerous instances occurring among us of assaults and murders of Indians and violations of Indian women, which either receive no punishment at all or else punishment so light as to be hardly better than a farce. If the life of an Englishman is taken by an Indian, even when there are many extenuating circumstances, no mercy is shown; with almost absolute certainty the Indian must pay with his life. But when the committer of the crime is an Englishman and the victim is an Indian, the situation is entirely different. Under no conditions must an Englishman be hanged or shot for anything he does to a native of the country. A small fine or a short imprisonment, or in extreme cases both, are the most that he must ever be allowed to suffer. Our British-administered courts, continues Mr.

Mozumdar, seem usually to "value Indian lives at from fifty to a hundred rupees (from seventeen to thirty-three dollars) each." In cases where an Englishwoman is insulted no penalty is too severe. But not so when the victim is an Indian woman.

"There are dozens of cases in which Indian husbands and fathers have been compelled to submit in utter despair, without any legal recourse to the grossest outrages committed on their wives and daughters, in tea-gardens, on board steamers, in railway carriages and stations, and in the vicinity of military encampments, where the helpless victims have either died, or preferring death to dishonor, have committed suicide. With the exception of one solitary instance, no serious notice has ever been taken (so far as I have known or have been able to learn) of these abominable crimes, which go on unchecked, embittering public feelings."

In the Allahabad *Independent*, under date of October 7, 1920, Mr. Motilal Nehru, a man of the highest standing, President of the Indian National Congress in 1919, a lawyer who had had a practice of 37 years in the law courts of India , publishes an article in which he says :

"Coming to the courts of India, we all know what kind of justice is to be expected in criminal matters under the special procedure prescribed for the trial of Europeans. During the last 150 years every Indian who has met with death at the hands of a European has either had an enlarged spleen or his death has turned out to be the result of pure 'accident.' There has not been a single case, so far as I am aware, of murder pure and simple."

In other words, a "special procedure" is provided "for the trial of Europeans" so that they may have special favor shown them as superior persons, and not be subject to the penalties that would be pronounced against them if they were Indians. And as a result, during a century and a half of British rule not a single Englishman, so far as Mr. Nehru is aware, has ever been indicted "for murder pure and simple"; but in every case, the excuse has been found that the victim had some kind of bodily infirmity which caused his death, or that his death was the "result of pure accident."

Sir Henry Cotton, in his book "New India" (p. 57), slightly differs from Pandit Nehru; he has information of two cases in which Europeans have been punished with death for murdering Indians. He says:

"Assaults on natives of India by Europeans have always been of frequent occurrence, with sometimes fatal consequences. The trial of these cases, in which Englishmen are tried by English juries, too often results in a failure of justice not falling short of judicial scandal. During the past half century there have been only two cases in which capital punishment has been inflicted on an European for the murder of a native, and in both these cases no stone was left unturned by Anglo-Indians to obtain a reversal of the sentence. . . . If a tea-planter (British) is charged with an outrageous assault upon a helpless coolie, he is tried by a jury of (British) tea-planters, whose natural bias is in his favor; but if, in any circumstances, a conviction should ensue, the whole volume of English opinion finds expression in denouncing the verdict the anglo-Indian newspapers add fuel to the flame and give free vent to this protest in their columns, public subscriptions are raised to pay the expenses of the culprit, and influentially signed memorials are addressed to the Government praying for his release. An Anglo-Indian Defense Association has been organised in Calcutta for the express purpose of defending such cases. A paragraph is published in the newspapers headed, 'A Planter in Trouble,' and forthwith all the flood-gates of passion and prejudice are let loose." *

There is a tradition, an understanding, firmly fixed in the minds of the British in India to the effect that the British must never give in to the

* Sir Henry Cotton, "New India," pp. 57, 58,

Indians—that in the case of any crime alleged to have been committed by an Englishman against a "native," the Englishman is probably innocent, or, if proved to be guilty, must either go free on some legal technicality, or at least must escape with only a nominal punishment. This understanding is so deeply ingrained in the British mind in India, that Lord Curzon, when Viceroy, actually came near being "hooted and pelted out of Calcutta." if not driven out of India, because, as his historian says, in the case of an Englishman who had beaten a coolie to death, he, the Viceroy, had insisted on a trial and a penalty which had in them some real justice—which were more than farces enacted to shield the British criminal.

I give two more testimonies.

Says Mrs. Annie Besant, President of the Theosophical Societies of India:

"It is argued that Great Britain has bestowed upon India justice and good government. She has been just in quarrels in which Europeans had no concern; but in matters between Europeans and Indians she has shown, and still shows, the greatest injustice."*

Says Mr. S. R. Wagel, the eminent Indian Economist:

"The courts of justice in India are reasonably good so long as the dispute is between Indian and Indian. But when it is a political case, or when it is a dispute between an Indian and an Englishman, there is no justice at all in nine cases out of ten."†

Says Mahatma Gandhi:

"In ninety-nine cases out of a hundred justice is denied to Indians as against Europeans in the courts of India. This is not an exaggerated picture. It is the ex-

---

* *Navayuga*, May 11, 1924.

† Letter in *New York Times*, October 30, 1915.

perience of almost every Indian who has ever had anything to do with such cases."*

In the face of such facts and testimonies as the above, is there any conclusion but one that can possibly be drawn by intelligent and fair-minded men, regarding British legal "Justice" in India, and the claim that it is of so high a character as to justify British rule?

Let no one understand anything said in this chapter to mean a denial that Englishmen generally, love justice, care for justice, desire to be just. It is not questioned that in England, and among European peoples—indeed, among peoples everywhere who are free and of their own race, they are probably as just as any men in the world. The trouble in India is in the conditions under which they are placed. They are a part of a great system of injustice; how then can they be just? The situation changes their psychology, their moral standards, for the time being their very nature, and makes them unjust. It is well-known that, in domestic slavery, the slave masters, however just they may be in their dealings among themselves and among their equals, can never be depended on for justice to their slaves. A race eminently just among its own people, is often shamefully unjust in its conduct toward a race which it regards as inferior, especially if it has that race under its domination. Here is the explanation of British injustice in India. The British have undertaken a great unjust job, that of ruling another nation without its consent. In the very nature of things such a job cannot be done without constant injustice. Rebel against the thought as much as they may, and

* Quotation from his address made at his trial, March, 18, 1922.

some of them do rebel against it, they simply *must* make unjust laws. Unjust ends necessitate unjust means. The trouble is in the job. This means that the chief blame should be placed, not upon the Englishmen in India who made the unjust laws (though they should be regarded as by no means wholly blameless), but upon the infinitely unjust system of foreign domination existing in India with which they have allied themselves, and before all and above all upon the nation which, in the light of this twentieth century, and in disregard of the constant protest of the Indian people, maintains this barbarous domination.

Where is the remedy for India's legal injustices ? There is none so long as she is ruled by aliens.

CHAPTER IX

THE KIND OF "PEACE" BRITAIN HAS GIVEN INDIA

(India's Pax-Britannica)

There lies before me as I write an old number of *The Atlantic Monthly*, dated June, 1908, containing an article, by Mr. J. M. Hubbard, on British Rule in India, in which I find, among much else of a similar nature, the following statement regarding the great blessing of peace which the Indian people were alleged to enjoy as the result of the conquest and government of their country by Great Britain. Says Mr. Hubbard :

> "India is enjoying peace which has not been disturbed for 50 years; a peace which is not that maintained by force of arms, but which arises from pure contentment. Nowhere else in the world is there such contentment by people under a foreign yoke."

At the very time this article appeared, India was seething with discontent ; all Bengal was boiling with excitement and indignation over Lord Curzon's partition of the province; bombs were being thrown; there were arrests without warrant and imprisonments on every hand, and Lajpat Rai, because he had presumed to plead for a place for India in the Empire like that of Canada, had been seized and hurried away to imprisonment in Burma.

I call attention to these statements of Mr. Hubbard because similar utterances have been coming to us in great numbers for fifty years, all praising Great Britain's so-called Pax-Britannica in India. Indeed, nothing is urged oftener to-day in justification of British rule there than the claim that the rule has rescued the Indian people from perpetual wars and bloodshed, and given them the great blessing of peace, such peace as they had not known for centuries, if ever.

Is the claim true? Was India a scene of perpetual conflict before the British came? Did Britain come bringing peace—such peace, such rescue from war and bloodshed, such security, and therefore such contentment, as has justified her in the past and as justifies her to-day in robbing the Indian people of their freedom and holding them in forced bondage?

If Britain brought peace to India, was it peace only after forcing on her long and terrible wars, wars of conquest, wars bloodier than any she had ever known?

And if the British gave India *internal* peace, did they give her also *external* peace? Or did they force upon her participation in foreign wars almost without number, which cost her the blood of hundreds of thousands of her sons?

Still further. What was the *nature* of the internal peace, such as it was, which they gave India? Was it of a kind which meant happiness, health, strength, sanitation of the country, freedom of the people, prosperity of the people? Or was it a peace which meant foreign exploitation of the country, neglect of education, neglect of sanitation, impoverishment and starvation of the people, loss of national freedom, enslavement and degradation of the nation?

Not all kinds of peace are better than war. Has the so-called peace which Britain has given India been better than war? Or has it been, as many Indians and not a few Englishmen believe, worse than any wars that India had ever known before the British came?

Let us see just what are the facts?

First, as to the condition of India before the British made their advent. Was that condition one of such war and bloodshed as the British represent.

So far as we can learn from the best historical records we possess, India, during most of its history before the British came, was more peaceful than Europe. For more than twelve hundred years—from the third or fourth century B. C. to the tenth A. D.—its leading religion was Buddhism, and, as is well known, Buddhism has taught peace more strongly and secured it among its followers more effectively, during all its history, than has any other great religious faith known to the world.

At the time the British made their appearance in India there was unusual tumult. The great Mogul Empire which had been the ruling power for several centuries was just breaking up. That, of course, caused, for a period, much conflict and bloodshed. The British took advantage of that, and by shrewdly and often shamelessly taking the part of one native state or one warring faction against another state or faction, secured such a foothold in the land as otherwise they could not have obtained. From this beginning they pushed on their conquests, by the use of much the same arts, until they have obtained supremacy everywhere. But it cannot be too strongly affirmed that much of the time before the British came, India was better fitted to teach peace to Europe than any European nation was to teach peace to her.

It is true that from time to time in its past history India had had wars on a more or less extensive scale between states or provinces or cities or native princes, such like the wars during the Middle Ages between the states and dukedoms and princes of Germany and France and Italy and England, and occasionally she had suffered more or less serious raids from outside like the cruel border raids of Scotland, with at long intervals a temporary great and devastating raid such as that of Nadir Shah. But never, in all her history, had she experienced any wars involving such vast destruction of life and property as the Thirty Years War of Germany, or the wars of Napoleon, or even the Civil War in the United States; and as to the Great War in Europe of 1914 to 1918, she had never known anything in any way to be compared with that.

Indeed, the bloodiest wars India has experienced in modern times, if not in all her history, have been those which the British themselves forced upon her,—first those fought to conquer the country, lasting almost a century, and then, later, that connected with what the British call the "Mutiny" or "Sepoy Rebellion" but which the Indians call a "War for Independence." Said the London *Spectator* of April 27, 1910: "We took at least 100,000 Indian lives in the Mutiny." But that was only one war and a very short one; the number of Indian lives taken in the wars, and wars following wars of conquest, was many times greater, reaching into the millions.

Sir George Otto Trevelyan, the British historian and Statesman, tells us in his book, "Cawnpore," published in 1865, that the British soldiers in India had killed more of the Indian people in a single year than the missionaries had converted in a century.

The world has little conception of the amount of Indian blood shed in the long succession of wars waged by the British to subdue all the different Indian peoples and states,—wars continuing on for nearly a hundred years, from Clive's battle of Arcot in the South, in 1751, to General Gough's battle of Gujrat in the North-west, in which the brave Sikhs were finally crushed, in 1849. And it should not for a moment be forgotten that on the part of the British these wars were pure aggression—fought to gain forcible possession of a country to which they had no right ; whereas on the part of the Indians, they were all patriotic wars, fought against invaders, fought to retain control of their own land.

British historians of India, desiring to justify their country before the world for conquering a great civilized nation and holding it in subjection, are wont to pass lightly over the terribly sanguinary character of these wars. Says Dickinson :

> "We (the British) are accustomed to consider the battle of Waterloo, one of the most sanguinary ever fought; yet the losses in some of our Indian battles of conquest were about double the loss at Waterloo. The loss in our Sutlej battles in 1846 was much more severe than that of Waterloo."

Does it become a nation, which, on coming to India, proceeded for a hundred years to pour out India's blood in such torrents, to boast of bringing her peace ?

But, not only did Great Britain shed rivers of Indian blood in conquering the country and later in putting down the so-called "Mutiny" of 1858 ; but, from the very first until the present time she has all the while compelled (virtually compelled) Indians in large numbers to serve in her armies, in carrying on wars largely of aggression and conquest, many of them on borders of India, against neighboring peoples, to gain possession of their territory, and others in distant lands to enlarge or strengthen the British Empire there.

Notice first the almost continuous nearer wars which the British have fought (or forced their Indian soldiers to fight) along the borders of India to conquer contiguous peoples so as to annex their lands.

I wonder if my readers are acquainted with John Morley's description of the way in which Great Britain, during all her history in India, has been constanly encroaching on her neighbors. Not only is it very illuminating, but it is especially interesting as coming from one who for some years was the Secretary of State for India in the British Cabinet. He calls it "The Rake's Progress."

Writes Morley :

"First, you push on into territories where you have no business to be, and where you had promised not to go ; secondly, your intrusion provokes resentment, and resentment means resistance; thirdly, you instantly cry out that the people are rebellious and that their act is rebellion (this in spite of your own assurance that you have no intention of setting up a permanent sovereignty over them); fourthly, you send a force to stamp out the rebellion; and fifthly, having spread bloodshed confusion and anarchy, you declare, with hands uplifted to the heavens, that moral reasons force you to stay, for if you were to leave, this territory would be left in a condition which no civilized power could contemplate with equanimity or with composure. These are the five stages of the Rake's Progress."

In other words, these are the steps by which Great Britain has insidiously and persistently extended the bounds of her Indian Empire.

A lurid light is thrown upon all this (that is, on the way Britain has *given India peace*) by a

Parliamentary Report made in 1899 in the British House of Commons, on the demand of John Morley, showing just how many of those border wars there have been, in what localities and their exact nature. The Parliamentary Report revealed the amazing fact that during the 19th century Great Britain actually carried on, in connection with India, mainly on its borders, not fewer than one hundred and eleven (111) wars, raids, military expeditions and military campaigns. Think of the almost unbelievable number—nearly all, as Morely makes clear, wars and raids of pure aggression. Of course, more or less plausible excuses or pretexts were always found to justify them,—a "quarrelsome neighbor," a "dangerous neighbor," a neighbor that had encroached upon India in some way and needed to be "punished," the necessity for a "better" "more natural" or "scientific "boundary" or "frontier" for India, etc., etc. But with scarcely an exception, their real object was to grab new territory.

Upon whom did Britain put the burden of carrying on these wars and campaigns—the burden of fighting those battles and shedding this blood? Mainly the Indians. And, why not? For was not Indian blood cheaper than that of Englishmen? But was it a great Benefit to India, a great improvement over former conditions, for the Indian people to be thus saved from local conflicts such as they had formerly known—from local wars, longer or shorter, of Indian States against Indian States and Indian Princes against Indian Princes,—and instead, to be compelled to lose their lives in those British wars after wars, and campaigns after campaigns, almost without ceasing, against neighboring peoples and nations, and all for the purpose of increasing the territory and augmenting the power of their foreign conquerors and masters? *

It will be illuminating if I give a list of the wars and campaigns, most of them on the borders of India but some of them far away carried on by Great Britain during the last half of the nineteenth century (from 1859 to 1900),—campaigns and wars in which Indian troops were compelled to fight, in any cases to do the main fighting. The list, not quite complete, is as follows:

Two wars in distant China. in 1860 and 1900; the Bhutan war of 1864-65; the distant Abyssinian war of 1868; the Afghan war of 1878-79; after the massacre of the Kabul Mission, the Second Afghan war of 1879-80; the distant Egyptian war of 1882; the Burmese war of 1885; ending in the annexation of Upper Burma in 1886; the military expedition to Sitana, 1858; on a small scale, and on a large scale (the Sitana Campaign) 1863; to Nepal and Sikkim in 1859; to Sikkim in 1864; a serious struggle in the Northwest Frontier in 1868; military expeditions against the Lushais in 1871-72; against the Nagas in 1875; against the Afridis in 1877; against the Rampu Hill tribes in 1879; against the Wuziriz and Nagas in 1881; against the Akhas in 1884; a military expedition

---

* Says an Indian writer with biting sarcasm: "Great Britain has always been greatly concerned to save the Indian people from themselves. She loves them so much, she feels such a deep responsibility on them as their guardian and protector, that she can't think of *letting them shed one another's* blood. It is so much *better* that their blood should be shed by *Christian Englishmen.*" Commenting on this, an eminent British writer adds with sarcasm not less sharp, "This is a splendid moral view. It is unfortunate that the people of India are so steeped in barbarism that they do not appreciate what a blessing it is to be killed by *civilized foreigners rather than by one another.*"

to the Zhob valley in 1884; a second to the same valley in 1884; military expeditions against Sikkim, against the Akazais (the Black Mountain expedition), and against the Hill Tribes of the Northeast in 1888-89; another Black Mountain military expedition in 1890; a third in 1892; a military expedition to Manipur in 1890; another military expedition against the Lushais in 1891; one into the Miratzel Valley in 1891; the serious Tirah Campaign in which 40,000 men were engaged, in 1897-98; the military expedition against the Mashuds in 1901; that against the Kabalta in 1902; the invasion of Tibet in 1904. To these should be added the sending of Indian troops to distant Malta and Cyprus in 1878, and the expenditure of some $10,000,000 in military operations to face what was described as the "Russian Menace" in 1884.

Let it be noted that this list, almost unbelievably long as it is, includes none of Britain's wars or military expeditions, some of them of large magnitude and importance in which Indian soldiers had part, occurring in the nineteenth century *previous to the year 1859*, nor, of course, does it include any of the wars fought by Great Britain (largely with the aid of Indian troops) in the *twentieth century* culminating in the Great War of 1914 to 1918, in which the soldiers of India did remarkably effective (and sanguinary) fighting in France, Palestine, Syria and Mesopotamia. But the list is sufficiently full to show how almost constantly Great Britain has been carrying on wars during all her Indian history—some of them to enlarge the boundaries of India and some in distant parts of the earth—all of them fought purely *in the interest of the British Empire*, not one of them fought *in the interest of the Indian people*, yet *India's sons compelled to* *do a large part of the fighting, suffering and dying* !*

In view of all those rivers of blood which British rule has drawn from the veins of India's sons, we can well understand the lines wrung from the anguished soul of one of India's gifted woman poets :

"Lo, I have flung to the East and the West
Priceless treasures torn from my breast,
And yielded the sons of my stricken womb
To the drum-beats of England, the sabres of doom.
Gathered like pearls in their alien graves,
Silent they sleep by the Persian waves;
Scattered like shells on Egyptian sands
They lie with pale brows and brave broken hands,
They are strewn like blossoms mown down by chance
On the blood-brown meadows of Flanders and France.
. . . . O, England! O, World!
Remember the blood of my slaughtered ones,
Weep for my dead, my martyred sons." †

So much then for *one side* of the *Pax-Britannica* which Great Britain has given India, a side which Britain persists in calling "peace," but which India calls very bloody and terrible wars.

There is *another side*. Is it any better? Has it brought any more good, any less suffering, or any less loss of life to the Indian people, than the cruel *war side* has done.

We have already said, there are kinds of peace that are worse than war. Has Britain given India such peace ?

Practically all Indian authorities and also many eminent Englishmen deny that India's *pax Britannica* has been on the whole in the sum total of

---

* In the light of such revelations as these, one can hardly wonder at the words of Richard Cobden : "We British have been the most aggressive, quarrelsome, warlike, bloody nation under the sun."

† Sarojini Naidu.

its effects—any more a benefit to the Indian people than was the old *pax-Romana* a benefit to the nations of the ancient Mediterranean world. Why was not that Roman peace a good? Because it was created by force. And therefore, as is now recognized, it was really a peace of helplessness, of emasculation; a peace of nations reduced to such weakness, exhaustion and poverty, such loss of men and resources, such destruction of courage and hope, such physical, intellectual and moral decadence, that it was simply impossible for them to fight longer, and they were, therefore, compelled to submit and become subjects and political slaves of Rome. Looked at superficially and as to its immediate and temporary effects, the *pax-Romana* may have seemed a good. But looked at deeply, as we look at it to-day in the light of history, it is seen to have been a terrible calamity. Instead of advancing the progress of the nations concerned it arrested their progress, probably for several centuries.

Peace caused by intelligence, justice and good-will is always a good. It always tends to produce progress and civilization. But peace caused by force, by war, by destroying the ability of nations to fight, by reducing nations and peoples to such a degree of poverty, helplessness, emasculation and despair that they cannot fight,—such a peace in the very nature of things is an evil—an evil far outweighing any seeming or superficial good that men may associate with it.

It is in *this light* that intelligent students are more and more judging, and that future generations will *wholly* judge, the lauded *pax-Britannica* which by blood and slaughter, by all the horrors, ravages and destructions of war Great Britain has forced upon the Indian peoples.

Just what kind of an India has Britain's

lauded "peace" produced? The answer is seen in India's lack of schools and education, in her want of sanitation, in her unparalleled poverty (according to British high authorities one-third of her population never knowing what a full meal is) the untold millions of Indian men, women and children who have died from famines, from plague, cholera, fevers, influenza, malaria and other preventable diseases, who need not have died if the enormous sums of money wickedly spent by the Government for militaristic and imperialistic ends and needlessly paid to foreigners in the form of fat salaries and pensions, been expended for India's good—for her prosperity, intelligence and health.

Says the *Modern Review* of Calcutta (December, 1920, p. 675) :

"England claims to have given India the benefits of 'undisturbed peace.' Our reply is : What kind of peace has it been? What has it brought to India? Not only has India's blood been poured out in rivers at home and abroad, but India to-day is poorer, more illiterate, more famine-stricken, more disease-ridden, and inhabited by a worse fed and physically weaker population than any civilized country in these continents. During the many decades of this 'undisturbed peace' which England has blessed us with, India has lost more of her population by death than any other equally populous area on the earth even where peace has been most disturbed and wars worst.',"

Let me give some terrible facts about the single matter of birth and death-rates in India as compared with other lands. The average annual death-rate in England is only 13 per 1,000 of the population and in the United States only 12 per 1,000. But *in India it is from 24 to 25 per 1,000 or fully twice as great.* The average expectation of life (length of life) in England is 48 years, and in the United States 56 years. In impoverished India, *it is only about one-half as long.*

Who can estimate how many millions of unnecessary deaths this means annually? And to this loss should be added, as a British writer has pointed out,

"The incident suffering of those who die, the widows and orphans and other dependent ones left to suffer as the result of the death of heads of families. Also the loss of productive energy, to the country."

The high death-rate in India is sometimes attributed to climate and sometimes to malaria. But Lt. Dunn, of the Indian Medical Service, says this is incorrect. He declares that if the laws of health were regarded in India to the same extent as in England, and if the same proportion of public money was spent on sanitation, the death-rate in India would be no larger than in England. He avers that one-half of the death-rate is preventable, being due to the want of public health provisions, and the poverty and starvation of the people.

Consider malaria, which causes more suffering and larger numbers of deaths in India than anything else except poverty and famine. Mr. Arnold Lupton, an Englishman who speaks with authority, says in his recent book, "Happy India:"*

"What a magnificent country India would be if only its malaria were abolished! And I am quite certain of this, that if instructions were given to the engineers in the employ of the British Government in India to abolish malaria, and if they were allowed the requisite sums of money, they would soon make a great change..... The banks of the Panama Canal were made into a place that could be visited as a sanatorium in consequence of the successful effort of the American engineers in charge to abolish malaria; and the malaria of the Panama Canal was the deadliest kind the world has ever known.....If only the rulers of India could give their minds to those questions which concern the lives and health and well-being of the Indian people, instead of wasting their energies on other matters of no importance, India might be made a Sanatorium."

---

* *Indian Journal of Economics*, January, 1924.

A high medical official connected with the British army in Bombay, who for 24 years had been in medical charge of extensive districts in various parts of India, told me in 1914 that the death-rate in India ought to be little or no higher than in England; because, he declared, where proper sanitary regulations are observed, India is essentially as healthy a country to live in as England. Her high death-rate is preventable. It is caused by want of sanitation and public health regulations, bad water which the government should remedy, poverty and consequent starvation, and by the want of schools in which the laws of health can be taught to the children. *

In the face of all these various facts, if we are honest and fair-minded, how can we avoid asking the questions: How great a boon to India has Britain's boasted "*pax Britannica*" been? Even if Britain has saved India from the loss of some thousands or tens of thousands of lives in internal wars, does that atone for or should it hide from our view, the vastly greater number of Indian lives she has destroyed in her border and foreign wars, and above all, the uncounted millions who have perished at home from starva-

---

* Thirty or forty years ago, under Spanish rule, Cuba a tropical land like Southern India, had a very high death-rate, and suffered from malaria, typhus-fever, cholera and other devastating epidemic diseases as much as India has ever suffered. But now, under self-government and proper sanitary regulations, all is changed. Cuba's death-rate has become nearly the lowest in the world, and the land has become one of the healthiest known. Sanitary engineers and medical authorities tell us that exactly the same change can be wrought in India, if only the country can get a Government which will use the country's revenues for sanitation, education and the good of the Indian people, instead of to promote the militaristic and imperialistic interests of foreign masters and to enrich a foreign nation.

tion, insanitation and disease for whose deaths she is largely responsible?

Some years before his death, William Jennings Bryan made a visit to India to study conditions there. After his return, he wrote and published a pamphlet on British Rule and Its Results, in which he said:

> "The British have conferred some benefits on India; but they have extorted an enormous price for them. While they have boasted of bringing peace to the living they have *led millions to the peace of the grave.*".

Says Mahatma Gandhi, and no man weighs his words more carefully than he:

> "The kind of peace which British rule has brought to India, has been *worse than war.*"

As has already been said, Rome had her *Pax Romana.* It was the prototype of England's *Pax Britannica* in India. The historian Tacitus in describing that of Rome wrote the grim sentence, *Solitudinem faciunt, pacem appellant.* Indian scholars employ this sentence of Tacitus to describe the work of the British in India, translating it, "*They have made a graveyard, and they call it peace.*"

CHAPTFR X.

INDIA'S OPIUM CURSE. WHO ARE RESPONSIBLE?

India produces more opium than any other country in the world. Roughly speaking, one-half of it is consumed at home and the other half is sold to other countries. That which goes out of India cannot be considered here for want of space although it is a matter of very serious concern to the world as a whole; for wherever it goes it proves to be one of the most terrible evils with which humanity has to contend.

Says an eminent American medical authority:

The greatest menace that confronts the world to-day, next to war, is opium, and the efforts to overcome this menace will never succeed until opium production and opium traffic in India have been wiped out. India produces about five times as much opium as is necessary to supply the whole world with all the opium and derivatives needed for legitimate purposes, that is, needed for medical and scientific uses."

Leaving out of consideration, then, the evil consequences of the Indian opium which is sold to other countries, let us see what are the effects of the large amount which is retained for consumption in India itself. *

---

* In justice to Great Britain, it should be stated that in 1926 the Government of India made the gratifying announcement that it had decided to reduce the quantity of its sales of opium to foreign coutries by one-tenth each year, beginning at once, which would have the effect of bringing to an end in ten years the terrible evils which Indian opium has so long inflicted upon the outside world. This commendable measure, if carried out faithfully,

Although India produces so large a quantity of opium, it is not because the Indian people want to produce it. Its production and sale are purely government affairs, carried on for the purpose of revenue, against the will of the people. The amount of opium consumed in India is about 1,780,000 pounds a year, provision for its sale being made everywhere, through some 7,000 shops licenced by the Government. It is generally taken in the form of pills, eaten by persons of all ages—much of it being given to babes.

It seems amazing that a government claiming to be civilized and Christian can plan to obtain revenue by selling to its people a poison such as opium is declared by the highest British medical authorities to be. What is its excuse?

The excuse, the justification, which it puts forward oftoner than any other and as its strongest defense, is a report of an old Government Commission of 1895 which purports to describe the condition of things existing in India at that time. * In order to be as fair as possible and show the strongest case that the Government is able to

---

will be of incalculable benefit to many lands outside of India. But the question at once arises, sharply and painfully: Why is India itself discriminated against? Why is not the same reduction to be made early in the quantity of opium to be sold at home, so that in ten years the people of India, as well as those of foreign lands, may be relieved from the curse which has rested on them so long? Are they not as worthy of protection as the people of other countries? Is not the British Government of India under as much obligation to the people it rules and of whom it claims to be the "guardian" as to foreign peoples? The attention of lovers of justice everywhere should be called to this amazing and wholly unwarranted discrimination made by Great Britain against the Indian people.

* This Commission was appointed in 1893, but it did not make its report until 1895.

make out for its opium policy, we will quote that Report at some length. Says that document (we condense) :

The opium habit as a vice scarcely exists in India. ......Opium is extensively used for non-medical and quasi-medical purposes, in some cases with benefit, and, for the most part without injurious consequences....... It is not necessary that the growth of the poppy and the manufacture and sale of opium in British India should be prohibited except for medical purposes. . . . . .Inherited experience has taught the people of India discretion in the use of the drug, and its misuse is a negligible feature of Indian life. . . . . .The great majority of Indian opium eaters are not slaves to the habit. They take small doses as required and can and do give up the allowance when the need of it is past. . . . . .Opium is the commonest and most treasured of household remedies accessible to the people. It is taken to avert or lessen fatigue; as a specific in bowel complaints as a prophylactic against malaria, to lessen the quantity of sugar in diabetics, and generally to allay pain in sufferers of all ages. . . . .The use of opium in small quantities is one of the most important aids in the treatment of children's sufferings. ...To prevent the sale of opium except under regular medical prescription would be a mockery; to many millions it would be sheer inhumanity."

Here we have the British Indian Government's defense of its opium policy, the strongest that it offers, or is able to offer.

Before proceeding to give the other side, the side against opium, the side of the Indian people as distinguished from that of their foreign masters, the side of progress and reform, the side of that large and growing body of men and women in all lands who are opening their eyes to the terrible curse which opium is, whenever it is used for other than strictly medicinal purposes,—before proceeding to that, several observations should be made regarding the character of this particular Report which Great Britain is putting forward so prominently and relying upon so confidently as a justification of its practice of selling to the Indian people practically unlimited quantities of the most insidious and dangerous poison known to the modern world. We say "practically unlimited quantities," because, although there are "government regulations" connected with the selling, they are of such a nature as to accomplish little else than to give government approval and respectability to the sales ; their limiting effect is really *nil* ; they leave the situation such that any one by a little effort,—by conforming to the government's "regulations" can obtain practically any amount of opium he may desire. Indeed, why should anybody expect the government to make regulations really to limit sales ? It is sales that it wants ; the larger its sales, the larger its revenue.

The observations regarding the Report that need to be made are four :

1. The Report is over thirty years old. Much has occurred in India, as everywhere else, in three decades. Even if it describes correctly the situation existing in India thirty years ago, it does not describe that existing there to-day.

2. Thirty years ago, not nearly as much was known regarding the nature of opium and its effects upon individuals and nations as is known now. It was then used even by physicians in ways which now are recognized as perilous. Its danger as the worst of habit-forming drugs was then comparatively little realized. So that a body of investigators, even if honest in purpose and reasonably intelligent for that time, simply could not produce a report on opium fit to be regarded as a standard to-day, or which the Government of India for a moment is justified in using as a basis for an opium policy in this time of so much greater knowledge.

3. And yet much more was known about

opium even at that time than this report indicates; indeed, enough was known to brand the report as worthless. One member of the Commission which made the report refused to sign it, and wrote a minority report, telling a very different story. And (a fact of tremendous significance which should not be overlooked) three years earlier, in the year 1892, a public declaration had been made by 5,000 medical men in Great Britain declaring that opium smoking or eating is physically injurious and morally debasing, and that in India, just the same as in England, opium ought to be classed and sold as poison.

4. As a fact, that Commission Report of 1895 was never regarded by the opponents of opium either in India or in England, as intelligent, fair or just. It was, and is, considered a partisan report, a "whitewashing" report,—something obtained by the Government of India for the purpose of giving a show of justice to an iniquitous opium policy. Evil, however black, alway tries to paint itself white.

I now go forward to present briefly the case against opium in India; the side of the suffering Indian people; some present-day facts which cannot be escaped, and which every lover of justice should heed.

1. If anyone questions the determination of the British-Indian Government to preserve its opium revenue and resist all attempts to reduce it, he may have his doubts removed by reading the report of the "Government Retrenchment Committee" of 1923 (page 225), which emphasizes "the *importance* of *safeguarding opium sales* as an *important source* of *revenue*" and recommends "*no further reduction.*"

Writes Reverend C. F. Andrews:

"In 1921 the Rev. J. N. Roy, a Christian missionary, introduced a resolution into the Assam (India) Legislative

Council proposing that the sales of opium in Assam should be reduced 10 per cent. each year, until opium was prohibited except for medicinal use. The resolution was carried by an overwhelming majority, the only persons voting against it being Government officials, Europeans and several Indian title-holders. Yet the Government, having the executive power in its hands, has refused to carry into action the will of the Legislature ...The criminal conduct of the Assam Government in continuing to allow and encourage the use of opium, is destroying the Assamese people, one of the noblest races in India." *

When the followers of Mr. Gandhi, by a temperance and anti-opium campaign in Assam, reduced opium consumption in the province by 50 per cent., the Government *intervened* and *put 44 of the 63 campaigners in prison.*†

2. The people of India are very, very poor. Scores of millions are all the while on the verge of starvation. And yet, for generations, an area of from 200,000 to 400,000 acres of the very richest and best land in the country has been diverted, by the desire and practically by the compulsion of the Government, from the production of food for the people to the production of poison.§ Has this ever been justifiable ? Is it jusifiable to-day ? Ought it to go on ?

3. It is true that the opium evil existed in India before the British arrived; but it was in a light form and on a limited scale; the religions of the country condemned it; it was regarded as a vice; and the governments discouraged it. Says Mr. Gandhi,

---

* *Modern Review*, Calcutta, 1925, p. 638.

† "Opium as an International Problem," by Professor W. W. Willoughby, Johns Hopkins University Press, 1925, p. 445.

§ In the United Provinces (the section of India where the production is largest) the area devoted to opium was reduced in 1922-23 to 141,000 acres, and in 1923-24 to 134,000 acres. Opium in smaller quantities is produced in other sections.

"No government in India until the British came ever fostered the opium evil and organized it for purposes of revenue as the British have done."

4. The British Government constantly gives out the impression that consumption of opium in India is very light and not at all a danger to the people. In answer, some figures may be cited. The normal consumption of opium for medicinal purposes, as decided by the League of Nations, is 6 seers (a seer is about two pounds) for each 10,000 of the population. But the amount consumed in many parts of India is many times that. For example, in some districts of Assam the average consumption ranges from 106 to 227 seers, and in the whole province it is over 52 seers, per 10,000. The average in Burma and Bombay is only a little lower. In Calcutta, it is 144 and in Rangoon 108 per 10,000. In the Punjab, where the population has long been among the most hardy in India, opium is making terrible inroads, as seen in the fact that the average consumption in Lahore is 40 seers, in Ludhiana 49 seers per 10,000 of the population. In other words, in large areas and among large populations of India from 6 times to 39 times more opium is consumed than the opium authorities of the League of Nations declare to be legitimate for medicinal uses.

5. It is shocking to the Indian people that Great Britain enacts stringent home laws declaring opium a very dangerous poison, and carefully protecting its own people in England against all traffic in it and all uses of it except for strictly medical purposes; and yet allows it to be used in India almost as a food, gives the people there no protection whatever

against it, actually encouraging and promoting its virtually unrestricted and dangerous use. Yet Britain professes to be India's conscientious "guardian," claims to be ruling her "for her good!"

6. The British hide behind the peoples of other countries, and claim that so long as others produce opium they must ; no nation can reform alone. They declared that, as things are, the opium traffic in India simply cannot be stopped: if the Government did not furnish the drug to the people, it would be smuggled in. Therefore, the Government may as well supply the demand and get the revenue.

The answers to be made to these assertions and claims are three.

First : The opium *traffic can* be stopped, and stopped in the *Orient*. This has been *demonstrated more than once.* (a) The American Government stopped it in the Philippine Islands where it had long been carried on. (b) In the years between 1907 and 1917, in China, where its ravages had been the most terrible ever known in the world, it was almost wholly abolished, and there seems to be every reason for believing that it would have remained so but for the influence of foreign nations. (c) In Formosa, where it has been bad, Japan at the present time is carrying out with marked success a plan of wiping it out gradually in ten years.

Second: *Smuggling of opium can* be prevented. How ? in the manner urged at the Geneva Opium Conference of 1924, by Honorable Stephen S. Foster, Chairman of the American delegation to that Conference, namely, by international agreement limiting the production in the world to the quantity required for medicinal and scientific purposes.*

---

* For full reports of the Geneva Opium Conferences,

Third: The final answer to be made is, that of Bishop Brent:

"It is monstrous to argue that because people in their ignorance and weakness are willing to be debauched, therefore, it is justifiable to debauch them, or to maintain that if we do not reap a golden harvest from a nefarious trade, somebody else will, and therefore we are foolish not to do it."

To this may be added the equally pertinent answer made by the editor of *The Christian Patriot* of Madras:

"Why should the British wait to do right until other nations do right? Lord Cecil saying that Britain cannot give up her wicked opium business until this, that and the other country give up theirs, seems to us like a thief saying to a judge, "I cannot stop stealing until John Smith and Bill Jones do."

7. The British Government in India claims that it furnishes the people opium because they want it. But who want it? The addicts and nobody else. Practically the whole vast body of the untainted Indian people are against it. The intelligence of the country is against it. So are the teachings of the religions of the country Hinduism, Mohammedanism, Buddhism and Christianity. Even the addicts themselves, when in their right minds are against it. It is only when the fearful appetite created by the drug seizes them and for the time being destroys their intelligence and their will that even they want it. And this very appetite which is their deadly enemy has been created by the opium temptation placed before them by the Government. When children want things which we know will destroy them, we do not gratify

---

see "Opium as an International Problem," by Prof. W. W. Willoughby, and "The Geneva Opium Conferences; Chinese Statements," by S Alfred Sze. Both published by the Johns Hopkins Press.

their desire. These opium addicts are weaker than children. The duty of a good government is to help these miserable slaves to overcome their evil appetite by removing the temptation.

Says the *Bombay Chronicle* of May 31, 1923:

"The people of India whole-heartedly endorse the American proposal made at the Geneva Opium Conference [to limit opium production to medicinal needs] and utterly repudiate the opposite view put forth by the representatives of Great Britain in India's name."

The Rev. C. F. Andrews says:

"The English Government is imposing the poison of opium upon India, while hypocritically pretending that it is simply fulfilling the wishes of the Indian people. And it stops its ears to India's indignant protest."*

8. Great Britain argues that because India is poorly supplied with trained physicians able to direct the use of opium scientifically and safely, therefore, the untrained people in their ignorance should be permitted to have it and use it as freely as they please. The reasoning should be the opposite. If there is lack of physicians to insure the safe use of opium, the Government should do two things: one is, keep the dangerous poison away from the people, as parents keep razors and loaded guns away from their children; the second is, make plans to promote medical education in the country to an extent many times greater than we now see.

9. British apologists for the free use of opium in India claim that Orientals may use opium safely where Occidentals cannot. There is no ground whatever for this claim. Said Mr. Porter, who had made the most careful and intensive investigations on the subject:

"All authorities agree that the Oriental suffers the

* *Modern Review* (Calcutta), June, 1925, p. 637.

same harmful effects as the Occidental. The reaction to the drugs is the same. The only difference lies in the Orientals' helplessness to protect themselves from the traffic."

Every medical man who has had experience in the East and the West knows that this is so. Japan fully understands it and acts upon it, as is seen in the fact that the Japanese Government has enacted laws just as strict as those of England or the European continental nations or the United States, confining the use of opium to medical purposes under the direction of trained physicians.

10. As a matter of fact, the British Government *knows* that opium *is* a terrible injury to the Indian people. Said Warren Hastings, the first Governor-General to sanction traffic in opium for revenue :

"Opium is not a necessary of life, but a pernicious article of luxury which ought not to be permitted except for the purposes of foreign commerce alone, and which the wisdom of the Government should carefully restrain from internal consumption.*

Here we have the highest official in India confessing that opium is something so bad that the Government ought not to allow its consumption by the Indian people. But alas! while Hastings' conscience would not allow him to sanction the sale of opium at home, it did allow him to sanction and favor its sale to the people of China, and against the wish of the Chinese Government.

From Warren Hastings' day to our own there have been innumerable testimonies to the evil effects of opium in India and in every other country where its use outside of strict medical control has been allowed. Says the London

---

* Quoted by Ellen N. La Motte, "Ethics of Opium" p. 540.

Times of April 7, 1923: "In all countries with European civilizations, there are no two opinions as to the physical and moral ruin wrought by these so-called 'drugs of addiction;' of which opium is the most dangerous.

11. Terrible effects of opium upon the user are almost beyond description. In the year 1880, the Chief Commissioner of Burma submitted to the British Government a Report on the subject in which he says: "The habitual use of these drugs (opium and its derivatives) saps the physical and mental energies, destroys the nerves, emaciates the body, predisposes to disease, induces indolent and filthy habits of life, destroys self-respect, is one of the most fertile sources of misery, destitution, and crime, fills the jails with men of relaxed frames predisposed to dysentery and cholera, prevents the due extension of cultivation and development of the land-revenue, checks the natural growth of the population, and enfeebles the constitution of the succeeding generation.

Commenting upon this report, the Rev. John Liggins, formerly an American Episcopalian missionary in China, remarks in his brochure on opium:

"Before it was conquered by British forces and annexed to the Indian Empire, opium was as rigidly excluded from every part of Burma as it now is in Japan, those Asiatics knowing as well as the Chinese that there was nothing but ruin for them if it was admitted. But no sooner did England obtain control of the country than British subordinate officials distributed opium gratuitously among the natives to create a market for it; and now the results in the demoralization, impoverishment and ruin of the people are fearful."*

12. The ravages of opium in India were

* Quoted by Dr. Taraknath Das in "Hearings" before the Foreign Affairs Committee of the United States House of Representatives, early in 1923.

never greater than they are to-day. Says Mr Herbert Anderson, Secretary of the Calcutta Temperance Federation :

"It is one of the commonest sights of Calcutta to see a crowd of persons standing before the barred window through which drug sales are made, often blocking the pathway, and pressing upon one another to secure their daily quota of poison." Again he says : "The majority of the retail opium shops are so situated as to afford the most direct temptation to all classes of the community. The Government shelters itself under the delusion of doing a 'legitimate trade,' but by its policy it has fastened the shackles of a habit, condemned by Hindu and Moslem authorities alike, upon the community at large, and the chain gets stronger and stronger each year."*

Says Gertrude Marvin Williams in a letter to the New York *Nation* written from Calcutta, India, under date of July 2, 1925 :

"Two thousand three hundred men and women were recently counted entering a single one of Calcutta's many government-licensed opium shops in a single day. I visited a shop a block from Chowringhee, Calcutta's Fifth Avenue. Squatting on a counter, behind a small, iron-barred window, sat a man rolling cubes of sticky brown opium in a green leaf, and wrapping them with a deft turn of his wrist, in a bit of newspaper. Besides him sat a man taking a steady stream of one-anna piece (two cents) to exchange for the bits of opium. The line of men waiting to push into the shop were of all sorts. Two cents buys six and three-quarter grains of opium. A friendly man of about fifty told me that when he began using it four years ago two cents worth lasted three days, two doses each day. Now he takes that amount in one day. He asked me if I was going to buy, and solemnly warned me that four cents worth would kill a beginner. Old addicts, however, take as much as thirty-five cents worth at a time. Defenders of licensing system make a great point of the fact that the shop is permitted to sell only a limited amount to any customer. On inquiry I found that the limit is one *tola*, 188 grains, but the customer *may buy this every*

* "Excise Administration in Bengal," 1921, Pp. 9 & 16.

day. Also there is nothing to prevent him *making the rounds* of the shops or *returning to the same shop five minutes later*. This is "government regulation" of the opium traffic. One of the most serious phases of India's opium problem is the drugging of babies. The women who work in the mills of Calcutta and Bombay give their babies opium in the morning so that they will sleep all day and not interrupt their mothers at work by crying to be nursed. The women in the villages who work in the fields dope their babies before they go out, so that they may not waken and cry in their mother's absence. A physician in the Central Provinces estimates that 90 per cent. of the babies in his district are doped. There are estimated to be over 50,000,000 people in India who never are able to satisfy their hunger. Poor women of this class who have not enough milk to nurse their babies give them opium to stop their crying from hunger. Dr. Mistri, a woman doctor holding a government appointment in the west of India, estimates that 90 per cent. of the Hindu children and 75 per cent. of the Mohammedan children are continuously drugged from birth until they are two years old."

Bishop Fisher of Calcutta declared in a public address delivered in New York, May 14, 1924, that of every 100 babies born in some sections of India only 28 live to be two years old, the causes of this appalling death-rate being the poverty of the people, poor sanitation, but mainly opium fed to these babes from their birth.

Says Rev. C. F. Andrews:

"In India a man or woman may go into a shop and freely purchase enough opium to commit suicide. I took up a Bombay paper this morning and saw as a common piece of news the account of a woman who had just committed suicide by opium poisoning, and side by side with it was the report of the death of a baby from an overdose of opium. The number of such deaths which are never even reported is large. Only a few weeks ago, the wife of the British Governor of Bombay, Lady Wilson, called attention to the shocking fact that in a recent year the annual infant mortality in Bombay had reached 666 per thousand. She also stated that she had been told by her own physician that 98 per cent. of the mothers who work in the Bombay factories dose their children with opium regularly before going to their work. From my own experience I can confirm this statement of the wife of the Governor. I myself have seen little babies, with their shrunk, old, wizened faces lying drugged with opium on the floors of the wretched hovels of Bombay." *

On these figures of Lady Wilson being cited in the House of Commons in London, Earl Winterton, the Under-Secretary of State for India, derided them, declaring them a gross exaggeration. When word of this reached India, such overwhelming testimony corroborating them was produced that the Under-Secretary found himself a few days later compelled to withdraw his denial, and to acknowledge that the original shocking figures were correct.

Says Mr. Badrul Hassan in his book (1923) "The Drink and Drug Evil in India":

"The Government's drug policy has tempted the strong and demoralized the weak; it has exploited the rich and the poor; it has ruined both the young and the old, the strong and the infirm, of all classes and creeds and races." †

Such are a few of the facts, of which India is full, showing the appalling effects of opium in a land under the control of foreigners and therefore helpless to protect itself.

---

* *Modern Review*, June, 1925, pp 638-639.
† Pages 124-125.

CHAPTER XI

INDIA'S DRINK CURSE. WHO ARE RESPONSIBLE ?

As soon as one begins to study the subject of intoxicants in India he is confronted with three facts, namely :

1. The drink evil is widespread in the land and serious.

2. India is not primarily responsible for it. It was brought to her, virtually forced upon her, by "Christian" nations of the West.

3. India deplores the evil, feels deeply the terrible nature of it, struggles constantly against it, and would prohibit the manufacture and sale of intoxicating liquors of all kinds to-morrow, if she could. But she cannot, because she is not free. She is a subject land, and the foreign power that rules her wants revenue, and therefore refuses to listen to her protests, petitions and prayers.

When the British came on the scene, India was a singularly sober nation. This had been its character for thousands of years. The reasons are easy to discover.

India is a land of great religions ; and it is significant that all of them teach strict temperance, and at least two of the most important enjoin total abstinence. The Tantrik or some Sakta forms of Hinduism allow the use of certain intoxicants in connection with some of its religious ceremonies, but on the whole its influence for temperance is strong. Buddhism wholly forbids the use of intoxicants. One of its "Eight Commandments" is : "Thou shalt not indulge in intoxicating drink." Ever since the sixth century B. C., the Buddhist religion may well have been called a great organized prohibition movement. When, much later, Islam came into India, it was with a temperance message essentially in harmony with that of Buddha. The Arabian Prophet strongly condemned all intoxicants. Although in wealthy and luxurious society there has been some violation of the commands of the Koran, it would probably be no exaggeration to say that for the past thousand years the most powerful and effective temperance movement in the world (with the possible exception of the Buddhist religion) has been Mohammedanism.

Vasco da Gama, the first European to reach India by sailing around the Cape of Good Hope, tells us that he found no class of the Indian people addicted to intemperate habits. Warren Hastings has left us the following testimony :

> "The temperance of the people of India is demonstrated in the simplicity of their food, and their total abstinence from spirituous liquors and other substances of intoxication."

These facts make clear the condition of things in India, so far as temperance was concerned, when Europeans began to gain influence there.

These foreigners from the far West came first seeking trade and wealth, and then power and domination and exploitation and more and more wealth. In the beginning the comers were Portuguese, Dutch, French and British ; but soon the British drove out the others, conquered the whole country and ever since (for nearly 200 years) have been its rulers.

With the very first trading posts (or "factories") there were established saloons or places for the sale of rum and other intoxicating drinks. The traders, who were avaricious for gain, generally had little conscience, and when they found they could create a growing appetite and market for their wares, with large profits, they availed themselves eagerly of the opportunities before them. In this way began that odious business of poisoning the peoples, not only of India but of the whole Orient, with the liquors of the supposedly more civilized and "Christian" West.

The story of the complicity of the British rulers with the liquor trade, is a dark one. Under the rule of the East India Company it was bad enough, but under the British Government itself it has been even worse.

Because the British nation was professedly Christian and claimed superior enlightenment, the people of India long hoped, hoped even against hope, that sooner or later their rulers would recognize the disastrous effects of the intoxicants everywhere offered for sale and pressed upon the public, and would take action to remedy the evil. But no ! instead of taking the side of the people, the Government early allied itself with the liquor interests, and has steadily maintained that alliance to the present time. Not only have the earnest protests of thousands of individual Indians of eminence in all parts of the land been ignored ; but the same is true of the strong and repeated petitions and protests of temperance societies local and national, and such strong and influential organizations as the Indian National Congress, the Indian Industrial and Social Conferences, the All-India Theistic Conference, Provincial Conferences, the Brahmo Somajes, the Arya Somajes, the Theosophical Societies, and the Christian Churches. The Government wanted money to enable it to carry out its imperialistic and militaristic plans for holding the land securely in subjection, and exploiting it for Great Britain's benefit and enlarging its boundaries ; and so the expedient of obtaining funds through the drink traffic—through the impoverishment and degradation of the people—was seized upon and maintained. The Government's revenue from its excise department in the year 1922-1923 was the great sum of 12,282,000 pounds sterling, or about $60,000,000. Think what suffering and wretchedness this means in a land of such dire poverty as India !

Let me relate some personal experiences. During one of my visits to India, made just before the Great War, I had occasion to spend some time in Ceylon (which is virtually a part of India), lecturing in the Ananda (Buddhist) College in Colombo and speaking in other places, which took me to different parts of the island and brought me into contact with many leaders. They told me that for some time they had been having an extensive and very earnest temperance campaign in which prominent representatives of all the religious faiths, Buddhists, Hindus, Mohammedans and Christians had taken part. The drink evil in the country had long been serious and was growing more so. The campaign had two aims in view, one was to create everywhere a public sentiment against the drink habit, to persuade those addicted to the use of intoxicants to reform, and to prevent non-drinkers, particularly the young, from forming the habit. The other was, if possible, to induce the government (British) to lend its aid, preferably by prohibition, but at least by granting local option, or by considerably reducing the number of saloons and places where intoxicants could be obtained. But they found the government adamant. Sometimes the officials would reply to their appeals courteously, or even express in a general way sympathy with the aims of the reformers, and the pious wish that nobody might carry drinking to excess; but as for doing anything in any way to imperil the large revenue received by the Government from the liquor traffic, no! that could not be considered for a moment.

In one of my journeys to the Orient a part of my duty was to execute a commission given me by the Unitarian churches of England to visit the Brahmo Somaj societies in all parts of India and confer with them as to ways in which the English Unitarians could most effectively help them in their important work of educational, social and religious reform. Everywhere I found warm and grateful appreciation of this offer of aid. In the many conferences held with the Brahmo Somajes regarding the matter, various kinds of aid were suggested as important and acceptable,—money, literature, trained and sympathetic workers sent out from England, etc. But to my great surprise the answer I received oftener than any other was: Tell the Unitarians (and also all other Christians) in England that the most important single direction in which they can help us or India, is in our struggle against intoxicating drink. We want to get rid of our terrible drink evil, but we can do nothing effective without the sympathy and help of England, which is the seat of influence and power. The Christian churches of Britain can give us not only help but *victory, if they will.* How? By creating a strong public sentiment in Great Britain (such a sentiment *can* be created by the churches if they will so determine and will combine for the purpose)—a public sentiment so strong and so commanding as to compel the government in India to cease its wicked policy of obtaining revenue through the physical and normal degradation of the people ; and, what is hardly less important, so strong as also to compel the British officials in India to stop setting everywhere the fashion of drinking, by using liquor, as most of them do on their own tables, and especially by furnishing it lavishly and with display, as is almost universal at their banquets and on all public festive occasions. The effect of such use and such display is of course, to create the impression that drinking is "the thing." The princes and upper social classes naturally imitate their rulers. Thus the fashion of drinking, set in the most influential quarters, spreads and spreads like the plague. A great banquet given by the Viceroy, or by a Governor of a Province, or by the Mayor of a great city, in which champagnes, wines, brandies and whiskies are conspicuous, and are reported by the papers as a notable feature of the festivities, has an influence for perpetuating and extending the drink curse which cannot be overcome by a thousand Brahmo Somaj leaders, or Christian missionaries, or other temperance workers.

Seldom in my life have I seen such misery or heard such tales of suffering caused by drink, as among the people of India. And the worst is that the liquor revenue, and therefore the misery, steadily grows. The government is not idle or indifferent in the matter, but active and determined. Such is its power, such is its callousness to the people's interests and protests, such is its determination to obtain money for its ends from any source, such is its astuteness in creating the fashion of drinking among the princes and social "upper classes" (as has been pointed out) by always serving liquors at its banquets and public functions, and such is its license system (making it to the interest of the liquor handlers to push their sales to the utmost), that the government's income from liquor has more than tripled in the last thirty years, and increased nearly seven-fold in the last forty-eight years.*

Writes the Secretary of the Bengal Temperance Federation : "The rapidity with which our souls and bodies, our hearths and homes are being devoured by the Drink Demon is frightful. The tempter, the grog shop, lurks everywhere ; it brings revenue to the Government and so the Government makes sure that it shall nowhere be absent. Go about the streets of our cities, it is on every side ; go into our villages, it is there ; go to factories and mines, it confronts you. Have you ever been to the coal fields ? O, the misery wrought by liquor ! All the week the workmen labor hard from early morning till late night to earn their morsel. Pay-day comes and they receive their meager wages. But at the gate stands the liquor shop, beckoning, enticing ; they are tired, weak, discouraged, how can they help entering to drive away a little of their misery ? Without intending it and almost before they know, they spend a large part if not all of their hard earned money. Often their whole week's pay goes ; and the workmen, bereft of money and devoid of strength crawl to their homes to meet their weeping wives and starving children. Statistics show in some places that as high as 80 per cent. of our workmen are victims of these grog shops.

"What does the Government do to save these poor souls ? Nothing, and less than nothing. Indirectly it is a partner in all this miserable, this devilish business. Is it

* From 1,561,000 pounds in 1874-75 to 12,284,000 pounds in 1922-23.

not the duty of a true government to do what it can to save the people from temptation? To make it easy for people to do right and difficult to do wrong? How can the Government of India justify itself for placing temptation at every corner throughout the land?"

Says *The Indian Messenger* (Brahmo Somaj), of Calcutta:

"Every year our British ruler record with evident satisfaction the increasing revenue which they obtain from their liquor licenses. We are amazed that they can be so indifferent to the shocking fact that behind all this increased revenue are increased poverty, squalor, crime and degradation.

Says another Calcutta weekly:

"The Government gives license to liquor sellers to poison the people wholesale. But who gives authority to the Government thus to debauch and demoralize a nation?"

Of course, the Government tries to justify itself. It says it must have revenue or else it cannot exist. With a pious face it declares that it does not compel anybody to drink; and its desire is that nobody shall drink to excess. It simply does not believe in sumptuary laws. It is unwilling to take away the people's freedom to regulate their own eating and drinking. These are the kind of excuses made by all governments, everywhere, that rule peoples for ends of revenue and power and not for the benefit of those ruled.

Doubtless there may be some real grounds for an argument in favor of saloons and unrestricted sale of liquor in England, America and other countries where there is an important section of the people who want liquor; but in India practically nobody wants it except drunkards and the small European element, and by no means all of those. As has been said, all the religions of the country oppose it, and the sentiment of the nation as a whole is overwhelmingly against it. If the people had self-rule, they would sweep it away once for all.

Says *The Christian Patriot*, of Madras :

"There is on all sides an insistent and growing demand in India for prohibition. The last National Social Conference issued the following public statements :

1. This Conference declares that Indian public opinion is strongly in favor of total prohibition of the manufacture, import and sale of intoxicating drink and drugs, except for medicinal purposes.

2 Provincial, municipal and local governments are moving in this direction. Already one of the largest Provincial Governments, that of Bombay, has distinctly declared in favour of prohibition.

3. The total abstainers in India, of all races and creeds, far out-number the drinkers and drug-takers, moderate or excessive. If only the real judgment of the vast majority of the people can be made to prevail, prohibition is assured."

In the July, 1926, issue of the *Modern Review* (Calcutta), Mr. Frederic Grubb, Secretary of the Anglo-Indian Temperance Association, has an article on "Prohibition for India" in which he gives a full, careful and authoritative survey of present conditions. He says :

"One cannot follow the development of Indian affairs from day to day without realizing that the need for temperance reform is accepted by all sections of opinion. Public conferences, the proceedings of legislative bodies, the declaration of ministers (Indian), the almost complete unanimity of the Indian press, testify to the strength of India's conviction on the subject, and the determination of her people to suppress a traffic which menaces their present and future well-being. A fact to be noted is that consideration of the subject is rarely excluded from the programs of gatherings which are primarily concerned with other political, social and economic issues. Trades unions, for example, find it incumbent upon them to make complete pronouncements upon this question. So far as can be ascertained, there has been no single instance of resolutions of an opposite nature passed by any religious, political, social, commercial, or communal organization in the whole of India."

The only important opposition anywhere is from the Government. The question of Prohibition was brought before the National Indian Legislative Assembly in September 1925. The only speeches opposing it were made by Englishmen. Sir Basil Blackett, Finance Member of the Government of India, declared that prohibition was impracticable, contrary to ethics, and unthinkable, and that no change in the present policy of the Government regarding the sale and use of intoxicants was called for. The resolution (supporting prohibition) was passed, 69 to 39, absolutely all the elected Indian members of the Assembly voting in the affirmative ; those voting in the negative consisting of 25 Europeans and 14 Indians who were officially connected with the Government and therefore were not free to oppose it.

Nothing could show more clearly two things : first, how strong and universal is the desire and determination on the part of the Indian people to be rid of the curse of intoxicating drink; and second, the determination of the Government to defeat their desire.

Mr. Grubb concludes his article by saying :

"When self-rule comes, India will be mistress of her own house in regard to the drink evil and every other social problem."

One undeniable fact alone, even if there were nothing else, proves the responsibility of the Government for the grog shops of India and their ravages,—proves that the Government, instead of wanting the sale of liquor to be stopped or even restricted, is determined that it shall not stop or be restricted. That unescapable fact is, that the

Government has arrested and imprisoned thousands of persons in different parts of the land for temperance work, especially for "picketing," that is, for standing in front of places where liquor is sold and trying, peacefully and with no suggestion of violence, to persuade their neighbors and friends not to buy the cursed intoxicants which would only injure them; and, which, indeed, most of them would not buy except for the temptation of the everywhere present drink shops. Says the Reverend C. F. Andrews:

"To my knowledge the Government has imprisoned over 800 persons in one relatively small section of India—the Assamese districts, for perfectly peaceable temperance work."

It is well known that one of the offences of Gandhi which the Government was most unwilling to forgive and which led to his imprisonment, was the mighty movement which he was leading against drink, by which the Government found its revenues being reduced.

Nowhere is the evil influence of the Government's liquor policy felt more keenly than among the Christian missionaries and the Christian churches. They want it understood everywhere that Christianity is a temperance religion; that it, as well as the other faiths of India, stands for opposition to intoxicants. But how sharp is their pain when they find the people around them pointing to the "Christian" Government of the land as a refutation of their claim; and declaring that it is Hinduism, or Buddhism, or Islam (as the case may be) and not Christianity, that is the temperance religion. More than once in India (and alas! in China and Japan too) I have heard saloons called "Christian" saloons; and I was told that this is by no means an uncommon name given them. Think of the difficulty of the work of the missionaries and the churches in the midst of such conditions!

The subject need not be pursued further.

Such is a brief sketch, I believe a fair and truthful one, of the liquor situation in India, as it has existed during the past century and a half and as it exists to-day, under foreign rule. The facts cited should do something toward helping the people of America and the world to judge whether that rule is so great a benefit to the Indian people that it should be continued. Everywhere you go in India the word is the same. The leaders of all classes tell you that they see no hope of ever getting rid of India's liquor curse until they have a government of their own.

CHAPTER XII

THE EMASCULATING INFLUENCE OF FOREIGN RULE

There is no more certain way to emasculate a nation, to destroy its soul, and to turn it into a flock of human sheep, than to subject it for a considerable time to foreign domination. This the whole history of the world shows. If you destroy a nation's spirit, you might about as well destroy the nation itself and the most effective way to destroy the spirit of a nation is to rob it of its freedom.

The ancient Greeks, after their conquest by the Romans, lost their intellectual vigor and much of their fine character, and became a very commonplace nation. The cause was plain. The same disastrous effects followed the conquest and domination of the Italians by Austria. The rule of England over Scotland in the fourteenth century and that over France in the fifteenth, are recognized by all historians as having been productive of distinct decadence for a considerable time in both Scotland and France. Mr. Asquith has more than once in his speeches and writings employed such expressions as "the degrading influence of foreign rule," "the intolerable degradation of a foreign yoke."

Says Professor E. A. Ross, of Wisconsin University: "Subjection to a foreign yoke is one of the most potent causes of the decay of nations." He maintains that there is no case in history where the subjection of one people to another has not tended powerfully and irresistibly to produce intellectual and moral deterioration in those held in subjection. Even in those cases where the domination is of the best type known, he declares that "the alien dominion has a distinctly blighting effect upon the higher life of the people."

The English ought to have learned this lesson thoroughly from their own early experience in connection with the conquest and rule of their country by the Romans. For four hundred years England was governed by Rome. If rule by foreigners is ever a good, it ought to have been a good in this case; for the people of Britain were what we call barbarians, and the Romans were supposedly the most enlightened nation in the world. But what does history tell us?

When the Romans came to Britain, they found a people as independent, as manly, as vigorous and as brave as they had ever encountered in all their history,—a people who fought them so determinedly that Caesar after two attempted invasions was strongly inclined to give up his project of conquering the land, and it was only after a third attempt that the Romans were able to gain a permanent foothold.

During their long domination of the country, the Romans built strong fortifications everywhere, constructed excellent roads leading to all sections founded and developed flourishing cities, built for themselves hundreds of luxurious villas like those of Italy, and tried to plant Roman civilization and the Roman tongue permanently in the island.

What was the result? Absolute failure, and worse. The Britons, originally so heroic and masterful, had become so utterly cowed, and weakened by their long subjection that when their foreign masters left they were unable to defend themselves, and at once fell an easy prey to the Jutes, Angles and Saxons, from beyond the North Sea, who had never been emasculated by foreign domination.

The verdict of history seems to be that the four centuries of Rome's rule of Britain left behind it almost absolutely nothing of value. Its chief traces to-day are some old fortifications and walls built for military defense, remains of paved roads here and there, foundations of places, theaters, baths and other buildings, and old Roman pottery, personal ornaments, household utensils, etc., discovered by excavations in various places, and a few Roman names of towns, chiefly those that were military headquarters and camps.

The one and only deep and lasting result of the Roman domination seems to have been the degradation of the spirit of the people of the land,—the transformation of a manly, resourceful and heroic nation, able long to beat back the attacks of mighty Rome, into a nation of weaklings unable to defend themselves from any formidable foe.

Why has not England learned the lesson which blazes from every page of this long and tragic experience of her own,—that forced subjection to a foreign power, anywhere, everywhere in the world, in the very nature of the case means the degradation and emasculation of the nation robbed of its freedom and held in bondage ? Why does she not see that this lesson applies in full measure to India ?

Perhaps the ablest defense ever penned of the British Colonial policy and of the conquest and rule and India, is that given us by the eminent English historian, Sir J. R. Seeley, in his "Expansion of England." What is Professor Seeley's final judgment concerning it all ? He declares that the British Government of India is "at its best only a good specimen of a bad political system ; "and he expresses his grave doubt "whether our (Britain's) rule is benefiting the people, or whether it may not be sinking them lower in misery." And he declares further, that "subjection for a long time to a foreign yoke is one of the most potent causes of national deterioration."

This is in harmony with the strong statement of Ramsay Macdonald in his "Awakening of India" (p. 213) :

"In all attempts to govern a country by a 'benevolent despotism,' the governed are crushed down. They become subjects who obey, not citizens who act. Their literature, their art, their spiritual expression go. They descend to the level of mere imitators and copyists....... When we recall the riches of Indian civilization in the past it becomes plain that the loss of initiative and self-development has been greater in India than in almost any other country."

Modern educational principles and modern psychology are enabling the world to see as it never saw before, that freedom and self-direction are absolutely necessary conditions of healthy life, and especially of progress, alike in individuals and in nations ; whereas, repression and domination by outside influences, are fatal. If you would destroy a child's spirit and make him a moral weakling, keep him under a regime of constant forbids, constant dictation by others, constant defeat of his own natural, healthy and right desire to be independent and think and act for himself. Treat a child habitually in that way and you do all in your power to make him a dunce, or else a rebel against all restraint and all law. If you want to turn a man into a coward, a toady, a sycophant, a shirk, a creature without moral backbone or honor or even self-respect, put him in a situation where for a long period he is obliged to submit to being looked down upon, despised, bossed and bullied. If there is anything on earth that will take all manliness and spirit out of him, (or else put the devil into him), that will do it.

All this applies to nations as well as to individuals. It applies exactly to India, one of the greatest nations of the world, robbed of its freedom, its power, self-direction, its self-respect, looked down upon, made a mere appendage to a foreign power, its people bullied, their hopes and ambitions blighted, their power of initiative everywhere checked, their genius despised, permitted to do nothing without the consent of their alien masters, reduced to the humiliating and disgraceful condition of political and economic slaves.

For nearly two centuries the British have been dealing with India in precisely the way to destroy her soul, in some degree ignorant of the result they were producing, but none the less imposing on her exactly the kind of government tending to produce it.

Looting the country of its wealth, as in the old days of Clive and Hastings, was bad. Exploiting the country, draining away it resources to England and impoverishing it in all the long years since, has been not less evil in its effects. But worst of all has been the conscienceless robbing of the nation of its freedom, its power of self-direction. Jesus said of a man, "What shall it profit him if he gain the whole world and lose his soul ?" If it is a sin that cries to heaven, to destroy the soul of a man, what is it to destroy the soul of a nation ?

Rev. C. F. Andrews, who came to India in sympathy with British rule, after a score of years of observation of the effects of that rule became convinced that if India would save her soul she simply must become independent and self-ruling. He declares that :

"Her soul is being lost under the influence of the mechanical and materialistic civilization which British rule fosters, and which it really forces on the Indian people."

Foreign rule destroys patriotism. Where it exists what is there to be patriotic about ? The people have no country. What used to be their country or what ought to be their country, is owned by foreigners. Says John Stuart Mill,

"In a country governed by a despot, there is only one patriot and that is the despot himself."

Attempts to be patriotic on the part of the people are regarded as sedition or treason, for which they are liable to be arrested and sent to prison, if not shot.

One of the last words of the eminent Hindu scholar and teacher, Swami Vivekananda, was,

"My countrymen, pray to the Great Mother for manhood : manhood is the great need of the Indian people."

But how can a nation get manhood in slavery ? The indispensable condition for the creation of manhood is freedom to stand on one's own feet and shape one's own life.

Said Sir Henry Campbel-Bannerman, Liberal Premier of Great Britain :

"Good government is no substitute for self-government. The atmosphere of subjection is poisonous, killing all that is virile and worthy, and fostering all that is vile and ignoble. I must remind my countrymen that Britons have stooped to Prussian and Russian methods in the government of India."

Says *The Indian Messenger*, the Calcutta organ of the Brahmo Somaj :

"British Rule has done more to emasculate the Indian people than was done by Mohammedan Rule in its worst period."

The Honorable G. K. Gokhale, the eminent Indian statesman, describes the blighting influences of British rule, as follows:

"A kind of dwarfing or stunting of the Indian race is going on under the present system. We must live all the days of our life in an atmosphere of inferiority, and the tallest of us must bend. The upward impulse which every schoolboy at Eton or Harrow may feel, that he may one day be a Gladstone or a Nelson or a Wellington, and which may draw forth the best efforts of which he is capable, is denied to us. The height to which our manhood is capable of rising can never be reached by us under the present system of foreign domination. The moral elevation which every self-governing people feel cannot be felt by us. Our administrative and military talents must gradually disappear owing to their disuse, till at last our lot, as hewers of wood and drawers of water in our own country, is stereotyped."*

Another eminent Indian leader, the Honorable Bhupendranath Basu, thus confirms and supplements Mr. Gokhale's testimony:

"A foreign bureaucratic government, holding all, power in its hands and undertaking all responsibility, has acted as a dead weight on the Soul of India, stifling in us all sense of initiative, for the lack of which we are condemned; atrophying our nerves of action, and, what is most serious, necessarily dwarfing in us all feeling of self-respect."†

The very education of the country, planned by the Government, is planned steadily and systematically, not to create free, strong and independent minds, as education always should; but to create really slave minds, docile and

* "Gokhale's Speeches," G. A. Natesan and Company, Madras. Appendix, pp. XLII, XLIII.

† Quoted in Mrs. Besant's book, "Shall India Live, or Die?", p. 27.

obedient minds, minds dominated by an "inferiority complex," without ambition, without patriotism, content to be subjects of a foreign power, content to belong to a nation that has no recognition in the world as a nation.

Professor S. Radhakrishnan, an eminent Indian educator, makes this clear in an address as President of the All-Bengal College and University Teachers' Association (reported in *The Modern Review*, Calcutta, May, 1927). He says :

"The educational policy of the government trains men into docile tools of an external authority, it does not help them to become self-respecting citizens of a free nation. Love of one's native land is the basis of all progress. This principle is recognised in all countries. But in our unfortunate country it is the other way. A conquered race feels its heart sink. It loses hope, courage and confidence. Our political subjection carries with it the suggestion that we cannot consider ourselves the equals of free nations. Indian history is taught to impress on us the one lesson that 'India has failed.' The worst form of bondage is that of despair and dejection, which creeps on defeated peoples, breeding in them loss of faith in themselves. The aim of true education should be to keep alive the spark of national pride and self-respect. If we lose our wealth and resources we may recover them to-morrow, if not to-day ; but if we lose our national consciousness, there is no hope for us."

Mrs. Annie Besant tells us of the weakening, denationalizing and degrading influence of this kind of education as she has observed it in India for more than thirty years. She writes :

"The stunting of the Indian race under British rule begins with the education of the children. The schools (which are under British control) differentiate between British and Indian teachers ; the colleges do the same. The students see first class Indian teachers superseded by young and third-rate foreigners ; the principals or presidents of colleges must be foreigners ; foreign history is more important than Indian : to have written on English villages is a qualification for teaching economics in India: the whole atmosphere of the school and college emphasizes the superiority of the foreigner. The whole education of the country is planned on foreign models, and its object is to serve foreign rather than native ends, to make docile government servants, rather than patriotic citizens. High spirit, courage, self-respect, are not encouraged, and docility is regarded as the most precious quality in the student. Pride in country, patriotism, ambition, are looked upon as dangerous. English instead of Indian ideals are exalted; the blessings of a foreign rule and the incapacity of Indians are constantly inculcated."*

The British often charge the Indian people with weakness, obsequiousness, lack of manliness, lack of courage and spirit, and even lack of honor and integrity, and declare that because of these deficiencies they are not fit to rule themselves, but must be governed by Britain.

But if this is true, *who is to blame but the British?* To a very notable degree the people of India were strong and virile before the British came and reduced them to political and moral subjection. During the long centuries and decades when India stood on her own feet, ruled herself and developed her own great civilization, no nation stood higher in every characteristic that distinguishes an influential, honored, brave, illustrious people. It was India that was first able to check and turn back Alexander the Great in his career of world-conquest. Surely Indians were not weaklings and inferiors then. According to the Greek writers of the time the civilization of India stood essentially on a level with their own, and the Indian people were represented as bearing the highest character. The Greek Flavius Arrian, the historian of the campaigns of Alexander, wrote of the Hindus:

"They are remarkably brave, and superior in war

* "The Case for India." pp. 32, 33.

to all Asiatics ; they are remarkable for integrity ; they are so reasonable as seldom to have recourse to lawsuits, and so honest as neither to require locks to their doors nor writings to bind their agreements. They are in the highest degree truthful."

The celebrated Chinese traveller, Houen Tsang, who made an extended visit to India in the seventh century A. D., assigns to the Indian people as high a general character and as elevated a place in civilization as did the Greeks of Alexander's time

Travellers from Europe visited India from time to time in later centuries, and nearly or quite all brought back praise of the country for its fertility, rich products, and wonderful scenery ; and hardly less praise of the people, for their industry, general prosperity, honor, culture, and high character.

One of the most noted of these visitors was Sir Thomas Roe, who, early in the seventeenth century, was sent by the King of England as an ambassador to the court of the Indian Emperor, Jehangir, in Agra. Roe wrote much about India, highly lauding the country, the people, whom he represented as comparing favorably with the people of Europe, the remarkable architecture of the land, and other forms of high art, the wealth of the upper classes, the splendor of the courts of the rulers, and so on.

This general high estimate of India, not only of the country for its attractiveness and wealth, but of the people, for their intelligence, culture, courage and high attainments, continued right on, until these comers from the West began to turn into greedy coveters of India's wealth, and plotters to get possession of it by fair means or foul. As soon as this change took place, and the English and other Europeans entered upon that career of spoliation, robbery and domination of the country which forms one of the darkest chapters in modern history, then at once the world began to hear a very different estimate of the Indian people. Almost in a day from a nation of high civilization, culture, character, and honor, they sank into barbarians.

It is the old story : as soon as we wrong a man, we instinctively begin to defame him. This unjust and shameful disparaging of the Indian people, this representation of them as low in civilization, low in character, an inferior race, "half devil and half child" (in Kipling's words), not fit to rule themselves, and the like, continues right on down to the present day.

And why not, if British domination of that country is to continue ? Really what else is to be expected ? Unless the world can be made to believe that the Indian people are only half-civilized, and an intellectually and morally inferior race, how can England find even a shadow of an excuse for continuing to force her rule and her exploitation on them ?

Suppose the British people themselves to-day were ruled by foreigners, as the Indian people are, could they long keep their present strength of character ? Would their subject condition have no weakening and degrading effect on them ?

Those very pertinent questions were asked and answered many years ago by a distinguished British official in India. Said Sir Thomas Munro, (Governor of Madras from 1819 to 1826) :

"Let Britain be subjugated by a foreign power to-morrow : let the people be excluded from all share in the government, from public honors, from every office of high trust or emolument, and let them in every situation be considered as unworthy of trust and all their knowledge and all their literature, sacred and profane, would not save them from becoming, in a generation or two, a low minded, deceitful and dishonest race. If we pay the same price for integrity, we find it as readily among Indians as among Europeans."

That the Indian people have become so little weakened, demoralized or debased by their long subjection; that they are still, on the whole, so morally strong, trustworthy and admirable; and that within the last thirty or forty years (since their determined struggle for freedom began) they have developed such an able, strong, courageous, forward-looking and altogether remarkable body of leaders, is a testimony of the highest order as to the inherently superior, intellectual and moral qualities of this ancient, historic, and (in spite of all their discouragements, and all the degrading tyrannies to which they have been subjected) this *still great race of men.*

India's subject condition cannot always last. To believe it perpetual is to despair of the human race. To preserve one's sanity we must believe that the world is moving forward. If it is, then India must and will once more have a place among the world's leading nations. And when she comes into her own, she will not come empty-handed, but as the bearer of important gifts to her sister nations. Mr. Gokhale was right in his vision:

"When the emasculating influence of India's subjection is over, and she once more becomes free, and when, therefore, Indian men and women become able again to grow to the full height of their stature and proclaim to the world the mission which is to be theirs, then a great stream of moral and spiritual energy, long lost to view, will have returned to its channel, and East and West—white and dark and yellow and brown—will all have cause alike to rejoice."

CHAPTER XIII

CRUSHING OUT THE GENIUS OF A GREAT AND GIFTED NATION

It seems to be true that the world has produced no nation more gifted intellectually and spiritually than India, that is, possessing higher or richer, intellectual and spiritual genius; unless we ought to except ancient Greece.

Has Great Britain, in conquering and ruling India, recognized this fact, and treated the Indian people as the world had a right to expect and demand, in view of their high intellectual qualities and the great contributions they had made to human civilization?

The answer that has to be made is No. Amazing as the statement seems, the British have ignored India's civilization as something of little or no value, and instead of showing appreciation of India's rich genius, guarding it, preserving it, fostering it, developing it, as something of priceless value to mankind, they not only have been indifferent to its existence, and unsympathetic toward it, but they have actually shaped their governmental policies in India in ways to disparage it, to discourgae it, seriously to limit its spheres of activity, to cripple it, and, at least for the time being, in large measure to crush it.

In other words, the shocking fact confronts us and confronts the world, that Great Britain, by depriving India of its freedom, by despising its ancient and high civilization, by ignoring and crippling the genius of its people for nearly two centuries, and by insisting on the baseless pretense that a great people which has ruled itself for three thousand years is not competent to rule itself to-day, has practically robbed the world of one of its most important nations, turning this historic, renowned and highly gifted people into (if I may be allowed the figure of speech) a stagnant pool, giving forth almost nothing of benefit to mankind; instead of allowing it to be what, if free, it would have been, a great flowing river pouring the abundant waters of its activities and its rich genius into the great and growing civilization of the modern world. How can any intelligent mind fail to recognize this loss, this robbery, this crime against India, as a calamity to mankind of the first magnitude?

As has often been pointed out by eminent Englishmen themselves, the average British mind seems unable to understand any civilization but its own; therefore, it habitually looks down upon all others with indifference, if not with contempt. This appears to account for the contemptuous treatment which from the beginning the British government has extended to the important civilization of India, and its seemingly fixed design to crowd that civilzation into the background, and, so far as possible, destroy it, with the purpose of planting that of England in its place.

It is hardly an overstatement to say, that to the great mass of Englishmen in India, every Indian custom, institution, habit of the people, even to dress, furniture of houses and manner of eating, if different from those of England, is bad, and should be changed. Systems of education, forms of government and ideals of life that have been built up as the result of thousands of years of experience count for nothing. Schools from lowest to highest must be patterned after those of London, Harrow and Oxford. The history taught must be primarily that of Europe and especially of Great Britain; and if the history of India is taught at all, it must be given a secondary place; and moreover, it must be written not by Indian scholars who are "sympathetic" with their nation's institutions and ideals and who give the story of her past as India herself sees it, but by Englishmen or others in sympathy with British ideals and with British rule, who portray India's past unfavorably, as Britain sees it, and wants the world to see it. Both in the higher institutions of learning and in the public libraries wherever the British have control, the extensive and important literature of India must be crowded into the background and that of England must be kept at the front. Even the language of the country so far as possible must be made that of the foreign nation that rules the land. English must be insisted on as the official language everywhere. All communications with the Government must be written in English, all government business must be transacted through the medium of English, all studies in the universities must be carried on in English and all examinations must be conducted in the same foreign tongue.

The Government sees to it that public buildings are built in European styles and not in any of those of India, although some forms of Indian architecture are unsurpassed in beauty by any in the world. The British officials furnish their homes in English fashion, for the most part importing their furniture from England. They have specially comfortable and luxurious cars on the railways reserved for Englishmen, and luxurious clubs of their own from which Indians are excluded.

Thus everything possible is done to disparage and belittle the great civilization of India, to destroy the pride and interest of the people in their own country and to keep them ignorant of the great place it has filled in the world ; to make them look up to the British as their superiors in everything ; to break their spirit ; to destroy their power of initiative and their ability to think and act independently ; thus making impossible the development of their national genius, preventing them from making those important intellectual contributions to the world which they are naturally so well qualified to make, and transforming them from what throughout so many ages of the past they have been—a great nation with a unique genius and a proud mission in the world, into a flock of sheep, meekly and helplessly obeying the voice of foreign shepherds ; or, in other words, into a vast mass of spineless imitators of English ways.

How long will the world consent to such a humiliation and degradation of one of its greatest, most gifted and historically most important nations,—one which, according to distinguished Englishmen themselves (including Lord Curzon), has made contributions to the civilization and higher life of mankind not second to those of any nation, even Greece.

In an address delivered before the London Positivist Society, February 16, 1908, Mr. Henry Ellis, an eminent leader in that body, said: "We Englishmen are fond of saying to the world that we are governing countries like Egypt and India, not primarily for our own advantage, but for theirs. It is a specious plea which appeals at first sight to our altruistic sympathies ; but it will not bear examination. We know, in fact. that no nation is so disinterested as to undertake such a labor and responsibility without the expectation of a *quid pro quo* of some kind. The root of the evil which we are inflicting on these nations is, that we are depriving them of their freedom; and what is life worth to men who are not free? It is only in a state of freedom that a nation is enabled to show of what it is capable and these people are consequently prevented by us from developing their natural tendencies, their natural gifts and powers, their natural genius. We seem to be acting on the principle that our precise form of civilization is the only one that is important; that it is superior to all others; and that if we could but succeed in establishing a number of little Englands throughout the world, its happiness would be greatly increased. This is a gross piece of presumption. Who are we that, in view of the social misery that exists among ourselves—our extremes of wealth and poverty—our shameless luxury on the one hand, and our destitution and crime on the other—who are we that we should seek to stereotype universally our particular form of society, as if it were the last word to be said?

"The world would be a dull place if it were all patented one color, and that color a 'dockyard drab.' What would become of all the mystery, the glow, the charm, the romance of the East if all its cities were converted, under British rule, into so many copies of Birmingham of Sheffield; and if a glimpse of the Himalayas could be obtained only by peeping through a forest of factory chimneys? How much would be left under such a dispensation, of the legends of Saladin, and Haroun-al Raschid, and the Arabian Nights,—to say nothing of the more ancient and sacred memories of Menu and Buddha and Zoroaster.

"No! What is wanted in human life is not more of the hideous uniformity which now prevails, or is aimed at, in accordance with our Western ideas, but more variety. Each race has its own traditions, and can furnish its own valuable contributions civilization. Do not let us seek to crush all into one procrustean bed of 'Competitive Industrialism," with its Jargon of 'Supply and Demand,' its brazen 'Law of Wages,' its ferocious 'Class War,' and its brutal gospel of 'the devil take the hindermost. And, especially, let us not inflict all these evils on helpless nations and people under the hypocritical plea that we are doing it for their good."

British rule in India has been very significantly compared to a banyan tree. Under a banyan tree little or nothing can grow. The tree overshadows and kills essentially everything beneath it. The only growths that can live and thrive are the stems or slender branches sent down to the ground from the tree itself; these take root and develop; nothing else can.

So in India, everything that has any chance of life is what comes down from the all-powerful, all-overshadowing British banyan-tree government.

Here we have the strongest of all reasons why the Indian people desire to escape from foreign domination. They feel that their very life depends upon their gaining freedom to stand on their own feet, to be men and not slaves or nonentities, to think their own thoughts, to follow their own ideals, to cultivate their own national and racial genius, to develop their own important civilization, to shape their own destiny as they can never do under the chilling, discouraging, dwarfing, character-weakening, initiative-killing, ambition-destroying, hope-blighting shadow of the banyan tree (or upas tree) of a haughty, unsympathetic foreign tyranny.

Professor Pual S. Reinisch says in his work on "Colonial Government:"

"The essential thought in dealing with native societies should be that they must on no account be deprived of their morale, and of their feeling of responsibility for their own destiny."

Here England has failed absolutely and disastrously in her treatment of the Indian people. She has taken their destiny out of their hands into her own. Politically she rules them wholly. Financially and industrially they feel that they are constantly at her mercy. The influence is to break their spirit. There is no incentive for ambition. Young men, no matter what their talents or education, have little or nothing to look foward to. A situation more depressing it is hard to conceive. England tries to justify herself by the claim that she can rule the Indian people better than they can rule themselves. This is the claim of tyranny the world over.

The surest way to destroy the physical strength of a man is to deprive him of the possibility of physical exercise. The most brilliant minds may be reduced to dullness, and the most powerful to weakness, by being deprived of opportunities for activity. Just so, there is no other way known so effectually to weaken and degrade a people as to deprive them of liberty and the power of self-direction. The highest end of government is not law ; it is not even order and peace. These may be present under the most monstrous oppression. The highest purpose of government is the creation of the capacity for self-government. The sufficient condemnation of all vassalage and of all government of weaker peoples by stronger is, that thus the weaker peoples are deprived of their right to plan for themselves, and to work out their own self-development.

This is something which the better minds of India feel very deeply. Especially is it felt by ambitious, earnest, educated young men, who want to make the most of their lives, who desire to do something for their communities and their country, and to become leaders in movements for social, industrial, educational, political and other reforms.

On every hand such young men are met by the fact that neither they nor the people are free. They are forever under foreign masters. If they make plans for public improvements, their plans can come to nothing without the assent and co-operation of the Government, because it has all power. The very fact that the plans are initiated and carried on by Indians—by "natives," is very likely to be regarded as a sufficient reason why the Government should ignore or oppose them. The Government wants it understood that it never follows "native" lead, it never welcomes, or, if it can help it, even tolerates, native initiative. That would lower its "dignity." That would destroy its "prestige." The government stands on the lofty height not only of supreme power, but of supreme wisdom, and it cannot stoop to be instructed or directed, even to have suggestions made to it, by the "inferior" people of the land, who, of course, do not know what is good for them or what the country requires.

Thus initiative on the part of the people is chilled and killed. They soon learn to say, "What is the use ?" Educated young men, who, in free lands where the people have a voice, would look forward to influential public life, to careers of public usefulness and service, to doing something of value for their country, have in India little or no such possibility before them. They have no country. The English rule it, monopolize it, treat the Indians as strangers and foreigners in it. King George calls it, "My Indian Empire." And when Indians presume to interest themselves in public matters and make suggestions as to reforms and improvements which in any way touch politics, they at once find themselves in danger of being arrested and sent to prison as pestilent "agitators and "seditionists;" or if they escape that, then they are likely either to be ignored, receiving no co-operation and no encouragement from the superior powers, or else they get the virtual reply: "Mind your own business. Who are you, that you presume to teach us how to manage this country?"

Sir Henry Cotton tells us that the British policy in India has always been to discourage, and so far as possible to suppress, native ability and native initiative, He tells us of hearing Sir William Harcourt say in a speech in the House of Commons;

"The officials at the head of the Government of India have never encouraged men of ability and force of character. They have always hated and discouraged independent and original talent, and have always loved and promoted docile and unpretending mediocrity. This policy they have inherited from the Roman Tarquinius Superbus. Although they have not actually 'cut off the heads' of the 'tall poppies,' they have taken other and more merciful means of 'removing' any persons of dangerous political eminence."*

I shall never forget an experience I once had in Poona. I was there attending the session of the Indian National Congress. One afternoon I went out for a stroll with a company of young men who were students in the Ferguson College. After walking an hour or so we all sat down under a great tree for a long talk. They were keen-minded, earnest fellows, all of them desirous of making something worth while of their lives, and all ambitious to serve their country. But in

* "Indian and Home Memories," Chapter XXI.

a land where everything was in the hands of foreign masters, how could they do either? If ignoring their country's needs and forgetting her sorrows, they would consent to be docile servants of their alien rulers, shaping their education so as to fit themselves for employment as clerks, accountants and subordinate helpers of one kind or another in the offices of the Government or of British merchants, then places would be opened for them where they could gain at least a meagre living, with the hope of some slight advancement later, and thus their paths for the future would probably be fairly smooth.

But if, standing on their own feet as men, they determined to shape for themselves independent careers, and to make their lives of real service to the land they loved, what was there for them? This was the pathetic, the tragic question, asked by all those young men, again and again and again. The government had many low positions—too low to be accepted by Englishmen—to offer them, and a very few fairly high ones. But all persons permitted to occupy these positions must give up their patriotism and their manhood, keep out of politics, be loyal to the alien Government, that is, must not criticize it or advocate any reforms, and be dumb and docile servants and satellites of their British lords. Could these earnest, patriotic, splendid young sons of India, of the holy "Mother" whom they loved and worshipped, stoop to this humiliation and this shame?

Alas! that afternoon I realized as I never had done before how bitter, bitter a thing it is for educated young men, in whose breasts burn the fires of a patriotism as true and as holy as was ever felt by any Englishman or American, to know that they have no country; to realize that their country, as dear to them as their lives, has been taken by force, and is held in subjection by the sword of the foreigner!

This Poona experience illustrates and emphasizes the undeniable fact that one of the very grave evils of British rule in India is its influence in crushing out the native genius of the Indian people,—thus robbing not only India but also mankind of something very precious. There is nothing in the world that is of higher value and therefore that should be more sedulously guarded than genius—the peculiar genius of nations and of races; and there is nothing which when destroyed is a more serious or a more irreparable loss.

What a loss to the world was the destruction of the remarkable indigenous civilizations of early Mexico and Peru. What a loss to mankind was the disappearance of the ancient and wonderful civilizations of Babylon, Assyria, Persia, Egypt and Crete! Scholars in our day are making enormous efforts, and vast sums of money are being spent in excavations, to rescue such fragments and relics of them as may be possible. The civilization of India is far higher, richer and more important than any of these. Then shall we despise it? Would not the loss of it be among the greatest of possible calamities? Is not the neglecting, crippling or degrading of it a crime against humanity?

Writes James Russell Lowell:

"All nations have their message from on high,
Each the Messiah of some vital thought;
For the fulfilment and delight of men
One has to teach that labor is divine,
Another freedom, and another mind.
And all, that God is open-eyed and just,
Aye, each a message has from God's great heart;
And each is needed for the world's great life."

Who can estimate how great would have been the disaster to humanity, if, by foreign domination or otherwise the genius of Greece had been cut off before it reached its splendid flowering in art and literature?

I will not persist in comparing the genius of India with that of Greece, although some eminent scholars both in Europe and America have done so. But I will say, what no competent scholar denies, that no other nation in Asia has shown in the past so rich and splendid, intellectual and spiritual genius as India has manifested in many forms and throughout a long series of centuries. That genius should be preserved, fostered, and developed, not only for the sake of the Indian people, but for mankind's sake, for civilization's sake, as a precious contribution to the world's higher life.

How can this be done? What is the indispensable condition of the efflorescence, nay of the very existence of genius anywhere? It is freedom. But India is not free. This is her calamity; it is also the world's calamity. So long as she continues to be humiliated, disgraced, crippled, emasculated by being held in bondage to a foreign power, by being robbed of her proper place among the nations, by being deprived of the right to direct herself and shape her career, it will be impossible, in the very nature of things, for her naturally rich genius to rise to its best, or anything like its best, and thus for her to make that important intellectual and spiritual contribution to the world's civilization that her past history gives the world the right to expect and demand. Thus we see that India's freedom is a matter of concern not to herself alone, but to mankind. Her bondage is a world-disaster—a great and shameful crime against the world's higher life.

CHAPTER XIV

INDIA AND JAPAN. WHY JAPAN IS IN ADVANCE OF INDIA.

Why does small (comparatively small) Japan occupy so conspicuous a place in Asia and the world? And why does India, a country so very much larger, more populous, and older in civilization, occupy a place so much less conspicuous and less honored?

Is it because the people of Japan are by nature a superior people, and the people of India inferior?

As for myself, I think very highly of the Japanese. I have had much acquaintance with them, both in America and in their own country; and I regard them, whether in their intellectual ability, their character or their civilization, as not inferior to the average white nations, and as distinctly superior to some.

But are they superior to the people of India? And even if they are to-day, were they when the Indian people fell under British domination, a little less than two centuries ago? Or were they when Japan emerged from her long seclusion, three-quarters of a century ago?

If at either of those dates, Englishmen or Americans who were best acquainted with the Orient, had been asked which of the two nations in their judgment, was the superior, as to their civilization, their intellectual ability and their character, I think they would have assigned to India a place distinctly above Japan.

Certainly until recent years Japan has had a very inconspicuous place in the world ; indeed, she has hardly been known even by the other nations of Asia. On the other hand, India has occupied a very great place. Let us see how great.

From time immemorial India was known not only throughout practically all Asia, but in eastern Europe and in parts of Africa. At the time of Alexander the Great she was so famous in Greece that it became the supreme ambition of that great conqueror to lead his armies to India, and add to his empire that most renowned country of Asia. And he did push his conquests to India, where he found a civilization which he recognized as little if any inferior to that of Greece, and great kingdoms with armies so strong that after fighting a great battle he decided that wisdom required him to retreat.

Two or three centuries before Christ the Buddhist religion, which had its rise in India, was carried by its missionaries all over central and Western Asia, to the very borders of Europe, if it did not even penetrate that continent ; and a little later it spread over nearly all eastern Asia, carrying Indian thought and influence wherever it went.

There was much knowledge of India among the Romans, and considerable overland commerce, bringing to Rome the valuable products of India—jewelry, precious stones, fine silks and so on. Later, the wealth of Venice, Genoa and other Mediterranean cities was built up largely by their extensive and profitable commerce with India. For more than two thousand years, up to very recent times, numerous great caravans were all the while moving between the Mediterranean countries and India.

It was to discover a sea route to India, so as to give Europe easier access to Indian products and Indian wealth that Columbus sailed over the Atlantic ; and when he found America he thought it was India,—hence the incorrect name, "Indians," given to the natives of the American continent.

The glory that came to Vasco da Gama from his discovery of a passage around the south of Africa came mainly from the fact that it gave the European nations, what they had so long desired, an all-ocean way to India. As soon as that route was discovered all the leading sea-going nations of Europe, Portugal, Spain, France, Holland and Great Britain, became rivals in extending their trade by sea to India, and it was not long before the Dutch, French and English were fighting to gain, first, commercial and then political, dominance in that wealthiest and most renowned country in the greatest of the continents. And when Great Britain drove out her rivals, and became the conqueror, possessor, exploiter, and despoiler of the land, drawing from it a stream of riches greater than the stream of gold and silver which Spain drew from Mexico and Peru, all the nations of Europe were jealous, and ever since have regarded Britain as having obtained the greatest prize (robber prize !) in all the world.

Surely such a country, thus famous from as far back as history extends, ought to-day to occupy a conspicuous place in the world.

Why does it not ? Why is it so far outstripped and overshadowed by Japan ?

Compare the past history of Japan, and her past and present resources and natural advantages with those of India.

Japan is very small in area, only about one-seventh as large as India, and possesses only about one-fifth as great a population. Instead of being located centrally in Asia, as India is, it is located far to the east, and not even on the continent at all. Its known history does not go back nearly so far as India's, and the beginning of its civilization is much more recent. During much of its history it has been a sort of hermit land, its people having little to do with other nations. Until the American Commodore Perry, less than eighty years ago, broke up its isolation and compelled it to open its doors to foreign intercourse, it was very little known even in Asia, and had practically no place at all among the nations of the world. Whatever literature it had created, was unknown to other peoples. Its chief religion was borrowed from a foreign country, India. Its art, although in some of its forms excellent, was limited, and at least to a degree was an imitation of that of China. It was almost wholly an agricultural land, its manufactures being few and its foreign commerce very restricted, neither one comparing at all with those of India. It had little iron or other mineral resources and its coal was limited, whereas the iron, coal and other resources of India were immense. Its wealth was very small compared with the vast wealth which India possessed before her conquest and exploitation by the British.

And yet, within the last two generations, Japan has become the foremost nation in Asia, and one of the foremost in the world, while India has lost its leadership in Asia which it had maintained for twenty-five centuries, and has now no recognition at all among the world's nations.

What is the explanation of this amazing difference which we see between the two countries to-day,—the splendid advance of little Japan in almost every respect, and the astonishing stagnation and decadence of great, historic India ?

Can any intelligent man anywhere, in this country or any other suggest any possible explanation but one ? And is not that one the fact that Japan is and has been free, while India, for nearly two hundred years, has been in bondage to a foreign power ?

It is universally agreed to-day that, after freedom, the prime condition of advance, I may say the prime *creator* of advance, among nations in the modern world, is education ; and that with the exception of bondage, the prime cause of the stangnation and decline of nations, is want of education. Let us see how this applies to Japan and India. Has education flourished equally in the two countries ? Have the governments of the two been equally interested to promote education ?

In Japan, as soon as the nation decided to give up its policy of isolation, and put itself into contact with the other nations of the world, the government saw the importance of *universal education* for its people, As early as 1869 it issued an educational ordinance of a very radical character, which read :

> "*Education is essential for all persons ; and whereas in the past learning has been looked upon as a means of securing official position, henceforth the whole population of the country regardless of classes, must be educated so that no village shall contain a person devoid of learning, nor any house contain an illiterate inmate.*"

Accordingly, schools of all grades were established, primary, secondary, and high ; as also colleges and universities. Particular attention was paid to agricultural, industrial, and technical education. And, what the government clearly saw the importance of, young men in large numbers were sent abroad to study in the best colleges, universities, and agricultural, industrial and technical institutions, of America and Europe, so that they might become teachers and leaders at home.

On the contrary, from the beginning of British rule in India, the foreign government there adopted an educational policy almost the opposite of that of Japan. It feared and distrusted education, realizing that a people kept in ignorance would be most easily controlled and kept under British power. True, after a while, it established an educational system of a sort, but it was very limited in its scope. It reached only a small fraction of the children of the nation ; and as for higher education, that was shaped mainly with a view to fitting young men for the service of their British masters. Scientific and industrial education, and all kinds of training calculated to fit young men and women to serve India, to develop her material resources, to build up her industrial life, and to put the Indian people into contact with the other peoples of the world—these kinds of education were seriously neglected or wholly ignored. Instead of sending students abroad to get the best training obtainable there, as Japan did, the British government of India indirectly discouraged everything of the kind. Especially was this true in the case of young men desiring to come to America to study, because it feared the influences of freedom and democracy with which in this country they would be surrounded.

Dr. Sudhindra Bose (Lecturer in the State University of Iowa) has put the whole matter very clearly. Says Dr. Bose :

"Although technological institutes and agricultural schools are a prime necessity in the economic uplift of any country, there has not been and is not any adequate provision for the creation of these in India. Had

India possessed, like Japan, a national government free to rule its own destiny, the situation would have been very different. Seventy years ago Japan was industrially no better off than India. At that time Japan was a feudalistic agricultural country, with a strong aversion to foreign trade or commerce. The nation was sharply divided (her divisions were quite as great as any existing in India) into many classes and sub-classes, of which the Samurai, the warrior class, was the most powerful faction. With the advent of Commodore Perry, Japan turned over a new leaf. The Japanese government decided to make their country the leading industrial land of the Orient. And how did the Japanese government go about it? Japan had little or no modern industrial knowledge or experience. It was entirely without models for industrial organization and without financial machinery. At this juncture the government took hold of the situation. It established schools and colleges, where all branches of applied science were taught. Says Baron Kikuchi: 'There were official excursions into the domains of silk-reeling, cement-making, cotton and silk spinning, brick-burning, printing and book-binding, soap-boiling, type-casting and ceramic decoration. Domestic exhibitions were organized by the government for the encouragement of the people in undertaking those industries; and specimens of the country's products and manufactures were sent under government auspices to exhibitions abroad. The government established a firm whose functions were to familiarize foreign markets with the products of Japanese artisans. Steps were taken for training women as artisans, and the Government printing bureau set the example of employing female labor, an invasion which soon developed into large dimensions. In short, the authorities applied themselves to educate an industrial disposition, and as soon as success seemed to be in sight, they gradually transferred from official to private direction the various model enterprises, retaining only such as were required to supply the needs of the state.' The result of all this was, that whereas in the beginning of the Meiji era, 1867, Japan had virtually no industries worth the name, in thirty years she possessed no less than 4595 industrial and commercial companies, either joint-stock or partnership, with a paid-up capital of two hundred million dollars; and to-day the number of companies and the capital invested are almost beyond belief."

Is it surprising that Japan is now the most

advanced and the most prosperous industrial country in Asia? Is there any room for doubt that, if the Indian people had possessed a national government of their own like that of Japan, India, with her natural resources almost infinitely greater than those of Japan, and with her unlimited labor supply, would have prospered as well as or better than Japan, and would to-day, industrially and commercially, have been quite abreast of Japan if not in advance?

Says Rabindranath Tagore:

"The Japanese have made remarkable progress, but given equal opportunity, India would do as well. We are not intellectually inferior to the Japanese. Possibly we are in some crafts: but in pure thought we are superior; and even in the crafts in which they excel, we were once quite their equals, and would be now if not fettered and hindered. The Japanese have been free to educate themselves, and to send their young men to all universities of the world to acquire knowledge. But every Indian feels, and every candid investigator of the subject must admit, that England has conceived it to be her interest to keep us weak, and has discouraged education. In the laboratories she dislikes us to acquire science and to pursue research. In almost every way she has persistently striven to repress and cramp our economic development."

Let us compare a little more fully what Japan's government has done for the Japanese people with what India's has done for the Indian people.

1. As we have seen, Japan's government set out from the first to give education to all the people, so that there should not be an illiterate person in any home in the land; and as a result her Year Book shows her to-day to be one of the most highly literate nations in the world.

On the other hand, India's government (by foreigners) has persistently refused the people's demand for education, so that now, after a hundred and sixty years more than ninety per cent. of her people are illiterate.

2. As we have seen, the government of Japan set out from the beginning to foster every kind of manufactures and industries, so that now she is the leading manufacturing nation in Asia.

On the other hand, India's foreign government, by her tariffs and in other ways, has deliberately destroyed India's extensive native manufactures in the interest of those of England, and has done all in her power to reduce India from the condition of a great industrial nation to that of a producer of raw materials to build up the industries of Great Britain.

3. The government of self-ruling Japan, from the beginning, in every way possible, has fostered foreign commerce and trade and ship-building, with the result that now Japan is not only the first commercial nation of Asia but one of the first in the world.

On the contrary, India's British government, by its patronage bestowed upon British merchants and shipping companies, and its discriminations against those of India, has practically killed the extensive foreign commerce and the ship-building of India as formerly carried on by the Indian people, so that now India's foreign commerce for the most part is British, controlled by the British and enriching Britain instead of India; and the shipping which transports this commerce is built in Great Britain instead of in India, thus again taking away from India a legitimate industry and giving it (with the wealth it creates) to the nation that holds her in subjection.

4. From the beginning the Japanese government has done everything in its power to build up the wealth of Japan, in the ways already mentioned and others.

On the contrary, the government of India, in addition to its destruction of those industries which would have promoted the wealth of the Indian people (in the ways already pointed out), from the very beginning has deliberately and persistently drained away her wealth to Great Britain, in enormous quantities, by tariffs ; by purchases made in England that ought to have been made in India ; by drawing from her large sums to pay the expenses of Britain's imperialistic wars which in no way benefited India ; by filling nearly all the more important official positions in India with Englishmen at high salaries, when they might have been filled quite as efficiently, and often very much more so, by Indians at salaries one-third as great ; by conferring on those English officials, after a brief service of only twenty-four years, fat pensions to support them in England all the rest of their lives ; until in these various ways the country has been drained of its very life blood (as an eminent Englishman has said, has been "bled white").

If we ask the explanation of this contrast, can any possibly be given except, that Japan has had a government of her own, while India has had a government of foreigners ?

There are those who try to account for the fact that Japan is so far in advance of India to-day, by saying that the Japanese are a practical people, and the Indian people are not.

On the contrary, as already pointed out, up to seventy years ago the Japanese people were anything but practical, according to our western ideas of practicality. They were a shut-in nation, with few manufactures and little commerce, living their own secluded almost wholly agricultural life. If to-day they are what we call eminently practical, they have become so within less than two generations, and as a result of their contact with the world, their education, and, above all, their freedom. On the other hand, India, besides her thinkers, her scholars, her poets, her philosophers, her religious teachers and devotees—her dreamers if one chooses to call them so—has had, as has been shown, whole great classes, numbering millions and millions, not only of agriculturists, but of artisans, of traders, of soldiers, of practical men of every known kind.

This point needs to be emphasised, even at the risk of some repetition, there is so much misunderstanding regarding it. The fact is, there is probably no great people in the entire world among whom the practical things of life, that is, the practical activities, occupations, and industries which accompany civilization, have been more fully developed than in the people of India for two or three thousand years, up to the time of the coming of the British. This is shown by the fact that their wealth was so great. It was their wealth that attracted the British. This wealth was created by their vast and varied industries. Nearly every kind of manufacture or product known to the civilized world,—nearly every kind of creation of man's brain and hand, existing anywhere, and prized either for its utility or beauty, had long, long been produced in India. India was a far greater industrial and manufacturing nation than any in Europe or than any other in Asia. Her textile goods—the fine products of her looms, in cotton, wool, linen and silk, were famous over the civilized world; so were her exquisite jewelry and her precious stones cut in every lovely form; so were her pottery, porcelains, ceramics of every kind, quality, color and beautiful shape; so were her fine works in metal—iron, steel, silver and gold.

She had great architecture—equal in beauty to any in the world. She had great engineering works. She had great merchants, great business men, great bankers and financiers. Not only was she the greatest ship-building nation, but she had great commerce and trade by land and sea which extended to all known civilized countries.

Such was the India which the British found when they came. Can such a nation be spoken of as lacking in practical ability? Can any one who knows anything of the history of the Orient believe for a moment that the reason why such a nation has fallen behind Japan is that her native ability, genius or skill in any practical direction, was less than that of Japan in all those ages when she was free, or would be less to-day were it not for the shameful fact that for more than a century and a half she has been in bondage, and that her foreign rulers for their own advantage have destroyed a large part of her manufactures, her native industries, her finances, her most important lines of home industries, her ship-building, her foreign trade and commerce, and at the same time have refused to give her scientific or technical school or any except the most meager and inadequate industrial and practical education?

Is it said that the British Government in India is handicapped by caste, as the Japanese government is not, and on account of this cannot give universal education to the Indian people? The unanswerable reply is: Some of the leading Native Indian States, where caste is as strong as anywhere in India, namely, Baroda, Mysore, Gwalior, Indore, Tranvancore and others actually are giving their people universal education. It is true that caste creates a difficulty; but these native States overcome it. It could be overcome in all British India if the British Government so willed.

Is it said that the British Government of India could not give universal education to the Indian people, as Japan has done to the Japanese people, because the population of India is so great and the country is so poor? The answer is: the natural resources of India are not only incomparably greater than those of Japan, but they are far greater *in proportion to population*; so that if Japan can find financial means to maintain universal education, much more could India if she would. The fact is the government of India has never lacked money for education; it has only lacked *will*. It always has plenty of money for its own militaristic and imperialistic ends; for maintaining a great army to hold the country in subjection, and to fight Britain's battles in other lands; to maintain a Christian Church (a State Church) in India, for the support of which Hindus and Mohammedans are taxed; to pay the high salaries and pensions of the Englishmen who are robbing the Indian people of the right to govern themselves; to create government buildings of various kinds in all parts of the land, often far more costly than necessary, to gratify British pride; to give the government of India the luxury of spending seven months every summer in the mountains, at an expense to the poor taxpayers of many millions of dollars; to hold from time to time great and gorgeous "*durbars*," rivalling in pomp and show the utmost display of the monarchs of barbaric ages, having for their aim to impress and over-awe the people, but costing them tens of millions of dollars; and to build a wholly unneeded new Capital City, new Delhi, showy and magnificent, to impress the people with the splendor and power of the British Empire, but adding to the crushing burden of the taxpayers many times "tens of millions" of dollars.

If even a quarter part of the vast sums of money spent upon these things, most of which have solely British interests in view and are of no value whatever to the Indian people, were devoted to schools, India could not only equal Japan in education, but surpass her. And who can doubt that it would have done so, if India had been as free as Japan, with a government not of foreigners but of her own eminent leaders ?

The exceedingly significant fact should not be overlooked that the new awakening of Asia, caused by contact with modern European thought and modern science, began in India ; it did not begin in Japan. India has always been more closely in touch with Europe than has Japan. Asia's renaissance began with Ram Mohun Roy and Ishwar Chandra Vidyasagar in Bengal, where important literature, alive with the modern spirit, was produced a full half century before Japan ceased to be a closed land, uninfluenced by modern progress. The awakening of Asia which thus begun in Bengal, ought to have continued, grown, spread, borne rich fruit not only in India but in all Asiatic lands.

I think the whole situation may be briefly summed up somewhat as follows :

Japan has had her wonderful development and has attained her conspicuous and honored place among the nations of the world, because she has been free. In 1852, when our American Commodore Perry knocked at her closed door and insisted on her opening it to the intercourse and trade of the world, he did not conquer her, reduce her to subjection, and begin robbing her. He respected her independence and her rights, took her by the hand and introduced her to the fellowship of free peoples. That was what made possible her splendid career. It is because she has been free, and not subject to foreign domination and spoliation, that she has attained a position among the nations abreast of Great Britain, France and the United States; that her children and youth are in school; that her people are well-fed; that her sanitation is equal to the best in the world; that her manufactures are flourishing; that her commerce is found in all lands and her ships on all seas; and that her wealth is her own and not another's. If America or any European power had seized her, made her a dependency, disarmed her, set up a foreign government to rule her, filled all her most important offices with strangers, refused to give her education, denied to her people power to make or alter a single one of the laws which they must obey, taken control of every yen of her national revenues, is there any reason whatever for believing that to-day she would have been any farther advanced than is India, if as far?

On the other hand, if India had been treated as Japan has been, given the hand of friendship, permitted to retain her own wealth for her own uses, and to develop herself in freedom along the lines of her own genius, can any intelligent person for a moment doubt that, with her not inferior intelligence, her far greater material resources, her earlier start and her advantages of many kinds, she would to-day have occupied a place in the world at least as prominent and as honorable as that of Japan?

In the careers of modern Japan and modern India we have one more illustration among the many which appear in history, of the tremendously important fact which the whole world should lay to heart, that everywhere the prime and absolutely indispensable condition of growth, of development, of achievement, quite as much in nations as in individual men, is freedom; while everywhere bondage, subjection, means stagnation, degradation, blight, virtual death.

CHAPTER XV

DEMOCRACIES AND REPUBLICS IN INDIA

It is common to speak of Asia as a land of despotisms and absolute monarchies, where political freedom and popular self-rule are not known and never have been, and where the habits and the very nature of the people are far removed from interest in self-government or capacity for it. These ideas are put forward as a justification of British rule in India. We are told that the Indian people have always had despotic rule, and if the British despotism were withdrawn they would set up despotisms of their own. Democracies and republics are the creation solely of Europe and European civilization, and not for centuries, if ever, may we expect to see Asiatic peoples establishing them, able to maintain them, or even desiring them.

Is this view of Asia and India true? No. It is very far from true, as is seen as soon as we begin to look at the real facts in the case.

When the Philippine Islands threw off the tyranny of Spain and obtained their freedom, what did they do? Set up a monarchy? No. They set up a republic, with a constitution fashioned closely after that of the United States of America.

When China broke the yoke of its Manchu rulers, what did it do? It proceeded at once to establish not a monarchy but a republic. And, although it has had a hard time to get a unified and settled government, largely because of the obstacles thrown in its way by the foreign powers, it nevertheless shows no sign of surrendering its republican hope and ideal.

Democratic ideas have long been in the minds of many of the leaders of Persia, and there is some ground for believing that, but for hostile European influences Persia before this time would have become a republic.

Turn to Turkey. As soon as possible after the Great War of 1914 to 1918 was over and the Turkish people were able to free themselves from the intrigues and shackles of European diplomacy, they proceeded at once to establish not a monarchy but a republic.

Turn to Russia. Russia is hardly less an Asiatic power than a European. What did it do when it had overthrown the despotism of the Czars? Did it set up another monarchy? It founded a republic.

Turn to India. Is there any sign that the great movement there to obtain freedom from British despotism means a desire on the part of the Indian people to set up a monarchy or a despotism of their own? Not the slightest. The ideal of practically every public leader in British India, of whatever party or name, is essentially that of Abraham Lincoln, a government "of the people, for the people, by the people." In other words, the almost universal desire is for a great Republican Nation, to be known by some such name as "The United States of India" in which all the individual states or provinces shall have their places as smaller and subordinate republics, with local self-rule like that of the individual States of the American Union or the individual Provinces of the Dominion of Canada.

Thus we see how false is the idea that Asia does not want and is not fit for democratic or republican institutions, and that India, because an Asiatic nation, is not fit for freedom. That fact is, not Europe but Asia seems to have been the cradle of political liberty, the cradle of democratic and republican government, in the world. Ethnological, linguistic and other forms of historical research make it clear that the democratic and republican institutions of Europe and America actually send their roots back to Asia, and especially to India. Republics actually existed in India at least as early as the days of Buddha (the sixth century before Christ), and as late as the fourth century after Christ. They were situated in the extensive region stretching from the Punjab in the west to Behar in the east, and from Nepal in the north to the southern borders of the Central Provinces. The republican form of government in ancient India had a duration of at least a thousand years. We have records of no other country, ancient or modern, where republics have existed and continued for so long a period.

Even more important than her republics has been the spirit of freedom and democracy which has manifested itself in many forms among the Indian people from the earliest ages. The Vedas show that the principles of representative government were held by the ancient Aryans twelve or fifteen centuries before the Christian era.

Buddhism, which was born in India and which had there a great career of more than fifteen hundred years, was democratic in a very high degree, and when it disappeared from the land it left behind it everywhere democratic traditions and influences.

Mohammedanism, which to-day has a large following in India than in any other country, is hardly less democratic than was Buddhism.

As compared with Christianity it is distinctly more democratic than the Latin-Russian or Oriental churches, and quite as much so as most forms of orthodox Protestantism.

Even Hinduism, which is fettered by its undemocratic caste system, is nevertheless admirably democratic within the limits of each individual caste.

But more effective than anything else as creators and preservers of the spirit of freedom in India have been her everywhere present village communities or village republics. For more than three thousand years these have been training the people of the whole land in self-government. This is why the Indian people are so law-abiding and such ardent lovers of peace.

India is pre-eminently an agricultural country. More than eighty per cent. of its population gain their subsistence from the soil. They live in villages, which number more than 650,000. In their character these villages are democracies,—as much so as are the towns (or townships) of New England. Sir Charles Metcalf, the eminent British administrator in India, thus describes them:

> The village communities of India are little republics having nearly everything they can want within themselves, and almost independent of any foreign relations. They seem to last where nothing else lasts. Dynasty after dynasty tumbles down; revolution succeeds to revolution; but the village community remains the same. The union of the village communities, each one forming a little state in itself has, I conceive, contributed more than any other cause to the preservation of the peoples of India through all the revolutions and changes which they have suffered, and is in a high degree conducive to their happiness, and to the enjoyment of a great portion of freedom and independence."

From time immemorial these village communities have chosen their own officials and managed their own affairs. What a training in fundamental democracy that has been!

Dr. Sudhindra Bose, Lecturer on the History and Institutions of the Orient in the University of Iowa, says on this subject:

"Democracy is not the exclusive monopoly of the West; it is to be found in the East as well. Oriental democracy has its roots in the common life of the people. In the Orient, sovereignty has always been shared by local bodies and communal groups. The Asian State may be thus described as a political federation with a very large share of local autonomy in village communities; communal assemblies; guilds, and village unions. The political history of Asia, especially China and India, is an unbroken record of group institutions, which have been practically self-sufficient and self-governing. The central government has rarely interfered with the local democracies."*

It is true that India in the past has known much despotism, as have England and France and all Europe but India's despotisms (I refer to those of her own rulers, before the coming of the British) were generally such as only very slightly affected the affairs or the liberties of the people. Only rarely did the Kings or Emperors or other rulers of India disturb the local self-government of the village republics, where the spirit of freedom, seldom failed to burn with a steady flame.

Having thus had three thousand years of training in democracy, is it any wonder that India to-day regards herself fit for self-government?

Our American historians are fond of telling us that our New England and other town meetings and town governments, in our colonial days, were the schools that made possible our national republic. They affirm that the training and experience which the people of the colonies gained

---

* *Modern Review*, Calcutta, August, 1927.

through this long management of their town affairs, fitted them as nothing else could have done, for the larger task of creating and maintaining a republican government for the several States and for the whole Nation.

If this is true, what is to be said of the similar and far longer training for republican institutions and self-government, received by the Indian people through these village democracies ?

Where did our colonial town-meeting system come from ? Our historians trace it to England, and beyond that to Germany. But they cannot stop with Germany. To find the beginnings they are obliged to go to Asia and especially to the village republics of India. Thus India proves to be, in a sense, the Mother of Republican America.

Do not the foregoing facts prove that Asia, and especially India, is as much the natural home of liberty, of democratic government, of self-government, as is Europe or America ?

CHAPTER XVI

CASTE IN INDIA: SHOULD IT BAR HOME RULE?

We are often told by those who favor the continuation of British rule in India, that the Indian people are not capable of self-government because they have among them so many castes. By counting up all the castes, and sub-castes, and semi-castes and semi-subcastes, and social divisions and distinctions of the most minute kinds, existing in any part of the land, they make out, or profess to make out, a total number of several thousands—3000 or more.

Unquestionably these many distinctions are interesting and more or less important in connection with studies of India's social and religious life. But what relation have they to her political life? They have none. They no more concern Indian political matters than American or English social and religious customs concern political matters in America or England. Caste regulations principally affect marriage and eating; they do not affect voting or carrying on the affairs of government. If the different castes can work together under British rule, as they do, why can they not under home rule?

Any one who is at all acquainted with India knows that in political matters all castes co-operate freely. The movement for self-rule is democratic, it belongs to all the people irrespective of social or religious distinctions. All persons who have ever attended the meetings of the

Indian National Congress or any other large political gatherings, know this. Those assemblages are made up of persons of all classes and names—Hindus, Buddhists, Mohammedans, Parsis, Jains, Sikhs, Christians—all meeting on a level politically, to carry on the political ends which they have in common.

An incident in my own personal experience illustrates the separate character of caste and politics. During one of my visits to India I had occasion to go to one of the cities in the South to deliver a lecture,—a city where caste was very strong. It chanced that the man who entertained me, in his attractive home, was the mayor of the city, whom I found to be a highly interesting, capable and cultured gentleman. Before leaving I made a discovery concerning my host as to his caste-standing. He was a Hindu, but to my surprise I found that he did not belong to any caste—being actually below all castes—a so-called "outcast" and yet politically he was at the head of the city. That is to say, he was so much respected by all classes, and was so influential, that the people, without reference to cast, had elected him to their highest political office. Such facts as these show how utterly groundless is the claim that the existence of religious and social caste in India means that the people are incapable of self-rule and need to be governed by a foreign nation.

I have no desire to minimize the evils of caste, for when carried to the lengths to which we see in religious and social circles in many parts of India (not in all parts) I believe it to be a tyrannical and often a cruel institution, which seriously hinders the social and religious progress of the people. But it does not help us in our battle against it, to misunderstand its character. We may perhaps get a little light if I quote the following statements from an eminent Hindu scholar. Writes Mr. B. N. Basu of Calcutta:

"Caste is a social and religious institution, and does not hinder political unity or the growth of the spirit of nationalism among the people. With all its drawbacks (and it has many), an Indian caste is absolutely democratic within its own fold; there the lowest is equal to the highest. And as to different castes, though they are divided by the *jus connubium*, they are united by many ties in common; and in village life even an untouchable has a well defined and not unimportant position; there is a distinct bond of relationship between him and the entire village circle. Even the social divisions of caste are fast losing their sharpness, and the time is not far distant when under the influence, of Western ideas, caste will cease to be a serious barrier even in social intercourse."

Perhaps it may help us a little if I compare caste in India with some things nearer home.

In this country, and in most of the countries of Europe, we see scores and actually hundreds of different kinds of associations and societies and guilds and leagues and fraternal orders and organizations representing different classes and sorts of people. Indeed, they are found in connection with nearly or quite every kind of trade and vocation and calling and profession and station in life and class of persons, high and low, rich and poor, white and colored, old and young, educated and uneducated,—in city, village and country,—bankers, merchants, manufacturers in a hundred different lines, farmers, university professors, engineers, railwaymen from conductors to track-walkers, college women, coal miners, cabmen, shop-girls, bootblacks, and thus on and on and on. All these are for this country and Europe in no small degree what the castes are for India. But they do not interfere with our political life. There are in this country more than 160 different religious sects, each of which is a sort of caste. Yet they all vote together and work together in political affairs.

Let me venture to suppose (if such a supposition does not mean insanity or idiocy) that a set of persons in this country, counting up all our labor unions, fraternal orders, social clubs and circles, religious sects, together with all our aristocratic families and families who pride themselves in their genealogies, and, finding that these make a total of 3000 or more, straightway declare this to mean that we as a nation thus divided are not capable of governing ourselves and need to be ruled by some foreign power. What would we think? Would we hasten to accept this reasoning? Hardly! Then why does anybody accept essentially the same reasoning regarding India?

The claim that the existence of caste is a reason for claiming that the Indian people are unfit to rule themselves is supported by no facts.

Brahmins, the highest caste, fill all grades of political office. So do Sudras, the lowest caste. Even "outcasts" may be active and influential in politics, as in the case of the mayor of a southern city already mentioned. The Gackwar of Baroda, the ruler of the most advanced Indian state, is a Sudra. So is the Maharajah of Gwalior, an important state. The Maharajah of Mysore is a Vaisya, the next to the lowest caste. The Honorable G. K. Gokhale, who was long a member of the Viceroy's Council, and was regarded as the greatest statesman that modern India has produced, belonged to one of the lower castes. The same is true even of Gandhi.

All these facts show how entirely separate are caste and political affairs.

Why do persons who believe that caste is an evil and that India needs to get rid of it, desire the continuation of British rule? Do they think British rule is opposed to caste? If so they are quite mistaken. As a fact the British Government has always been friendly to it. Of course, it could not openly legislate in its favor, because of the British policy not to interfere with the religion of subject peoples. But from the beginning the Government has quietly given its influence to keep caste strong, for two reasons, first, because this policy tended to win the favor of the high caste Brahmins, an influential class, and second, because caste divisions (as all other divisions) tend to make the British task of holding the people in subjection more easy, on the principle of "divide and govern."

Thus we see why persons who desire to have India freed from the evils of caste should not favor British supremacy, but should be in sympathy with the struggle of the Indian people for a government of their own. Mr. Gandhi, during his short career in India, has done incomparably more to expose the evils of caste and to set on foot influences for their abolition than has been done by the British Government of the country in all its history.

The forces in India that are working against caste are : (1) Christian missions, which are using all their influence to discredit and destroy it ; (2) the two important religious reform movements of the country the Brahmo Somaj and the Arya Somaj which are working earnestly to the same end ; (3) the Mohammedans, who constitute nearly a third of the population. who have no caste system and oppose it ; (4) the Theosophists, with Mrs. Besant at their head ; (5) Western ideas coming from Europe and America through education, literature and commerce, which are tending slowly to undermine the whole caste conception : and above all (6) the political movement in the land for self-rule. By far the greatest hope for the abolition or amelioration of caste evils is to be found in the great new awakening of the people,—in the growing spirit of independence, self-respect, brotherhood, democracy, which is pervading all castes and classes, from highest to lowest, and uniting them in one determined demand for freedom from the galling yoke of the stranger, and in one burning desire to see their country again, as in the past, occupying an honoured place among the nations of the world.

The truth is, the caste which is the most galling of any to the Indian people, and which they most desire to see reformed or removed, is that of their arrogant foreign lords and masters, who, with some honorable exceptions, treat them as serfs.

CHAPTER XVII.

INDIA'S ILLITERACY: SHOULD IT BAR SELF-RULE?

One of the arguments much used as a proof that the Indian people are not fit for self-government, and need to be ruled by others, is their "illiteracy."

This argument seems strange as coming from the British. For who are responsible for the illiteracy of the Indian people? There is only one possible answer. The chief responsiblity rests on the British themselves. One would naturally suppose, therefore, that they (the British) would try to cover up and hide from sight a fact so damning to themselves as this illiteracy is. Instead of being a proof that they ought to stay in India, its existence there after more than a century of their supreme and unhindered domination, would seem to be a clear evidence that their rule has been a failure, has been an evil, and ought not to be continued.

The responsibility of the British for India's illiteracy seems to be beyond question. All the people of India except the very lowest (and many of *them*) prize education highly, they earnestly desire it, and for fifty years their leaders have been pleading for it as for almost nothing else. Moreover, there is plenty of money to give India universal popular education —education equal or superior to that of Japan, if only the resources of the country, instead of being consumed on unnecessary salaries and pensions to Englishmen, and on worse than unnecessary military and other outlays for the benefit of the British Empire, were expended in the interest of the Indian people.

I say universal, popular education, equal to that of Japan. It is true India has a much larger population than that of Japan, to be provided for ; but it is also true that she has vastly larger resources, resources which, in proportion to her population, are much larger than Japan's. So that, if her revenues were not taken away from her by foreigners, she could not only equal, but actually outdo, Japan, in giving education to her people, and thus nearly or wholly wiping out the illiteracy of India. The British hide these facts, the world does not know them, but the Indian people understand and realize them in all their bitterness.

Let us study India's illiteracy, to see exactly what it is, and to find out whether, bad as its effects are, it is of such a nature that it ought to prevent her from having self-rule. Even if we grant that literacy, a much greater amount of literacy than exists in India, is necessary for self-government in our Western World where everybody depends for knowledge upon reading, where there is little knowledge or intelligence except what is obtained from books and newspapers—does it follow that there is the same need for literacy in a country like India, where the people are so much less slaves to books and papers, where they depend so much less upon these for their intelligence, and have so many other sources of knowledge besides the printed page?

Is it true that nations in the past which have been self-governing have always been literate ? Have there not been nations many, in Asia and Europe and other parts of the world, with very much less literacy than India possesses to-day, that have ruled themselves, and done it well—much better than any foreign power could have ruled them?

In the first place, it should be borne in mind that not all the people of India, by any means, are illiterate. The literate elements, while small in comparison with the 320,000,000 of India's entire population, are really large. Let us see how large.

Beginning with those who are literate in English, how many of these are there ? Turning to the Statesman's Year Book of 1926, we find the number of persons literate in the English language given as 2,500,000. Do we realize that this number actually exceeds that of the population of any one of thirty-nine of the forty-eight states which compose the American Union ? In other words, do we realize that there are more persons in India who read, write and speak the English language than the whole population of Virginia, or Tennesee, or Kentucky, or Wisconsin, or Iowa, or California, and more than the combined population of Maine, Vermont, New Hampshire and Rode Island ? Should such an amount of literacy as this count for nothing in estimating the fitness of India for self-rule ?

But this is only a beginning. India has a literacy of another kind, many times larger than this, and for purposes of Indian citizenship much more important. I mean, literacy in the vernaculars. What is the number of persons literate in one or more of the languages of India ? Turning again to the Statesman's Year Book, we find the answer to be 22,600,000. These figures may well be a surprise. Add this great number to that of the literates in English (making allowance for all duplicates), and we have in India actually more than one-half as many literate persons—persons who can read, write and speak some important language—as the total population of England, Wales and Scotland, more than one-half as many as the whole population of France, more than one-third as many as the total population of Germany. With all these not fewer than twenty-four or twenty-five millions of literates distributed throughout the whole of India, one wonders with what consistency the British Government can refuse self-rule to the Indian people because of illiteracy.

But this is by no means all that is to be said. In a country like India, why should the question of literacy or illiteracy, as related to self-rule, be given anything like so great importance as the British give it? Literacy is important, very important, in connection with culture, for enlargement and enrichment of life, and for uses in many directions; but in a country like India is it not possible for men to be good citizens, valuable citizens, intelligent in nearly or quite all matters fundamental to citizenship, and yet be technically illiterate? Even if we say that ability to read and write is indispensable to good citizenship in America and Europe, are we quite sure that it is so in lands with different civilizations from ours? We in the Western World almost universally regard literacy as always and everywhere necessarily identical with intelligence, and illiteracy as necessarily identical with unintelligence or ignorance. But a mistake could hardly be greater. A man who does not know a letter of the alphabet and who cannot sign his name may be a person of large intelligence, and, on the other hand, a man who can read and write half a dozen languages may possess very little knowledge of any practical value.

The truth of this is well illustrated by the case of a prisoner in the State Prison at Auburn, New York, in the year 1926. The intelligence tests of the 1,300 prisoners in that institution showed that the very highest intelligence of all was found in a man (45 years old) who had come into the prison wholly illiterate, unable either to read or write. His intelligence was proven to be higher than that of any of the high school or college graduates. And this by tests the most rigid.

The truth is, there is amazing ignorance in our whole American and European world as to the real relation of literacy to intelligence. The reason we identify the two is because we of the West are fed on books and other reading from our babyhood, and get almost all our knowledge from the printed page. Thus our minds become artificialized, our conception of knowledge becomes narrowed down to that which we get from reading, other avenues for obtaining knowledge, outside of reading, become largely closed to us. And yet these other avenues are of enormous importance. Taking the great past as a whole, very little of the intelligence of mankind has been obtained from books or letters. Books and letters are comparatively modern things, and relatively very artificial. The great means of gaining intelligence throughout by-gone ages, and the far more natural means, has been speech, not writing, has been personal contact with others—children learning from their parents, knowledge slowly gained by observation and experience, and handed down by word of mouth from generation to generation, wise sayings and teachings of sages committed to memory by the people and transmitted orally, and thus preserved from age to age as intellectual gold.

Up to very recent times the great teachers of mankind have never been teachers through books or reading or writing, but always through personal contact and speech. Jesus taught his disciples orally. Buddha devoted himself to teaching all his long life, but so far as we can find out his instruction was mainly if not wholly oral. Socrates, Plato, Aristotle and the great philosophers and teachers of Greece communicated their knowledge and thought by speeches—gathering their pupils and followers into groups and small companies, in gardens, groves or temples and there instructing them through conversation, with probably little or no use at any time of anything so artificial as a book or a manuscript.

Many of the greatest men of the past, ever since writing and books have been known, (to say nothing of the long ages before letters were invented), have been illiterate,—kings, statesmen, commanders of armies, governors of provinces, managers of great business enterprises, discoverers, inventors, leaders in every department of life. Nobody ever dreamed that these men, or the nations to which they belonged, were incapable of ruling themselves and needed to be held in subjection by foreigners because of their illiteracy. Then why does anybody say that the illiteracy which exists in India (especially when it is remembered that by its side there exists the very large amount of literacy which has been mentioned) makes it necessary for the Indian people to be governed by aliens from beyond great oceans, most of whom come to their governing tasks in almost absolute ignorance of India, indeed with far, far less knowledge of India's history, civilization, institution, customs and real needs, than is possessed by millions and millions of the Indian people who are stigmatized and looked down upon by their egotistical British masters as illiterate ?

Up to within a century or so of the present time, the literacy of Great Britain herself was very low. When she wrote her Magna Charta, and when she established her Parliament and made her Kings answerable to it, only a small minority of her people could read and write. But that did not prevent her from ruling herself.

Large numbers of the early pioneers of America, who penetrated its wilderness, subdued its forests, and laid the foundations of its governments, were nearly or wholly illiterate, according to our present understanding of the word. But what men they were ! How many of us with all our book-learning are their equals in intellectual and moral strength ? It has been estimated that less than half of the people of the thirteen American Colonies at the time of the Revolution could read and write. Yet how nobly they wrought for freedom, and what a nation they founded !

Americans should not forget that the staunch and virile American stock from which Abraham Lincoln came was largely illiterate. The great Appalachian Mountain region of West Virginia, Kentucky, Tennessee, the Carolinas and Georgia, contains a white population of about 6,000,000, nearly all native Americans for six or seven generations. The statistics of the draft at the time we went into the European War indicated an illiteracy in that region of nearly 80 per cent. Would it not be possible to find six millions of graduates from our schools, including many graduates of our colleges and universities, who could be better spared from the nation than these independent and sturdy mountain people, so large a portion of whom cannot read or write ?

The large South American Republic of Brazil, according to a recent census, has an illiteracy of over 80 per cent. Yet Brazil is self-ruling and well-governed. Several other South American nations have a rate of illiteracy nearly as high, and yet have reasonably good governments, far better than any foreign rule could be.

Many of the people of India who cannot read and write not only possess large knowledge of things outside of books, but actually have an amount of knowledge of books (obtained by hearing them read or recited by others) which amazes the Westerner and often puts him to shame. The last time I was in India they told me that the lyric poems of Tagore were known by heart (had been committed to memory) by millions, and were recited and sung all over Bengal and far beyond.

I suppose it would not be beyond the truth to say that a larger proportion of the people of India, even of those who are called illiterate, are reasonably intelligent about the two great national (and almost sacred) Epics of their country, the Mahabharata and the Ramayana, and have large portions of them committed to memory, than the proportion of Europeans or Americans who are intelligent about our Bible and have relatively equal portions of that committed to memory. It is not uncommon for Hindu men and boys who have never been to school a day, to be able to repeat actually by the hour passages from these two great national poems or other esteemed Hindu literature, and hardly less is to be said of the Mohammedans as to their knowledge of the Koran and other Islamic literature.

Max Muller (in his "What India Can Teach us") says :

"There is such a thing as social education and education outside of books; and this education is distinctly higher in India than in any part of Christendom. Through recitations of ancient stories and legends, through religious songs and passion plays, through shows and pageants, through ceremonials and sacraments, through fairs and pilgrimages, the Hindu masses all over India receive a general culture and education which are in no way lower, but positively higher, than the general level of culture and education received through schools and newspapers, or even through the ministrations of the churches, in Western Christian lands. It is an education, not in the so-called three R's, but in humanity."

Mr. Romesh Dutt, than whom there is no more trustworthy authority, says :

"There are few if any groups of ten or twelve villages in India that do not contain men of influence, men of intelligence and some education,—men who are respected in their neighbourhoods, cultivators of the soil on a large scale, village priests, village physicians, village schoolmasters and others."* These men are the natural leaders of the people. In political affairs they are usually "willing to come forward for election, to represent their communities, and to serve the Government."*

Facts like these should be pondered by Englishmen or others who so lightly and ignorantly declared that the great historic nation of India is not fit to rule itself, but must remain subject to foreigners because of its so-called "illiteracy."

In conclusion. The whole subject of illiteracy in India as related to self-government, may be concisely and fittingly summed up in the two following questions, which it is believed, in the very putting of them answer themselves :—

1. Should India be ruled by a small body of foreigners, who are in the country only temporarily, whose supreme interests are in a distant land a majority of whom are haughty and overbearing

* "Life and Work" (of Romesh C. Dutt), by J. N. Gupta, p. 110.

towards the Indian people, and unsympathetic toward India's civilization and Ideals, whose knowledge of India and its needs, in the very nature of the case, is and can be, only very imperfect and superficial? Or,

2. Should India be ruled by her own natural leaders, namely: (1) the 2,500,000 Indians who are literate in English; plus (2) the 22,600,000 Indians who are literate in one or more of the languages of India; plus (3) the still larger number of millions of Indians, who although technically illiterate, are men of large practical intelligence, whose home is India, who love their native land as Englishmen or Americans love theirs, whose whole interests are in India., and whose knowledge of their own country and the needs of its people is incomparably greater than the knowledge of these possessed by any transient foreigners?

I say, which of these are best fitted to rule India? I am sure the questions answer themselves.

Let nothing that has been said in this chapter be understood as meaning that the writer estimates lightly the value of reading, writing and books, or the importance, for many uses and in many directions, of the knowledge to be gained through them. As has been pointed out, India deeply needs and craves, and has long been pleading with her rulers to give her, this knowledge. The crime of her rulers in withholding it has been very great.

But, notwithstanding the illiteracy which is India's unfortunate lot, she unhesitatingly and earnestly declares that she is *fit for self-rule,* and by every principle of human justice is *entitled to it.* Furthermore, she wants the world clearly to understand that *one* of the *very strong reasons why she demands self-government* is, because *only through it* can she see any *hope of ever getting rid of her illiteracy.*

SUPPLEMENT

The article printed below, which appeared in *The Modern Review* for February, 1928, supplements the arguments of this Chapter.

The question whether illiteracy should bar self-rule has been very ably discussed in our present issue by Dr. J. T. Sunderland. Literacy and the education which it enables people to receive are undoubtedly of the highest value. But the argument that those who are illiterate should not be allowed to rule themselves, proceeds from selfishness and love of power. It also betrays ignorance of or wilful blindness to the facts of history. A time there was when all peoples of the earth were illiterate. That was before the invention of the art of writing. But in those days there were independent peoples, and they were all illiterate. They did not have to import literate rulers from the planet Mars or some other member of the solar system. In civilized ages, how much book-learning, if any, did Akbar and Sivaji possess ?

Even within historical times, many nations which are at present both independent and literate were largely illiterate. England has enjoyed representative institutions for centuries, but education has been widely diffused there only during the last century. In the age of King John, when the barons wrested the great charter from him, many of the nobility could draw spear-heads more skilfully than the letters of the alphabet ;—book-learning was despised by them. In later ages of parliamentary history, too, literacy was not a prominent feature of English society. Robert Lowe, Viscount Sherbrooke, familiarly known as Bobby Lowe, went to the Education Office as vice-president of the Council in Lord Palmerston's ministry. He felt then and still more after the Reform Act of 1866 that it would be necessary to educate the people whom that Act had given the vote. He said in his address to the Edinburgh Philosophical Institution in 1867 that it was necessary "to induce our future masters to learn their letters." This shows that in Great Britain even so recently as the Sixties of the last century the extension of political rights did not follow but was followed by the spread of education. When Lord Durham's report led to the grant of self-rule to Canada, it was stated in that report :

"It is impossible to exaggerate the want of education among the habitants. No means of instruction have ever been provided for them, and they are almost and universally destitute of the qualifications even of reading and writing."

Not to speak of others in Canada, there even "a great proportion of the teachers could neither read nor write." It was to such a people that representative institutions were granted.

When representative government was established in Japan in the sixties of the last century it was mainly the Samurai who were literate. Even in 1873 only 28 per cent. of the childern of school-age were at school. By 1923—5 that percentage had risen to 90. It is practically cent. per cent, now. So in Japan representative government has not come after universal literacy, but universal literacy has been the result of representative government.

But let us take other countries under other forms of government.

The countries of Europe are now vying with each other to honour and welcome King Amanullah Khan of Afghanistan. His country is independent. But it has never been famous for the prevalence of literacy. In fact, some five years ago, the Statesman's Year-book for 1922 had nothing to say in regard to public instruction in that country. But the same book of reference for 1927 records among other educational arrangements that "elementary and secondary schools exist throughout the country. Elementary education is free and compulsory, and higher education is also free." What are the causes of such a wonderful change in the course of five years? They are, we presume to be found in the following facts stated in the same annual for 1927:

"On November 22, 1921 a treaty between Great Britain and Afghanistan was signed at Kabul, in accordance with which Great Britain recognises the complete independence of Afghanistan, and agrees to an interchange of diplomatic representatives; while Afghanistan accepts the existing Anglo-Afghan frontier."

"The Government of Afghanistan is, since 1922, a constitutional monarchy with Legislative and State Assemblies, and a cabinet presided over by the King himself."

So, Afghanistan has been preparing for universal literacy after establishing full independence, a constitutional government, a legislative assembly, etc.

"In Abyssinia "education is restricted to the teaching of the secular and regular clergy. There are schools at Addis Ababa and Harar, at which however, the attendance is practically negligible. The people are in consequence illiterate and ignorant." Nevertheless, the country is self-ruling and independent.

But let us return to the British Empire itself. There is Home Rule among savages in this very empire. These people live in the Gilbert and Ellice Islands in the mid-western Pacific Ocean. The Gilbert Islanders are nearly always naked, but wear a conical hat of pandanus leaf. It was they who have an armour of plaited cocoanut fibres. Their canoes are made of cocoanut wood boards. Mr. E. C. Eliot, Resident Commissioner in these islands, contributed an interesting article on them to the December (1915) number of United Empire, the journal of the Royal Colonial Institute, in which he wrote:—

"To-day a state of 'Home Rule' exists which is probably unique among native races under the protection of the British Crown. With their own code of native laws, revised and amended by a King's Regulation, the people are wisely and justly ruled by their own councils of Chiefs and Elders."

A perusal of Mr. Eliot's article and consideration of the British objection to allow India to be self-ruling lead to the conclusion that barbarism like that existing in the Gilbert and Ellice Islands fit their inhabitants to be self-ruling and civilisation like that prevalent in India for milleniums disqualifies her children for self-rule.

There are other parts of the British Empire which in some respects afford a better parallel to India than the above-mentioned small islands inhabited by savages.

In the Union of South Africa the non-European population, mostly illiterate, numbered 54,09,092 and the European males, more literate, numbered 7,82,035 in 1921. In Kenya the European males and females number 12,529 and the Africans 26,82,848. In Nyasaland the European males and females number 1,656 and the Africans 12,90,883. In all these countries, and in many other vast regions about which similar statistics might be quoted, the numerically very small number of literate Europeans settle among them and manage the affairs of those lands inhabited for the most part by natives who are generally illiterate. These Europeans differ from these Africans in race, language, religion, complexion, manners and customs, standard of living and the most other things. Yet they are thought to be fully qualified to manage the affairs of the countries they inhabit. In India the literates and the illiterates do not form separate sects, racial groups, linguistic groups, castes, occupational groups, or any other kinds of groups. Within the same sects, castes, sub-castes, linguistic groups—nay, families—some are literate and some illiterate. Literates and illiterates are one another's kith and kin in India. Yet, the literates in India, many of them far more highly educated and more intellectual than any Europeans in Africa are thought to be disqualified to manage the affairs of their country, because they form the minority and the illiterates the majority. But in Africa the European literate minority are deemed qualified to manage the affairs of the country inhabited in common with them by the African illiterate majority. It therefore, comes to this, that the fault of the literate Indians is that they are not "white" Europeans, and are, in addition, not aliens from a distant continent but are autochthonous to India and blood relatives of the illiterate majority.

In opposing the attainment of self-rule by Indians, Britishers lay great stress on literacy. But in actual practice, they do not attach any importance to it. Literacy is not a factor which finds a place as a qualification for electors. This is not, of course, peculiar to India. But, if literacy were really considered a *sine qua non* for self-rule in India, one would expect all illiterates to be excluded from the franchise. As regards candidates for election to the legislative bodies, illiteracy is nowhere mentioned as a disqualification. The barest literacy appears to be insisted on, because the candidate is required to sign his nomination paper and certain other declarations and notices connected with his candidatures. Consequently, in discussing the advantages and disadvantages of a residential qualification, Mr. E. L. Hammond I. C. S., C. B. E., writes in his book on "The Indian Candidate and Returning Officer" (p. 35):

"Against this restriction must be set the fact that it may unduly limit candidature and result in the return of a worthy but uneducated rustic, unable to understand, though he may impede, the proceedings in Council."

So, though Britishers profess to consider literacy essentially necessary for self-rule, they have provided us with a form of so-called representative government in which the electors may be absolutely unlettered and the legislators" uneducated rustics, "just able to sign their names!

CHAPTER XVIII

INDIA'S "MANY LANGUAGES AND RACES." SHOULD THESE BAR HOME RULE?

PART I.

One of the arguments oftenest used in justification of British rule in India is the many races, tribes and peoples alleged to be found there, and specially the many languages alleged to be spoken. One British writer urges the necessity of British rule by telling us that there are 130 different languages in India, another says 170, another 185; and by including minute variations and dialects the number has been swelled to more than 200. It is hardly possible to read any book or extended article on India, from a British source, without having such figures as these put before us as an unanswerable evidence that Britain is needed there, and must stay.

But really what do these appalling figures and numbers signify? Anything in justification of British rule? or the opposite? Why should numbers even ten times as great make it necessary for the land to be ruled by foreigners and strangers? Are men born and reared in distant countries, who are without knowledge of these various Indian peoples, who are ignorant of their institutions, customs and needs, and who are unable to speak a single one of their languages, better fitted to govern them—govern them wisely and safely—than are their own intelligent and trusted leaders, born and educated among them, having life-long knowledge of their institutions, habits and wants and able to speak their tongues? Such a claim is amazing. And yet we hear it constantly made by the British, and repeated parrot-like in America.

The existence of many languages in India can be no more an argument against Home Rule there, and no more a proof of the need of foreign rule than is the existence of many languages in countries other than India a proof that those countries should be ruled by foreigners. Turn from India to Russia.

During all her later history Russia has had more languages, and also more races and tribes and nationalities, than India, yet nobody has contended that therefore Russia was incapable of self-government and ought to have been conquered and held in subjection by a foreign power.

As a matter of fact, the United States of America has more languages and more nationalities than India. In order to get any such numbers of Indian tongues as we are told that India possesses, there have to be included the languages and dialects of all the small and unimportant hill and mountain and jungle tribes that live in remote and often almost inaccessible places,—similar to the small tribes of our American Red Indians. In the United States we have people from all the nations of South and Central America, from all the nations of Europe, from nearly or quite all those of Asia, Africa and the principal islands of the sea. Now count the languages of all these, and to them add the nearly two hundred languages and dialects spoken by our own Red Indian tribes, and it is easy to understand the truth of the statement that we have more languages in this country than has India. But does anybody believe it necessary, on this account, for some nation beyond the sea, say Japan or Russia or France or England, to conquer and govern us?*

Canada would hardly like to have the claim made that it is unfit to govern itself because of its many languages, natonalities and religions. Yet according to recent statistics Canada has 178 languages, 53 nationalities, and 79 religious faiths. That is to say, considering the number of its population, † Canada has a far greater diversity of languages (as well as nationalities and religions) than has India. Yet Canada rules itself and has done so for much more than half a century with great efficiency.

As a matter of fact, the main, the really important, languages of India are not many, but few,—fewer than those of Europe. India has a population as great as that of all Europe outside of Russia. Yet what may properly be called the main tongues of non-Russian Europe are as many as ten or eleven, if not more: whereas the main languages of India do not exceed nine or ten; and these to a surprising degree are closely related,—the Tamil and the Telugu in the South being almost twin sisters (Dravidian), and all those in the North being children of the Sanskrit (Aryan), and therefore sisters.§

---

* A recent census of New Bedford, Massachusetts shows that in that relatively small American city 58 languages are spoken.

† In 1921, the population of Canada was 8, 788, 483 and that of India 318, 942, 480.

§ India has a very important common language, which goes far toward uniting the whole land in speech.

It is also true that the main and most important *races* in India are few. When the Aryan people came into India from the Northwest, they found it for the most part inhabited by a race known as Dravidians. The Aryan invaders pushed on and on until they had possessed themselves of a large part of the country, except in the South, driving out or amalgamating with the somewhat civilized but not so highly civilized Dravidians.

The India of to-day is nearly all Aryan and Dravidian,—but with a relatively small Mongolian or partly Mongolian element (about one-thirtieth of the whole population) in the North and Northeast; a slight Persian and Afghan element in the Northwest, and certain small miscellaneous elements in the hills and remoter regions here and there, which are remnants of a primitive people or peoples somewhat like our North American aborigines.

Thus we see how baseless is the claim that India is extraordinarily or seriously conglomerate or divided racially. As a fact, it contains less diversity of races than Europe, and far less than the United States of America, which, as already said, contains nearly all the languages and races of the world.

Why do not Englishmen, who urge that India is unable to govern itself and must be ruled by the British because of its diversity of tongues

---

Mr. Gandhi tells us that 'out of a population of somewhat less than 320 millions there are not more than 38 millions, living in the Madras Presidency, who are unable to follow a Hindustani speaker; that a majority even of the Mohammedans in that Presidency understand Hindustani; and that Hindustani (a resultant of Hindi and Urdu) is rapidly becoming the *lingua franca* of India.' See "Modern India," by Dr. V. H. Rutherford M. P., P. 265.)

and peoples, apply the same principle to their own empire as a whole? The British Empire contains all the diversities of every kind that are found in India, and at least two or three times as many more. Do Englishmen think that therefore they are unfit to rule their Empire, and that it ought to be ruled by some outside power?

The fact is, this whole argument that India contains a large number of languages and peoples and therefore needs to be ruled by foreigners is hollow, is a bogey, is something devised in order to furnish seeming justification for Great Britain's remaining in a country where, for selfish reasons, she wants to remain, but where she has no right to be. It is strange that any sane mind can fail to see instantly that the greater the number of peoples and languages there are in India or any other country, the stronger becomes the reason why it should be ruled *not by foreigners* but by its *own sons*, who *know most about these languages and peoples*.

The claim is made by many Englishmen that the diversities of language, race, and so forth, found in India, destroy her *unity*, make it incorrect to think or speak of India as *one*, or as *a nation* at all: and for *this* reason she cannot govern herself.

This argument, which is accepted as true by many who know nothing to the contrary, has been answered many times over, and with great thoroughness, both by Indian scholars and by Englishmen, who have shown that, notwithstanding all the diversities that have been mentioned, deep down below them all India is profoundly one, that as a fact she has a unity older and more fundamental than that of any other extensive country or great people or nation in the world with the possible exception of China. Let us see what are some of the evidences of this as shown by historians and scholars.

Perhaps the most widely circulated and therefore the most mischievous statement we have of the claim that India has no unity, is not a nation, is that made by Sir John Strachey on the opening page of his well known book, "India." There he says :

> The first and most essential thing to be learned about India, is, that there is not and never was an India possessing according to European ideas any sort of unity, physical, social, political, or religious ; no Indian nation, no people of India of which we hear so much.

This alleged condition of things he claims to be a clear justification of British rule. What answer is to be made ? A more than sufficient answer is furnished by a high British official, writing much later than Sir John Strachey, who has given us two of our most trustworthy books on India. In his important work, "The Government of India," Mr. Ramsay MacDonald, at one time Premier, declares that India is one in absolutely every sense in which Mr. Strachey denies the unity. Here are his words (pp. 28, 29) :

> India from the Himalayas to Cape Comorin, from the Bay of Bengal to Bombay, is naturally the area of a single government. One has only to look at the map to see how geography has fore-ordained an Indian Empire. Its vastness does not obscure its oneness ; its variety does not hide from view its unity. The Himalayas and their continuing barriers frame off the great peninsula from the rest of Asia. Its long rivers, connecting its extremities and its interior with the sea, knit it together for communication and transport purposes ; its varied productions, interchangeable with one another, make it a convenient industrial unit, maintaining contact with the world through the great ports to the east and west.
>
> Political and religious traditions have also welded it into one Indian consciousness. This spiritual unity dates from very early times in Indian culture.
>
> An historical atlas of India shows how again and again the natural unity of India has influenced conquest

and showed itself in empires. The realms of Chandragupta and his grandson Asoka (305-232 B. C.) embraced practically the whole peninsula, and ever after, amidst the swaying and falling of dynasties, this unity has been the dream of every victor and has never lost its potency.

Says Vincent Smith, than whom there is no higher historical authority:

India, circled as she is by seas and mountains, is indisputably a geographical unit, and as such rightly designated by one name, Her type of civilization, too, has many features which differentiate it from that of all other regions of the world; while they are common to the whole country in a degree sufficient to justify its treatment as a unit in the history of the social, religious, and intellectual development of mankind." ("Early History of India.")

William Archer in his "India and the Future" devotes a chapter to "The Unity of India" in which he declares that Indian unity is "indisputable."

There is no greater uniting force known among peoples and nations in the world than religion. This applies with pre-eminent emphasis to India.

Many centuries before the Christian Era, Hinduism spread over virtually the whole peninsula of Hindustan. Although originating among the Aryan peoples of the Northwest, it soon extended beyond, and was widely accepted by the Dravidian peoples occupying other parts. Thus it became early, and it remains still, an all India religion, exercising a strong uniting influence upon practically all the inhabitants of the land and all Indian history and civilization.

Hardly less is to be said of Buddhism, the child of Hinduism. It spread everywhere in India, and its influence everywhere was to create a spirit of unity and brotherhood throughout the whole country.

Writing of the unifying influence of Hinduism and Buddhism Lord Acton says:

"Just as Christianity attempted during the Middle Ages to provide a common civilization for Western Europe, on the basis of which the various nations and races might combine in a common State, in the same manner Hinduism provided, during many centuries, a common civilization for India, which has made and still makes the Indian continent a political unity in spite of a thousand disintegrating forces. To Hinduism, with its offshoot, Buddhism, belongs this great glory that it was not content with a narrow racial boundary, but included the whole continent in its embrace from the Himalayas to the farthest shores of Ceylon. There are few more imposing spectacles in history than this silent peaceful penetration of Hindu civilization, till the farthest bounds of India were reached."*

Mohammedanism, which came into India much later, has sometimes been called a divider. But even if in certain respects this is true, in a large and truer way it has been a uniter. The very fact that it has penetrated to virtually all parts of India, has tended to give all parts a common interest in one another and therefore to bind all-together. Having become an all-India faith, like Hinduism and Buddhism, it has tended to unify the whole land.

The truth is, if there is a real nation in the world, a nation with a unity so long-standing and so deep (the growth of thousands of years) that it has become a part of the very intellectual and moral fiber of the people, an ingredient of their very life blood, that nation is India. Compared with the unity of India, that of every American and European nation is superficial and ephemeral.

It is true that India's unity is made up of variety; many constituent elements enter into

---

* Quoted by C. F. Andrews in the *Hindustan Review* of February, 1911.

it. But of what important national unity is not this true ? *E pluribus unum*, "one formed of many" is the motto of the United States ; showing that our own American nation glories in the fact of its composite and comprehensive character. Canada is also one formed of many. Every large nation of Europe is formed of numerous smaller political units gathered into one, and most of the nations of any considerable size contain peoples of different races, religions and languages. But these differing elements do not prevent them from being true nations, or from possessing a real unity. Rather is their national life larger and richer because of the many and diverse elements of which it is made up.

This is essentially the condition of things that exists in India. Her eminent poet, Rabindranath Tagore, expresses it well :

> "We (the Indian peoples) are one all the more because we are many ;
>
> We have made room for a common love,
> A common brotherhood, through all our separatenesses.
> Our unlikenesses reveal the beauty of a common life deeper than all,
> Even as mountain peaks in the morning sun
> Reveal the Unity of the mountain range from which they all lift up their shining foreheads."†

---

† A new kind of unity in India has been created by British rule, a kind not foreseen, much less desired, by the foreign rulers, but now conspicuous and ominous and growing rapidly, namely, the unity of a common desire and determination to throw off a hated yoke.

Professor Moon in his "Imperialism and World Politics" (p. 297) tells us that even if the Indian people had no bond of union before, Britain has given them a powerful one in a common "antagonism to British rule,"—a burning sentiment which has brought Brahmin and Pariah, Hindu and Moslem, Marathi and Bengali into unity. All these have been "welded together in the heat of resentment

But even if this were not so; even if all the statements made by Sir John Strachey and the rest of the imperialists, as to the lack of unity in India, were true, still what right would that give the British to be there, forcing their rule upon an unwilling people?

A century ago, Italy was regarded as having no unity. Would Britain have been justified for that reason in conquering and ruling Italy? In the seventeenth and even as late as the eighteenth century, Germany was divided into some two or three hundred kingdoms, princedoms, and other petty sovereignties of one kind and another, with hardly a shadow of real unity among them. Did that give England a right to subjugate and govern Germany? China to-day has very imperfect unity.

---

against what they consider as wrongs done them by England."

Practically all the Indian people are now united in their realization of the wrong of being ruled by a foreign nation, of the degradation that it entails upon them, of the humiliating arrogance toward them of their rulers, of the heavy and galling financial load laid on them by an expensive foreign government, of the exploitation and impoverishment of their country in the interest of foreigners, of the injury done their children by the refusal of the Government to provide adequate schools and education. These and many other injustices have strongly and increasingly tended to unite all sections of the Indian people by giving them a deep grievance which they all share; a common reason for complaint and protest, a common battle to fight. As Mr. H. W. Nevinson has said, "Every act of injustice and tyranny on the part of the British rulers, has promoted India's sense of unity, by creating, among all classes, a realization of common suffering, and a new and united impulse to shake off the tyranny and thus end the suffering." As a fact, there is no other such uniter of any people anywhere in the world as a common feeling that they are oppressed, and a common fight for freedom. This kind of unification is now strong in India, and is steadily and irresistibly deepening and becoming more intense.

Does any one claim that it would be right for Britain or Japan or any other foreign nation to conquer and rule China? There have been times in England's own history when she had little unity, when for long periods she was distracted by many and serious divisions. Does any Englishman believe that those divisions gave any foreign power a right to come and subdue and govern England?

Then why would want of unity, why would divisions, in India, even if they existed to the monstrously exaggerated degree affirmed by men like Sir John Strachey, give Great Britain even the shadow of a right to conquer the land and rule it by the power of the sword?

One further thought.

The British declare that they cannot give India (India as a whole) self-rule, because she lacks unity. But there are great Provinces, great States, really great Nations in India which even they themselves (the British) do not deny possess unity,—unity quite as complete and perfect as that of France, or Germany, or Italy, or the United States. Why is not self-rule given *at least to these*? In other words, why does not Britain grant self-government to such great and important populations as the Bengalis in the East, the Mahrattas in the West, the Telugus and Tamils in the South, and others, who are united in language, in race, in history, and in every other important respect, who have literatures, arts and cultures of their own, and whose number are greater than those of most of the European nations?

What interpretation is it possible to put upon the fact that all these States and Provinces in which there is no lack of unity are held in subjection just as firmly and relentlessly as is India as a whole, except that the question of unity has little or nothing to do with the case? and that the British hold India simply because they want to hold it, for their own advantage, the alleged lack of unity being merely a convenient, and, to persons ignorant of India, a plausible, excuse? Is this interpretation false? If so, why do not the British correct it, as they easily may, by giving self-rule at least to those great sections of India which nobody can deny are as united as England itself?

PART II

Instead of Britain refusing to give India self-government because of lack of unity, she ought long ago to have learned the lesson taught by history a hundred times over, that nothing is so effective in *producing* unity among divided peoples as *self-government*,—in other words, as the bringing of all parties and classes and sections together for common thinking, common planning, common working for the common welfare; and that is just what democratic self-government means. When men, however, far apart, begin to plan and work together, and bear responsibilities together, in the interest of a government which they feel is *their own*, in trying to promote the safety and prosperity of a nation which is really *theirs* they inevitably tend to grow serious, constructive and united. Many illustrations of this might be mentioned. It will be sufficient if I cite two; the case of the British Colonies in America which became the United States, and that of Canada.

In the case of the former, few persons have any adequate understanding at all of the wide differences and divergencies of almost every kind that existed among them. The Colonies were very widely scattered—extending all along the Atlantic seaboard from near Nova Scotia in the North to near the Gulf of Mexico in the South. Their inhabitants were from different countries of Europe; they had different religions and spoke several different languages. Their industrial and commercial interests were very different, and in many cases antagonistic. It was widely declared in England that these thirteen different Colonies (virtually thirteen little separate nations), with so many differences, rivalries and contentions, could not possibly unite in one government, or rule themselves; and that without the overlordship of Great Britain there would be disorder, anarchy and local wars throughout the land.

Says the historian Lecky:

> Great bodies of Dutch, Germans, French, Swedes, Scotch and Irish, scattered among the descendants of the English, contributed to the heterogeneous character of the Colonies, and they comprised so many varieties of government, religious belief, commercial interest, and social type, that their union appeared to many incredible.*

An English traveller named Burnby made an extensive tour of observation through the American Colonies in 1759 and 1760, and on his return to London published an account of the same, in which he said:

> Fire and water are not more heterogeneous than the different Colonies in North America. Nothing can exceed the jealousy and emulation which they possess in regard to each other. The inhabitants of Pennsylvania and New York have an inexhaustible source of animosity in their jealousy for the trade of the Jerseys, Massachusetts Bay and Rhode Island are not less interested in that of Connecticut. The West Indies are a common subject of emulation for them all. Even the limits and boundaries of each Colony are a constant source of

---

* "England in the Eighteenth Century," Vol. IV, p. 12.

litigation. In short, such is the difference of character of manners, of religion, of interest, of the different Colonies, that I think were they left to themselves, there would soon be a civil war from one end of the continent to the other, while the Indians and negroes would watch the opportunity to exterminate them altogether.

As a matter of fact, the differences and antagonisms between the Colonies were so great that, even after the Revolutionary War had been fought and their independence from Great Britain had been won, it was difficult to persuade them to unite, and very difficult for them to form a Gevernment acceptable to all. But no sooner was a common government set up, with its parliamentary or representative system, which placed all the colonies on a level and set all to the task of working together and planning for the common good, than the old differences and antagonisms began to disappear. And it was not long before the new nation, the United States of America, was as united, as peaceful, and as efficient a government as probably existed in the entire world.

Turning to the history of Canada, we find a situation in many respects the same, and with the same lesson to teach. For a long time Canada was denied self-rule ; she was regarded as not fit to govern herself, partly because her area was so great, stretching from the Atlantic to the Pacific ; and partly because her people were so divided in race, language and religion,—her white population being about one-half French, speaking the French language and professing the Roman Catholic faith, and the other half being English, speaking the English language and professing the Protestant faith, while in the land, scattered throughout all parts, were scores of tribes of aborigines, or native "Red Indians," all having separate customs and cultures, and all speaking different tongues, and still in addition to these, there were in the far north various tribes of Eskimos, with strange languages, and with customs and modes of life different from all other peoples.

How could a country of such vast extent, and with a population so scattered, divided and diverse and possessing so little unity of any kind, govern itself ? Surely it would be full of anarchy, wars and bloodshed, resulting in ultimate division into smaller nations forever fighting one another, if England withdrew her hand.

Was this what happened ? It was the exact opposite of what happened. So long as the foreign rule of Great Britain continued there was discontent, ever-increasing discontent, with insurrections and rebellions breaking out here and there, and others forever threatening. There was no feeling of general unity, no assured general peace and no general contentment until the country was given self-rule, that is, until it was given its present dominion status, with freedom and power to manage its own affairs. Then a marvellous change came. A feeling of unity such as would have been forever impossible under a foreign rule began to make its appearance; the different parts of the country began to develop a common interest, and to draw together for promotion of the common welfare, and there was such contentment and peace, and also such efficiency of government, as had never been known before.

In these experiences,—that of the American Colonies which separated themselves from Great Britain and under independence grew united in spirit and strong; and in the experience of Canada which also found that self-rule mean unity and strength, there is a very important lesson for both India and Great Britain. It is folly to claim that because of differences of race and language and religion India requires to be ruled by foreigners. What India needs to make her *united and strong*, is *self-government.* Nothing in the world would be so effective in causing the people of India to forget their differences of race and language and religion and to become united, and, when united, peaceful and efficient and powerful, as to set up for themselves responsible government of their own, and begin the practical work of ruling themselves. That would mightily increase their self-respect, their confidence in themselves, their moral stamina, their interest in one another, their desire to promote peace in the land, and their ability to defend India in case of danger.

If the British, with all power in their hands set up in India a government responsible to the Indian people when Lord Ripon (in 1880-1884) made so fine a start toward it (which India hailed with delight but which the British thwarted) we may well believe that, by this time, all the Indian peoples outside of the "Native States," and probably with some of them included, would have been working together through their representatives as harmoniously, and, so far as can be seen, well nigh or quite as efficiently, as Canada or the United States.

CHAPTER—XIX

INDIA'S GRAVE SOCIAL EVILS: SHOULD THEY BAR HOME RULE?

(Rather, do they not make Home Rule imperative?)

PART I

India has many and serious social evils. Nobody is more conscious of them, or more desirous of getting rid of them, than are the Indian people—the intelligent and educated leaders of the Indian people—themselves.

In having serious social evils to contend with, India is simply like all other nations. Probably her social evils are no more numerous and no worse than were those of Europe or America a hundred years ago. Any of us who are disposed to look down on her because of her supposed inferiority or our supposed superiority in these respects may well turn our thought to the past of our Western nations and call to mind our own terrible social and other evils and crimes—for example, the hideous "Inquisition" in Europe, carried on for hundreds of years and continuing right on down to the beginning of the nineteenth century—an institution of cruelty and terror unequalled in all Indian history; the witchcraft persecution, costing the lives of thousands of good men and women; more than a hundred kinds of crimes, some as trivial as sheep-stealing, punished by death (in England); the horrors connected with the

Tower of London, the Bastile of Paris, and numerous other prisons and dungeons; the unspeakably cruel slave trade carried on by England and the United States and lasting well into the nineteenth century; slavery in the British Colonies, not abolished until 1833, and slavery in the United States of America lasting until 1864. Many of these equalled, and some of them exceeded in cruelty, anything found in India.

And turning from the past to the present, what ground have we for boasting over India to-day? India to-day knows nothing so bad as our American lynching and roasting alive of Negroes; or our present American crime record, which is the highest in the world—from five to ten times as high, in proportion to population, as that of India. It is to be noted, too, that according to the best statistics and records that we possess, prostitution, sex crimes and sex diseases seem to be worse both in Europe and America than in India.

These facts should cause us to think of India's social evils certainly not with arrogance or haughtiness but with modesty, and with feelings of sympathetic interest toward India's many social reform organizations and the great numbers of men and women in all parts of India who are laboring earnestly and self-sacrificingly for the abolition of the evils which afflict their nation.

Yet (and here we have a curious anomaly!) in the face of all the past and present social evils and crimes of England, of the Continental European peoples and of America—some of them actually worse than any of the social evils of India—we see it argued, urged, proclaimed to the world, from influential quarters, that *India* on account of *her* social evils is *not capable of ruling herself and needs to be held in bondage and ruled by a foreign nation*; while at the same time *no voice is raised in any quarter*, so far as is discoverable, arguing or declaring that our *Western* nations on account of *their* social evils are incapable of ruling themselves and need to be held in bondage and ruled by foreigners.

Why is this strange anomaly ? Is not justice the same in all lands ? Is not "sauce for the goose sauce for the gander ?" If bondage to a foreign power is the penalty, the just and proper penalty, or if it is the cure, for social evils in India, is it not the same in England and France and Italy and America ?

I believe it was once publicly declared by George Bernard Shaw, that, in view of America's horrible lynching and burning alive of Negroes, the United States is not fit to rule itself, and ought forthwith to be taken in hand and civilized and governed by some foreign nation, say England or France or Japan. Did the American people assent ? Hardly.

Just what are India's principal and worst social evils ?

1. Probably the most serious is *child-marriage.*

Greatly exaggerated accounts of this evil are widely circulated in America, England and elsewhere. What are the exact facts ? They are as follows : Extensive classes of the Indian people do not practise child marriage, and never have. In several of the self-governing States of India where it formerly prevailed, it has been abolished. It needs to be understood that the expression "child marriage" does not mean in India what it does with us in the West ; there it means only *betrothal.* The parties are not married in the full sense, and do not come together as husband and wife, until puberty. Indeed, in some parts of India cohabitation does not begin until even later than that ; and everywhere movements are on foot to get the age raised still higher. As a matter of fact, careful records in maternity hospitals show that in large parts of India the age of mothers at the time when their first childern are born is well over eighteen years, and, of course, the fathers are older still, often much older.* This is very different from the sensational reports widely circulated in the west.

Nevertheless, there is no denying, and Indian authorities have no desire to deny, that marriage in vast numbers of cases in India is too early, much too early, and that this is a very grave evil. It stands in the way of the proper education of girls and young women, and it unquestionably tends to produce degeneracy in the race.

2. Closely related to child-marriage is the evil of *enforced widowhood*, and the *hard conditions under which widows are compelled to live.* There is no denying that these conditions are severe ; and yet, only in exceptional cases are they anything like so bad as is often reported, in the West. The status of the high-caste Hindu widow is somewhat like that of the nun in Christian lands. She may not marry ; she is denied ornaments and luxuries, and is expected to devote herself closely to the service of the family with which she is connected. Many chafe under this and are very unhappy. But many develop the same spirit of cheerful, unselfish, loving ministration to others seen in the best nuns. Some of the most spiritually beautiful, noble and beloved women of India are found among her widows. Moreover, the old rigors required by

* See Report of Dr. M. I. Balfour, *Times of India.* October, 11, 1927.

orthodox Hinduism are being gradually softened. Public opinion is slowly changing in favor not only of better treatment of widows, but of widow-marriage. As a fact every year sees more and more widows actually marrying.

However, all this does not mean that, taken as a whole, the condition of widows in high-caste Hindu circles is not still bad. It is bad. It is one of the grave social evils of India and must be changed. Happily, all the most important social and political leaders of the nation, except the ultra-conservatives, want a change, and are working in one way or another to bring it about.

3. *Purda* in India—the custom of *secluding* the women of the higher social classes in apartments of their own, too often the darkest, poorest and least sanitary in the home, and forbidding them to see any men other than their very nearest relatives, or to go out, except heavily veiled and attended by a masculine member of their own family—this is a cruel social evil.

But it is an error to suppose that it is by any means universal. As a fact, it is confined to a minority, a relatively rather small minority, of the women of India. The large majority wear no veils and mingle with the other sex in their homes and outside of their homes almost as freely as do the women of Europe and America. But the purda system, *so far as it extends*, is unquestionably an evil. It is cruel to the women; although many, having been all their lives accustomed to it, do not to any considerable degree feel it so. It tends to keep women ignorant, to limit their interests and their outlook, to narrow their lives, and to prevent progressive ideas from coming into the family. It also prevents that healthy and important community social life which naturally develops where men and women mingle freely in the home and outside. Last but not least, this confinement of women tells badly on their physical health. For example, it is found that tuberculosis is much more prevalent among purda women than among others who have a freer life and more fresh air and sunshine, and also much more prevalent than among these purda women's husbands and sons, who, of course, are not confined.

4. The institution of *caste*, at least when carried out in the rigorous ways that it has been in the past, and as it is now in soundly orthodox high-caste Hindu circles, is a very serious evil. It is a mistake, however, to suppose that caste is universal in India. Among very large sections of the Indian people it does not exist. It is also a mistake to suppose that even where it does exist it much affects business relations or political affairs. But in social matters its results and its influence are often cruel and deplorable. Happily, with the advance of education, the increase of travel, and the coming of the telephone, the radio, and all the other agencies that are breaking down division walls of every kind, and with the growing influence of such distinctly anti-caste organizations as the Brahmo Somaj, the Arya Somaj, the Theosophical Society, the Christian Church and others, caste lines are showing signs of giving way at many points, and caste rules are growing less rigid. This is the encouraging side.

5. The keeping of *devadasis*, girls and young women, "married to the gods," that is, prostitutes, in some of the *temples* is a shocking evil, which all the world justly condemns. But let us not do India the injustice of believing the evil to be more extensive than it is. Instead of being an all-India affair, it is confined mainly, if not wholly,

to the temples of a single religious sect, and to Southern India. And there is a strong and growing public feeling in all parts of India against it. Already it has been banished from several Indian Native States.

6. India is cursed with the *opium evil*, and on a pretty large scale. The people are fighting it; but they can effect but little, for the British Government supports and protects it.

7. India is also cursed with the *drink evil*. This, too, the people would drive out if they had the power: but the Government prevents.

8. One more very great and very grave social evil I must mention. It is perhaps more widely known to the world than any other; and wherever it is known it is deplored and condemned. I refer to the existence of India's *depressed classes*, her *outcasts*, her so-called "*untouchables*." These number about thirty millions. Their position in society, that is, their relation to the higher classes, is almost unbelievably degrading and shocking. They have often been compared with the slaves held in America in the old days, before emancipation.. Many of them actually suffer worse for want of adequate housing, clothing and food than the American slaves ever did. But in one thing their lot is superior. They cannot be bought and sold as chattels; wives cannot be sold from husbands and husbands from wives, and children cannot be sold from parents. They are free and independent, even if in a very low sense; they are persons, not things. This is of infinite importance. And one of the most cheering signs of progress in India today is the fact that a great movement for the uplift of these classes, to recognize them as men, to secure to them their rights as human beings, is springing up in all parts of the land, and has become so strong that it is being taken up by the poli-

tical parties. Gandhi is giving it his powerful support. The number of university graduates among these classes is increasing year after year.

So much, then, for India's social evils. There are others; but they seem of less importance, and hence, for our purpose, need not be considered here.

Also there are serious evils that are *partly social* and *partly economic*, such as the terrible poverty of the country, want of good water, want of sanitation, want of public measures to give the people better homes, and to prevent malaria, tuberculosis, cholera, plague and other preventable diseases. But these too may here be passed by with only a mention.

We are ready now for some questions, suggested at the beginning of this chapter,—questions for which all that has gone before in this chapter has been written—to which it has all been leading up. They go down very deep. India asks Great Britain to consider and answer them. She asks the world to consider and answer them. These are the questions.

1. Is it true, as we are so often told, that India's social evils, those described above (and others), mean that she needs to be kept, and ought to be kept, longer in bondage to a foreign power?

2. India has been in bondage to Great Britain more than a century and a half. In all this long period, has Great Britain done anything to prevent or to cure any of the social evils mentioned above?

3. Have the Indian people any reason to believe that if she *continues* her rule—continues it for no matter how long she *will* cure any of these evils, or do anything of importance looking toward that end?

4. In the very nature of things, can the foreign rulers of any country, whose primary interests are not in the country and in the people that rule, but in a foreign land and nation, be expected to take much interest in the social reforms of the country, and to spend the amounts of money (of the country's revenues) needed for promoting reforms, when they want the money for themselves (for their own salaries, pensions and the like), and for their own foreign and imperialistic purposes ?

5. Would not an Indian government, if India had such a government consisting of her own trusted sons, who know India's needs as foreigners cannot, and whose interests are in India and not in a foreign land, be practically certain to do many times over more to cure India's evils, all her evils, social and other, and to promote her welfare in every way, (among other ways, of course, by enacting needed laws and appropriating needed sums of money) than the British (foreign) government of India has ever done, is doing now, or can be expected ever to do?

6. In other words, is bondage ever anything but a curse to any nation? And has India any right to expect ever to secure the removal of her social evils or any other evils, or to attain progress or prosperity in any direction or of any kind, except through freedom and a government of her own ?

PART II

The foregoing questions are not mere idle vaporings. They are serious, they are practical, they are pressing, they penetrate to the very heart of the Indian situation, and they cannot be evaded.

Certain it is, that India's most eminent, most intelligent and most trusted leaders believe almost to a man, find themselves *driven* to believe, that India has no ground for hope of ever getting rid of her social evils through a foreign government, or until such a government is replaced by one of their own. This conviction is shared by not a few Englishmen too.

Let us see what Indian leaders and Englishmen are saying on the subject and what are the exact facts regarding the whole matter.

For more than thirty years a national organization, the "All-India Social Conference," has been working earnestly to promote social reforms of all kinds. One of its greatest handicaps, perhaps its very greatest, all the while, has been the want of sympathy and co-operation, and sometimes the positive opposition, of the Government. At its annual session in December, 1927, the Conference voiced strongly its regret and disappointment at this attitude of the Government and expressed its earnest conviction that "the time has come for the State to address itself boldly and comprehensively to the task of social legislation." It also went much further and declared its belief that the way, and the only way, such necessary helpful social legislation can be obtained is by securing *home rule.*

This action of the All-India Social Conference shows how tired the leaders of social reforms in all parts of the country are coming to be, of trying to carry on their reforms in face of the indifference and opposition of an all-powerful foreign government, and how earnestly they desire a government of their own which will sympathize with and aid them in their immensely important work of ridding India of its social evils.

An illustration of the indifference, and worse

than indifference, of the active opposition, of the present foreign government to essential social reform legislation, is seen in the fact that, during the year 1927, at least three bills were introduced into the national Indian legislature and the legislatures of the Bombay and Madras provinces, to do away with child-marriage. All were supported by strong Indian influences, including the leading women's organizations of the country. At the time of the writing of these words (May, 1928) all three bills were opposed by the British government of the country, and were either defeated or seemed likely to be.

In his book, "Miss Mayo's Mother India, A Rejoinder" (p. 10), Mr. K. Natarajan, one of India's most widely known and trusted social reform leaders, says :

"In legislation upon matters of social reform the Indian government has always thrown its weight upon the side of the *status quo*. The social reform movement has had to work without any countenance from officials"

In his book, "Father India," Mr. Ranga Iyer (a member of the Indian Legislative Assembly) says :

"The social reformer in India who urges the granting of Dominion Status (Home Rule) to the country, does so on the ground that a people's government alone can have a sanction behind it to introduce and carry forward social reforms. As things are now, with foreign rule, the social reformer is handicapped."

One of the evidences that the British Government is a hindrance to social reforms, and that the hope for such reforms lies in a self-governing India, is the fact, often pointed to by social reformers, that in several of the Native States which have self-rule (Baroda, Mysore, Indore and others) social reforms, such as the abolition of child-marriage, promoting the education of girls, protecting widows, lifting up the "untouchable" classes, restricting the evils of caste, etc., are distinctly farther advanced than in British India.

There are persons who say that the people of India should carry on their social reforms themselves, alone, without reference to the government; that the responsibility is not at all on the government but wholly on them. The answer is, can these persons point to any nation in the world that has ever carried out social reforms on any considerable scale, that were effective and enduring, without the aid of legislation, without the aid of laws ?

The American anti-slavery reformers might have carried on their agitation for ever for the freedom of the slaves, and nothing would have been accomplished unless something more had been added. The agitation was important, but it had to be supplemented by legislation. For the slaves to become free, that had to be made so by law. England's social as well as other reforms have all been achieved largely through legislation; without which not one of them would have been effective.

From these illustrations we see how foolish it is for anybody to assert or imagine that it is possible for India to achieve the reforms so essential to her life without government aid, without the assistance and support of laws.

India sees this clearly. Says Mr. Indra Vidyalankar, writing in the *Vedic Magazine* of May, 1928, on "Legislation and Reforms :"

"In all civilized countries where social evils are rooted out it has to be done largely by the force of legislation. The same is true of India."

Says *The Indian Messenger*, (Calcutta), July 17, 1928 :

"Our hope lies in making India a modern nation, and this can only be done by the aid of legislation. The

Indian people are more and more realizing that legislative interference and help in matters social are a necessity. Our social wrongs must be mended or ended, and that can only be done by the aid of legislative enactment."

This is why the Indian people of all parties are demanding a government of their own which will give them the legislation which they see to be absolutely necessary if they are ever to get rid of their social evils.

The Manchester Guardian has called attention to the great disadvantage that a foreign Government is under in connection with social reforms: it points out that because the government *is foreign*, it "cannot safely meddle with social customs and prejudices." If it did, there would be rebellion.

In the nature of things, all reforms which interfere with "social customs and prejudices" must be carried on by the Indian people themselves, and not by foreigners. This is why self-government-home-rule—is imperatively necessary if India's social evils are to be cured. Instead of the existence of these evils being a reason for the continuance of British (foreign) rule, they are a powerful reason for its discontinuance.

Mr. J. A. Spender, the distinguished English publicist, going to India and studying the situation on the ground (as he recently did), sees that this is true. He sees that there is and can be little or no chance for reforms under a government of timid foreigners (this exactly describes the British Government in India) who dare not enact laws against such crying evils as child marriage, prostitution in temples and "untouchability" for fear of antagonizing religious prejudices; and that the only hope for India is in getting a government of its own, which will have no such fear. Mr. Spender's significant words are :

"Only a government trusted by Indians and to a large extent manned by themselves, will be able to combat the religious and caste prejudices which impede reform and in a hundred other ways impoverish the people and retard their progress."

Again Mr. Spender says:

"It is extremely difficult for the alien ruler, with his wholly different mentality, to identify himself with the life of India, or to perform the services for it which Western peoples expect from their rulers. Fundamentally the *case for Indian Home Rule rests on this radical fact.*"*

No one to-day speaks on Indian subjects with greater knowledge, candor or weight of judgment, than the eminent Englishman—college professor, clergyman and publicist—the Rev. C. F. Andrews. We cannot better conclude than by quoting at some length from a remarkably clear, broad-minded, courageous and weighty discussion of the subject of "India's Social Evils and the Relation of the Government to the Same" which has recently appeared from Mr. Andrews' pen in several of the leading periodicals of India, England and America. He says:

"British rule in India constantly stands in the way of progressive social reform, acting as an obstruction to it. So often has this happened of late, in practical experience, that most thoughtful Indians have bitterly come to the conclusion that without self-government being attained by the Indian people, further social advance is almost hopeless.

"British rule in India is a tragedy—a tragedy in the old Greek sense, that there is a fatality in it, which can only be prevented by a discontinuance of the rule. The tragedy lies in the foreign element. The British rulers, however well-meaning, are building up something which has a fatal poison in it bound at last to burst out in death. The poison is the foreign element which will not, cannot, mix to make an organic whole.

"The lack of intimate contact between the foreign

* "The Changing East," pp. 157, 194.

ruler and those over whom he rules paralyses all great efforts of statesmanship.. The foreign ruler fears, to an inordinate degree, the excitement and disturbance which may be caused by any social change wherever religious practice may be even remotely affected. For this reason the foreign ruler is apt to throw himself almost blindly on the side of reaction, with the excuse that *laissez faire* is the only wise policy. It is time in India that this 'tragedy' of foreign rule should be brought to an end, and full self-government should be granted, whereby India may take her place in the League of Nations, no longer under the tutelage of Great Britain, but in her own sovereign right.

"It has been my daily experience for nearly a quarter of a century to watch the course of events in India, with an eager longing for advance in humanitarian directions. Every day my own convictions—slowly and painfully formed—have grown stronger, that the rule of the foreigner is now definitely standing in the way of healthy social reform. In the Legislative Councils the official vote is continually given for reaction."*

Mr. Andrews continues :

"It may be asked whether the depressed classes would stand to gain or lose under India's self-government. Unhesitatingly I reply that to-day the strongest forces working for their emancipation are to be found outside of government circles. By far the most powerful movement for their upliftment is the National Movement (the movement to obtain self-rule). If the

* Mr. Andrews says (what every one acquainted with the history knows) that, of all the social evils of the country which the Indian progressive leaders have been fighting for more than a century, the only one in which they have had any at all effective assistance from the Government was the abolition of *sati* (or suttee). And the credit for that is due quite as much to the eminent Indian leader, Ram Mohun Roy, as to the British Government. Indeed, the Government would not have acted at all except for strong pressure from a powerful Indian movement led by the great Indian reformer just named. Mr. Andrews declares that this instance of the British Government using its power against a great social evil is the exception which proves the rule. There has been nothing else kin to it since. And that was a hundred years ago.

British rule were to cease to-morrow, the advancement of the depressed classes would at once be brought into the foreground of the national programme.

"Let me answer two vital questions:

(1). Will the acknowledged social evils, which have grown up with the caste system, especially those relating to child-marriage and widow-remarriage, be remedied more quickly under Indian self-government?

(2). Will the purdah system, leading to the unhealthy seclusion of women among the higher classes, be brought more quickly to an end under self-rule, or will it be strengthened?

"I answer: My own personal experience has been that *all these necessary changes are being retarded, rather than accelerated under the present British government in India. In social reform work in India* it is probably true that *progress* would be *doubly rapid if Indian statesmen had the helm instead of British.*"*

---

* *Foreign Affairs* (London) February, 1928; *The People* (Lahore), March 8, 1928: *The World To-morrow* (New York), March, 1928.

CHAPTER XX.

HINDU AND MOHAMMEDAN RIOTS: SHOULD THEY BAR SELF-RULE?

There are in India about seventy millions of Moslems and two hundred ten millions of Hindus.

Disturbing reports come to us from time to time of hostilities and riots between these two great religious communities, sometimes resulting in considerable bloodshed and loss of life. As is well-known, these riots are claimed by the British to be clear evidences that their rule in India is necessary, absolutely necessary, to prevent the Mohammedans and Hindus from destroying one another in great numbers, and plunging the country into devastating wars. Is this claim well founded?

As soon as we begin to examine the situation with care and a desire to be unbiased, we discover that there are two exactly opposite views of the case. One is that of the British, just suggested namely, that the hostilities and riots are very bad; that the responsibility for them rests wholly upon the Indian people; that were it not for the presence of the British Government, the Hindus and Moslems would be at each other's throats and the country would be deluged with blood; and therefore for India's sake, the British must stay.

The other view, which is that of a large part of the most intelligent Indian people, denies that the hostilities and riots are as numerous or serious as the British reports indicate; and as to responsibility for them, it places that primarily on the British, and only secondarily, if at all, on the Hindus or Moslems.

It puts the case essentially in this way: The Hindus and Moslems of India are not naturally hostile. When left to themselves, that is, when not stirred to hurtful rivalries or to antagonisms by outside influences, they are as kind and peaceful neighbors and friends as are to be found anywhere in the world. Living side by side in nearly all parts of India, no one would know them apart except for possibly some slight difference in dress or in religious practice or rite, which does not affect at all their business relations or their neighborly relations or their friendship and goodwill to one another. Why then should there be riots between them? Is it not necessary to look for some outside cause?

Wherever in India the British are most in evidence, there the riots are usually worst; wherever the British are least in evidence, there riots are generally fewest.

Before the British came to India, there seems to have been little hostility between Hindus and Moslems; everywhere they seem to have lived together for the most part peacefully and harmoniously.* In the Native States to-day, where there are few

---

* It is true that before the coming of the British there were sometimes wars between Hindu and Mohammedan princes and Hindu and Mohammadan states. But they were not wars of religion, but simply wars caused by political quarrels, or by the ambitions of rulers to gain new power or territory. Hindus lived in security and peace under Moslem rulers, and Moslems in peace and security under Hindu rulers. Hindu princes appointed Moslems to high official positions, sometimes to the very highest, and Moslem princes were as generous in placing responsibilities and conferring honors on Hindus.

British and where British rule is least felt, there are very few riots, and very little enmity is seen. It is only since British rule in India began, and in those parts of the country where British rule is most directly and strongly felt, that hostility becomes noticeable and riots of any importance appear.

The only conclusion, therefore, that it seems possible to draw is, that, instead of the British being needed in India to prevent hostilities and riots, it is their presence that is mainly responsible for such riots or other hostilities as exist.

Going more into details, the Indian view of the case may be stated somewhat as follows:

The British policy in India has been from the beginning that known as "divide and rule," or that which the old Romans described by their well-known Latin words, *divide et impera.* This has been the policy of all great conquerors and rulers of foreign peoples, from those of ancient Babylonia, Assyria, Persia and Egypt down to Napoleon in Europe and Clive in India. All the British conquerors of India used it, and did not hesitate to boast that they did. Indeed, without employing this policy of stirring up hostility between states, between princes, and between parties, and taking the side of one against the other and thus gaining control over both, the British could never have conquered the land. Later British rulers of India have employed the same policy of fostering divisions among the people, knowing well that divisions always weaken a nation and render it easier to hold in subjection.

Since the time of the early conquerors of India this policy has been kept as much as possible out of sight; and sometimes it has been denied; and yet not infrequently eminent officials have been frank enough boldly to declare and defend it. As early as 1821, a British officer, signing himself "Carnaticus" wrote in the *Asiatic Review* of May of that year:

Divide et Impera should be the motto of our Indian administration, whether political, civil or military.

About the time of the Mutiny, Lieutenant Colonel John Coke, Commandant at Moradabad, wrote:

"Our endeavor should be to uphold in full force the (for us fortunate) separation which exists between the different religions and races, not to endeavor to amalgamate them. *Divide et impera* should be the principle of Indian government."

Lord Elphinstone, Governor of Bombay, in a minute, dated 14th. May, 1850, wrote:

"*Divide et impera* was the old Roman motto, and it should be ours.*"

Sir John Strachey, an eminent British Indian civilian and writer on India, said:

"The existence side by side of hostile creeds among the Indian people, is one of the strong points in our political position in India."

Mr. Gandhi tells us that Mr. O. A. Hume, for almost a life-time a high official in India, once made to him the frank confession that the British government was "sustained by the policy of Divide and Rule."

All this has been perfectly natural; and, if it is right for one nation to conquer another and rule it without its consent, then it has been perfectly consistent and perfectly right for Great Britain to employ this policy of fostering

* For the three preceding quotations see "Consolidation of the Christian Power in India," by Major B. D. Basu, Chapter VI, pp. 74, 75. (R. Chatterjee, publisher, Calcutta. 1927.) Also *The Modern Review*, Calcutta, May, 1926, p. 556.

divisions among the Indian people so as to make her rule secure. A united nation is not only more difficult to conquer, but it is also more difficult to govern, to keep under subjection, than one that is divided into opposing factions, parties, classes, or religions. It would be very strange, therefore, if the British had not borne this fact in mind and taken advantage of it in practically all their government of India.

Of course, the question arose early with them what particular division could be taken advantage of that would be likely to be most effective? The answer was not far to seek. Religious divisions generally strike deepest. Just as in Christian lands rulers have often availed themselves of the divisions of the people into Catholics and Protestants, arraying one of these religious communities against the other to serve their own political ends, so it was natural that the British in India should take advantage of the great and conspicuous religious division of the Indian people into Hindus and Moslems to serve their own British political ends. Perfect political unity between these two great communities would mean practically the unity of all India. But a united India would be a danger to British rule. The British well knew that a revolt, a strike for independence, undertaken by a united India, could not be put down. They would have to surrender their dominance and give India self-rule. Hence why should they not take every means in their power to keep the Indian people politically divided? Which, of course, is only another way of saying, Why should they not avail themselves of what seems now, and always has seemed, the most promising way of attaining this end, namely, fostering estrangement between Hindus and Moslems? Although it has been denied that this has been the policy of Great Britain, the evidences of it, both in the past and in the present, are overwhelming.

The particular ways most employed by the British to keep the Hindus and Mohammedans apart have been, and are, two, namely, *favoritism shown by the Government to the Mohammedans*, which, of course, tends to create jealousy on the part of the Hindus, and therefore estrangement; and, of late years, *communal elections*.

The favoritism shown by the Government to the Moslems has taken many forms, and it has generally been hidden and elusive; but its existence has been, and is, unmistakable.

Ramsay Macdonald, in his "Awakening of of India," (p. 283), calls sharp attention to the widespread

"Suspicion that sinister influences have been and are at work on the part of the Government; that Mohammedan leaders have been and are inspired by certain British officials, and that these officials have pulled and continue to pull wires at Simla and in London, and of malice aforethought sow discord between the Mohammedan and Hindu communities, by showing to the Mohammedans special favors."[1]

India does not forget an address delivered some years ago by Sir Bampfylde Fuller, Lt. Governor of E. Bengal, in which that high official, employing a significant figure of speech, represented the British Government in India as having "two wives," Hindu and Moslem, and the Moslem wife was the Government's "favorite."

A year or two ago, Lord Olivier, who was Secretary of State for India in the Ramsay Macdonald Government, wrote a letter to the London *Times*, confessing in the plainest words this favoritism. He said:

"No one with a close aquaintance with Indian affairs will be prepared to deny that on the whole there is a predominant bias in British officialdom in favor of the Moslem community, partly on the ground of closer sympathy but more largely as a make-weight against Hindu nationalism."

This statement made a great stir in London, and Lord Olivier was widely censured. Much of the feeling was caused by what was regarded as his indiscretion in letting the public know something which the government thought should be kept secret. He had "Let the cat out of the bag," which was a grave offense.

Passing to the Communal Elections,—the influence of these in estranging different sections of the Indian people, especially Hindus and Moslems, is so obvious that no one dares to deny it. Just what are the Communal Elections? The plan of these, or to employ another name, the plan of Communal Representation, is a scheme by which men are elected to office not to represent the people as a whole, but a section of the people, a class, a division, especially a religious sect. The electorates are divided into compartments, so to speak, social, racial and religious; that is, the people who vote do not vote all together, as citizens all on an equality, and for representatives to represent them all as Indians, without reference to their social status or their religious faith, as is the case in this country and Canada and England and nearly all other countries. Instead of that, the members of different religious faiths, and different social classes, and different races vote separately, and for candidates to represent them as belonging to separate and distinct faiths and classes and races.

For example, the Bengal Legislature of one hundred thirteen members has not been elected

* Quoted in *The People* (Lahore), of July 18, 1927.

and does not exist as a legislative body of one hundred thirteen *Indians*, representing *all* the people of Bengal, or *all* the people of this, that and the other *district* of Bengal. On the contrary, forty-six members of the Legislature have been elected as Hindus to represent Hindus; thirty-eight as Mohammedans to represent Mohammedans; sixteen as Europeans to represent the relatively very small number of Europeans; two as Eurasians or Anglo-Indians to represent that section of the people; five as landholders to represent landholders, etc., etc., Of course, the influence of such a dividing political system, of such a broken-up elective and representative plan, is in the greatest possible degree to destroy all feelings of citizenship, to crush out all patriotism, to prevent all interest in India as such or Bengal as such, and to destroy all care or concern for measures aiming to promote the benefit of the nation, the province or the city. Its influence is to cause all voters to concentrate their interest on the narrow and selfish affairs of one's own particular class or race or religion. Could human ingenuity devise a political system in its very nature more certain to produce political, social and religious divisions and antagonisms, or better calculated to make religious, social and political unity in India impossible?

Community representation means representation, not, as in the United States or Canada or England, according to numbers of population, but representation according to classes, and groups (religious, racial, social and others), that is, a certain number of representatives is given to the Mohammedans, a certain number to Christians, a certain number to non-Brahmans, etc., irrespective of whether these classes or groups are many or few.

Perhaps in order to be perfectly fair to the government, it ought to be said that the officials who framed the system of communal elections and secured its adoption did so under the plea that thus they were giving representation to minorities. But how could any intelligent statesmen or government administrators in the world fail to see that granting unjust favoritism to one religious community as opposed to another, must, in the very nature of things, create jealousy and a deep sense of injury in the mind of the religious community discriminated against, and thus prove a firebrand everywhere ?

Do the Indian people want the Communal system ? The answer is, a few do. Extreme partisans, and narrow-minded sectarians, whether Hindus, or Mohammedans, do ; and extremely selfish men who care for nobody but themselves, and for no interests but their own or those of their own sect or class or party, these do. But these do not constitute the great body of the Indian people, or include the ablest and most trusted leaders. The Hindus, who constitute more than two-thirds of the population of the nation, are against it almost to a man. The three or four millions of native Christians are the same. The more intelligent, more progressive and better element among the Mohammedans are against it. Who is responsible for this system ?

Of course, the Government is. The Government created it, and insists on keeping it.

It is true that the National Indian Congress in 1916 made the mistake of accepting the communal elections idea. But very soon it discovered its error. For some years past, strong efforts have been put forth from nearly all the more intelligent classes in India, of whatever name or faith, to induce the government to abolish this divisive and evil system. But the government has been unwilling to listen.

About 1890, a number of Mohammedans under the lead of Sir Syed Ahmed Khan besieged the government of special concessions for more political places and privileges than were their due according to their numbers. But the move was opposed by many Mohammedans. The *Moslem Herald* strongly condemned it as something sure to

"Poison the social life of districts and villages and make a hell of India."

India owes the inception of the communal system seemingly to Lord Minto (Viceroy from 1905 to 1910), or perhaps to Lord Minto and Lord Morley together, in connection with the so-called "Morley-Minto Reforms" of 1909.*

Says Sir Surendranath Banerjea in his book "A Nation in Making," (p. 283) :

"India owes to Lord Minto the system of Communal representation for the Legislative Councils, from the meshes of which it will take her many long years to emerge."

The *Indian Messenger* (Calcutta) of May 20, 1926, also lays the responsibility for communal electorates or communal representation in India primarily upon Lord Minto. It says :

"British imperialism has never failed to do all in its power to keep India divided, by pitting minorities against majorities ; and in this way making British interests safe and secure."

---

* On December 6, 1904, Lord Morley wrote to Lord Minto as follows : "I won't follow you again in our Mahometan dispute. Only I respectfully remind you once more that it was *your* early speech about their extra claims that first started the Muslim hare," Morley's "Recollections," Vol. II. p. 325

In this connection it quotes Lord Minto as saying :

"I am firmly convinced that any electoral representations in India would be doomed to mischievous failure which aimed at granting a personal enfranchisement regardless of *the beliefs* and *traditions* of the *communities* composing the population of this continent."

That is to say, Lord Minto declares that the people of India ought to be represented in their municipalities, their legislative assemblies, etc., not according to their numbers, as, for example, one representative for 10,000 people, or 5,000 people, or some other number, thus treating the people all alike as all standing on an equality ; but they should be represented according to their "beliefs and traditions ;" in other words, persons of certain beliefs and traditions should be favored, while persons of other beliefs and traditions should be discriminated against.

Colonel Josiah Wedgewood M. P., declares tha the minds of those who formed the present Constitution of India (the "Government of India Bill" of 1919—"Dyarchy"), were so full of the idea of communal elections that

"The very thought of *India* vanished from the Bill, to be replaced by consideration for the separate communities of *Hindu*, *Mohammedan*, *Sikh*, *Mahratta*, *non-Brahmin*, *Indian*, *Christian*, *Anglo-Indian* and *English*."
—that is to say, representatives to the Assemblies and elsewhere, were to be elected not as Indians but as Hindus, Mohammedans, Sikhs, Christians, etc. ; and not to serve India, their common country, but to serve primarily their own *particular classes* and *religious sects*.

As already said, no scheme could possibly have been devised more destructive of national unity, or more certain to create jealousy, rivalry and hostility among all religious sects, especially between Mohammedans and Hindus.

As Mr. Lajpat Rai has pointed out, an absolutely clear proof (even if there were no other) that the British find in the plan of communal electorates an effective means of keeping India divided and therefore of making their own mastery of her secure, is seen in the fact that this plan receives the enthusiastic support of the British press of India and the Tory press of Great Britain—in other words, of all parties that want to strengthen Britain's hold on India; as it receives no support from any one who wants to see India united and advancing toward self-rule.

Although the communal election scheme is so shaped as on the whole to favor the Mohammedans above the Hindus, it is well-known, as has already been seen, that by no means all the Mohammedans "bite at the bait" (of excessive offices and other favors) which the British Government holds out to them. Not a few of their ablest, most honored and most influential leaders see what these favors mean and reject them with indignation, realizing that the true and permanent interests of Mohammedans as well as of Hindus can be secured only through a united India.

To cite conspicuous illustrations. As I write this I have before me the Presidential Address of the President of the All-India Moslem League of 1915, in which that highly representative Mohammedan deprecates all antagonism between Hindus and Moslems and urges in the strongest terms the elevation of the Indian nation above all sectarian interests. He says:

"When the question concerning the welfare of India arises I am not only an Indian first, but an Indian next, and an Indian to the last. Favoring no community and no individual, I am on the side of those who desire the advancement of India as a whole. In the affairs of my country I stand for good-will and close co-operation between all communities, with a single eye to the progress of India, the mother-land alike of Moslems and of Hindus."

These words from the man holding the highest position within the gift of the Indian Mohammedans.

Another eminent Moslem, the Honorable Syed Sirdar Ali Khan of Hyderabad says in *The Times* of August 1st, 1925:

"No sane Mohammedan wants communal differences to be perpetuated. We want them to be eliminated...... The great majority of us trust that by co-operation of Moslems and Hindus we may attain self-government that will be, not a Hindu government, but a government that will really represent India and will give to the Mohammedans that share in assisting the well-ordered progress of the country that they deserve by their numbers, their merits and their traditions."

Said Sir Syed Ahmed, one of the wisest Mohammedans that India ever produced:

"Hindus and Moslems are the two eyes of India, and one cannot exist without the other."

In August, 1927, Mr. Shaukat Ali, an eminent Mohammedan Leader, Secretary of the India Khilafat Committee, issued and circulated widely a strong public statement deprecating the estrangement which (after a long period of "most remarkable amity and good-will,") had sprung up of late between Hindus and Moslems, owing largely to the communal election system, and appealing in the most earnest way for harmony and co-operaation between the two religious bodies, declaring that a united and self-governing India was the desire, the goal and the imperative need of Mohammedans as truly as of Hindus. He added that the whole Khilafat Working Committee was earnestly endeavoring to promote unity between the Mohammedans and the Hindus.

Thus we see that the evidence is simply overwhelming that the responsibility for the existence of the communal election plan rests wholly upon the British; and that if not their sole, at least their primary, object in maintaining it, against the protest of a large majority of the Indian people, is to create and preserve sufficient hostility between the two great religious communities of India to prevent their political unity and co-operation,—in accordance with the principle of "divide and rule," which has been the British policy in India from the beginning.*

Do the British officials really want to stop the riots? Many of the Indian people find themselves compelled to believe that they do not; they say "If they *wanted* to stop them, they *would* stop them; for they have the power." Not a few Indians believe that the British regard the riots as a valuable asset,—as one of the best excuses they have for staying in India.

To be sure, the British proclaim to the world that they deprecate the riots, are pained and shocked by them, and want them to stop. The Indian people reply, "If what you say is true, why do you do the things which promote them, and refuse to do things which would prevent them? In other words, why do you insist on keeping the communal elections when you see that everywhere they create divisions and antagonisms

* As showing the good feeling between Moslems and Hindus when not estranged by outside influences, it is worth while to notice that, from the first, Mahatma Gandhi a Hindu, has been almost as much esteemed and honored by the Mohammedans of India as by the Hindus. Some of his strongest supporters always have been and are to-day distinguished Moslem leaders. Another thing which shows the fundamental friendship between the two religious communities, is the almost unanimous election to the Presidency of the 1927 Indian National Congress, of Dr. Ansari, a Mohammedan, notwithstanding the fact that fully three-fourths of the members of the Congress are Hindus.

and the spirit which tends to produce riots; and why do you refuse to give us in their place such elections as other civilized nations have, which tend to foster unity and peace?"

In August, 1927, Lord Irwin, the Viceroy of India, delivered a speech in Simla, the Indian Summer Capital, calling public attention to the riots which he represented as serious, giving statistics as to the number of persons killed and and wounded during the preceding year and a half, and appealing to the officials of the nation and to the people to do all in their power to promote harmony and unity between the Hindus and Moslems so that the riots might be brought to an end. And yet, amazing as the fact seems, the speech did not contain even an intimation of willingness on the part of the Viceroy to do away with the communal election system which everywhere creates the divisions and hostilities from which the riots spring.

Lord Birkenhead, Secretary of State for India in a speech delivered in the House of Lords, in March 1927, declared, with an air of high and austere righteousness, that the Indian people need expect no concessions looking in the direction of self-rule so long as "sectarian violence" between Hindus and Mohammedans continued. And all the while his Lordship, himself, possessed the power to stop that sectarian violence, by changing the form of the Indian electorates; yet he refused to take even a step in the direction of stopping it.

An English writer has summed up in two sentences what he declares is the exact Indian situation:

"We, the British, put on a face as long as the moral law and say to the Indian people, 'You want self-rule; we are preparing you for it, and will grant it to you when you are *united*,—of course, we *cannot before*.' And then we turn round, grinning like the devil, and say to ourselves, 'We've got them in our power, and by the Eternal we will *never let them become united*, until water runs up hill and the sun rises in the west,"

The present writer declines to adopt as his own the utterance of this Englishman; but he sees enough truth in it to desire to give it to his readers, and to commend it to the thoughtful attention of the Secretary of State for India and the British government.

It is difficult to understand just what is the attitude of the British officials toward the riots. They seem both to want them to continue, and not want them to continue. They declare that they deeply regret them and are trying to prevent them; and at the same time they continue persistently to maintain the communal election system which, they know, produces them; and also they continue to use them as a seemingly prized and and cherished argument for convincing the world that they (the British) must stay in India to protect it.

The situation is a puzzle. Certainly we are unwilling to think of men like Lord Birkenhead, the Secretary of State for India, and Lord Irwin, the Viceroy in India, as knowingly playing a double part, or as being otherwise than sincere when they solemnly declare that they deplore the riots and are trying to prevent them. Perhaps the kindest view to take is, that in setting up the communal system of electorates as a means of keeping the Hindus and Moslems apart, they have created for themselves a "Frankenstein," a something which they themselves cannot control—an agency which, while accomplishing the object which they intended, of dividing the people, has got out of hand and caused riots which they sincerely deplore. They attempt to wash their hands of responsibility for the riots, and place the blame upon the Indian people. But the attempt is in vain. They created the cause; therefore, they themselves are responsible for the effects.

They can get rid of the riots, and other forms of dangerous hostility, in one way and only one. And that is by ceasing to show favoritism to the Mohammedans or to any other community or party; and by giving to India electorates and elections so planned as to *unite* the people and cause them all to vote together as citizens of a *common country*, and in the *interest* of their *common country*, instead of electorates and elections planned in their very nature to *divide* the people, by setting them to voting as *Moslems*, as *Hindus* as *Parsis*, as *Sikhs*, as *Christians* and the *rest*, in *the interest* of *their rival sects*.

There is absolutely nothing fundamentally antagonistic between the Hindus and Mohammedans of India. They have lived together for the most part entirely peacefully and happily for more than seven hundred years, and are living together happily now in essentially every respect except as stirred to rivalries, jealousies, and temporary hostilities by the persence and plannings of a foreign government, whose constant policy is that of the old Romans, *divide et impera*.

To conclude. Nothing is more certain than that the Indian people earnestly desire to get rid of riots and all forms of hostility between their two great and honored religious communities. How is it to be accomplished?

In the very nature of things, it can never be done through *foreign rulers* whose *interest* is, and always must be, to keep them *divided* so as to make their *foreign rule secure*. It can be done only through a government of *their own*, some form of real *home rule*, whose *interest is unity*, and whose *security* is to be *ensured through unity*.

CHAPTER XXI.

IF THE BRITISH WERE GONE, WOULD INDIA "RUN WITH BLOOD?"

One of the claims oftenest made by Englishmen—a sort of favorite claim, one in which many seem to take peculiar satisfaction is, that the presence of Britain in India is necessary in order to prevent the country from falling into "chaos," "anarchy" and "blood-shed." Staying and maintaining their rule is something which the British do unselfishly, for India's safety (generously bearing thoir share of the "white man's burden").

Nor is it strange that this claim is a favorite one. It is dramatic, and quickly attracts attention; people who do not know India, easily accept it as true ; and it takes away something of the obloquy naturally resting upon foreign rulers, by representing them not as enemies but as friends and benefactors of an inferior and helpless people. One travelling in India is fairly startled to find how constantly the British justify their domination there by this claim—saying to him: "You see, we are here simply because we must be. The 'natives' can't govern themselves. If we withdrew to-morrow, the barbarous or only half civilized people would fly at one anothers' throats, and the land would "run with blood from the Himalayas to Cape Comorin."

Travelling in England, one finds Englishmen there saying the same. Similar statements are made again and again in Parliament. There, however, they are not made without rebuke and denial; for not a few members of that body are reasonably intelligent about India, and refuse to listen in silence to what in their judgment is a perversion of facts. Nevertheless the claim is repeated over and over. The Master of Elibank is reported as declaring, without a blush, in a speech on the budget: "For us to abandon India would be in effect to hand her over to the most frightful anarchy." Members quote Sir Charles Elliott, who, some years ago published an article in the *Imperial Review*,* in which he went into particulars and painted the following hair-raising picture:

"If we English abandon India to-morrow, no organized government would be formed. There would follow, not a despotism under Surendranath Bannerjea, or any other leader of the advanced party, not a democratic Government of elected representatives of Bengal, Baboos or Mahratta Brahmins, but a prompt invasion from Afghanistan in the north-west and Nepal in the north, and the wild tribes on the frontier of Assam in the north-east. The Princes of the Native States, with their well-trained armies would re-commence their old internecine quarrels and annex adjoining territory, and there would be an orgy of murder and rapine."

This kind of thing is talked so much and written so much by the British that three-quarters of the world actually believes it. I find it on all hands accepted as true in America. Even a man as intelligent as President Roosevelt declared in a public address:—

"If English control were withdrawn from India the whole peninsula would become a chaos of bloodshed and violence; all the weaker peoples, and the most industrious and law-abiding, would be plundered and forced to submit to indescribable wrong and oppression, and, the only beneficiaries among the natives would be the lawless and blood-thirsty."

As I write these words, there lies before me

---

* August, 1909.

an American paper that tells of a Boston man visiting the city of Calcutta and asking an Englishman what would happen if the English withdrew from the country. Pointing toward the Zoological Garden, the Englishman replied: "If you should open the cages and let out the lions, tigers and other wild animals you would see what would happen." The innocent American, knowing no better, accepted it all as true, returned to Boston, told the story, and fervently praised the British for their great service to India in keeping the benighted and barbarous people from tearing one another to pieces like wild beasts.

What is to be said in answer to this amazing claim made by so many persons interested in the perpetuation of British rule in India, and so widely believed? Is it true? Or, like so many other things which are told and believed by credulous multitudes, is it a fiction, a scare, a mere "bugaboo," something *imagined* to be true because men *want* it to be true?

At least one thing to be said is, that if the claim is true, if after being so long under British rule, the Indian people, as a result, have sunk to such a condition of savagery as this claim implies, the fact is a most shocking *indictment of British rule.* For more than 2,500 years before the British came, the Indian nation was one of the greatest, the most influential, and most enlightened in the world. It was distinctly the leading nation of the greatest of the World's continents—the continent which has been called the mother of civilization. India produced great literatures, great art, great philosophical systems, great religions, great legal and moral codes, great men in absolutely every department of life. Can we believe that during the domination of the British of 160 years or so, it has sunk to the condition indicated by the claim which we are considering—a condition analogous to that of wild beasts just escaped from a zoo,—a condition such that it is unable to govern itself, but must be kept under the control of foreigners to prevent its people from flying at one anothers' throats and plunging the whole land into anarchy and bloodshed ? If the situation in India is such as these Englishmen assert, one would think they would hide it, cover it up, blush with shame at the thought of it, be the last persons in the world to acknowledge it. Instead of its being a reason why the British should remain in India, surely it is a most unanswerable evidence that they never should have gone there, that their rule has been nothing short of a calamity and a crime : and that the only hope for India is for them to leave, and allow the Indian people once more to manage their own affairs and govern themselves, as they did for so many centuries before the British came on the scene. Plainly this is the first thing that ought to be said by honest men, concerning British rule in India, if the claims made by Sir Charles Elliott, the Master of Elibank, and the rest are true.

But are they true ?

Sir Charles Elliott is more specific in his statements, goes more into details, than any other. Let us examine his statements, to see whether they prove to rest on a basis of reality, or only on one of imagination.

This eminent Englishman tells us, as we have seen that if the British ever go away, there will immediate "invasions of India from Afghanistan and Nepal" and by the so-called "wild tribes on the borders of Assam," and a general uprising of the "Princes of the Native States of India," with "their well-trained armies," to invade and "annex" adjoining territory" and to create a general "orgy of murder and rapine."

Certainly this is a dark picture. Where does he get it? Just what are Afghanistan and Nepal? Are they great, powerful, and dangerous countries invasions from which would be a peril to India? These armies of the Native Princes, are they large. And these wild tribes at the north-east, how formidable and dangerous are they? Let us see.

Afghanistan is a country located on the far side of great and lofty ranges of mountains from which invaders can reach India only through difficult, dangerous, and easily defended passes. Its population, although vigorous and hardy, totals only about six millions, a number which does not seem to be very alarming when placed beside India's three hundred twenty millions. The population of Nepal is about the same, no larger. Thus the two nations compare with India in population and in strength, well, say about as six or seven years old boys compare with full grown men of twenty, or if I may be allowed a less dignified illustration, about as Rat-terriers compare with Mastiffs, Great Danes, or Newfoundland dogs.

As for the so-called "well-trained armies" of the Princes, which are to spread such havoc and carnage over the land, just what is their strength? If we turn to the Statesman's Year Book of 1926, we find that all the Native Princes of India (that is, the rulers of all the Native States) possess armies (well-trained or ill-trained), all combined, numbering only 27,000, or to be exact, 27,030. Is that number to be regarded as very dangerous in a *great nation like India*? And then as to the *character* of these Native Princes, is it such as we are given by Sir Charles and the rest to understand? We know that some of them are among the most enlightened and peace-loving rulers to be found anywhere. Where does Sir Charles get his authority for representing all of them or any of them as bandits, only, restrained by British control from plunging into war with one another and inaugurating a nation-wide orgy of "rapine and murder ?" One would like to ascertain his authority. As for ourselves, we have never been able to discover any evidence that the great majority of the Indian Princes are any less peaceful or law-abiding than the British themselves.

As for the "wild tribes on the borders of Assam," what is the truth about them? I myself happen to have a little personal knowledge bearing on this question. It was my fortune some years ago to spend two weeks on horseback travelling among two of these tribes, on a missionary journey to visit some little mission churches which existed among them. I had to travel on the back of a "pony" (or else on foot) for there was not a wheeled vehicle of any kind, or a road for one, anywhere in the region; the only way of getting from one of the scattered villages to another, being by foot-trail or "pony path." What kind of people did I find ? Dangerous savages ? I travelled with a single companion, a member of one of the tribes, who acted as my guide and interpreter. We carried no arms more formidable than an ordinary pocket-knife. When my journeyings were nearly at an end, I spent an evening with the British official who had charge of the region. He said to me, "You have probably wondered sometimes whether you are entirely safe going about among the people of these wild and far-away hills, But I assure you that your only cause for fear is the tigers and leopards in the jungles and ravines; and even they will not trouble you unless you travel in the night. As regards the people, you need not have the slightest apprehension. They are manly and self-respecting; they know how to fight if their rights are trampled on; but when treated justly and fairly they are as kind and peaceable and trustworthy as any people in the world. I have lived here now nearly a dozen years. Before coming here, I lived in London. And I want to say to you that you are actually safer going about among these people than you would be on the streets of London."

Does it look very much as if these "wild tribes" are likely under any circumstances to rush down from their hills to the plains and cities and spread havoc and destruction over India?

Such, then, seem to be the actual facts regarding the peril which Sir Charles Elliott, the Master of Elibank, and others imagine threatens India if the British go away and if the Indian people are left to rule themselves. Do the facts show that there is any reason whatever to believe that such a peril exists anywhere else except in the imagination of the men who proclaim it as a justification of British rule?

Sir Charles tells us one thing more which we have not yet considered, but which demands attention. He gives us to understand that if the British leave India, they will do so *without making any provision for another government to fill their place*. In other words, they will not, before leaving, he thinks, take any steps, or permit the Indian people to take any, to organize a republic or any other form of rule, under Surendranath Banerjea or any other Indian leader or leaders; but will deliberately and intentionally leave the country without a government, thus taking the course which they believe will be most likely to produce universal anarchy and bloodshed, and wreck the country. This seems to be the clear meaning of the talk of Sir Charles and the rest about universal bloodshed and anarchy following the departure of the British.

The British hold all power in their hands ; they know that the Indian people want self-rule, and to that end desire a government of their own, under the management of their own competent leaders, of whom they believe they have no lack. The British can, if they will, make provision for such a government ; they can easily arrange for a nation-wide election in which the Indian people will be able to choose their best and most trusted public men and statesmen to set up and maintain a system of rule which will be Indian, and which will serve their needs, as they believe, incomparably better than they can possibly be served by any foreign government. Having made such provision for a reliable government to succeed them, the British can take their departure with every reason to believe that all will go on in India essentially as safely and peacefully as one king succeeds another in England, or as one political administration follows another in America. And making such preparation before they go is just what they should do, and the very least that they can do in justice or in honor. Will they not do it ?

For nearly two centuries they have been holding India in subjection without her consent, exploiting the country, and in a hundred ways gaining prestige, commercial advantages and pecuniary wealth from what they have proudly called their great "Indian Empire." Surely after India has done and suffered so much for them, and after they have reaped such enormous benefits from her, if they are actuated by any principles of honor or even decency, they will desire to see her safe and prosperous when they are gone, and will gladly do all in their power to insure such safety and prosperity. To do less than this will be on their part the basest ingratitude and the most shocking injustice.

As to the matter of the British government leaving India *suddenly, and without making provision for any other government to take its place,* of course that would probably be temporarily a dangerous thing ; but only for the same reason that it would be dangerous for any government in the world suddenly to drop everything and go away, without providing a successor to take up its responsibilities. If the government of the United States, or Canada, or England, or France, or Germany, or any other nation, left suddenly with no successor provided for, it would create confusion and more or less of temporary anarchy. The same is true if the government of New York City, of Philadelphia, or Buffalo, or Chicago, or any other city, were suddenly to abscond, with no provision for successors. But the disturbed and more or less lawless condition which would exist in the interval before a new government could be organized and put in operation, would not mean that the peoples of these nations or cities are not able to govern themselves and need to have foreigners from a distant part of the earth come and govern them. Instead of having any such meaning at all, it would mean only, as has been said, that the proceeding government had been criminally neglectful in not making provision for a competent and adequate government to follow it.

Of course, if the British *want* India to fall into such a condition of bloodshed and anarchy as is portrayed, they can doubtless bring it about. How ? In the way already indicated, that is, by going away and leaving the nation without a government, and as inexperienced, helpless and defenseless as possible. But the resposibility and the crime will rest wholly on the British. For one, I cannot believe that they will for a moment contemplate such a crime.

And yet, and yet, much as one regrets to say it, it has to be confessed that there has been from the beginning a very dark side to Great Britain's management of India. It looks much as if from the very first it has been her fixed plan and policy to keep the Indian people just as weak in a military way as possible, and therefore just as unable as possible to protect themselves from bloodshed and anarchy, if left to govern themselves; and it looks very much as if that is her policy to-day.

Let us examine the actual situation in India as to military protection. The present strength (1926) of the Indian army maintained by the British-Indian Government (this does not include and has no relation to, the small and insignificant armies which the Native States are permitted to possess) is 187,437. This Indian Army is maintained by the British for two purposes. One is to help them to guard against any possible revolts or revolutions—any possible attempts of the Indian people to throw off their foreign yoke. The other object is, to be ready at the summons of the Empire to go abroad and help fight the Empire's battles in various parts of the world.

This Indian army is so constituted, trained and managed as to keep it strictly *under British control* and make it as efficient as possible for serving *British* ends; but *nothing beyond that.* It is not permitted to learn to direct or manage itself, and it is kept as weak as possible for any independent operation against the Government and in favor of freedom for the people. Both when in India and when taken on campaigns abroad, it is kept strictly under British officers. There are plenty of of Indians who would make as good officers as the British. Indians are not inferior to the Japanese, and it is universally recognized that Japanese military officers are equal to those of any European nation; Indian officers would be equally efficient if they were allowed like the Japanese to receive training as officers, and to hold high and independent commands. But this the British will not allow. Indians are not permitted any training or any experience that will make them independent of the British or enable them to command or lead or think or plan for themselves, and thus endanger the supremacy of their British masters. And not only is the Indian army kept strictly under British (or other European) officers, but certain parts of the military service are reserved solely for the British Indians not being permitted to enter them. Thus only British men (or other Europeans) are allowed in artillery regiments. With the exception of a few light mountain batteries drawn by mules, all artillery is kept strictly in the hands of the British; The same is true of the air service, the tank service and others. Furthermore, whether in India or serving abroad, Indian troops are not trusted by themselves not only must they be commanded by British officers, but they must have British troops in close contact with them all the while, so that in case of any sign of disloyalty or revolt British rifles and British cannon can be turned on them, and British airplanes can drop bombs on them from the air.

Thus everything possible is done to keep India in a military sense weak, untrained, unable to stand on her own feet, wholly dependent upon British masters.

In case an Indian government were set up

in place of that which now rules, the present Indian army if it were officered by trained and competent Indians as it ought to be, as the British ought to have caused it to be, would be abundantly competent to protect the country against any danger that threatens, or is likely to threaten, from Afghanistan, Nepal or any other source.

Another thing of great importance should not be overlooked. The present Indian army is only a very small part of India's possible military strength. Beyond this she has a further resource of tens of millions of men, as good fighters when trained as there are in the world, who, under an Indian government, would be available as soldiers if there were need. But under British rule all these men are kept untrained; India is kept without military officers of her own; the whole nation is deprived of arms; even the soldiers who are taken away to fight, as in Europe and Mesopotamia and Palestine in the Great War, on returning home and receiving their discharge, are disarmed. Such fear has Britain constantly that India will revolt and strike for freedom. The weaker she can keep the Indian people in a military way, the easier it is to hold them down.

Of course, if the British should leave India, and if, in connection with leaving, they should *commit the crime* of *refusing to set up an Indian government* or *allowing the Indian people to set up one*, to fill the place and take over the functions of its British predecessor, thus leaving the country *without a government*, and at the same time *without military protection*, if the British should do that, then, doubtless, as already said, there would be more or less confusion and anarchy *until the country could recover from the result of the shameful conduct of the British.*

Here we have India's only danger; and, as

we have seen, it is one wholly of Britain's creation.

What the British ought to have been doing throughout all these long years past, was, *making India strong,* both *civilly* and *militarily, instead of deliberately keeping her weak.* They ought to have put competent Indians freely into all government positions, from lowest to highest,—certainly there should have been as many Indians in these places as Britons. There should have been at least as many Indian as British officers in the army, the highest military commands should not have been withheld from trained and competent Indians. The Military Member of the Viceroy's Executive Council should often, at least half the time, have been a trained and experienced Indian.

What the British Indian Government should now do, is to *remedy* these shameful delinquencies (these persistent wrongs) of the past, as soon as possible.

As the best Indians and some Englishmen are urging, only a short time is necessary for the present British masters of India to arrange for elections everywhere, and thus aid the peeple to set up a carefully planned and competent government. It is believed by many men of weightiest judgment that all could be accomplished in a single year's time. But if not in one year, then in two, or five ; what India wants is not haste, at least not unwise haste, but *certainty*, something which she can depend on, and an end to promises of pots of gold at the foot of a rainbow.

Since India has been and still is, so shamefully deprived of trained and experienced military officers of her own, and also of higher police officers, doubtless, on obtaining self-government she would desire to engage a considerable number of British military and police officers for a time as trainers of her own men and to fill important positions of military and police command until Indians were ready. Probably, too, some would be retained permanently, but of course under India's control, as Canada's army is under Canada's control, and as Australia's and South Africa's are under control of these Dominions.

With such careful provision made for setting up a proper Indian government to take the place of the retiring British one, and with such adequate military and police arrangements made for protection in case of possible immediate need, as already has been said there should be no more disorder or confusion or danger connected with the turning over of the control of India to the Indian people, than in turning over of the control of England to a new political party after an election. For the people of India are not less law-abiding and peaceful than the people of England.

India, once on her own feet, and free to organize and equip and officer and train an army of her own, as large as necessary, would have no more reason to fear Afghanistan or Nepal or her own so-called "wild tribes" than the United States has to fear attacks from our red Indian tribes or from Cuba or Nicaragua.

Supplement

Englishmen manifest great concern over what they imagine is the danger of blood-shedding and blood-running in *India*. Would it not be well if they directed their first attention to a region nearer home, namely, *Europe*? India has never known such vast holocausts of blood and slaughter as "civilized" and "Christian Europe has experienced again and again and again.

Europe boasts of its superiority over India in

civilization, and especially in science. But to what use does it put its civilization and particularly its science? We are told on what seems to be the best of authority that the scientists of Europe (and alas! of America too) are actually devoting more of their time, money and effort to creating inventions and instrumentalities for killing people than to any other single object. Who invented all the immensely effective and fast-growing enginry of modern war—to make ever more and more vast and pitiless the wholesale slaughter of human beings,—improved rifles and revolvers; murderous machine guns; cannon to shoot twenty miles and more; deadly dynamite and still more deadly T. N. T.; horrible bombs; armored war tanks; battleships which are monsters of destructions and death almost beyond imagination; submarines which turn the oceans into hells; poison gas and germs of the most horrible diseases, to be let fall from aeroplanes and thus destroy whole cities—men, women and children, every living thing; I say, who invented these fiendish agencies for wholesale human slaughter? Was it the people of India? No! Every one has been the creation of so-called civilized and Christian Europe (or America).

With so large a proportion of Europe's science, brain power and money devoted to the production of machinery for murder on the largest possible scale, is it any wonder that she has wars the most numerous and terrible in the world? The truth seems to be that Europe has vastly more need of foreign control to prevent blood-running than has India.

Englishmen liken the people of India to wild beasts of a zoo. If there is a land on earth where nations and peoples have over and over, and for long periods of time, acted like wild animals of the zoo or the jungle—springing at one another's throats and devouring one another, that land is not India, it is Europe. Then why should any European nation seek to control India for purposes of civilization and peace? If only for a century or two India could control the nations of Europe, then perhaps at last they might learn what peace and real civilization mean.

CHAPTER XXII

THE KIND OF MILITARY PROTECTION BRITAIN GIVES TO INDIA

PART I

Great Britain makes constant and strenuous claim that she is in India for its military protection. The Indian people, she declares, cannot protect themselves, and so she generously and unselfishly renders them this great service. When they complain, as they constantly do, of the enormous proportion of the country's revenues spent by their foreign rulers for military purposes, the reply is made: "You should not complain; all this expenditure is for your good; and it is far less than your own expenditure would have to be, if we were not here and you had to protect yourselves. We maintain our army in India solely to guard you, to prevent you from being attacked, invaded, subjugated by a foreign power. Even our mighty British navy, for which you have no expense, we use to guard you from danger. This is a matter of pure generosity on our part, for which you should be profoundly grateful. You are in the highest degree fortunate thus to have the powerful protection of the great British Empire."

What reply is to be made to this claim of Great Britain?

The reply which the Indian people make is to deny that there is any truth whatever in it.

They declare that Britain, instead of being their protector, is a usurper that has deprived them of their dearest possessions on earth, namely, their country and their freedom; that she refuses to give these back; and therefore, that the foreign nation which, far more than any other, they need to be protected from, is Britain herself.

India puts her case essentially like this: "Britain, a far-away power, having no just claim on us and no right to be on our soil, has conquered us, is holding us in subjection against our will, and is exploiting our country. All that Britain's army and navy do for India is to make more firm her grip on us. That is to say, Britain has taken possession of our country by conquest and duplicity; and by means of the army which she keeps here (which India has to pay for), and by the aid of the British navy, she (Britain) holds us down, and at the same time prevents any other power stealing from her her ill-gotten property—her big valuable Indian Empire. This is the sense, and the only sense, in which Britain gives India military and naval protection."

India says to us in America: "Our Indian situation is much what yours would be if Germany had conquered and was holding in subjection the United States, and was maintaining a big army there (at your expense), and was using her navy, to prevent you from revolting and throwing off her rule, and to prevent any other nation—say England or France—from taking you away from her. Would you regard Germany as your protector? Would you have reason to be very grateful to Germany for using her army and navy to make secure her possession of her stolen American empire?"

Really to protect a country is to protect its freedom: is to protect its people, its rightful owners, from having their country taken from them by foreigners, or from being ruled and exploited and despoiled by foreigners. Britain does nothing of this kind for India; but the exact opposite. Instead of protecting India against foreign conquerors, foreign domination, foreign exploitation and foreign tyranny and injustice, Britain uses her military and naval power to rivet all these upon India.

If somebody takes my house from me by force or other unrighteous means, I do not care much to have him protect himself against having the house stolen from him by some other person. That does not benefit me. What I want is the return of the house to me, its rightful owner. That is protecting me in my rights; nothing else is. In like manner, really to protect the Indian people is to give them back their country, of which they have been deprived. Nothing else can ever be.

I repeat: what Britain maintains her army in India for, and what she uses her navy for, is not at all to protect the Indians in their right to liberty and justice, but to protect *herself* from what she regards as two possible dangers to herself in India, namely (1), that of the Indian people rising, shaking off their foreign yoke (the British yoke), and recovering possession of their own country; and (2) the danger that some other nation may drive her out of India and thus steal from her the country (the rich possession) which she has taken from the Indian people.

Thus we see that the only protection the British give India in return for the crushing military burden that she is compelled to bear is the infinite injustice and wrong of subjection, bondage, exploitation, loss of freedom, deprivation of the place which she has a right to occupy among the great nations of mankind.

And now as to the cost of all this to India.

As already has been said, Great Britain claims not only that she protects India but that she does it at a far less expense to the Indian people than they would have to bear if they protected themselves. They have to pay nothing for the service of the great British navy; and the cost of the Indian army, great as it is under British rule, is less than an army of their own would cost if they were independent. This is the claim. Is the claim true? India answers, no, it is not.

The Indian people have studied the matter carefully, and there seems to be clear evidence that their military budget now under British rule is considerably larger than it would need to be under independence; in other words, that they are now paying considerably more for British "no-protection-at-all" than it would cost to maintain an army and a navy of their own which would give them real protection.

Where do they get their evidence? A substantial part of it from Japan.

Japan is more dangerously situated than India. It has more threatening enemies than has India. Russia, which Britain has always regarded as India's only peril, is far nearer to Japan than to India; indeed, Russia's Asiatic possessions extend to Japan's very door, while, on the other hand, she is separated from India by hundreds of miles of space, by lofty and difficult mountain ranges and by buffer States. Yet Japan's army and navy, which afford her ample security, and by means of which she actually fought a victorious war against Russia, entail upon her a *military and naval expenditure considerably less than that borne to-day by India.*

Let us see exactly what are the figures—the figures which nobody can deny.

According to the Statesman's Year Book for 1926 (and there is no higher authority), Japan's total estimated expenditure for her army and navy for the year ending March 31, 1926, was $146, 612, 270. By the same authority the total estimated military expenditure of India for the same period was $200,735,660. Thus we see that India has to pay actually over *$50,000,000 a year more* for military domination of foreign rulers, called" protection," (which is not protection at all but subjection), than it costs Japan really to protect herself with her own army and navy, and have freedom.

Nor is even this all. Notwithstanding India's much larger military expenditure, India has not a War College, or a Naval College, or an Army General, or Naval Commander, or a battleship, or an aeroplane, or a fort, or a regiment of soldiers, or a cannon, or a rifle, that she is allowed to call her own. In Japan there are all of these; and they belong not to foreigners but to the Japanese people, and are used wholly for their benefit.

In these facts and figures we see the ground for India's claim, not only that Britain's so called protection is a sham, but that under freedom she could provide for herself real protection at a considerably lower cost than she now pays for the sham.

PART II

The latest and crowning movement of Britain for the "protection of India" is that of creating a "Royal Indian Navy." The plan for building such a navy has caused much discussion in Parliament and elsewhere and some opposition, but it seems to have been finally decided affirmatively.

To the world looking on, and also to some of

of the Indian people, it has seemed at first sight as if now India will have something of a military kind which will be really her own, which she herself will be permitted to control, and which will really protect her. But—this illusion has been dispelled. It has turned out that the plan is one formed not at all for India's benefit, but wholly for Britain's. Its real object has proved to be to increase the *British* navy, under the name of India and at the expense of India.

To be specific ; it has three objects in view, as was made clear in the debate on the subject in the British House of Commons, April 5, 1927. In that debate three Amendments to the Bill creating the Navy were moved, all of them aiming to give India some real ownership and some real control. But all were defeated by heavy majorities of more than two to one. The Ammendments proposed were to the following effect.

1. That the Indian Navy, paid for by India, should be used only for the defense of India, in Indian waters, and not for the defense of the Empire, in distant waters.

2. That if sent to distant waters, in defense of the Empire, the cost of the same should be borne by the Empire and not by India.

3. That it should not be sent to a distance, in the service of the Empire, without the consent of both Houses of the Indian Legislature.

But as already stated, these amendments were defeated by large majorities.

It was definitely decided by the British House of Commons :

1. That the so-called Indian Navy, notwithstanding the fact of its being built wholly by Indian money, is to be really a part of the Imperial Navy, to be used anywhere and for any imperial purposes that the British Admiralty may order.

2. That the cost of using it outside of Indian waters and for general imperial purposes may at any time be placed on India, if Parliament shall so order.

3. That the Indian Legislatures (that is, the Indian people) shall have no control over it whatever.

Thus the so-called Indian Navy is placed upon exactly the same footing as the Indian Army. While paid for wholly by India, it is to be King George's "My Indian Navy," and a constituent part of his "My Indian Empire"—that is, it is to be owned wholly by Britain, controlled wholly by Britain and used wholly for Britain's ends. *

What about "protecting" the Indian people? As for *really* protecting them (from the tyranny,

---

* In this connection attention ought to be called to a question which is being asked in not a few quarters. The question is, whether, in creating this Royal Indian Navy, as an auxiliary to and really part of her British Navy, Great Britain does not violate her promise made in connection with the Washington Conference for the Limitation of Armaments. At that Conference, she in connection with several other nations, engaged to limit her naval construction in a certain specified degree. Technically she seems to have kept her promise: that is, she appears to have limited her *home* naval construction exactly as agreed. But what about this naval construction of hers *in India*? Does she not here really *break her promise*? It is noticeable that in the debate in Parliament this question came to the fore, members seriously urging that the creation in India of a "new Navy of capital ships, submarines, cruisers, and the rest," to be used anywhere and in any manner the British Admiralty may direct, even including being ordered to China to suppress her struggle for freedom, is a *clear violation of Great Britain's duty and pledge* to assist in promoting naval disarmament in the world.

The matter is one which is troubling not a few minds outside of Great Britain. Evidently British statesmen will make a mistake if they treat it lightly.

domination and exploitation of a foreign government, which is the only protection they need), the new Navy is to have no such function at all. Its sole purpose is to be that of *protecting Britain* from the danger of *losing India* either by rebellion or through attack and invasion by some other nation.

What about the *cost* to India? We have found that before the building of the New Navy, the amount which India has paid for her so-called protection (military and naval) has been $200,735,660 a year, some fifty million dollars a year in excess of what, if free and independent, she would have had to pay for real protection like that of Japan. Now let us add to that great sum the heavy cost of building this new navy and the further heavy cost of its perpetual up-keep. Then we shall be able to get some idea of what the impoverished Indian people will be required to pay when Britain's scheme of an "Indian Navy" shall have been put in operation.

Will be required to pay *for what purpose?* As we have seen, not for *protection* at all, but for the support of a military and naval system the object of which is to *rivet more firmly India's chains.*

CHAPTER XXIII

COULD INDIA, FREE, PROTECT HERSELF?

Does any one question whether India, if free, would have sufficient men, sufficient fighting ability, and sufficient material resources to enable her to protect herself against external aggression? Let us see what are the facts.

1. First as to physical location and surroundings. There is probably not a country in the entire world better situated for natural security, for natural safety from attack, invasion or aggression by other nations, than India. It is a vast peninsula which nature has thrust, all by itself, far down into the Indian Ocean. On its northeast, north and northwest, that is, on practically the entire land border, it is surrounded and to a most extraordinary degree protected, by vast ranges of mountains the loftiest and most difficult of passage in the world. The rest of its boundary is ocean, with no country within thousands of miles from which there is probably the slightest danger of attack.

2. As to men.

India has a population of 320,000,000 from which, to draw soldiers in time of need. This is twice the number of Russia, five times that of Germany or Japan, more than six times that of France or Great Britain.

In 1918, an estimate of India's available military man-power, that is, the number of her men between the ages of twenty and forty was made. It was found to be over 40,000,000. Here is a source of supply for soldiers greater than exists in any other nation in the world except China.

3. What about the fighting quality of these men ?

It is true that the Indian people as a whole are more peacefully inclined than Europeans. But all history shows that peaceful nations often produce the bravest and most effective armies known, when there is need to defend their liberties and their country. Such armies fight from duty, from principle, from true patriotism, their courage is moral, not merely physical ; and they come nearer than any other soldiers to being invincible.

But as a fact, fully one hundred million of India's population consists of what is known as her "fighting races,"—her Sikhs, Rajputs, Pathans, Mahrattas, and others.

As for the qualities of Indian soldiers, notice some testimonies of British authorities.

The English historians, Kay and Malleson, in their "History of the Indian Mutiny," tell us of the bravery and great efficiency of the Indian soldiers in the armies of the East India Company (fighting mainly under Indian officers too, not under British commanders)—"how they fought in the attack on Madura, how they fought in the defense of Arcot, how they crossed bayonets, foot to foot, with the best French troops at Gudalur."* Large bodies of troops, sometimes composed partly of Indians and partly of Europeans and sometimes of Indians alone, were sent out on hazardous enterprises under Indian commanders, with the result that they achieved successes quite equal to those of troops under British commanders.

---

* Quoted by Major Basu, in his "Consolidation of the Christian Power in India, "p. 71.

But we do not need to go back to the early days of the British in India to find evidences of the bravery and efficiency of Indian soldiers. There are abundant proofs of the same right up to the present.

No Englishman of the last generation knew India better than did Lord Curzon, for five years its Governor General and Viceroy. In an article in the *North American Review* of July, 1914, speaking of the native army of India which at that time contained in the neighborhood of 150,000 men, Lord Curzon called it "one of the finest fighting forces in the world."

Sir Valentine Chirol, in his last book on India declares that

> The Indian army has a fine record for gallantry, and is a great fighting engine.*

He tells us of a remark once made by the German Kaiser, that the Sikhs of India were the only foreign troops against whom he feared to pit his own German infantry.

General Allenby, whose conquest of Palestine was achieved largely by the use of Indian troops, reported in the highest terms of their bravery and efficiency, declaring that in every quality required to constitute good soldiers they had no superiors.

Says General Sir Ian Hamilton :

> There is material in the north of India sufficient and fit, under good leadership, to shake the artificial society of Europe to its foundation ; and diffusion of knowledge will produce leaders.†

As is well known to every one at all perfectly acquainted with the history of the Great War in Europe, it was the splendid Indian army,

* "India," p. 277.

† Speaking of Indian soldiers and British soldiers in the same campaigns, General Hamilton declares that in nearly every kind of fighting and service the Indian

brought over with the greatest possible haste to France when war was declared, that turned the tide at the first battle of the Marne, beating back the German advance and saving Paris from capture.

India free could easily meet an invading army with a fighting force of five millions, or, if necessary, ten millions, of such soldiers as these, should any nation on earth be insane enough to attempt an invasion.

Does any one say that India could not protect herself without a strong navy ? There is no ground for such a declaration. The experience of the British at Gallipoli, even if there were no other evidence, proved once for all that a navy, with such forces as it can carry, is powerless against strong land fortifications and an adequate land army. But even if India should find herself requiring a navy, we have found in another chapter that she can provide herself with one as strong as that of Japan, which ranks third in the world, at an expense no greater than that of her present military budget. And as for the qualification of her men for sea service, it should not be forgotten that before the British came India was one of the greatest sea-faring and ship-building nations in the world. Why under freedom should she not become the same again ?

Is it claimed that, whereas Indians fight well under British or other European officers, they would fail under officers of their own ? That while they make good soldiers in the ranks,

---

troops are actually superior to the British : and he confesses that the British officers among themselves recognize this, but they try to keep it "secret" only "whispering it with bated breath." "A Staff Officer's Scrap Book During the Russo-Japanese War." Vol. I, pp. 7, 8.

they have not the intellectual ability to make competent military leaders?

This is what the British claim. Is the claim well founded? No. It is refuted by the testimony already quoted from Kay and Malleson. Moreover, there is further overwhelming evidence to the same effect coming from many sources. More than once in the conquest of India, British armies were beaten by Indians under their own commanders. In the Mutiny of 1857-58, it was the same. Indeed, the probability is strong that in that bloody struggle the British would have been defeated and compelled to leave the country except for the aid received from the brave Sikhs of the Punjab. In all the long centuries of her past history, India has seldom lacked competent leaders, military as well as civil. As pointed out in another chapter, it was an Indian army under Indian generals that checked the conquering career of Alexander the Great. The Indian Emperor, Asoka, whom H. G. Wells declares to have been one of the six greatest men of all time, was not only a great statesman and civil ruler, but also a great military commander. A great general as well as a great emperor and statesman was Samudragupta, in the fourth century A. D. Vincent Smith calls him the Indian Napoleon. Baber, the founder of the Mogul Empire, ranks among the great military generals of the world. The Emperor Akbar the Great, the contemporary of Elizabeth of England, the equal of any civil ruler that Europe ever produced, was a general of extraordinary ability. Europe has produced few, if any, commanders of armies of greater genius than Sivaji, the hero of Mahratta history. Many of the Rajput military leaders in the Age of the Rajput Ascendancy (800 to 1200 A. D.) and several of the leaders of the Sikhs during their striking career (1469 to 1846 A. D.), were men of military genius seldom equalled in any country.

The British in all their later history in India have kept their Indian troops strictly under European officers, seldom, if ever, allowing any Indian to rise to a position as high even as second lieutenant. But this has not been because of lack of Indian military ability : it has been solely a matter of caution ; it has been because the British have feared to allow Indians to receive training or experience in military leadership or command lest they use the same in creating movements of revolt against the foreign government of their country.*

Other Asiatic countries—Japan, China, Persia, Turkey—possess able military leaders. Japan in her war with Russia produced generals in her armies and admirals in her navy quite the equals of those of her European antagonist. The Indian people are not inferior in ability or genius to the peoples of any of these countries. There is every reason to believe that if she were free, and if there were need, India could and would produce military and naval leaders and commanders equal to those of any nation.

4. Finally, has India material resources with which to carry on successfully a war of defense:

---

* The Indian troops that fought in the World War came partly (the larger number) from British India and partly from the Native States. Those from the Native States were commanded by Indian officers, who showed no lack of efficiency as compared with the British. Those from British India were commanded by European officers ; but when these were killed or disabled, the Indian officers took command, and so far as reported, with complete success. There seems to be no evidence from any source that Indians are any less able than the British to fill high commands (even the highest) if allowed to have proper training and experience.

coal, iron, timber, water power (electrical power), oil, and others? It is well known that to-day these are as important as men. Is not India wanting here? No, she is not. She has all these in abundance, probably beyond any nation of Europe except Russia. Indeed there are not more than three or four nations in the world that possess these indispensable requisites for war in such quantities as does India. Japan has shown herself able to defend herself both by land and sea, and yet her material resources, of all the kinds named, are scarcely more than infinitesimal compared with the vast resources of India.

From all these facts it will be seen how utterly without foundation is the claim that India needs the so-called "protection" of any foreign power; or that, if once master in her own house she would not be able to make herself as secure from outward molestation as any nation in the world.

The condition of things in India as regards the ability of the Indian people to protect themselves from foreign aggression, seems to be exactly this: The British say to them: "However it may have been in the past, to-day you have no military strength. Deprived of our help you could not possibly defend yourselves against foreign invaders. For your own sake therefore we must stay in India. How terrible it would be if we should leave and some nation should attack you, conquer you and hold you in bondage!"

What is India's reply? It is this: "Are we not in bondage! now? What is your so-called protection but bondage? Even if another nation should conquer us, would it be any worse to be in bondage to them than to you? Why do you mock us? What we want is, to be free from all bondage, yours as well as that of any other power.

And believe us, once free from you, we would never be in bondage again; for then we could have, and would have, an army of our own command, trained, efficient, equal to any need, able to protect us against any possible aggressor."

Mr. Srinivasa Iyengar, of Madras, in his Presidential Address before the Indian National Congress of 1926, declared (I condense):

> There is absolutely no truth in the idea that India, if free, cannot defend herself by the creation and maintenance of not only an adequate army, but, in case of need, an adequate navy as well. Indians—both Hindus and Mohammedans—organized and led armies with singnal success in the past, before the British came on the scene and deprived them of all opportunities of military leadership and command. There was always plenty of martial spirit among them. Not only were they adventurous on land, but they were also an adventurous sea-faring race, with far-flung colonies and navies to protect them. India, if and when she is free, can and will create and maintain both an army and a navy on modern lines. Japan has done so. India can do the same. It is simply a question of finance and of training. Give her freedom and what other nations have done and are doing she can and will do.

Few living persons know India so well as Mrs. Annie Besant who has resided there for more than thirty years. Says that eminent Englishwoman.

> If to-day India is helpless in a military way, or unable to defend herself, it is because Britain has made her so. How dares Lord Birkenhead to mock her helplessness, when it is the British government that bars her way to self-defense? Give to Indians the same military training that is given to the British—give them the same training not only in the infantry but in the artillery and the air service, and give them trained Indian officers, of all grades from lowest to highest, and India can defend herself as perfectly as any nation on earth. British generals themselves confess that there are no braver or more efficient soldiers in existence than those of India.*

* *The Hindu* Madras, December 8, 1927.

Sooner or later India will be free, either with the freedom of equal partnership with Great Britain like the freedom of Canada and South Africa, or with the freedom of absolute independence, No future event is more certain than this. And the date of the attainment of this freedom cannot be long delayed without disaster to Britain as well as to India.

Although a free India will possess great military strength, no nation will have cause to fear her. Notwithstanding her vast population and her unexcelled potential military resources, she will not be a danger to any people, as so many nations are. On the contrary, cherishing ideals of peace and good-will, as she does, her freedom and her occupancy of an important place in the world will be a powerful influence in favor of world peace. The fact that her most influential leaders to-day are such peace lovers as Ghandhi and Tagore is a sufficient guarantee of this.

Many Indians. following Gandhi, believe that India, when free, will need nothing for her protection from aggression by other powers except her own peaceful spirit and her determination to deal with all nations justly, fairly without aggression on her part and without giving any ground for offense. And yet most of her leaders, Gandhi and Tagore among them, are strong believers in treaties of peace and arbitration; and there is every reason to believe that when she becomes master of her own career, she will, among her ealiest acts, seek to make her security doubly secure by negotiating with all the leading nations, treaties of complete arbitration like those proposed by Secretary Kellogg of the United States, pledging India on the one hand and those nations on the other to settle all their disputes and differences by reason and justice, and not by force, thus—making war between them impossible. Thus she will be relieved from that shameful and shocking necessity of being compelled to waste on a great army and navy the nation's revenues which are so sorely needed for education and the welfare of the people.

However, if India finds, much against her spirit and her earnest desire, that she must arm, that she can obtain safety in no other way, then the world may be perfectly certain that *arm she will, and to the full,*—making herself as formidable as Japan, and far more, because her supply of men and material resources are so much greater. *And she will be unconquerable.* Never again will the great Indian people allow themselves to be robbed of their freedom and their nationhood by any foreign power. The lesson they have learned in the last century and a half will last them a thousand years.

CHAPTER XXIV

ARE THE BRITISH (OR ANY OTHER FOREIGNERS) FIT TO RULE INDIA?

Can any nation in the world be ruled well and safely by transients—by persons from a distant country, who come with no intention of permanency, stay a little while, and then go? That is the way India is ruled.

Could England be ruled safely or well in that way? Could the United States? Could Japan? Could China? Then why does any intelligent person believe that India can be, or is?

I

The British who go to India to carry on the government never for a moment think of the country as home; it is merely their temporary tarrying place, their "inn," while they are "enduring their term of banishment" from England which they never cease to think of and to call "home." Edmund Burke described these British countrymen of his by the striking phrase, "birds of passage and of prey." The expression was so wholly true to the fact, that it has persisted. Let us see exactly what it means.

The British in India are no part of India; they do not settle down to make homes there; they do not belong there. They come as government officials or as traders; they make their 'piles' and return to their own country, where all who have been in government service continue all the rest of their lives to draw fat pensions from India. While in India, except small sums spent for house-rents, and for servants, for bread and milk and vegetables, and probably for some curios of the country, practically all the money they spend goes into the pockets, not of the people of India, but of Englishmen. Their hams and bacons, their jams, their pickles, their beefs and 'tinned' muttons, they import from England. The clothes of their wives, of their children and of themselves, their jewelry, and the furniture of their houses, come from their own country. Seldom do they patronize Indian merchants selling Indian goods, no matter how excellent the goods may be. Except fresh vegetables and bread and the most perishable articles, they purchase almost exclusively English or European things. India is called by most of them a 'land of exile,' and a 'land of regrets.' They are always counting the days that remain before their furloughs begin or their pensions become due. Thus from the day of their arrival in the land to the hour of their departure they are aliens and exotics. Even their children are essentially foreigners.

As for the child of the *Indian*, of course, *he* is not only born in India, but is brought up and educated in India, is identified with India from his earliest life, works and dies in India. On the contrary, the child of the *Englishman* in India goes to his father's far-off western home to be educated there, and to spend the most impressionable years of his life there ; then if he returns to India it is as to a foreign land. Thus the Englishman in India has little or nothing in common with the Indian people. As a rule, he does not share their aspirations or their fears, their hopes or their ambitions their joys or their sorrows.

He lives a life cut off from the real India; his heart is always turned toward England which he thinks of as home.

Such a state of mind as is here described is perfectly natural in men who feel themselves foreigners in a foreign land. We need not blame them for their feelings. But *are such foreigners, such transients, such "birds of passage and of prey," fit to rule India?*

The British in India have also been called another very appropriate name, and one that Americans can easily understand, "carpet-baggers." America has had not a little experience with "carpet-baggers." Some of our Western States learned to their sorrow what it was in early pioneer days to have speculative bankers from the East start business with no other property than they could carry in their carpet-bags, and abscond when they failed. But that was not the worst. After the Civil War, during the "reconstruction period," our Southern States learned to their still greater sorrow, what it meant to have Northern political adventurers ("Carpet-baggers") come South and by the help of the negro vote "steal" control of the government in large areas, even in whole states.

British rule in India has been called "carpet-bag rule" by Englishmen themselves. And with good reason, for exactly such it is; and it is actually of a much worse kind than that which prevailed for a few shameful years in our Southern States. Our American carpet-bag rulers were actually elected to office by a majority of the people over whom they ruled, even if many of the voters were ignorant negroes. But the British carpet-bag rulers in India are not chosen to their offices by any part of the people over whom they rule; they are distant foreigners placed in their offices by other foreigners ; they are not voted for by any Indian or even invited to come to the country by a single resident of the country ; they are pure transients, having no stake in the land except what they may be said to carry in their "carpet-bags."

All decent Americans soon became ashamed of the carpet-bag government in our Southern States, and as soon as the moral sentiment of the nation could be roused, they were swept away.

One of the anomalies of our age is, that many Americans who look back with humiliation to our own very brief carpet-bag government in the South, regard with complacency and even with approval, Britain's age-long government of the same kind in India, which has far less warrant in justice than had ours, which affects vastly larger populations, and which, while it brings prestige, power and wealth to the nation of the carpet-bag rulers, inflicts far greater injuries and wrongs upon the people ruled than our carpet-bag rule in the South ever inflicted.

II

In some respects the British are less fit to rule subject peoples than are some other nations. It is true that they have had large experience, and for this reason we think their qualifications for ruling are superior. But this is only partly true. Their large experience gives them a certain kind of valuable knowledge—knowledge of methods of administration and so forth. Thus as organizers, managers and manipulators of administrative machinery they excel.

But they possess certain mental qualities which are against them, and they lack certain qualities which they need. Their main lack is sympathy and imagination. The strong and conspicuous mental qualities which they possess, and which, while helping them in some ways, are on the whole hindrances to their real success as rulers, are their egotism, their arrogance, their over-bearing spirit and their narrowness of vision (their insularity). So far as these qualities mean self-reliance, strength of purpose and of will, power to decide, and to do promptly the things in hand, which to some extent is their meaning, they are good, and undoubtedly add to the efficiency of the British as administrators and rulers. But when, uncontrolled by sympathy, they are carried to the extreme which we see in so many Englishmen and Scotchmen in India and all the colonial possessions of Great Britain, and take the forms of haughty assumption of race and color superiority, of almost brutal discourtesy, and of willingness to trample on the feelings and rights of their assumed inferiors, then they are not good ; on the contrary, they are serious disqualifications for successful ruling, because they create dislike, distrust and antagonism, and a constant and growing desire on the part of the ruled to free themselves from the humiliation and injustice to which they are subjected. Of the various colonizing nations of the present time the British seem to have least sympathy with the peoples whom they govern, are least able to come into close touch with them, manifest most race and color pride and haughtiness, and therefore are probably least able to win their affection and really and deeply influence them.

The United States, although it has no more right to be in the Philippines than Britain has to be in India, yet is clearly doing much better work; probably because it carries to its work much more sympathy with the Filipino people, much more understanding and appreciation of the Filipino civilization, and much less color and race arrogance. The evidences of its superior work are many, perhaps the chief of which are, the very much greater amount of freedom and self-government that it willingly grants to the Filipino people, the very much larger extent to which it promotes popular education and public sanitation, and the incomparably lighter military burden (taxation for military purposes) that it puts on the country.

Perhaps no one has pointed out more clearly than Mr. Lowes Dickinson, of Oxford, what is undoubtedly the leading reason why the British are so little fit to rule India. Says Professor Dickinson: *

> Of all the Western nations the English are the least capable of appreciating the qualities of Indian civilization. of all the races they are the least assimilable. They carry to India all their own habits and ways of life; squatting, as it were, in armed camps; spending as in exile twenty or twenty-five years; and returning, sending out new men to take their place, equally imbued with English ideals and habits, equally unassimilable.

It is impossible for men to rule well any people when they do not understand, appreciate, or sympathize with, or any people whom they look down upon and despise.

We may not like the sarcasm of Emerson, but there is some truth in his words when he says:

> "The Englishman sticks to his traditions and usages, and so help him God, he will force his island by-laws down the throat of great countries like India, China and the rest."

Perhaps the psychology, the whole mental and spiritual make-up, of no two great nations in the world are farther apart than those of Great Britain and India. This means that their civilizations are

* "Essay on the Civilizations of India, China an Japan," pp. 18, 19. J. M. Dent & Sons, London.

fundamentally far apart. If the civilization of India were fundamentally a material one, primarily interested in getting on in the world, money-making, physical pleasure, sport of rather brutal kinds, war, and domination of other peoples, then it would be comparatively easy for the British to understand and appreciate it. But a civilization which makes money-getting, material gain and physical pleasure secondary, and which puts kindness, sympathy, things of the mind and spirit, and religion, first—such a civilization baffles the average British official in India, whether civil or military,—it is a world strange and unreal to him, and because he is unable to understand it, he takes for granted it is worthless, and despises it.

III

Said Abraham Lincoln:

"There never was a people good enough to govern another people."

Is Great Britain an exception? Does she manage her own home government so supremely well that she is entitled to undertake the political management of other nations? Then what mean her frequent upsetting of parties, and changes of ministries, and appeals to the electorate, with the hope of correcting past legislative and administrative mistakes and getting a wiser government? Are a people who at home thus "muddle along," groping their way blindly in political matters, and committing what they themselves confess are blunders on blunders, likely to become wise and skilled when they undertake to conduct the complicated political affairs of a distant foreign nation, about whose affairs and needs they are ten times more ignorant than they are about those of their own land?

If the men sent by England to India, to rule there, to fill the chief government positions, national and provincial, to make and administer the laws, and to do all those things which the rulers of a great country are required to do, were superior in intellectual ability and in character to the Indian leaders who are available for the same places and to do the same work, then there would be some excuse (or at least a greater approximation to an excuse) for British rule in India.

But while it is true that some of the Englishmen who go to India are excellent and able men, equal (but not superior) to the Indians with whom they are to be associated, it is also true that many of them are distinctly inferior. Largely they are the sons of well-to-do fathers who want "careers" for their boys, and who choose India because the service there is honorable and lucrative, and is made additionally attractive by its short duration, (twenty four years, four of which may be spent on leave of absence) followed by large pensions for the rest of life.

Generally, these prospective Indian officials come to India young, often very young, only just out of college, and enter at once upon the responsibilities of managing the affair of a great foreign nation of which they know almost absolutely nothing. They are saved from utter disaster only by the fact that under them are placed efficient Indians who help them in their ignorance and do what they can to prevent fatal blunders.

It is the commonest thing to see Indian scholars and officials of confessedly very high ability, of very fine training, of long experience, serving under these ignorant young Englishmen, who in England would not be thought fit to fill a government or a business position above the second or even third class.

The fact is (the world is not allowed to know it, but the people of India know it to their sorrow) the ignorance concerning India of the ordinary Englishman who comes there to manage the vast, intricate and immensely important affairs of the Indian nation, would be in the highest degree ludicrous if it were not shocking.

Englishmen themselves confess this. Sir Bamphylde Fuller, long a high official in India, declares in his book, "Studies of Indian Life and Sentiment :"

Young British officials go out to India most imperfectly equipped for their responsibilities. They learn no law worth the name, a little Indian history, no political economy, and gain a smattering of one Indian vernacular. In regard to other branches of service, matters are still more unsatisfactory. Young men who are to be police officers are sent out with no training whatever, though for the proper discharge of their duties an intimate acquaintance with Indian life and ideas is essential. They land in India in absolute ignorance of the language. So also with forest officers, medical officers, engineers, and (still more surprising) educational officers .-It is hardly too much to say that this is an insult to the intelligence of the country.

Says *The Pioneer*, of Allahabad, which is perhaps the leading British organ in Northern India, and which therefore can be trusted not to put the case against the British too strongly :

It may be affirmed, without fear of contradiction, that there are less than a score of English civilians in these Provinces who could read unaided, with fair accuracy and rapidly, even a short article in a vernacular newspaper, or a short letter written in the vernacular ; and those who are in the habit of doing this, or could do it with any sense of ease or pleasure, could be counted on the fingers of one hand.

Such are the men who fi. the lucrative offices of India, and who rule the land because they are so much "better fitted" to do so than are the *educated Indians* !

Few Englishmen have given so much attention to Indian matters during the last fifty years as has Mr. H. M. Hyndman. Says this eminent publicist:

The British who came to India to rule it have been brought up and educated in accordance with methods as remote from, and as irreconcilable with, Asiatic ideas as it is possible for them to be. In their work and in their pleasure they keep as aloof as possible from the people they govern. The head of the government, who himself is brought out fresh from Europe and entirely ignorant of India, does not remain in office more than five years (thus leaving as soon as he begins to get a little knowledge). His subordinates return 'home' frequently for their holidays, and go back to England permanently, to live on a considerable pension paid by India, after their term of service is completed. The longer this reign of well-meaning but unsympathetic carpet-baggers continues, the less intimate do their general relations with the Indian people become. The color and race prejudices which were only slight at the beginning of English dominance, now become stronger and stronger every year. In India itself, men of ancient lineage, beside which the descent of the oldest European aristocracy is a mushroom growth, are considered in the leading cities, as well as on the railways, unfit to associate on equal terms with the young white bureaucrats just arrived in the country.*

Mr. Hyndman quotes a prominent British official in India as saying:

It is sadly true that the Englishmen in India live totally estranged from the people. This estrangement is partly unavoidable, being the result of national customs, language and caste, but largely it is contempt, growing out of ignorance. This tendency to aloofness is increasing.

Speaking of the ignorance of India possessed by many of the government officials, Ramsay Macdonald says:

I have met men in the Indian Civil Service who

* "The Truth About India," Series 1, p. 10. New York.

had been there for a score of years. They knew few Indians, they had rarely discussed public affairs with them, they could not answer accurately some of the most elementary questions about Indian life, their opinions on current affairs were obviously the parrot repetitions of the club talk or newspaper statements. In fact, they were as separate from India as I am at home in London, and took their opinions of India in an even more second-hand way than I had taken mine before I ever set foot on Indian soil.*

He declares that it would be almost safe to say that the average intelligent American or other tourist at the end of three months knows as much about India as do a good half of the civil service officials who are carrying on the government of the country.

Mr. Macdonald, quotes Lord Curzon as saying that in former days the assumption of everybody who went to India to take part in the government was that he must learn what languages were necessary to enable him to speak with the people.

But the arrogance of these modern days assumes that that is quite unnecessary. The number of officers now who speak the vernaculars with any facility is much smaller than fifty or even twenty-five years ago, and the number devoting themselves to anything like a serious study of the literature of the country is diminishing year by year.†

In The Bookman of February, 1926, an Englishman (Mr. Aldous Huxley), gives the following description of the arrogance and egotism of his countrymen who are ruling India. He writes:

A young man goes out from a London suburb to take up a clerkship in the Indian Civil Service. He finds himself a number of a small rolling community; he has slavish servants to order about, dark-skinned subordinates to whom it is right and proper to be rude. Three hundred and twenty million Indians surround him; he feels

* "The Awakening of India," p. 261.
† "The Awakening of India," p. 236.

incomparably superior to them all, from the coolie to the Maharaja, from the untouchable to the thoroughbred Brahman, from the illiterate peasant to the holders of half a dozen degrees from European universities. He may be ill-bred, stupid, poorly educated; no matter. His skin is white. Superiority in India is a question of epidermis.

Mr. George Lansbury, Editor of the London *Daily Herald*, said in a speech in Essex Hall, December 11, 1920 :

There are more than three hundred million people in India; there are forty million of us English in the British Isles. We claim to know what is good for those people better than they do themselves. Was there ever impudence more colossal? Because our skin happens to be white we claim more brains than those whose skin has been browned by the sun. Whenever I look at Indians I feel ashamed of myself. How can I know more about India than they do?

The right Honorable Edwin S. Montague, Secretary of State for India, said in a speech in the House of Commons in July, 1917 :

The Government of India is too wooden, too iron, too inelastic, too antediluvian, to be of any use for modern purposes. The Indian government is indefensible.

Two years after these words were spoken, what is known as the "Government Reform Scheme" (Dyarchy) was given to India. It made many changes, a few of which were improvements; but others were of little significance, while others again were distinctly bad. On the whole, the people of India regarded it little, if any, better than that which was condemned so severely by Mr. Montague in 1917.

Sir Louis Mallet, when Under-Secretary of State for India, was reported as saying :

Nothing but the fact that the present system of government in India is almost secure from all independent and intelligent criticism, has enabled it so long to survive.

There are few English officials of any rank, no

matter how long they stay in India, who ever get a good knowledge of any Indian tongue. Even the Viceroys, as a rule, know no native language when they go to India, and seldom during their stay do they acquire anything more than the merest smattering of any. Such contact with the people as they have is mostly second-hand, through English subordinates or through Indians who speak English.

Said John Bright in a speech in Parliament:

> The Governor General of India (the Viceroy) goes out knowing little or nothing of India. I know exactly what he does when he is appointed. He shuts himself up to study the first volumes of Mr. Mill's "History of India," and reads through this laborious work without nearly so much effect in making him a good Governor General as a man might ignorantly suppose. He goes to India, a land of twenty nations, and he has not a glimmer of the grammer and pronunciation or meaning of these languages...He knows nothing of the country or the people. He is surrounded by an official circle, he breathes an official air, and everything is dim and dark beyond it. You lay duties upon him which are utterly beyond the mental and bodily strength of any man who ever existed, and which he therefore cannot perform... He has a power omnipotent to crush everything that is good. If he so wishes, he can overbear and over-rule whatever is proposed for the welfare of India, while as to doing anything that is good, I could show that with regard to the vast countries over which he rules, he is really almost powerless to effect anything that those countries require...I do not know at this moment, and never have known a man competent to govern India; and if any man says he is competent, he sets himself up as of much higher value than those who are acquainted with him are likely to set him.

This from John Bright, a man as careful in his speech and as just in his judgments as England ever knew.

When Mr. Edward Wood, now Lord Irwin, was appointed Viceroy of India in 1925, Colonel Josiah C. Wedgwood, M. P. wrote to Mr. Lajpat Rai, describing the new Viceroy thus:

"He will be very uncomfortable in India—an obvious martyr to duty. It is a grave drawback to him that he knows nothing whatever of India, and is therefore all the more helpless in the hands of the bureaucratic experts...I do not remember him ever even being present at an Indian debate."*

Think of a man who can be thus described by a distinguished member of Parliament, being appointed Viceroy, to govern the vast Indian nation.

Premier Asquith declared in 1909 that there are great numbers of Indians who are well-qualified to fill high official positions in India. He also called attention to the low and inadequate qualifications which are thought sufficient to fit Englishmen for those positions; and he affirmed that if high places were given to Indians half as unfit as are many Englishmen who occupy them, it would be regarded as a public scandal. †

Think of an Englishman wholly ignorant of Indian finance being appointed Finance Minister in the Viceroy's Council, the most difficult and responsible position in the land. I call no names.

Think of an unknown young man of twenty-five from England, appointed to the chair of Sanskrit in the Bombay University over Dr. Bhandarkar, one of the greatest Sanskrit scholars and investigators of the last fifty years, who had a European reputation.

Said the Honorable Mr. Gokhale in his budget speech of 1903 :

"It is difficult to describe the mischief that is done to the best interests of India and of British rule itself by the appointment of third and fourth rate Englishmen to chairs in government colleges. These men are unable to command the respect from their students which they

---

* Published in *The People*, Lahore, December 26, 1925.

† See *India* (The London Weekly), April 9, 1909, p. 209

think is due to their positions, and they make up for it by clothing themselves in race pride."

Mr. Ramananda Chatterjee, eminent both as an educator and as a publicist, after publishing a list of eminent Indian physicians and surgeons, connected with the government civil and military medical service and with medical colleges, some of whom have done important work in "original investigation," and all of whom "would do honor to the medical profession of any country," says:

"These eminent physicians and surgeons are compelled to spend the best years of their lives in subordinate positions as 'assistant' surgeons, while raw and callow English youths lord it over them and draw four to five times their pay."*

Mr. Chatterjee says still further:

"The rule of the government by which Indians, however competent, are practically excluded from the higher appointments in many departments of the Civil Service, is not only unjust and selfish, but is cowardly. It shows that Englishmen shrink from a fair competition with Indians. We challenge the sons of Great Britain to a fair competition. But our challenge is not taken up. The plain fact is, the British dare not take it up."

They know that if the higher positions were assigned to men according to their scholarship, their experience and their ability, there would be a complete revolution in many of the departments of the Indian public service.

---

* New Rules for the Indian Medical Service were issued by the Government in 1928, which, instead of remedying the old injustices, *reserved the majority of posts for Europeans*, threw the rest open, not to Indians alone but to Indians *and Europeans*, and *reserved none for Indians.*

CHAPTER XXV

BRITISH RULE IN INDIA COMPARED WITH THAT OF THE MOGUL EMPERORS

The impression seems to be widespread that India has seldom or never been independent,—that throughout its long history it has been generally, if not always, a subject land, ruled by foreign nations. It is common for Englishmen to justify British rule by declaring: "We are doing only what others have always done. If we were not in India, some other foreign power would be, which would not govern her as well as we do. Therefore, we feel wholly justified in continuing our domination." What is to be said in reply to this claim?

The reply to be made is that the claim is fiction. Instead of India always having been a subject nation ruled by a foreign power, never before in all her long history of 3,000 years is there any record of such an experience. The present British domination is the first rule of the kind that India has ever known.

To be sure, at different times, foreign raiders, as Tamerlane in the fourteenth century and Nadir Shah in the eighteenth, have swept with their armies across her borders, laying waste some of her villages and even cities, and carrying away much portable wealth. But always these sudden invasions, these raids, have affected only limited portions of India and have been of very short duration. The invaders have disappeared as quickly as they came. They never set up governments and became rulers of the land.

Probably the rule that these Englishmen have in mind is that of the Mogul Emperors who reigned over most of India during the centuries immediately preceding the coming of the British. But those Mogul Rulers were not foreign in any such sense at all as the British Rulers of India are. The first of their number, Baber, came from a foreign land; but he settled down in India and both he and all his successors made India their permanent home, identified themselves wholly with the interests of India and ruled the land as Indians, not as foreign sovereigns.

They were foreign only in the sense in which the sovereigns of England have been foreign since the time of William the Conqueror. William came from abroad, but he came to be an English, not a foreign, King, and all his successors have regarded England as their own country, and have reigned as English kings and queens.

The Mogul rulers of India were foreign only in the sense that all the Presidents of the United States have been foreign. All the Presidents have been descendants of men who came to America at some time from foreign lands. But they came to make America their home and to be Americans, and therefore their descendants are rightly thought of as American.

In exactly the same way the Mogul Emperors are rightly to be considered as Indian rulers, not as foreigners.

But the case of the present rule of Great Britain in India is wholly different. These British rulers are foreigners and transients and never become anything else. They are born thousands of miles from India ; they come to India for the distinct purpose of ruling the country as a foreign and subject land; as has been elsewhere pointed out, they never identify themselves with the people whom they rule; often they do not even learn to speak any Indian language, but are obliged to depend upon subordinates for communication with the people; they never call India home; as soon as their terms of office are over, they hasten back to England, the land where all their interests and hearts are.

It is as if a nation in a distant part of the world—say the Japanese—should come by a long sea-voyage to the United States, conquer this country, depose its own rulers, and thereafter, without the consent of the American people, govern the country arbitrarily, wholly by men sent from Japan, who never settle here and never identify themselves permanently with American interests, but are here as transients to exploit the country for Japan's benefit and return home to Japan as soon as their period of office expire. That is exactly the kind of rule which Great Britain maintains in India. Instead of being in line with previous Indian experience, it is something absolutely new in Indian history.

Furthermore, because the Mogul Emperors settled down in the country, became Indians and ruled as Indians, the Indian people felt all the while that they had a country, it was their as much as it ever had been; the Government itself was theirs, even when they did not like all its ways; they were still a great nation, and could hold up their heads as such among the leading nations of the world. Moreover, all the revenues of the land were spent at home. None were drained away to a foreign country. Thus the land was not impoverished.

But when the British conquered the country

and set up their rule, all was changed. These foreigners came to remain foreigners, and to rule as foreigners, not as Indians. They took possession of the land in the name of a foreign king and made it a part of *his domain.* Thus for the first time in their long history, the people of India had no country. Their great historic nation which had had such a long and distinguished career, had no longer a place among the nations ; it was no longer a nation at all, but only an "appendance" to a foreign nation, a land "owned" by a foreign power. This was such a humiliation as they had never experienced. And this is their condition to-day.

Nor is this all. Under the foreign rule of the British the land has been robbed of its wealth and impoverished as it never before was in all its history. Even the wealth stolen by the great raider, Nadir Shah, who with the rest of his plunder carried away the famous "Peacock Throne" of Delhi, was small compared with the vast amounts which have been drawn from India by the British during their rule,—first the enormous loot extorted by the East India Company under Clive and Warren Hastings, and then later the pitiless "drain" that has continued ever since, to pay the great salaries and pensions of India's foreign rulers, and to enable them to carry on their perpetual military aggressions and wars, for the benefit, not of India, but of the far-flung British Empire.

It is estimated that the amount of treasure wrung from the conquered Indian people and transferred to English banks between the Battle of Plassey and the Battle of Waterloo (fifty-seven years) was between £500,000,000 and £1,000,000,000 (between $2,500,000,000 and $5,000,000,000). *

* See "The Law of Civilization and Decay" by Brooks Adams, pp. 259-265 Swan, Sonnenschein & Co.

In the *Westminister Gazette* of London (April 24, 1900) the estimate is made that the later drain of wealth from India to Great Britain during the twenty-five years from 1875 to 1900 aggregated £500,000,000 ($2,500,000,000). And the drain goes right on and increases.

In a private letter received by the present writer from Mr. Dadabhai Naoroji, dated London, November 27, 1905, that eminent Indian leader (who for some years represented London in the British House of Commons), says :

"The lot of India is a very, very sad one. Her condition is that of master and slave ; but it is worse : it is that of a *plundered nation in the hands of constant plunderers* with the *plunder carried away clean out of the* land. In the case of the plundering raids occassionally made into India before the British came, the invaders went away, and there were long intervals of security during which the land could recuperate and become again rich and prosperous. But nothing of the kind is true now. The British invasion is continuous, and the plunder (under legal forms but not less terrible) goes right on, with no intermission, and actually increases and the impoverished Indian nation has no opportunity whatever to recuperate."

CHAPTER XXVI

IS BRITISH RULE IN INDIA "EFFICIENT"?

The British are accustomed to bestow high praise upon their government in India and to urge its continuance on the ground of its great efficiency.

Is the British government of India efficient? If so, in what ways and for what ends? The Indian people contend that it is efficient *only* in serving *British interests*, only in carrying on the affairs of India *for Britain's benefit*, and that it is *not* efficient, but woefully *inefficient*, in promoting the *Interests of India*.

Said the Honorable G. K. Gokhale:

"The efficiency attained by a foreign bureaucracy, uncontrolled by public opinion, whose members, again, reside only temporarily in the land in which they exercise official power, is bound to be of a strictly limited character, and it can never compare with that higher and truer efficiency which is possible only under a well-regulated system of self-government. The present form of administration in India is a strongly centralized bureaucracy in which the men at the center (the higher officials—the Governor-General, the Governors of Provinces, and others holding the supreme power) retain office for only five years. They then leave the country, carrying away with them all the knowledge and experience of administrative matters acquired at the expense of the country, and their places are taken by new men, who, in their turn, retire similarly after five years. As things are, there is no one ever in the government who is permanently interested in the country as only its own people can be interested. One result is that the *true well-being of the people is systematica y subordinated to militarism*, and to the service and the interests of the *English merchantile classes.*"*

---

* "Gokhale's Speeches," Appendix, pp. 146-7. Natesan and Co., Madras, India.

In his recent book, "Modern India: Its Problems and Their Solution" (p. 161), Dr. V. H. Rutherford M. P., examines the character and results of British efficiency, and pronounces it "one of the *chief causes of India's poverty.*" He declares that the British government in India is efficient *only* on behalf of *British* interests, only in carrying on the government and managing the affairs of the country for the *benefit of Great Britain.* As regards promoting the *welfare of India and the Indian people,* he declares it to be strikingly and shamefully *inefficient*; in proof of which he cites the government's

"*Neglect of education of masses; neglect of sanitation and medical services in the villages; neglect to keep order: neglect of housing of the poor; neglect to protect the peasants from the money-lenders; neglect to provide agricultural banks; comparative neglect to improve and develop agriculture; neglect to foster Indian industries; neglect to prevent British profiteers from capturing the tramways, electric lighting and other public services and neglect to prevent the manipulation of Indian currency in the interests of London.*"

Says the *Modern Review*, of Calcutta:

"It is not the desire of any Indians that the government of their country should be inefficient. On the contrary, we all want it to be more efficient than it is in British hands. We believe we can make it so. What are the tests of efficiency in government? The *tests are* that the *people should be educated and enlightened*; that they should be *well-fed, well-housed, well-clothed,* and *physically healthy and strong*; and lastly, that they should be *courageous and free* and *able to manage their own affairs.* Judged by these standards, is the British Government in India efficient? *No.* After more than a century and a half of British supremacy the country remains *woefully ignorant, industrially, backward, poor, insanitary, subject to epidemics,* and *subject to the rule of force and terrorism.* Do these things show *efficiency?*

In the light of these facts can we wonder at the words of Dr. Rutherford?

"British Rule as it is carried on in Inida is the *lowest and most immoral system of government in the world*—the *exploitation of one nation by another*." (Modern India, p. 77).

Says George Bernard Shaw:

"No Nation is fit to rule another."

Says Ramsay Macdonald:

"No race or nation can govern another justly."

Wrote Macaulay:

"Of all forms of tyranny I believe the worst is that of a nation over a nation.........The heaviest of all yokes is the yoke of the stranger."

The English poet, William Cowper, wrote the following lines as descriptive of British rule in India. Addressing his own country, England, he says:

"Hast thou, though suckled at fair Freedom's breast,
Exported slavery to the conquered East?
Pulled down the tyrants India served with dread,
And raised thyself a greater in their stead?
Gone thither, armed and hungry; returned full,
Fed from the richest veins of the Mogul,
A despot big with power obtained by wealth,
And that obtained by rapine and by stealth?
With Asiatic vices stored thy mind,
But left their virtues and thine own behind?
And having sold thy soul, brought home the fee,
To tempt the poor to sell himself to thee?"

Mr. Edward Thompson in his book, "The Other Side of the Medal," says (p. 118.):

"We (British) would repudiate the suggestion that our Indian Empire is a rule of masters over slaves. Yet *we judge as slave-drivers would, and we assess the virtues of our (Indian) fellow citizen as a hunter assesses the virtues of dogs*."

Some years ago, at the time of the Congo atrocities, an Irish author wrote:

"The English people love liberty for themselves. They hate all acts of injustice, except those which they themselves commit. They are such liberty-loving people, that they interfere in the Congo and cry, 'Shame'! to the Belgians. But they forget that *their heels are on the neck of India.*"

In his book, "Secret History of the English Occupation of Egypt." (p. 47), Mr. Wilfrid Scawen Blunt gives some strong and important testimony regarding British rule in India as seen close at hand and under the most favorable light. He was an intimate personal friend of Lord Lytton, who at that time was the Viceroy of India. Mr. Blunt went to India to make a study of the condition of things there. He belonged to the conservative party in British politics, and expected to find the British conduct of affairs in India worthy of the warmest approval. Moreover, he was taken charge of by the Viceroy and the highest officials, and was shown everything from their standpoint. What was the result? In spite of his prejudices in favor of the British—his own countrymen—and in spite of the pains taken to insure that he should see India as fully as possible from the English side, he was soon disillusioned. He found that British rule in India, instead of being a blessing, was *working India's ruin*. Of the British Imperial system in general he writes :

"It is one of the evils of the English Imperial system that it cannot meddle anywhere among free peoples, even with quite innocent intentions, without in the end doing evil. There are too many selfish interests always at work not to turn the best beginnings into ill endings." Of India he writes : "I am disappointed with India, which seems just as ill governed as the rest of Asia, only with good intentions instead of bad ones or none at all. There is just the same heavy taxation, government by foreign officials, and waste of money, that one sees in Turkey. The result is the same, and I don't see much difference between making the starving Hindoos pay for a cathedral at Calcutta and taxing Bulgarians for a palace on the Bosphorus...In India the "natives," as they call them, are a race of slaves, frightened, unhappy, terribly thin. Though myself a good Conservative and a member of the London Carleton Club, I own to being shocked at the bondage in which they are held, and my faith in British institutions and the blessings of English rule has received a severe blow. I have been studying the mysteries of Indian finance under the 'best masters,' government secretaries, commissioners, and the rest, and have come to the conclusion that, if we go on *developing the country at the present rate*, the inhabitants will have, sooner or later, to *resort to cannibalism*, for *there will be nothing but each other left to eat*."

Rev. C. F. Andrews in his recent book, "India's Claim for Independence," says:

"We see in the Italy and Austria of last century a signal instance of the fallacy of imperialism—of foreign rule. The Austrian Empire, with its Italian appendage—with Italy held in subjection by force—was a monstrosity. It could produce only hate, ever deepening hate, between two nations which ought to have been friends. The British Empire to-day, with its Indian appendage—with India held in subjection by force—is also a monstrosity. It can *produce only bitterness, ever-increasing bitterness*, and *estrangement, between India and England, two peoples that ought to be friends*."

To conclude. There is not a myth on the earth more baseless or more cruel than the claim put forth to the world that England is ruling great distant India well, or that she can by any possibility rule it well, or without constant blunders and injustices of the most serious and tragic nature.

Englishmen argue that because conditions in India are hard to understand, and the work of governing the country is difficult, therefore, they must stay—they alone are equal to the task. What reasoning! *Because a task is difficult, therefore put it in the hands of strangers, of persons who know least about it!* Fine logic! Why does not England apply the same reasoning to her own affairs, and when the difficulties of her home government are great, import foreigners who have never been in England to take charge and manage things?

She does not, because she knows, as all the world knows, that the greater the difficulties of any government, the more necessary it is that those who carry it on shall be men who know most about it. These cannot be foreigners and strangers, ignorant of the land,—its present, its past, its customs, its very language. They must be men born and reared in the land, who understand its language, its institutions, its history, its traditions, its peoples, its ideals, its needs.

This is why England can rule herself better than France or Germany or China can rule her. This is why we in America can rule ourselves better than Japan or Russia or England can rule us. And *this is the reason why India can rule herself better than England or any other nation on earth can rule her.*

CHAPTER XXVII

ARE THE PEOPLE OF INDIA COMPETENT TO RULE THEMSELVES ?

Does any one doubt the right or ability of England, or France, or Russia, or Japan to govern itself ? Then why of India, whose civilization is far older than that of any of these nations ?

Who is it that presumes to say that the Indian people are not capable of self-government ? It is the Indian people themselves ? No. They declare the contrary. They say they have proved by more than three thousand years of history their ability to rule themselves. Is it any friendly neighboring people who have had long association and dealings with them, and who therefore can judge with intelligence and reasonable fairness ? Not at all. No neighboring nation, so far as is known, doubts their fitness for self-government. Is it an authoritative commission of intelligent, impartial and competent men selected from different disinterested nations, who have visited India, studied conditions there in all parts of the land, acquainted themselves thoroughly with the Indian people, their history, their civilization, their character, their ability, what they have done in the past and their needs to-day ? Oh no !

Who is it, then, that presumes to declare anything so improbable, so unreasonable, so contrary to the whole experience of mankind, as that a great historic, civilized nation, compared with which all the nations of Europe are parvenus, is incapable of self-rule, and needs to be governed by strangers coming from the other side of the world ? Let an Englishman answer the question.

Some years ago, the Revernd John Page Hopps, an eminent Unitarian clergyman of London, published an article in *The Modern Review*, of Calcutta, answering the inquiry in a way that nobody has ever been able to refute. Wrote Mr. Hopps :

"Who says the people of India are not fit for home rule ? We, Englishmen, who profit by ruling them : we, who do not want to surrender power ; who in our egotism think we are the best and ablest rulers in the world. But it is an old cry. It was raised against the middle class in our own England ; it was raised against the mechanics of our great towns ; it was raised against our country farmers ; it has been raised against our women and in every case it has been raised, not for reasons of justice, but by the people in possession of power who did not want to lose their power."*

The nation which declares the Indian people unfit to rule themselves is the one among all the nations of the world which is least capable of udging fairly and justly in the matter, because, as Mr. Hopps points out, it is a deeply interested party, It is the nation which, some two centuries ago, not by right, but by force of arms, and for selfish ends, conquered the Indian people, and ever since has been holding them in subjection, because thus she secured and continues to possess increased political power and prestige in the world, large commercial and industrial advantage, much financial profit, and high and lucrative official positions, with fat pensions, for her sons. It is this nation that tells the world that the Indian people are incapable of ruling themselves. But, pray, what else can she be expected to tell the world ? How else can she justify herself for staying in India ?

* *The Modern Review*, Calcutta, June 1907.

This testimony, then, of a deeply interested, and therefore, of course, a deeply prejudiced party is the evidence we have, and essentially *all* we have, that the Indian people are not capable of self-rule.

On the other hand, an unanswerable proof of their ability to carry on the government of their own country, is the fact that, practically, they actually *are* carrying it on *now*, and long have been.

What do I mean ? I mean that Indians to-day are far more important factors in the government of India than the British are. I mean, as pointed out in another chapter, that the handful of Englishmen in India, with their necessary ignorance, of the country, its history, its customs, its institutions, its languages, its wants, indeed with their lack of knowledge of almost everything they need to know in order to rule the country properly, these foreigners ("birds of passage and of prey," as Edmund Burke called them) cannot possibly carry on the government without the absolutely indispensable help of the Indians in practically everything; if they attempted it, there would be collapse and ruin at once. The Government of India is now, and always has been, managed largely, almost wholly, by Indians, otherwise it could not exist. The British hold the supreme positions, have the authority and the power, get the prestige and the pay, and see that everything is shaped and directed *primarily for England's advantage*; but the *actual management* of the *machinery* of government, in all its parts, highest and lowest, most difficult as well as least difficult, is mainly in the hands of Indian sub-officials, Indian secretaries, Indian clerks, Indian assistants, who are real experts, who have the real knowledge, who are at their masters' elbows to furnish them with the knowledge which they lack, to save them from blunders which otherwise they would commit, and thus enable the government to go on.

What India asks, then, in demanding home rule, is not that the government shall be turned over to ignorance, or inexperience, or inability, but to these men of real governmental intelligence, and knowledge of government matters, these *real experts*.

Mr. W. W. Pearson, a Cambridge University "honor man," who spent ten years as a teacher in India. published a book in 1927 entitled "For India" in which he says (page 11):

> "How can it be argued that Indians lack ability to rule themselves when we find the actual British Government in India to-day full of Indians of all ranks, to such an extent that if to-morrow the British rulers of the land should leave India the machinery of administration would continue with very little change of outward form. The chief difference would be, that the Ruling Power, being no longer foreign, would have it for its primary object to *benefit India* instead of, as now, to *enrich England*."

Yes, the difference between India as it is to-day and what it would be if turned over with care and under proper conditions into the full management and control of the able and experienced Indians who are actually doing more of the real work of government now than the British officials are, is exactly, as Mr. Pearson has pointed out, the difference that, whereas *now*, the government is carried on primarily *for the benefit of Great Britain*, *then* it would be carried on primarily *for the benefit of India*, as by every principle of justice it ought to be.

The Honorable G. K. Gokhale, a member of the Viceroy's Council, than whom India never produced a higher authority, told us twenty years ago, that

23

in the administration of the government of India by the British at that time, the interests of the Indian people were not given the first place, or the second place, or even the third place; but a place actually *lower than the third.*

These terrible words are essentially as true today as when they were uttered.

Will there ever be a change? Will the venerable and illustrious Indian people, who have had such an influential past, ever again be ruled in the interest of their *own life*, their *own nationhood*, their *own great mission in the world*, instead of in the interest of *strangers?*

Yes, when they are *free*, and *rule themselves.* In the very nature of things, until then, *never!*

CHAPTER XXVIII

TESTIMONIES OF EMINENT ENGLISHMEN AS TO THE COMPETENCE OF THE INDIAN PEOPLE TO RULE THEMSELVES

It is the claim of the British Government that the people of India are not capable of ruling themselves, that is, do not possess the intellectual and moral qualities necessary for carrying on the government of their own country, and therefore require to be ruled by Great Britain.

In answer to this claim, the following testimonials are offered, from eminent Englishmen possessing large knowledge of India, most of them officials long connected with the Indian government. More than three times as many other testimonies of like import, and little if any less weighty, gathered during the last five years, lie before me as I write; but space compels me to limit myself to those given below.

In the light of these testimonies from the highest possible authorities, readers are asked to judge for themselves whether Great Britain has any just ground for her claim that India is not fit for self-rule.

The Testimonies

What is India's Place in the World's Civilization?

Max Muller, the eminent Orientalist, in his book "What India Has to Teach Us," says:

"If I were to look over the whole world to find out

the country most richly endowed with all the wealth, power and beauty that nature can bestow—in some parts a very paradise on earth—I should point to India. If I were asked under what sky the human mind has most fully developed some of its choicest gifts, has most deeply pondered on the greatest problems of life, and has found solutions of some of them which will deserve the attention even of those who have studied Plato and Kant, I should point to India. If I were to ask myself from what literature we here in Europe, may draw the corrective which is most wanted in order to make our inner life more perfect, more universal in fact more truly human, again I should point to India."

May We Look Down on India ?

Warren Hastings, the first Governor-General of India, tyrannized over and wronged the Indian people in many shameful ways. but he strongly rebuked all persons who looked down on them as lacking in civilization and in character, and declared that their literature, their writings,

"will survive when the British dominion in India shall have long ceased to exist and when the sources of wealth and power which that dominion once yielded to Britain are lost even to remembrance."

What Was India's Civilization When the British Came ?

When the British first entered India as adventurers and traders, did they find a civilization that was low, or one that was high ? This question was answered by Sir Thomas Munro, a distinguished Governor of Madras, in a statement made by him before a Committee of the House of Commons, in 1813 ("Hansard's Debates," April 12), as follows :

"If a good system of agriculture, unrivalled manufacturing skill, a capacity to produce whatever contribute to convenience or luxury ; schools established in every village, for teaching reading, writing and arithmetic ; the general practice of hospitality and charity among each other, and above all a treatment of the female sex, full of confidence, respect and delicacy, are among the signs which denote a civilized people, then the Hindus are not inferior to the nations of Europe ; and if civilization is to become an article of trade between the two countries, I am convinced that this country (England) will gain by the import cargo."

Burke on India's Civilization

In all his speeches in Parliament on India—those made in connection with his Impeachment of Warren Hastings and others—Edmund Burke invariably represented the civilization of India as high. In his speech on the East India Bill, he said :

"This multitude of men (the Indian nation) does not consist of an abject and barbarous populace, much less of gangs of savages ; but of a people for ages civilized and cultivated ; cultured by all the arts of polished life while we (Englishmen) were yet dwelling in the woods. There have been (in India) princes of great dignity, authority and opulence. There (in India) is to be found an ancient and venerable priesthood, the depository of laws, learning and history, the guides of the people while living and their consolation in death. There is a nobility of great antiquity and renown; a multitude of cities not exceeded in population and trade by those of the first class in Europe : merchants and bankers who vie in capital with the bank of England : millions of ingenious manufacturers and mechanics ; and millions of the most diligent tillers of the earth."

India's Great Place in the World

Mr. H. M. Hyndman, the eminent British publicist, thus describes the important place of India in the world's history and civilization :

"Many hundreds of years before the coming of the English, the nations of India had been a collection of wealthy and highly civilized people, possessed of a great language, with an elaborate code of laws and social regulations, with exquisite artistic taste in architecture and decoration, producing beautiful manufactures of all kinds, and endowed with religious ideas and philosophic and scientific conceptions which have greatly influenced the development of the most progressive races of the West. One of the noblest individual moralists who ever lived, Sakya Muni (Buddha) was a Hindu: the Code of Manu, dating from before the Christian Era, is still as essential study for the jurist as are the Institutes of Justinian. Akbar, the Mohammedan, was the greatest monarch who ever ruled in the East. And there are in India, in this later age, worthy descendants of the great authors of the Vedas, of the Mahabharata and the Ramayana, of the architects of the Taj Mahal, and of such soldiers and statesmen as Baber, Hyder Ali and Runjeet Singh.

"And yet, nine-tenths of what has been written by the British about India is so expressed that we are made to believe the shameful falsehood that stable and civilized government in Hindustan began only with the rule of the British."*

Are Indians Racially Inferior?

The Metropolitan (Church of England) Bishop of Calcutta, in a sermon preached early in 1921 is reported (in the *Indian Messenger* of April 17, that year) as saying:

"There are persons who conceive that to the White belongs, in virtue of inherent superiority, the inalienable right to rule over races of darker color than themselves. But facts are against them. Indians have achieved the highest distinction in the varied spheres of human activity, and by their success have refuted the charge of racial inferiority. Certain of those qualities which we (British) are apt to think rank highly may be less in evidence among them than among ourselves; but that is merely to say that they are different from ourselves; but difference may exist alongside of perfect equality." †

* "Truths About India," Series I, pp. 8, 9. New York (1923).

† In this connection it may be of interest to some to know that in his Encyclical published March 5th. 1927, His Holiness the Pope, declares that the belief that the dark-skinned races are inferior to the white, is

Should Indians Be Classed Among Inferior, or Among Superior, Peoples ?

Mr. J. A. Spender, long Editor of the *Westminster Gazette*, says in his recent book, "The Changing East," p. 23 (1927) :

"There is no Eastern country which has so many talented men in so many walks of life as India. Men like Tagore, whose writings are read all through Europe and America ; Sir J. C. Bose, whose researches in plant physiology are famous the world over, and whose zeal and originality as a teacher make an indescribable impression on those who see him at work with his students ; Major B. D. Basu, the historian of India ; Dhan Gopal Mukerji, the author of 'My Brother's Face ;' Cornelia Sorabji, the writer and lawyer,—to name only a few out of scores—would be highly distinguished in any European country, and most of them have followers and students around them who would do credit to any Western seat of learning. All of these should be respected and appreciated by us Englishmen and Europeans, as working on a plane of absolute equality with ourselves."

In 1911, Mr. J. A. Spender went to India to attend the Great Delhi Durbar. On his return, he published in his paper (January 29, 1912) the following interesting statement of the high impression he had received from the Indian people :

"India may impress one as poor, or squalid, as mediaeval, but never for a moment can it strike him as a crude, a barbarous country. Evidences meet him everywhere of art, originality and refinement. He will see more beautiful faces in a morning's walk in an Indian bazaar, than in any European city, and he will be charmed by the grace and courtesy of the common folk. It may surprise Englishmen to hear it, but many Indians seriously express the opinion that the Indian is mentally the superior of the white man."

---

a mistake. He affirms that long experience proves, that those alleged inferior peoples are fully equal in mentality to the white peoples.

Have Indians Intellectual and Literary Ability?

At the St. Andrews dinner in Calcutta in December, 1901, the English Vice-Chancellor of the Calcutta University spoke as follows of the Indian people, their intellectual ability and their great literature :

"Masterpieces of thought and language were produced in this country at a time when our ancestors as Englishmen were little better than savages : and though the age of masterpieces may have gone by, none of us who come into contact with educated natives of India to-day can doubt that their intellectual power is worthy of their ancestry."*

Has India Great Men?

General Smuts, Premier of South Africa in an address delivered in Johannesburg, August 26, 1919, called attention to the fact that the civilization of India instead of being low as some suppose, is high. He said :

"I do not look down on Indians ; I look up to them. Two with whom I have come into particularly close contact of late, Lord Sinha and the Maharaja of Bikanir, I regard as among the ablest men I have ever known. There have been Indians who have been among the greatest men in the history of the world. There have been Indians who have been among the greatest leaders of the human race, whose shoes I am unworthy to untie. Nor is there any one else here to-night worthy to do that."

On urging that commissions in the army, high as well as low, should be granted to Indians exactly as to Englishmen, he was asked if he would like to serve under an Indian. He replied at once.

"Why not? I would be glad to serve under an able Indian."

---

* *Indian Messenger*, December 27, 1901.

ARE INDIANS TRUTHFUL ?

Colonel Sleeman, an Englishman who lived long in India and mixed intimately with all classes, and who was extraordinarily well-qualified to judge, said,

"I have had before me hundreds of cases in which a man's property, liberty or life has depended upon his telling a lie, and he has refused to tell it."*

ARE INDIANS HONEST ?

Says Alfred Webb, President of the Tenth Indian National Congress :

'In Madras, in 1894, I conversed with a sewing machine agent, who had travelled and done business over the globe. His principal trade now was with Indian tailors, and seamsters—selling machines to be paid for by monthly instalments. I asked the proportion of bad debts in such business. He said he had found them as high as ten per cent., in England. 'How high in India ?' But one per cent., and such chiefly with Europeans. Practically we have no debts with Indian natives. If it comes that they cannot pay instalments, they will give back the machines.

"In open crowded bazaars or market-places on railway platforms in India are money changers. They sit at tables upon which are heaps of coins of various denominations. Could money be thus exposed at similar gatherings in Europe ?†

ARE INDIANS MORAL ?

At a meeting of the East India Association held at the Westminster Palace Hotel, London, in December, 1901, Sir Lepel Griffin, the President, is reported as paying the following tribute to Indian morality :

"The Hindu creed is monotheistic and of very high

---

* Dutt's "Civilization in Ancient India." Vol. II, p. 159.

† "The People of India," p. 51.

ethical value ; and when I look back on my life in India and the thousands of good friends I have left there among all classes of the native community, when I remember those honorable, industrious, orderly, law-abiding, sober, manly men, I look over England and wonder whether there is anything in Christianity which can give a higher ethical creed than that which is now professed by the large majority of the people of India. I do not see it in London society. I do not see it in the slums of the East End, I do not see it on the London Stock Exchange. I think that the morality of India will compare very favourably with the morality of any country in western Europe."

Are Indians Trustworthy ?

Sir Guy Fleetwood Wilson, long a distinguished British official in India, pays the following striking tribute to the trustworthiness of the many Indians filling responsible positions under his charge. In a speech made when he was retiring from the office of Finance Member of the Indian Government, in 1913, he is reported as saying :

"I wish to pay a tribute to the Indians whom I know best. The Indian officials, high and low, of my department through the years of my connection with them have proved themselves to be unsparing of service and absolutely trustworthy. When need arose, they have done ungrudgingly a double or triple amount of work. When their advice was sought, they have given it to me fully and frankly. As for their trustworthiness, let me give an instance. Three years ago when it fell to my lot to impose new taxes, it was imperative that their nature should remain secret until they were officially announced. Everybody in the department had to be entrusted with this secret. Any one of these, from high officials to low paid compositors of the Government Press, would have become a millionaire by using that secret improperly. But even under such tremendous temptation not one betrayed his trust. So well was the secret kept that a ship laden with silver in Bombay delayed unnecessarily its unloading for three days and was consequently caught by the new tax."

Have Indians Refinement, Spiritual Insight and Brain Power?

Sir Michael Sadler, Vice-Chancellor of the Leeds University, England, and President of the Calcutta (India) University Commission, in a Lecture delivered in Leeds, in 1919, is reported as saying:

"One cannot walk through the streets of any center of population in India without meeting face after face which is eloquent of thought, of fine feeling, and of insight into the profounder things of life. In a very true sense the people of India are nearer to the spiritual heart of things than we in England are. As for brain power, there is that in India which is comparable with the best in our own country."

Are Indians Competent Educators?

After his return from three months of study of education and educational institutions in India, Mr. Sidney Webb delivered an address before the Students Union of the London School of Economics on "What Are We to Do about India?" In this address (as reported in the London weekly, *India*, of December 6, 1912), he said that among the many colleges he had visited he could not avoid the conclusion that some of those which had, from the outset, been established by Hindus, managed by Hindus, and staffed by Hindus, without the intervention or co-operation of any European, were among the very best colleges that he had ever seen—alike for devotion of the professors, ability of the teaching staff, success in examinations, and what was most important of all, in the development of intellect and character in the students. He regretted to have to say that some of the Government colleges that he had seen, which were entirely managed by Englishmen, and nearly wholly staffed by English professors, compared very badly indeed with the exclusively Hindu colleges in various respects; and, unfortunately, often in the devotion and intellectual ability of the professors. He instanced particularly the building up of the Ferguson College at Poona solely by Indian scholars, and its great success; the organization of so great and pervading a movement as the Arya Samaj; the continued growth and development of the D. A. V. College at Lahore, wholly Indian; and the successful working out of the quite novel educational experiment of the Gurukula at Hardwar.

Are the Indian Leaders Inferior in Education or Culture?

Earl Winterton, Under Secretary of State for India, is reported as saying in a speech in Parliament, July 8, 1927:

"Owing to a long tenure of my present office, I have become personally acquainted with a larger proportion of the Indians of all parties who are in public life, than any of my predecessors, and I do not hesitate to say that in culture and in education the leading men among them are not behind the public men of any country."

A Great Englishman Ashamed

Late in his life, Sir John Malcolm, at one time Governor of Bombay, declared that he

"looked back with shame to the days when he had considered himself the superior of the Indians with whom he was called upon to associate."

Does India Hold a Place of Importance in the World's Intellectual Progress?

In his speech introducing the Indian Budget, March 1st, 1926, Sir Basil Blackett said:

"India long ago revolutionized mathematics, and provided the West with the key to the most far-reaching of all the mechanical instruments on which its control of nature has been built, when it presented to Europe through the medium of Arabia the device of the cypher (and the decimal notation) upon which all modern systems of numeration depend. Even so, India to-day or to-morrow, will, I am confident, revolutionize Western doctrines of progress by demonstrating the insufficiency and lack of finality of much of the West's present system of human values."

Does India Produce Great Men of Action as well as Great Thinkers ?

Sir Valentine Chirol, who is loath to give over-praise to Indians, says in "India," his latest book (1926), page 6 :

"At all times in her history India has produced some of the finest and most subtle intellects of which the human race is capable ; and great men of action as well as profound thinkers."

How Do Indians Compare with Englishmen ?

Mr. A. O. Hume, who served in India nearly forty years, and who held many high offices, among them that of Secretary of the Government, made the following statement before the Public Service Commission of 1886 :

"The fact is—and this is what I, who claim to have had better opportunities for forming a correct opinion than most men now living, desire to urge—there is no such radical difference between Indians and Britons as it generally flatters these latter to suppose....If both races be judged impartially, and all pros and cons be fairly set down on both sides, there is very little ground for giving the preference to either. If you compare the highest and best of our Indians with the ordinary run of the rabble in England, these latter seem little better than monkeys beside grand men. If you compare the picked Englishmen we often get in India, trained and elevated by prolonged altruistic labors, and sobered and strengthened by weighty responsibility, with the rabble of India, the former shine out like gods among common mortals. But if you fairly compare the best of both, those in each class would exhibit excellencies and defects less noticeable in the other, and neither can, as a whole, be justly said to be better or worse than the other.....The whole misconception regarding the people of India arises from the habit which Englishmen in India have acquired of regarding only the blackest side of the Indian and the brightest side of the English character, and from their theories as to the capacities of the two races being based on a consideration of the worst specimens of the one and the best specimens of the other."*

Are Englishmen Superior to Hindus ?

In his book, "The Expansion of England, "Professor J. R. Seeley denies that the English are superior to the people of India. He says :

"We are not cleverer than the Hindu; our minds are not richer or larger than his."

Are Indians Intellectually Equal to the English ?

Speaking in London, in May, 1904, at the annual meeting of the Society for Promoting Christian Knowledge, Lord George Hamilton, for some years Secretary for India, was reported as saying that

"There were hundreds of millions of persons in India whose civilization was much older than that of the English," that "They possessed a literature, architecture and philosophy of which any country might be proud,"

and that at the present time there were there

"tens of millions whose intellectual capacity was fully equal if not superior"

to that of the English.†

---

* Proceedings, Vol. VI, Section III. Sub-section 6.
† Report in *India*, the London weekly, June 3, 1904.

ARE THERE INDIANS EQUAL TO THE BEST ENGLISHMEN ?

In an article in the *Nineteenth Century and After*, of February, 1911, Lord Morley, Secretary of State for India, speaking of the most accomplished and highly trained native officials in India, declares them to be

"as good in every way as the best of the men in Whitehall."

ARE INDIANS CAPABLE OF COMPETING WITH ENGLISHMEN ?

Sir Valentine Chirol says in his last book, 'India," (p. 10) :

"There is a rapidly increasing class of Indians, not a few of whom are highly gifted, capable of mastering the literature, and, though more rarely, the science of the West, and qualified to compete with Englishmen in almost all the higher activities of modern life, in the public services, on the bench, at the bar, in the liberal professions in school and university teaching, in literature and in the press, and if more recently, in commerce and industry and finance.

"It is this new class of Indians who have assumed the political leadership of India, and it is they who to-day dominate the new representative assemblies designed to acclimatize in an Indian atmosphere parliamentary institutions and progressive forms of government presumed to be capable of future adjustment, to the newest conceptions of democracy."

Elsewhere Sir Valentine Chirol says :

"Indian brains, when given a fair chance are no whit inferior to European brains."

ARE THERE INDIAN LEADERS IN PRISON WHO ARE EQUAL IN CHARACTER AND CULTURE TO BRITISH MEMBERS OF PARLIAMENT ?

In a speech made in the British House of Commons during the India Debate in July, 1922, Mr. Ben Spoor, one of England's best informed men about India, said :

"At the present moment over 20,000 political prisoners are in jail in India. They include men of high character, men whose character has never been questioned. They include men of profound culture—of a culture, I submit, probably greatly in excess of that of the average Member of this House of Commons."

Are Indian Judges Equal to English Judges?

Sir Henry Cotton, in his book, "New India," (p. 140), says that the Lord Chancellor, the Earl of Selborne, testified as follows from his place in Parliament:

"My lords, for some years I practised in Indian cases before the Judicial Committee of the Privy Council. and during those years there were few cases of any imperial importance in which I was not concerned. I had considerable opportunities of observing the manner in which, in civil cases, the native judges did their duty, and I have no hesitation in saying—and I know this was also the opinion of the judges during that time—that the judgments of the native judges bore most favourable comparison, as a general rule, with the judgments of the English judges. I should be sorry to say anything in disparagement of English judges, who, as a class, are most anxious carefully to discharge their duty; but I repeat that I have no hesitation in saying that in every instance, in respect of integrity, of learning, of knowledge, of the soundness and satisfactory character of the judgments arrived at, the native judgments were quite as good as those of English judges."

Are Indians Fit, Morally and Intellectually, to Manage Their National Affairs?

Mr. Hodgson Pratt, long a prominent member of the British-Indian Civil Service, answers these questions as follows (in *India* the London weekly, November 10, 1905):

"As regards the possible qualities which have delayed the admission of Indians to a larger share in the management of their national affairs it cannot be said that there is any evidence of moral or intellectual unfitness. When posts of great responsibility, requiring qualities of no mean order, have been filled by Indians, whether in British or Native States, they have evinced high capacity as well as trustworthiness."

Have Indians the Qualities Necessary for Ruling?

Mr. G. F. Abbot, author of "Through India with the Prince of Wales," answers in the London *Nation* of July 1908:

"One often hears that the Indian lacks many of the qualities for rule upon which the Englishman prides himself. Among these qualities are a high sense of duty, impartiality, incorruptibility, independence of judgment and moral courage. Now, I submit, no better test for the possession of those qualities could be devised than the placing of the Indian in a position which demands the constant display of those qualities. Such a position he already occupies in the law courts. Every day the Indian judge is called upon to pass sentence in a variety of cases calculated to test his sense of duty, his impartiality, his integrity, his independence of judgment and his moral courage. How has he stood the test? By the confession of every European in India—including, amusingly enough, those who deny to the Indian the possession of those virtues—the Indian judge is not a jot inferior to his English colleague."

Are Indians Competent for High Executive Office?

Sir Henry Cotton, who served long in India, holding high offices there, and later was a prominent Member of Parliament, says in his book, "New India" (pp. 141-142):

"The natives of India are assumed to be unfit to have charge of districts; it is convenient to assume that all Englishmen are cool and wise in danger, while no natives are so, and that consequently only Englishmen, and no Indians, are competent to be trusted with independent charges. By a process of the grossest self-adulation, we persuade ourselves to believe that natives are only useful as ministerial servants, but that the work of a district, if it is to be done at all, demands the supervision of an English officer. The truth, however, is that the Indians, as of course they must be, are the backbone of our administration. The burden and heat of the day are already borne by Indian subordinates, and in the event (as occasionally must be the case) of an incompetent European being in charge of a district, the whole of the work is done by his Indian deputies and clerks."

Is India Fit for Self-Rule?

After his return from India, Keir Hardie declared :

"It cannot be alleged that the Indian people are unfit for self-government. The many Native States which are ruling themselves is a proof to the contrary which can not be gainsaid. A great educated class exists in India which manages universities and higher grade schools, supplies the country with lawyers, professors. newspaper editors, and the heads of great business concerns. Whereever these men have an opportunity they prove that, whether as administrators or as legislators, they have capacity of a very high order."*

Is India Fit for Freedom and Self-Rule ?

To this question Mrs. Annie Besant, after a residence in the country of more than thirty years, makes the following unhesitating answer, with which she ends her book, "India a Nation":

"You ask, is India fit for freedom and self-government ? I answer, Yes, and they are her right. What does India want ? She wants everything, and has a right to claim everything that any other nation has a right to claim. She would be free in India as the Englishman is free in England. To be governed by her own men, freely elected by herself. To make and break ministries at her will. To carry arms, to have her own army, her own navy, her own volunteers. To levy her own taxes; to make her own budgets, to educate her own people; to irrigate her own lands, to mine her own ores, to mint her own coins; to be a sovereign nation within her own borders. Does an Englishman ask for less for himself in England ? Why should an Indian, any more than an Englishman,

* The *Labour Leader* London, May, 1909

be content to be a thrall? India has a right to be free and self-governing. She is fit to be. It is a crime against humanity to hinder her."

ARE INDIANS INFERIOR TO ENGLISHMEN AS ACTUAL LEGISLATORS?

Dr. V. H. Rutherford, long a prominent English Labor Leader and Member of Parliament, tells us in his last book, "Modern India: Its Problems and Their Solution" (pp. 82—84), that after attending debates (in 1926) in the Indian National Legislative Assembly and in several Provincial Legislatures, where British and Indian members were speaking and working side by side, he "found a definite inferiority among the Englishmen as compared with the Indians." He declares:

"Although I have a natural bias in favour of my own countrymen, truth compels me to state that in these Legislative bodies the Indians far surpass their English rivals in brilliancy, wit, logic, knowledge, breadth of vision and ideals of statesmanship."

Asking the question,

"What station in life would these men have occupied if they had remained at home in England instead of coming to India?

He answers:

"Not more than one or two per cent. would have risen higher than a first class clerk in a government office. As a matter of fact, India is governed by first-class clerks from England, with a few lordlings thrown in as governors....One truth stands out like a beacon-light, namely that *Indians are infinitely better fitted to govern India than are their English overlords.* In sheer intellectual ability and parliamentary capacity Indians outshine their British adversaries."

In conclusion:

Such are a few of the many evidences which offer themselves to all who care to know, of the high civilization of India; of the undeniable intellectual, moral and practical qualities of the Indian people, their faithfulness, their trustworthiness, their honorable character, their eminent ability and efficiency in the discharge of the duties and responsibilities placed upon them, not only in private life but also in every kind of public, official and govermental position which they are permitted to hold.

We submit: Basing our verdict on the above testimonies, which are of the most reliable possible character, because they come from eminent Englishmen who know India best, have we not a right to affirm that in every quality needed for self-rule the people of India are little, if at all, inferior to the people of Great Britain, and that, as soon as they gain practical experience, which will quickly come with freedom, (but cannot come without it), they will be able to maintain a government not unworthy to rank with the fine government of Japan or the best governments of Europe?

CHAPTER XXIX

HOW PARLIAMENT GUARDS THE INTERESTS OF INDIA

We are often told with much assurance that the interests of the Indian people are safe, because they are carefully guarded by the British Parliament, especially by the House of Commons, that splendid group of 615 men representing the best intelligence and character of the British Isles. Of course, such a body of men do not, will not, and cannot neglect so grave a responsibility, so important a part of the Empire, as India, or fail to see that the Indian people are ruled honourably, efficiently and justly.

This sounds assuring. But what are the facts? Does Parliament give careful attention to India, or watchfully guard her rights? Indeed, do the majority of the members of Parliament know anything more about India than a schoolboy, or pay any attention at all to Indian affairs, unless there is an insurrection or some other form of serious trouble there? How can they? India is so far away, and they are so overwhelmed with matters nearer home that must be attended to!

When, at the fag end of a parliamentary session, a day is announced for discussion of Indian affairs, what happens? It is the signal for everybody to be absent who can possibly find an excuse.

Mr. Ramsay MacDonald, in his book, "The Government of India" (pp. 43 and 51), says,

"It must be admitted that Parliament has not been a just and watchful steward of India. Its seats are empty when it has its annual saunter through the Indian Budget.... Very few members of Parliament have any real knowledge of Indian affairs, and there is a deserted House of Commons when the Indian Budget is under consideration."

There lies before me, as I write, an extended report of the debate on India, in the House of Commons, July 17, 1927. According to the report, there were within call when the House was fullest 220 members ; but never in the Chamber at any one time more than fifty ; and the average attendance during the debate did not exceed twenty-five.

Writes Mr. Alfred Kinnear, M. P.,

"I recall thirty Indian Budget nights in the House of Commons. Scarcely one of the number drew an audience of fifty members, one-eleventh part of the membership. At a recent budget debate when a matter of very great importance was up for discussion, there were present, by count, fourteen persons—thirteen Liberals and one Tory. At another, there were twenty present ; at another, there were three on the Tory side and one on the Liberal."

In a letter written from London by Mr. Lajpat Rai, under date of July 22, 1926, and published in *The People*, of Lahore, August 15, that eminent Indian publicist says,

"Nothing proves so forcibly the absurdity and the unreality of the British Parliament's control over the Indian government, as the spectacle of a debate on India in the House of Commons. I have attended several such debates on previous occasions, and last night I attended another. Before the Under-Secretary of State for India introduced the subject of India, the House was full and everything was lively ; almost exciting, although there was nothing of any great importance on the tapis. But the moment the Under-Secretary for India got up, the House emptied. Soon the front benches were entirely unoccupied. Only a very few members remained. The whole scene was dull, and depressing. The speeches made were equally dull and uninteresting. There was no sign of life or interest anywhere."

Edward Thompson in his book, "The Other Side of the Medal" (Harcourt, Brace & Co., 1926, page 13), says :

"It has long been notorious, and a theme of savage comment by Indians, that the Indian Debate in the House of Commons has been regarded with indifference but the few who attended and with contempt by the many who stayed away. Sir Henry Fowler's noble appeal some years ago that every member should consider himself a member for India, since India was disfranchised in the assembly that controlled her destinies. won a spectacular triumph when made ; but it has been forgotten. Two years ago, a Member of Parliament of twenty years' standing asked a friend of mine, "What's happened to that fellow Gander—or some such name, who used to give us so much trouble ?'—thus showing that it is possible for one to be a British Privy Councillor and yet be utterly ignorant of the man in India who is our greatest British contemporary."

At a large meeting of the British Labor Party held in the University Institute, London in January, 1926, Major Graham Pole, M. P. described the interest, or rather the complete lack of interest, the British Parliament (that "sleepless guardian of India's interests") habitually shows whenever Indian affairs come before it for consideration. He declared that whenever "India Day" arrives and the Indian Budget is discussed there is almost invariably a "thin House of Commons, only barely enough members being present to form a quorum, and the few who remain for the most part spend their time in snoring while the Secretary of State for India makes his stereotyped annual statement," and that only when some "crisis" arises, like the "agitation caused by the Partition of Bengal, accompanied by boycott and bombs," or some "extraordinary condition of things threatening the loss of India or a disturbance of English investments," do the great majority of the House show any more interest in India, or the three hundred twenty millions of its people, for whom Parliament is supposed to be the responsible guardians, than if India were a province of the moon.

Let a single other fact of a different nature be cited, which shows in a tragic manner how closely in touch with Indian affairs the British Parliament is. On the 19th of April, 1919, the shocking Amritsar massacre took place, in which British soldiers under command of a British general attacked a peaceful religious assembly in a public park, and shot down in cold blood, killing or wounding more than 1,000 unarmed men, women and children. Did the British Parliament the very next day ring with hot protest and condemnation of the horrible transaction ? Not exactly ! It was more than seven months before the matter was even *mentioned* in Parliament. More amazing than that ! Can it be believed ? More than seven months elapsed after the horrible deed was done before Parliament *even knew what had happened* ! This makes entirely clear how well Parliament guards and watches over and protects India.

Let no one understand the above facts and contentions as indicating on the part of the author any want of respect toward the British Parliament (the House of Commons), which he holds in high esteem and honor. He believes that there is in the world no abler legislative body, and none more conscientious in the discharge of what it conceives to be its duties.

But (and here is the point not to be overlooked), even the British Parliament cannot perform the impossible, and should not be required to try.

Its members have mountains of responsibilities to carry entirely aside from India. Why should those of India be added? With the Scotch members charged with the duty of guarding the interests of Scotland, and the Welsh members the interests of Wales, and the members representing the counties and cities of England the interests of all these, and then, beyond the home countries, a great world-wide Empire entirely apart from India,—with all these pressing matters to look after and all these heavy responsibilities to discharge, what time or strength can this body of men have left, to make themselves intelligent about, and therefore be able to superintend with any knowledge or justice at all, the political and economic affairs of the vast Indian sub-continent, with a population equal to that of all Europe outside of Russia?

The blame to be put upon these heavily-burdened men is not because they fall asleep or go out of the House for a little needed rest when the time comes for discussing India—a subject so far away, so difficult, so enormous, and of which they know, and, in the very nature of the case, can know, almost nothing. The cause for blame is much deeper.

The guilt (in the eyes of a just God and of just men it *is guilt* and *heavy* too) which rests upon Parliament and upon the whole British nation, is that of the *Indian situation itself*,—is that of *seizing the government of India, wresting it out of the hands of the Indian people* where it rightly belongs, *placing the* stupendous *task of carrying it on, in the hands of distant, ignorant, over-burdened foreigners,* who can *no more discharge its enormous responsibilities intelligently and justly than the sun can rise in the west.*

About the middle of the last century, Mr. John

Dickinson declared in his book, "Government in India Under a Bureaucracy," page 136 (1853):

"Since India has come under British rule her cup of grief has been filled to the brim, aye, it has been full and running over. The unfortunate Indian people have had their rights of property confiscated ; their claims on justice and humanity trampled under foot ; their manufacturers, towns, and agriculturists beggared ; their excellent municipal institutions broken up ; their judicial security taken away ; their morality corrupted ; and even their religious customs violated, by what are conventionally called the 'blessings of British rule' . . . Parliament eases its conscience regarding these tyrannies and wrongs in India by exhorting those that govern there to govern 'paternally,' just as Isaac Walton exhorts his angler, in hooking a worm, to handle him as if 'he loved him.' "

Such is affirmed by an English historian to have been British rule in India at the middle of the last century. The Indian people declare that there has been little or no real improvement since. A few more offices or salaried positions are grudgingly assigned them ; but they are given no more power or authority in the management of the government of their own country, and their treatment by the British officials is actually more haughty and more humiliating than it was when John Dickinson wrote. As to Parliament, it is widely claimed by those who have fullest knowledge of the past and the present that this British legislative body actually knows less about India to-day and takes less interest in its affairs than at any time in the past.

Ramsay MacDonald says there is actually less Parliamentary control of the Indian administration now than there was in the days of the East India Company *

It should not for a moment be forgotten that

* "The Awakening of India," p. 265.

the extremely conservative House of Lords is a part of Parliament, that it is less intelligent concerning India than even the House of Commons, that it is constantly and notoriously opposed to liberal measures for India and favorable to those that are oppressive, that it openly sympathized with the ultra-tyrannical Rowlatt Acts of 1919 and that it actually defended and commended General Dyer for his horrible Amritsar massacre. Think of claiming before the world that such a body, which has to some degree veto power over legislation by the House of Commons, is a careful guardian of the interests of the Indian people!

One cause alone, even if there were no other, makes it absolutely impossible, in the very nature of the case, for the British Parliament to guard the interests of India with even an approximation of wisdom and justice. I refer to the fact that Parliament contains not a single representative of India.

Suppose New York or Massachusetts, or Michigan, or Louisiana, or California were allowed to send no representatives to the United States Congress in Washington, could such a wholly unrepresented State depend upon having its interests properly guarded? Suppose London, or Lancashire or Yorkshire or Wales or Scotland were not allowed to send a single representative to the British Parliament, could any one of those great constituencies be convinced that its interests would be safe?

How then about India?—a nation in a far distant part of the earth, which has a population nearly three times as great as that of the entire United States and more than seven times as numerous as that of the British Isles, and of whose languages, customs, civilization and needs, the British Parliament is almost absolutely ignorant.

It is astonishing how little knowledge of India seems to be possessed by many of even the most eminent members of Parliament. It is the commonest thing to find distinguished members of both Houses condescendingly referring to the Indian people as if they had no culture and no civilization. I find even Mr. Balfour, who is accounted a man of exceptional intelligence, actually insulting the Indian people by writing and speaking of them, not once, but again and again, and habitually, as if they were barbarians requiring to be civilized by Britain.

Is it anything less than lunacy to believe that an English legislative body, many of whose most conspicuous leaders are so ignorant of India, and which does not contain a single representative of that great and distant nation, can intelligently and justly guard its interests, even if we assume every legislator to be actuated by the most generous, honorable and altruistic motives?

Is it said that India does have one representative, if not in the British Parliament, at least in the British government in London, and near enough to Parliament so that his voice may occasionally be heard there? I mean the Secretary of State for India.

The reply is clear. Even if we grant that this official is a representative of India, what is *one*, under such conditions? A *hundred* would be utterly *inadequate* to present a country so enormous as India, and interests so vast as hers. But it is not true that in the Secretary of State India has even one representative. That eminent official is not an Indian, but an Englishman. He may never have been in India; probably he has not. Very likely he does not know a single Indian language. Most Secretaries of State do not. Furthermore, (what is vital), he is not chosen by

India, but by England, therefore, he is not India's representative at all, but England's. He never is, or can be, anything more than a make-believe representative of India, because he is not appointed or even credentialed by the Indian people; just as no man can be a real representative of a business firm or corporation who is not chosen or appointed or credentialed by that business firm or corporation. To be sure, he is one of the men who dominate and control the Indian people, but that is not because he is their representative, or has any right to control them, but because he is their master, put over them by Britain, without their having any part in the matter.

Is it said that even if Parliament fails, the English people themselves will not fail? They are a great liberty-loving and just nation, and may be depended on in some way, through Parliament or otherwise to see to it that India's interests are carefully protected.

Mr. H. W. Nevinson, the eminent English publicist who knows both England and India as well as any man, answers with the question:

"How many persons in England know anything about India, or can afford time to think about her? I doubt if one per cent of the British people gives to India a thought from year's end to year's end."

Dr. V. H. Rutherford, M. P., says, the British people "are never even consulted" about Indian affairs.*

The truth is, the whole claim or idea, so widely entertained in the world, that in the British Parliament the Indian people have an intelligent, careful, ever-solicitous and safe guardian of their

---

* "Modern India: Its Problems and Their Solution," Introduction, p. xi. (1927).

rights and interests, is a pure fiction. There is a fact to support it. *India has no such guardian*; and she *can have none until she becomes free and is therefore able to guard and protect herself.*

Said Thomas Jefferson :

"The people of every country aro the only safe guardians of their own rights."

CHAPTER XXX

THE TRUTH ABOUT THE AMRITSAR MASSACRE

The terrible Amritsar massacre of April, 1919, throws so much light upon British rule in India as it exists to-day, that the exact facts regarding it, as ascertained from the most trust-worthy authorities, ought to be given here as an important chapter of this book.

Besides a vast amount of testimony obtained through the Indian press, we have the extensive reports of two investigating commissions, one appointed by the British-Indian Government, consisting of five Englishmen and three Indians, with Lord Hunter, a British judge, at its head, and hence known as the Hunter Commission ; and the other, appointed by the Indian National Congress, consisting of five eminent Indians, and known as the Indian Congress Commission. With the evidence thus before us, as fully as we can ever expect to obtain it, what is the verdict ?

Turn first to the Hunter Report. We have here really two reports, which unfortunately divide on race lines. From the five Englishmen we have a Majority Report, which is too often thought of by the world generally as the voice of the entire committee. But it is not. This report in the main is favorable to the British. Nevertheless, it finds itself compelled to make admissions which are very significant. Its bias is so evident and so serious that the three Indian members of the Commission find themselves compelled to make a

Minority Report, which dissents at many points from that of the majority. The Majority Report is declared by all India to be a whitewash. In England the imperialists, the militarists, the extreme tories, the men who believe in holding India by the sword at no matter what cost, accept it, like it, find in it a "vindication of British rule." But these are by no means the whole nation; the entire labor party, all liberals and practically all independent investigators join with the people of India in condemning it as a partisan effort to bolster up a bad cause.

Such a biased report is only what was inevitable from the character of the Committee. For, (1), The Committee was appointed by the British-Indian Government, who was the culprit. Can a culprit be trusted to choose his judge ? Of course, the Government would appoint investigators who would make out for it the best case possible. (2), The Commission contained no representatives of India. To be sure, there were three Indians, but they were *not chosen by India*, and were *not men whom India would have chosen.* The Indian National Congress and the All-India Moslem League, the two great national representative organizations of the country, ought to have been represented and asked to be, but were refused. And yet the three Indians selected by the Government as presumably favorable to its interests, found the case against the Government so bad, that, as already stated, they refused to assent to the camouflage of the Majority Report. (3), The Congress Commission submitted to the Hunter Commission a large body of important testimony from persons intimately connected with the events to be investigated, but the Hunter Commission *refused to receive* it ; it would receive no testimony except that of its own choosing, and which came through its own official channels. Of course, therefore its findings could not be just.

Turn to the Indian Congress Commission Report. Does not this bear evidence of being as partisan as the other? It does not. Of course, it would have been better if the Commission could have represented both the Government and the Indian people. As has been said, this was what the Indian Congress tried for, and only when this failed did the Congress appoint a Commission of its own. Several things are to be said of this Commission:

(1) The men chosen to compose it were the least partisan possible; they were men kindly disposed toward the British, and bearing a record of absolute loyalty to the British Government; at the same time they were men widely honored and trusted among all parties in India. The determination from the first was to make the investigation and the report so thorough, so fair, so just, that it could stand the severest scrutiny.

(2) The Commission rejected no testimony from any source, if only it gave evidence of being trustworthy.

(3) Although the Hunter Commission would not admit valuable testimony offered it by the Congress Commission, the Congress Commission admitted all the testimony gathered by the Hunter Committee, and gave it due consideration in the formulation of its report.

(4) The Congress Commission examined the statements of over 1,700 witnesses, and the statements of 650 of the most important of these are given *in extenso* in its report, of two large volumes. All of these were carefully verified.

(5) The Report bears every evidence not only of thoroughness but of fairness, candor, and justice. Its entire freedom from harsh or vindictive expres-

sions, its studied courtesy and moderation of language, its charity of judgment, and its refusal to draw conclusions in any case unless they were supported by overwhelming evidence, are noticeable throughout.

Judging from all the evidence coming through all the reports, what in a general way, was the verdict compelled to be as to the alleged atrocities in the Punjab and elsewhere? Were the stories that came to the world at the time exaggerations? No, for the most part they were under statements; the censors toned down the accounts that were allowed to reach the world. The worst facts were largely suppressed.

Let us see what some of these fully substantiated facts were.

Was there "revolution" in the Punjab? Was there "a deep and widespread plot to overthrow the government" as was alleged? Even the Hunter Report admitted that no evidence of anything of the kind was discovered. So this excuse for the atrocities wholly failed.

Were there mobs and riots? Yes, in a number of places. These went so far in some cases as to burn or wreck valuable buildings, tear up railways and even take life. All together, seven Englishmen were killed, one English woman was severely beaten, and property to the amount of probably a million dollars was destroyed. This was serious. Of course, such riots had to be put down; and it was not strange if in their suppression the Government acted sternly and caused bloodshed. For this the world has given it no censure.

But did the Government confine itself to such measures as were necessary to suppress the rioting in the few places where it occurred? Let us see just what happened.

Was the first aggression by the people, or was it by the Government? It was by the Government. Was there any rioting until after the military began shooting the people? No, there was nothing of the kind anythere. The first shooting and the worst rioting were in the city of Amritsar. The people had been very much exasperated by many things that had occurred,—the heavy demand for enlistments in connection with the great war in Europe, indeed the virtual conscription; the unmerciful treatment of the men who went to the war; the refusal to grant commissions to any of the Indian soldiers, however brave or meritorious their military service; the heavy exactions of money from the people to meet the expenses of the war; the spying everywhere by the Government, and the wholesale arrest and imprisonment of persons against whom the spies or the police could find or manufacture any possible suspicion of disloyalty; the confiscation of books and newspapers; the prevention of freedom of speech; the harsh and arrogant attitude of the Government in all its dealings with the people; the unjust and tyrannical Rowlatt Acts, which had set all India aflame with indignation; and then last of all, only two days before the rioting in Amritsar began, the autocratic action of the Government in forbidding Mr. Gandhi, the nation's saint, from entering the Punjab on a mission of peace, and the sudden arrest and imprisonment, without charge, of Dr. Satyapal and Dr. Kitchlew, two of the most honored and beloved leaders of the people in Amritsar,—all these things, together had stirred the public mind to such a feeling of indignation, alarm and resentment, that it only required a spark to cause an explosion.

That spark came in the firing upon an entirely *peaceful procession* of people on their way to the residence of the British Commissioner to present *a petition* for the liberation of the leaders who had been imprisoned. The procession had gone a considerable part of the way when they found themselves stopped by the military. On attempting to proceed, they were *fired upon* by the *soldiers* and some *twenty of their number killed* and a much larger number wounded. This was too much. The sight of blood—of their dead and dying friends all around them—fired the passions of everybody, and turned a wholly peaceful company into a mob out of control, bent on retaliation and vengeance. The result was that in a very short time the railway where the shooting occurred was being torn up, public buildings were being attacked, looted and set on fire, and Englishmen were killed

Of course, in a little while order was restored, and there was no further disturbance worth mentioning. Such is the story of the Amritsar riot, which, as has already been said was the worst that occurred anywhere. If there were time to go into the details of the several other lesser disturbances in other places, we should find them generally closely resembling this. Always thoy were caused by the attempts of the military or the police to prevent or break up peaceful processions endeavoring to present petitions to the governing authorities, or to disperse companies of people assembled sometimes for purely religious purposes and sometimes to agitate for political reforms. The Government was angry because tho people dared to agitate for reforms, dared to oppose it in any way, however peaceful ; and tho military officials, always suspicious, scented in every large gathering something disloyal. And so all united in a common determination to "teach the people a lesson which they would not forget".—

"by force, force without limit,"—by that "frightfulness" plan, that *Schrecklichkeit* method, which at one time the British and others so severely condemned in the Germans.

We find the details of all this "frightfulness" so shocking that we de not wonder the Indian Government prevented knowledge of them from reaching the world, from reaching even the people of England, or Parliament, or Mr. Montagu the Secretary of State for India himself (as he affirmed), for eight long months after their perpetration.

Let us look at a few of the details. For a long time, judging from the newspaper reports, it was generally supposed that the number killed in the Amritsar (Jalianwala Bagh) massacre was about 500 and the number wounded 2000 or perhaps a little under. Then came the Hunter Report, putting the numbers at only 379 killed and 1,200 wounded, which everybody in Amritsar at once recognized as much too low. Finally appeared the full, detailed, carefully prepared report of the Congress Investigating Commission, which proved by ample and undeniable evidence that the number shot to death approximated *1,200* and the *wounded 3,600.*

And how could the numbers have been much, if any less, when fifty soldiers, armed with the most deadly rapid-firing guns, poured 1,650 rounds of ammunition, at close range, into a peaceful gathering of between 15,000 and 20,000 unsuspecting men, women and children, shut up in a walled-in garden from which it was almost impossible to escape?

General Dyer, the "hero" of the affair, who actually claimed praise for his deed on the ground that by it he had "saved India," attempted to justify what he had done by the plea that he had forbidden the gathering, and the people had disobeyed him in assembling. But it turned out that his proclamation had not been circulated in the part of the city from which the people came, that large numbers of those present were from the country, having come in wholly innocently for a religious festival, and that few persons in the crowd, if any, knew that the gathering had been forbidden.

That the gathering was the farthest possible from revolutionary or disposed to disorder or dangerous, is shown by the fact, established by abundant evidence, that only a few minutes before General Dyer came and began his massacre, it had actually passed practically unanimous resolutions condemning the riots and the destruction of property and life which had occurred two or three days before, and urging upon the public everywhere peaceful methods of procedure.

That the object of Dyer in ordering the shooting was not to disperse the crowd, but to vent his anger, to show the despised "natives" "who was who," and to "teach them a lesson that they would not forget," was proven by the facts, (1) That on entering the enclosure he did not order the crowd to disperse, but began shooting at once; (2) That he did not stop firing when the crowd broke up and tried by every means in its power to get away; And (3) That he did all he could to prevent the people from escaping, by directing the heaviest fire of his soldiers at those who were fleeing, and especially at the only places of egress, until those places were piled high and blocked with the dead and dying.

General Dyer confessed that he could doubtless have dispersed the crowd without firing at all; but, he said, they "probably would have come back and laughed at him!" There we have it.

Such an outrage, such a crime, as laughing at so exalted a personage as a British general, of course, had to be prevented, at any cost, at no matter what sacrifice of lives of innocent men, women and babes.

What provision did these butchers make for their dead and wounded? None. They removed not a single body from the bloodstained garden: they had not the mercy to convey a single mangled woman or child to a hospital or other place of aid. Some of the wounded received no care for twenty-seven hours,—British nurses, who could have gone to them, refusing to do so, and the alarmed and terror-stricken relatives and friends of the victims being prevented from rendering any but the most imperfect aid by harsh curfew orders and other savage restrictions imposed by the military officials and the police.

The following story of the efforts of one Indian woman (a woman of considerable standing in the community) to find and remove the body of her husband on the night following the shooting, will help us to understand the terrible situation. Madame Ratan Devi, residing near the Jalianwala Bagh, furnished to the Congress Investigating Commission the following statement:

"I was in my house near Jalianwala Bagh when I heard shots fired. I was then lying down, I got up at once as I was anxious, because my husband had gone to the Bagh. I began to cry, and went to the place accompanied by two women to help me. There I saw heaps of dead bodies and I began to search for my husband. After passing through the heaps, I found the deadbody of my husband. The way towards it was full of blood and of dead bodies. After a short time both the sons of Lala Sundar Das came there, and I asked them to bring a *charpai* (cot) to carry the dead body of my husband home. The boys accordingly went home and I sent away the two women also. By this time it was 8 o'clock and no one could stir out of his house because of the curfew order. I stood on waiting and crying. At about eight-thirty a Sikh gentleman came. There were others who were looking for something amongst the dead. I did not know them. I entreated the Sikh gentleman to help me in removing my husband's body to a dry place, for that place was overflowing with blood. He took the body by the head and I by the legs, and we carried it to a dry place and laid it down on a wooden block. I waited up to 10 P. M. I got up and started towards Katra. I thought of asking some student from the Thakurdwara to help me in carrying my husband home. I had not gone far, when some man sitting in a window in an adjacent house asked me where I was going at that late hour. I said I wanted some men to help me carry my husband's dead body home. He said he was attending a wounded man, and as it was past 8 P. M. nobody could help me. Then I started towards Katra again, and saw an old man. I repeated the whole of my sad story to him. He took pity upon me and asked the men to go with me. But they said that it was 10 o'clock, and that they would not like to be shot down. That was no time to stir out; how could they go out so far? So I went back and seated myself by the side of my dead husband. Accidentally, I found a bamboo stick which I kept in my hand to keep off dogs. I saw men writhing in agony, and a buffalo struggling in great pain. A boy about twelve years old in agony entreated me not to leave the place. I told him that I could not go anywhere leaving the dead body of my husband. I asked him if he wanted any wrap, and if he was feeling cold I could spread it over him. He asked for water, but water could not be procured at that place.

"I heard the clock striking at regular intervals of one hour. At 2 o'clock, a Jat belonging to Sultan village, who was lying entangled in a wall, asked me to come near him and to raise his leg. I got up and taking hold of his clothes drenched in blood raised his leg up. After that, no one else came till half past five. At about six, L. Sundar Das, his sons and some people from my street, came there with a *charpai* and I brought my husband home. I saw other people at the Bagh in search of their relatives. I passed my whole night there. It is impossible for me to describe what I felt. Heaps of dead bodies lay there, some on their backs and some with their faces upturned. A number of them were poor innocent children. I shall never forget the sight. I was all alone the whole night in a solitary jungle. Nothing but the barking of dogs, the braying of donkeys and the groans of the wounded, was audible. Amidst hundreds of corpses I passed my night, crying and watching. I cannot say more. What I experienced that night is known to me and God."

The investigations of the Congress Commission bring out other stories as touching as this; but this is sufficient for our purpose.

We must not suppose that the tragedy of the Jalianwala Bagh was all that Amritsar had to suffer; it was only the worst. Nor must we let the sufferings of Amritsar blind us to those of other cities and villages.

There was martial law of the severest kind in the whole of the Punjab Province. Sentences to death and transportation for life or long terms of imprisonment were pronounced on 581 persons; later, however, a Revision Court reduced or annulled some of these. The courts punished 1,179 persons; 18 death sentences were carried out, and 28 sentences of transportation for life; other sentences aggregating 400 years were put in operation. The whole Province was isolated by prohibition of travelling. Lawyers from outside were prohibited from entry to defend clients. "A reign of terror crushed the Press nearly out of existence."

In all parts of this Province innocent men were arrested on suspicion, and tortured to extort confessions. In many villages there were official raids and searches. Hostages were carried off. No man, however peaceful or loyal, felt himself or his home to be safe. In many places bombs were dropped from aeroplanes on peaceful gatherings—gatherings containing women and children as well as men. In Gujranwala, an assembly officially admitted to be dispersing, was bombed, resulting in 11 persons killed and 27 wounded. A bomb was dropped on a boarding house. In Lahore, because a public notice had been torn down by somebody, all the students of a medical college were compelled to walk 16 miles a day in the hot sun every day for three weeks.

The military officials seem to have racked their brains to discover unusual ways not only to inflict physical cruelty upon the people, but to humiliate and degrade them. Men were made to compose poems and sing them to the "honor" of the officials who were abusing them. The people were compelled to "salaam" to every British soldier they met, even those that had slaughtered their neighbors and kindred. Men were made to draw lines on the earth with their noses. *Sadhus* (religious men) were lime-washed and exposed to the scorching sun so that the lime might harden on their skin. Numbers of men were shut up in uncovered cages or pens, for many hours at a stretch, faced toward the burning sun.

For eight days all the people living in one of the short streets of Amritsar (that in which the English woman had been assaulted), and all having occasion to pass through the street, were compelled to crawl,—and not on their hands and feet, "like quadrupeds," but actually on their bellies, and if they attempted, as some did, to go "on all fours" they were struck on the back with the butts of the soldiers' guns and compelled to crawl flat on the earth "like worms."

There were hundreds of merciless public whippings, some of which were of school boys. At Kasur 40 men were whipped, the total number of stripes being 710. In Lahore 800 stripes were administered to 66 persons. In Amritsar many were whipped. We are given the following account of one of the public whippings of boys in Amritsar.

"Each of the boys was fastened to a *tiktika* (a large and strong, triangular frame) and given 30 stripes. One of them, Sundar Singh, became senseless after the fourth stripe, but after water was poured into his mouth by a soldier, he regained consciousness. The flogging was then resumed. He lost his consciousness the second time, but the flogging never ceased until he was given 30 stripes He was taken off the triangle bleeding and unconscious. The other boys were similarly treated, and the majority of them became unconscious while they were being flogged. They were all handcuffed, and as they were unable to walk, they were dragged by the police."

These fiendish outrages seem absolutely incredible. It would not be possible to believe that they occurred and were perpetrated by, or at the command of, Englishmen, except for the fact that they were proved by overwhelming and unimpeachable evidence.

Outside the Punjab there was much terrible work done by the military, though none quite so fiendish as in the Punjab. At Delhi, 14 persons were killed and 60 wounded; in Ahmedabad 28 were killed and 123 wounded (official reports).

Our space forbids us to go into further details.

In view of the terrible story which we have now passed in brief review, what ought to have been done? The Hunter Report recommended nothing in particular to be done—that is, nothing to any one connected with the story on the British side. As was to be expected, it placed the blame almost wholly on India. The iniquitous Rowlatt Acts were all right and must be enforced. All the other oppressive legislation must be maintained. With all the rest, the cities and villages of the Punjab which had already suffered most, must further pay large indemnities to the Government for its expense in "preserving order," that is, in shooting, bombing and imprisoning their people. Of course, it was to be regretted that such an inconvenient disturbance should have arisen. But when it arose, the Government simply had to do its duty. Probably here and there a British civil or military officer may have been a little indiscreet; may have erred in judgment as to the best method of doing some difficult thing, or in some urgent matter may have gone a little too far. But on the whole, there was little occasion for blaming any official and certainly little for punishing any official. If there was any exception, it was in the case of General Dyer; and yet the Report gave him more praise than blame. The whole Punjab matter was now a thing of the past; it was best to discuss it as little as possible; the least said the soonest mended. Such were the conclusions reached and the recommendations made by the Commission appointed by the British Government!

Not thus did the Indian Congress Report look at the situation. Instead of covering up the terrible wrongs which the people of the Punjab had suffered, that Report called for their just redress.

Was there any redress offered on the part of the Government? Was there any punishing done to those who had perpetrated these shocking atrocities? Very little. General Dyer was censured by the Government,—not, however, on the ground of his having fired on an unarmed assembly of men, women and children, but because he fired without first giving warning, and because he continued the firing too long. When his case came before the British House of Commons, the majority voted censure, 111 members dissenting. In the House of Lords, a strong majority refused to express any form of disapproval of what he had done. The feeling in India was so strong against him that he was removed from his Indian Command, and retired, first upon reduced pay and then on a pension. The militarists and imperialists of India, England and the Empire generally lauded him as a patriot and a hero. His friends and admirers in London presented him with a jewelled sword, and a purse of $150,000. A number of the lower officers in the Punjab were informed by the Government that their conduct was "strongly disapproved" as "injudicious and improper," and they were removed to other commands. The Governor of the Province, Sir Michael O'Dwyer, who sustained General Dyer in everything, and was really quite as guilty as he, if not more so, seems to have received no expression of censure or disapproval from either the Indian Government or the British Government in London. Judge Rowlatt, the father of the outrageous Rowlatt Acts, was honored and rewarded, by being decorated by King George with the insignia of Knight Commander of the Star of India.

The things brought to light above suggest several thoughts and inquiries:

1. Why were the terrible facts of the massacre and the other atrocities hushed up, and prevented by the censors from getting to the world except as they leaked out here and there? Why were the people of England and Parliament itself not allowed to know them except in the most inadequate ways for more than seven months? It was because they were so shocking that the Government of India knew they would be condemned by the whole world as soon as they were known. Governments based on tyranny and oppression always have to conceal. It is only governments of justice and freedom that need no concealments.

2. What was the explanation or meaning of these inhuman, these devilish deeds? Did they mean that the men who perpetrated them were by nature devils? On the contrary, Englishmen

under normal and right conditions are as just and honorable as Frenchmen, or Germans or Americans. The devil-deeds were the result of a condition; they were a part and an outcome of the great devil-business in which the men were engaged, the business which they were carrying on at the command of their government; namely, the business of robbing a great nation of its freedom, and ruling it by force. Such a devil-business necessarily involves devil-deeds. Angels from heaven could not carry it on without being compelled to do devilish work.

3. Where then rested the responsibility and the guilt? Partly on the men that committed the atrocities. They ought not to have allowed themselves to be engaged in such devil-business. The things they did were crimes—crimes against humanity, and the excuse that they were serving a government did not free them from guilt. But of course the greater guilt was on the government, on the nation, which was holding India in bondage and using them as instruments for carrying into effect *its supreme crime.*

4. Did the British Government follow up the Punjab atrocities, and in some measure atone for them, by at once making such provisions, creating such conditions as would insure that other atrocities, similar to these or worse, could not and would not be inflicted upon the Indian people in the future? It did nothing of the kind then, and it has done nothing of the kind since. The British Government has steadily refused to give the Indian people a Bill of Right for their protection, although they have urgently and persistently demanded it; and it has refused to put into their hands any power by which they can protect themselves. For aught they can know, a General Dyer may be inflicted on any city or a

Governor O'Dwyer upon any province, to-morrow, and there may be perpetrated again as brutal deeds as those of Amritsar. This is a possibility which hangs over the heads of the Indian people all the while. Is it said that they should trust the British? They did trust them; and the Punjab deeds were the result. Will it be any safer to trust them in the future than in the past?

5. Finally. It was claimed by the Punjab officials that their drastic deeds were compelled, were a necessity, in order to prevent a revolution, and the driving of the British out of India.

There are two answers to this claim. (1) The Hunter Commission itself declared that it found "nothing to show that the outbreak in the Punjab was a part of a pre-arranged conspiracy to overthrow the British Government." (2) But, if the Indian people did so hate the British Government that they were planning a revolution, and if the only way the British could stay was by perpetrating such deeds as the evidences showed that they did commit, then it was clear that they had no business to be there. The existence of such a condition of things—of such a horrible necessity (if it existed), constituted the strongest of conceivable proofs that staying was a monstrous crime, and that they had no justification for remaining a day longer than was necessary to turn over the country to a properly organized and responsible Indian Government, which, since they held all power in their hands, it was their duty to help the Indian people to form.

Supplement I. Tagore and Gandhi on the Massacre

Something should be said regarding the action of Mahatma Gandhi and Rabindranath Tagore in relation to the Amritsar Massacre and the rest of the atrocities.

Until after the passage of the Rowlatt Acts and especially the occurrence of the Massacre, Mr. Tagore had been friendly to the British regime and had freely co-operated with it, in recognition of which the British Government had conferred upon him the Order of Knighthood. But these crimes against his country, coming after so many others, were more than he could endure. He felt that to be silent, to refrain from protesting against treatment of India so uncalled for, so unjust, and so inhuman, would be a crime against his own conscience, against Indian people, against the cause of freedom and justice in the world, and against Britain herself. Especially he felt that he could not with honor of self-respect consent to retain a mark of distinction bestowed by a Government guilty of these things. Accordingly he wrote a courteous but outspoken letter to the Viceroy portesting strongly and with absolute plainness against what had been done, and declining to retain longer his Order of Knighthood.*

The attitude and action of Gandhi were much

---

* The letter contained besides others the following averments : "The enormity of the measures taken by the Government in the Punjab for quelling some local disturbances has, with a rude shock, revealed to our minds the helplessness of our position as British subjects in India. The disproportionate severity of the punishments inflicted upon the unfortunate people and the methods of carrying them out, we are convinced, are without parallel in the history of civilized Governments, barring some conspicuous exceptions, recent and remote. Considering that such treatment has been meted out to a population disarmed and resourceless by a power which has the most terribly efficient organization for destruction of human lives, we must strongly assert that it can claim no political expediency, far less moral justification."

the same as those of Tagore. Gandhi had always been friendly and entirely loyal to the British Empire. It is true that in South Africa he strongly opposed certain flagrantly unjust laws enacted by the Government of that Dominion against the Indians there, and endeavored to get the laws altered. But this he did, not in hostility to Great Britain, but in promotion (as he believed) of her true interests. In the Boer and Zulu wars, he warmly supported the British cause, rendering such valuable and distinguished service that he was "mentioned in the despatches" and was awarded medals of high honor. When the war in Europe broke out, in 1914, having left South Africa, he at once entered service on the British side, raising a volunteer ambulance corps in London and later undertaking to do the same in India. Even after the close of the war, he continued for some time his faith in, and loyalty to, the British Government. He believed that Britain would keep its promises to the Indian people, and, in return for their amazing loyalty and great service during the war, would deal with them less tyrannically than in the past, and would extend to them more privileges and increased justice and freedom.

When the Rowlatt Acts were enacted and the Punjab atrocities occurred, he was amazed and shocked beyond words ; still he could not, and would not, believe but that they were done more or less without the sanction of the higher authorities, and that the better and truer Britain would sooner or later awake, come to the front, assert itself, repudiate these terrible and "un-British" wrongs, atone for them, and at last, even if too tardily, endeavor to be just and generous to the Indian people. And it was not until he found the Government refusing to repeal the Rowlatt Acts when all India begged for their repeal, treating the awful Amritsar Massacre lightly and making excuses for it, siding with the officials who had committed the atrocities, refusing to utter a word of rebuke even to such high offenders as Sir Michael O'Dwyer, and instead of keeping its promises to reward India with increased justice and freedom as a just return for her great loyalty, self-sacrifice and service during the war, actually inflicting on her greater wrongs than she had ever known—it was not until then that Gandhi lost faith in the British Government, and came to the decision, which cost him more regret and pain than any other in his life, that India had nothing to hope for from her foreign rulers ; that they were determined to keep their grip on the land at any cost ; that they were maintaining their rule primarily for their own benefit and not for India's ; and that they would never grant the Indian people freedom except by compulsion.

It was as a result of this decision that Gandhi launched his movement for Non-Cooperation. He deeply disbelieved in war and bloodshed, and would not sanction a revolution that involved these. But was there not a way for the Indian people to gain the freedom, which was their right, by peaceful means ? Britain was wholly dependent upon Indians for carrying on her government in India ; without their aid she could not maintain it for a day. The Indian people had a right to withdraw their assistance. Was not here a way in which, without shedding a drop of blood or doing wrong to a single Englishman, they might gain their freedom and win back their country of which they had been robbed ? This was Gandhi's dream.

Was it only a dream ? Dreams sometimes come true. Sometimes dreams prove more powerful than bayonets, battleships and all the engineering of force and war. Gandhi believes that men and nations who dream of freedom need never despair. Why? Because he believes that God lives; that truth is stronger than error; that justice is stronger than injustice; and that

"He who ruleth high and wise,
Nor falters in his plan,
Will take the stars out of the skies
E'er Freedom out of man."

Supplement II. The Rowlatt Acts

The Rowlatt Acts had so much connection with the atrocities in the Punjab, that some information regarding their exact nature should be given here. Some of the leading features of the Acts were the following:

1. Sudden arrest without warrant of any suspected person and detention without trial for an indefinite duration of time.

2. Conduct of proceedings in secret, before three judges, who may sit in any place, and who may not make public their proceedings.

3. The accused is kept ignorant of the names of his accusers or of the witnesses against him.

4. The accused is not confronted with his accusers or the witnesses against him.

5. The accused has only the right of a written account of the offenses attributed to him.

6. The accused is denied the right of defending himself with the help of lawyers or counsel.

7. No witnesses are allowed the accused in his defense.

8. Usual legal procedure may be disregarded.

9. The right of appeal is denied.

10. Any one associating with ex-political offenders may be arrested.

11. Ex-political offenders must deposit securities.
12. Ex-political offenders may not take part in any political, educational or religious activities.

An Indian scholar has pointed out and published the following suggestive summary of points of similarity between these Rowlatt Acts and the infamous Star Chamber proceedings (in England) under Judge Jeffreys and those of the Spanish Inquisition.

1. Sudden arrest without warrant on mere suspicion, and detention without trial.
2. Conduct of proceedings secretly *in camera*.
3. The person under trial ignorant of the name etc., of his accusers or the witnesses against him.
4. The accused not confronted with his accusers or the witnesses against him.
5. The accused having only the right to a written account of the offenses attributed to him.
6. The accused not allowed the right of defending himself with the help of lawyers.
7. No witnesses allowed in his defense.
8. Arbitrary judicial procedure, different from the usual.
9. Trial and investigation of indefinite duration.

The Rowlatt Acts were felt throughout India to be a Star Chamber measure of the most unjust and tyrannical character, robbing the people of every vestige of political protection. They were enacted in the face of the most vigorous and earnest protest of the whole Indian nation. The Acts were later repealed. But were the people of India ever recompensed in any way for the terrible injustices and sufferings which they caused or did the British Government ever acknowledge their injustices or make any kind of apology for for them ? No. On the contrary, as has been seen, the Government bestowed a high honour on the author of the Acts.

CHAPTER XXXI

WHY INDIA REJECTED "DYARCHY"

Soon after the close of the Great War in Europe, the British gave to India a "Government Reform Scheme," (called "Dyarchy") which was proclaimed to the world as a great boon to the Indian people, as something which advanced them far on the road toward freedom and self-rule, and, withal, as something which showed the great generosity of the British toward India, and their constant solicitude for her welfare and progress.

Did the Indian people receive the Scheme as a great boon, and were they profoundly thankful for it, as Britain declared they ought to be? No, and for reasons which they thought were of the weightiest possible character.

Of course, *in a sense* they accepted the Dyarchy plan, they had to, it was forced upon them without their consent. A few thought that it was perhaps better than nothing, and so they said: "Let us make the most of it until we can get something more satisfactory." But it is not an overstatement to affirm that all India was deeply disappointed and hurt by it. Absolutely all parties, the most moderate and conservative as well as the most advanced, united in declaring that it was not what they desired or expected or deserved, and that it was not worthy of England.

Why were practically all the important leaders of India disappointed, grieved and pained? The reason which immediately presented itself and which would not down, was: The scheme seemed to them little or nothing but a "smoke-screen" to hide Britain's real mind and purpose. With the most careful and eager examination of it that they could make, they were unable to discover in it even the slightest evidence that their British masters intended to give them real freedom or real self-rule then or ever. It made a great show, a great pretense of advancing them far on the road to full attainment of both. But as a matter of fact. it gave them no advancement and no new freedom that amounted to anything; and it really promised nothing. All it did was to grant them a few new offices (some of them it is true with quite flattering salaries), and some new or enlarged legislatures, both national and provincial, in which they might talk and talk, discuss and discuss, and even vote and vote; but only upon such questions and subjects as the British graciously permitted them to vote or speak upon: in no case were they granted any *real power*; they were allowed to *control nothing*. ("Mock Parliaments" was the name given to the legislatures by an eminent Englishman). The real objects of the scheme seemed to be two, namely, to quiet the growing unrest of the Indian people by making them think they were getting something important (when they were not), and to produce a favorable impression upon the public opinion of the world by spreading the idea that the British were generous to India and were leading her as fast as seemed wise toward her desired goal of freedom and self-rule.

It is important to know the facts connected with the origin of the reform scheme.

When the great war of 1914 broke out in Europe, England found herself in a serious plight. In order to do her part in withstanding the

German attack on France, she was compelled to send for almost her entire Indian army, which was the first foreign contingent to arrive on the field of conflict, and without whose invaluable help the German advance could not have been checked and Paris would undoubtedly have fallen.

This sudden withdrawal from India of the military forces which were maintained there to hold her in subjection, naturally suggested to the Indian people that now was a favorable time to throw off the foreign yoke which was so galling to them, and to gain their freedom and independence. And why not? Would any other nation in the world, held in bondage for more than a century and a half, have refrained from taking advantage of such an opportunity?

It is easy to see how great, how tremendous was the temptation. How did the Indian people meet it? Did they say: "Now is the auspicious time; let us rise and be free?" On the contrary, the vast majority of them said: "England is in sore distress; she is fighting virtually for her life. To take advantage of her helplessness, to strike her when she is down, would be dishonorable, cowardly. We will not do it. Although she has robbed us of our nationhood, we will not turn on her in her time of peril. Until her danger is past, we will stand by her, we will be loyal—nay, we will even help her in her struggle." And they did. With insignificant exceptions they were absolutely loyal throughout the war. Largely they laid aside for the time being the political agitation for freedom which they had been carrying on for many years. India rendered to Great Britain great and invaluable aid both in men and money. It was amazing. It was almost incredible that a subject people longing for freedom should take such a course. It was unselfish, chivalrous, noble, beyond words. I am not able to recall in all history a national act, a national course of conduct so magnanimous or so noble.

The Indian people believed, and I think all the world believed, that when the war was over and England was safe, she would show appreciation of their marvellous loyalty and magnanimity, by treating them far better than she had done in the past, by righting their wrongs, and if not by granting them at once full and complete home rule like that of Canada, which was India's desire,—at least by setting them far on the way toward it, and by giving them a definite promise of its complete realization in the very near future.

Did England do this? No! Unbelievable as it seems, instead of meeting the magnanimity of the Indian people with a like magnanimity, instead of showing appreciation of their astonishing loyalty and their invaluable aid in her time of distress, instead of being even just to them, she proceeded to treat them with a degree of suspicion, oppression and cruelty beyond anything in the past, culminating in the Punjab atrocities and the infamous Rowlatt Act which virtually deprived India of even the protection of civil law. Of course, this was a terrible shock to the Indian people. It was a disappointment about as great as it is possible for any nation to experience.

But did Great Britain offer to the Indian people no return of any kind for what they had done? Yes, she offered them this so-called "Reform Scheme" (or Dyarchy) for their Government. This and only this was England's reward for India's amazing service and devotion.

Let us examine the Scheme a little more fully, so as to see exactly what were some of the more important reasons for India's dissatisfaction with it.

(1) The first disappointment, injustice, hardly less than insult, that India saw in the scheme, was Britain's spirit of high-handedness and arrogance, in claiming for herself all rights in the matter, and allowing India none; in setting out from the first to make *the* Scheme not what the Indian people had a right to and wanted, or what would have been just and acceptable to all parties concerned; but solely what she (Britain) wanted, and then thrusting it upon India.

The Scheme, to have been just, to have been anything that India could honorably accept, should have been mutual, something framed by India and Great Britain together, each recognizing the other's rights. But it was nothing of the kind. It was something designed to be a compact between two parties, but framed by one party alone and imposed upon the other. There was nothing mutual about it. It was a dictation; it was a command; it was the voice of a master to slaves. Britain, standing above, handed it down to the Indian people below. They must receive it on their knees. She owned India. She would manage it as she chose. She owned the Indian people. They must obey her.

Is it any wonder that a scheme framed and offered in such a spirit and with such aims, was not welcome to the Indian people? Is it any wonder that they found in it nothing to right their wrongs, nothing to set their feet upon a path leading to self-government?

Let me not be misunderstood when I speak of the Scheme as formed by Great Britain alone. I am quite aware that Mr. Montagu, the British Secretary of State for India, before formulating his plan went to India and consulted—candidly and honestly, I have no doubt—the various interested parties there;—on the one hand, the

Indian leaders and on the other the British rulers. That was fair so far as it went, but what a little way it went! What followed was that Mr. Montagu and other representatives of Great Britain proceeded themselves alone to draw up a plan for India's government, without associating with themselves in this great and serious task any representatives chosen by India; that is without giving India any real part or power in the matter. That was unfair; that was dishonorable. Such a one-sided body of men could not possibly produce a scheme that would be just to India or that India could accept. What ought to have been done was the creation of a Joint Commission with an equal number of British and Indian members, the Indian Members being elected by the Indian people and therefore empowered really to represent them; and this Joint Commission should have been instructed to draw up, and should have drawn up, such a scheme as seemed just and wise in their united judgment. That would have been fair both to England and India. And to a scheme thus created, the Indian people would gladly have given their assent.

(2) The second thing to be said about this so-called Reform Scheme is that, in its very nature it was self-contradictory, and therefore impossible.

The Scheme was given the very unusual name of "Dyarchy," which properly means the joint rule of two monarchs, as William and Mary in England. But in the present case it was supposed to signify the joint rule of the British and the Indians through an arrangement by which some matters connected with the Government were "transferred" or committed (under severe limitations) to Indian management, while others were "reserved" or kept wholly under British control. Exactly described, it was a plan which put side by side two radically different, two antagonistic forms of government—one, self-rule, the other, arbitrary rule from the outside ;one, democracy, the other, absolute autocracy or absolute monarchy (in the form of an alien bureaucracy) ; and expected them to work in harmony. It was an attempt to mix oil and water ; or to ride two horses going in opposite directions. Abraham Lincoln said ; "A nation cannot endure half free and half slave." The British ought to have known that neither can a nation be successfully ruled by means of governtal machinery, half formed for ends of freedom and half for ends of oppression. That is exactly what this scheme was and is.

What Great Britain ought to have done, instead of concocting such an impossible, misshapen, mongrel plan, is clear. She should have listened to India's just demands, and given her a government framed distinctly and honestly for ends of self-rule ; a government responsible, at least in all home matters, to the Indian people ; a real democracy essentially like that of Canada or South Africa, but of course adapted to the special needs and conditions of India. That would have been sane. It would have been straightforward and honest. It would have been practicable and to the infinite advantage of all concerned. On the one hand, it would have made India content, and on the other it would have removed all cause for anxiety or alarm on the part of Great Britain. It would have resulted in India's becoming as loyal a part of the Empire (or Commonwealth) as South Africa or Canada or Australia. That the very opposite state of things now exists, is the result of Britain's blind and arbitrary refusal to give to the Indian people what they so earnestly asked for, and what was their right ; and thrusting on them, instead, this impossible, self-contradictory vicious plan of "Dyarchy."

(3) A fundamental defect of the Reform Scheme or Dyarchy was the startling fact that it contained no Bill of Rights, no constitutional guarantee of any kind securing the Indian people against possible future injustices and tyrannies on the part of the Government. In view of the many wrongs that they had suffered in the past, this defect was fatal—something which alone, as they believed, was sufficient reason for rejecting the Scheme. They realized that without a bill of rights, or a constitutional guarantee of justice, they could have no sure protection, they would be at the mercy of their foreign rulers, liable at any time to have wrongs and cruelties inflicted upon them as great as any they had ever suffered. The British at home, in England, would on no consideration give up the protection which for hundreds of years they have received from their *Magna Charta*, which has shielded them by its great words:

"No freeman shall be arrested or detained in prison... or in any way molested...unless by the lawful judgment of his peers and by the law of the land."

We Americans could not possibly be induced to surrender the guaranteed protection which we possess in our Declaration of Independence, and especially in our National Constitution, which declares:

"Congress shall make no law abridging the freedom of speech or of the press, or the right of the people peaceably to assemble, and to petition the Government for a redress of grievances.

"The right of the people to be secure in their persons, houses, papers and effects against unreasonable searches and seizures, shall not be violated.

"Excessive bail shall not be required, nor excessive fines imposed, nor cruel and unusual punishments inflicted.

"No State or province within the nation shall deprive any person of life, liberty or property without due process of law, nor deny to any person within its jurisdiction the equal protection of the laws."

Such charters of rights, such guarantees of protection, are regarded by Englishmen, by Americans, and by all other free peoples, as absolutely indispensable in their own cases. Why did not Great Britain grant such protection to India?

What are the facts bearing in the case? They are startling enough. (See chapter XXX in this book). Within the last few years reports have come from the most trustworthy sources, of brutalities committed by British officials against the Indian people, which have shocked the world—houses searched without warrant; men seized and imprisoned without trial; men and women peacefully working in the field bombed from the sky; all the inhabitants in a certain street in a city forbidden to go along the street even to get water or buy food except by their crawling on their hands and knees; a great peaceful gathering assembled in a public garden on a religious festival day, fired on without warning, by troops, and the firing continued until the ammunition of the soldiers was exhausted, and 379 dead and 1,200 wounded men, women and children lay heaped on the bloody ground;* prisoners confined in a luggage van without ventilation, and in spite of their frantic cries for air kept there until more than 70 were dead; and many other brutalities and crimes almost as shocking.

* The Hunter Committee appointed to investigate the Punjab atrocities reported the number killed in the Amritsar (Jalianwala Bagh) massacre as 379, and the number wounded as about three times as many. These numbers, however, are very much the lowest given by any authority. The Investigation Commission appointed by the authorities of the National Indian Congress, whose researches were far more thorough, reported that they

If the new government Scheme for India, was to be of any value at all, ought it not to have guaranteed the people against such outrages in the future? Yet incredible, almost monstrous, as the fact seems, it did not.

The fact alone that the military forces of the country and the police were both wholly under British control—neither being responsible in any degree to the Indian people—made the recurrence of injustices and atrocities as bad as any of these, possible at any future time. The Scheme gave no guarantee whatever against the coming at any time of other Governor O'Dwyers, and General Dyers, and Jalianwala Baghs, and Moplah suffocations, and the rest. It provided protection for the British rulers of the land, but for nobody else. It did not guarantee to the Indian people police protection, or military protection, or civil protection; it did not insure to them freedom of speech, or of assembly, or of the press; or the right of trial in open court; or the privilege of *habeas corpus*; or any other of the essential rights and privileges which are the foundations and indispensable guarantees of liberty, justice and law. Is it any wonder that India rejected the Scheme? Is it not amazing that any nation calling itself civilized and Christian, in this age of the world, could have proposed such a Scheme?

(4) In the so-called "Reform Plan" offered to India in 1919, the British kept in their own hands not only all other kinds of power, but also all real legislative power. India was allowed no effective voice whatever in legislation. This statement applies to legislation in the Provinces, and

---

found unimpeachable evidence that the number shot to death was approximately, 1,200 and the number wounded approximately 3,600.

it applies still more fully and seriously to national legislation. It is true that the Scheme gave to India both national legislative bodies and provincial legislative bodies, which looked like real parliaments,—parliaments endowed with power to enact real laws. But on looking deeper, it was soon seen that this appearance was deceptive. They were not real parliaments or real legislatures at all as these words are understood in Europe and America. They were all under external control. Whatever they did could be overthrown.

In the national government, the Reform Scheme allowed Indians to hold a few more places than they formerly did. For example, in the National Legislative Assembly there were an increased number of Indians, enough to guard India's rights if they had possessed any real power. But they did not. As has been said, they were allowed to vote on some things, but not on all; on some they were not permitted even to speak. Matters were so arranged that in no case could they disturb the plans of the Government. Whatever legislation the British rulers desired, they enacted, whether the Indians favored it or not.

In the Provinces, the situation was similar. Each Provincial Legislative Assembly contained a majority of Indians, but here again they could legislate only upon such matters as the British rulers permitted; and even regarding these they had no final power; whatever laws they enacted could be overturned by the Governor in Council, or by the Governor-General in Council, or both. Even if a legislature voted unanimously for a measure, the Government might disallow it.

Is it said that even in democratic America the enactments of State Legislatures may be vetoed by Governors, and those of the National Congress, by Presidents? Yes, but these vetoes are not final. An American State legislature can pass anything it desires over the Governor's veto, and the American National Congress can pass anything it pleases over the veto of the President. In India nothing of this kind is possible. There, all final legislative authority, all real legislative power, whether national or provincial is in the hands of the executive. Notwithstanding the increased number of so-called legislators under the new Government Scheme, the British are still, just as before, the supreme, and really the sole, law-makers.

Of course, the fact that the dyarchal plan granted to members of legislatures considerable liberty of discussion, was not without value. It gave to the British overlords a better knowledge than they would otherwise have had of the feelings and wants of the people, and thus to some extent it may have influenced legislation for the better. And yet, one cannot help wondering how much. A prominent member of the British Indian Government said to an American :

"Oh yes! We listen to these Indian fellows, these natives, in our legislatures—to their talk, their discussions, their pleas for this and that, their demands for what they call their 'rights,' for 'home-rule' and the rest—we listen to them, they like it, and then—*we do as we damned please* !"

This is a cynical declaration ; but it describes exactly the amount of power possessed by the people of India under Dyarchy as regards enacting legislation on all subjects of highest importance, and in shaping all the really vital affairs of their own nation.* The fact is, the government of

---

* It may be claimed that the Dyarchal Scheme placed some vital matters—for example, education and public sanitation—in the hands of Indians, and hence, if any failures were found there the responsibility was with them. The claim is superficial. The truth is,

India continued just as autocratic and absolute after the introduction of the new plan of things as it was before. The power of "Certification" given to Viceroy made him virtually an absolute monarch, and placed all the Indian legislatures and all India virtually under his feet. It enabled him to defeat any legislation that he did not like by certifying that it was against the safety or interests of India (meaning the British Empire), and to enact any law desired by him by "certifying" that it was necessary for the interests or safety of India (the British Empire). As for the apparent check placed upon his certifications by the provision that they must lie two months before the British Parliament, before becoming operative, every-body knew from the beginning that that was meant only as a form.

The helplessness of the Indian legislatures under Dyarchy has been described in emphatic words by an eminent Englishman. In the winter of 1925-26, Dr. V. H. Rutherford, a member of Parliament and a prominent leader in the Labor Party, made an extended visit to India for the purpose of examining on the ground the working of the "Reforms."

The *Amrita Bazar Patrika*, of Calcutta, in its issue of February 2nd, 1926, published an interview with Dr. Rutherford, who is reported to have said :

---

the public revenue of the nation remained under dyarchy where it had always been, in the sole control of the British, who always use first of all as much of it as they want for their own military ,and imperialistic purposes and for other British interests (paying the high salaries and pensions of British officials, etc.), and Indian interests, however vital, whether education and sanitation or others, have to put up with what they can get from the small remainder. This is the prime reason why education makes so little progress and public sanitation and hygiene are so neglected.

"At Madras, Lahore and elsewhere in the Provinces, I have seen in action the Legislative Councils and Assemblies created by the Reform Scheme. My disappointment on account of the feeble powers which Great Britain has conferred upon them is boundless, as also is my indignation. My greatest disappointment and indignation, however, have been reserved for Delhi, the Capital, and the National Government there. The National Legislature is supposed to be the crowning piece of the anatomy of the Montague-Chelmsford Reforms; and on close inspection I have found it to be a mere make-believe, a mere pretence, a mockery, a legislative body in name but without power to form a government, or to displace a government in which it has no confidence; without power to appoint or dismiss ministers: without power of purse; without power to shift a nail or screw in the "steel frame" of bureaucratic control set up by the British; without the least shred or iota of control over the Viceroy, who can defy and damn at his pleasure all the representatives of the people, and who has, in fact, defied them again and again, 'certifying' the Finance Bill over their heads, locking up thousands of them in prison in disregard of all law, and doing whatever else he liked. Never in the history of the world was such a hoax perpetrated upon a great people as England pepertrated upon India, when in return for India's invaluable service during the war, she gave to the Indian nation such a discreditable, disgraceful, undemocratic, tyrannical constitution. No political party in Great Britain would tolerate these iniquitous semblances of parliamentary institutions for a single week."

Let it be borne in mind that these strong words were not spoken by an Indian, but by a Member of the British Parliament. In the light of such statements, coming from such a source, is it any wonder that India indignantly rejects the so-called "boon" of Dyarchy, as worthless and worse than worthless, and demands instead something incomparably better?

(5) A very prominent and evil feature of the Dyarchy Scheme which should not go unmentioned, is the fact that its whole spirit was one of negations, negations. From first to last, its constant aim was to forbid, to forbid.

Its most outstanding characteristic was its careful, specific and multiplied specifications and descriptions of privileges, rights, liberties and powers which the Indian people *were not permitted to have.* At every point where the Indian people came upon anything of first class importance, anything that would give any real power to India, there at once they were met with "reservations," "reservations." And the reservations were always in the interest of England, never of India. Even the "transferred" subjects "had strings to them." The great thing that the scheme constantly guarded against, was not India's danger, the danger that India might fail to get her rights, but the imagined danger that at some point or other England might suffer some loss of prestige, or privilege, or power. The scheme gave no evidence of being something prompted in any degree by a desire to right India's age-long and terrible wrongs; indeed, it contained no real recognition of the existence, then or in the past, of any such wrongs. Everything in it and about it showed that it was simply an effort on the part of Great Britain to *retain her grip on India at a trying time.* The scheme was an unintentional but clear acknowledgment that a great new spirit of freedom and independence had come into the world, and that India was feeling it mightily. This *alarmed England.* She saw that the Indian people were thinking, were rising from their knees to their feet, were becoming indignant at being held in subjection, were feeling humiliated and outraged beyond measure by the fact that they, who for so many centuries had been a great nation among the nations of the world, were now not thought of as a nation at all, but were regarded as a mere appendage, a mere possession of a nation six or seven thousand miles away.

It was distinctly with this in view, and because of this, that the new Government Scheme was offered to India. The Scheme was England's attempt to counteract all this, to quiet the unrest of the Indian people, to allay their humiliation, to soothe their wounded pride, to administer to them an opiate, to induce them to lay aside their dangerous ambition and be willing to continue loyal still to Great Britain, by offering them something which they were told was a great boon, something which England assured them meant increasing freedom, more and more privileges, more and more participation in the Government, an advance, with more and more advances to follow, on the road leading toward self-rule.

But alas! these promises when examined, when really looked into, when probed to the bottom, when tested, were seen to mean nothing of value to India. Their real purpose was not at all India's advancement, but her pacification, and England's security. They offered India no boon whatever. They merely promised her a pot of gold at the end of a rainbow.

(6) This brings me to a final indictment which remains to be made against Great Britain's new Government Scheme for India. The Scheme fixed no time. It left everything uncertain. Whatever promises it made, or was supposed to make of new rights or privileges, or of advances toward self-rule, were only to be fulfilled "some time," in an unknown future, and at the option of the British rulers.

This was fatal. It made the promises absolutely worthless. It is well-understood in law that if I give a man a note promising to pay him a sum of money, but without mentioning any time, my note is of no value. Nobody can collect anything on it. Or if I make my note payable at such a time in the future as I may then elect, still it is valueless. My promise to pay must state when the payment is due, in order to be of any worth. It is exactly the same with the supposed promise made in this Reform Scheme of future self-government to India. There was no date fixed. The fulfillment could be put off and put off until the end of time. It was no promise at all.

The fact is not to be escaped, that Great Britain did not in her so-called Reform Scheme, pledge to the Indian people anything whatever except that if they would cease their (to her) disagreeable agitations for reforms, freedom, self-government, and be dumb and docile, and do what she commanded (like good children, or rather, like slaves) and caused her no trouble, she would be kind and motherly to them, and at such time or times in the future as, in her superior wisdom, she might see fit, she might perhaps condescend graciously to grant them such limited new liberties as she might then consider safe, and such gradual advances toward some very far-off goal of self-government (Dominion status or some other) as she might then deem it best for them to receive.

To put the case in a word, this Scheme which has been heralded abroad and praised as offering so much to India, and as setting her feet securely on the road to self-rule, particularly to Dominion status like that of Canada, as a matter of fact, *gave her no assurance of being granted such a status, or any form of self-determination, in a thousand years.*

Can a great nation, with a proud history of three or four milleniums, be satisfied with such mockery ? Said the great and honored American Patrick Henry, "Give me liberty, or give me death." Said the great and honored Indian, Raja Ram Mohun Roy, "I want to be free, or I do not want to be at all."

In conclusion :

What are the lessons that Great Britain should learn from India's rejection of Dyarchy ? There are two which are clear as the light, if she will open her eyes to them.

One is that India refuses longer to accept stones for bread. She is fast waking up. All her leaders are awake now, and her people are fast following. She sees the world becoming free ; she sees Asia becoming free. Under such conditions she can no more be held in bondage than the rising tide of the ocean can be stayed.

The other lesson is, that if Britain persists in further treatment of India in the high-handed spirit of the dyarchy Scheme, if she attempts to force upon the Indian people another constitution as autocratic, as tyrannical, as defiant of their wishes and rights as the dyarchy Scheme was, she must be prepared for disaster,—the result certainly will be, acute, growing and probably permanent bitterness and resentment toward Britain on the part of India, and alienation between the two nations so deep that it probably cannot be healed. Why does not Great Britain recognize all this ?

Indeed, why was she not wise enough, brave enough, and noble enough at the close of the Great War in Europe, even if not earlier than that, to extend to India the same warm, strong hand of friendship, confidence, trust, comradeship, co-operation and real partnership in the Empire, which at the end of the Boer War she extended to South Africa ? That would have saved everything in India, as it did in South Africa.

Will she do it yet ? Will she do it before it is too late ?

CHAPTER XXXII

THE GREAT DELUSION: BRITAIN'S CLAIM THAT SHE IS "EDUCATING INDIA FOR SELF-RULE"

There is no greater delusion known to men than the idea that one nation can "educate another nation for self-rule," and especially that it can do so *by holding that other nation in bondage.* Yet that is exactly what Britain is doing or claims to be doing in India. How is it that any intelligent mind fails to see through the delusion?

Look at the situation carefully. India wants to rule herself, as she and all other nations have a right to do, and as she did with success for three thousand years before Britain reduced her to bondage. Britain, after holding her in bondage for a hundred and sixty years, says to her in effect: "You are not fit to rule yourself; but because you in your foolishness want and demand to do so (not appreciating your great privilege of being ruled by us), we, in our great desire to be kind to you, have undertaken the heavy task of making you, at least in a measure fit for self-government by educating you for it. How educating you for it? By holding you still longer in bondage. You ask: How much longer? We cannot tell; you must trust us; as soon as your prolonged experience of bondage has sufficiently educated you for freedom and self-government so that you seem to us *fit* to rule yourself, we will (perhaps) grant you self-rule."

I repeat: That is exactly what Britain's "educating India for self-rule" really means. Is it sane? Is it anything else but a delusion and a mockery? If conquering a nation and holding it in bondage a century and a half has deprived it of fitness to govern itself, by what legerdemain can continuing that bondage restore it to fitness, or have any other possible effect, except to make it still more unfit? The fact is, not since time began, so far as is known, has any nation ever obtained fitness or ability to rule itself through education given it by another nation; and certainly not by being held in bondage by another nation, as India is being held, and seemingly is to continue to be held, in bondage by Britain. It is by freedom that nations learn to govern themselves, and never by bondage. Also it is by their own experience, their own effort, their own practice, and never by so-called "education" or "training" imparted to them by other nations.

England long tried the policy of "educating" Canada for self-government, that is, of keeping Canada in virtual bondage, treating her people like children unable to take care of themselves, just as she is now treating India. Like any other self-respecting people they chafed, protested and rebelled, and England would have lost them, as she had lost her American colonies at the South, had not Lord Durham, who was sent to Canada to look into matters, returned home with a report which shocked the British people into sense, and caused the Government to grant to Canada greatly increased freedom—freedom to stand on her own feet and learn to govern herself by governing herself, by experience, the only possible way.

One of the most remarkable achievements of the modern world is the progress made by the negroes in the United States since their emancipation in 1863. Suppose that instead of freeing the slaves at once and setting them at once to the task of walking on their own legs, we had said as the British say of the people of India: "No, not now. We must go slow. Sometime, after many years, it may do to give them freedom; but we must keep them in bondage much longer and let their masters, overseers and slave-drivers 'educate' them for freedom. As soon as we think they are 'fit' to govern themselves we will grant them their liberty." Would they not all have been slaves to-day?

At the end of the Great War, when Poland asked for freedom, suppose she had been left for an unlimited series of years under her old masters, Russia, Germany and Austria, for them to "educate" her for self-rule, and grant it to her when they thought she was 'fit' to receive it. Would she ever have got it?

Suppose the South American nations, which are now prosperous, self-ruling republics, had been compelled to remain for an indefinite period under Spain, their old oppressor, to be "educated" by her for self-government, as India is being "educated for self-government" by her old oppressor, would any of them have been free to-day?

Does anybody claim that when China achieves peace and unity she ought then to be conquered by some European nation and held in bondage for a term of years for her conqueror to "educate" her for self-government?

Let us see what some very eminent men, Englishmen and Americans, who have had large observation and experience in the matter, say about "educating nations for self-rule," keeping them in bondage until they are "fit."

Long ago Macauley wrote the following words "Many politicians of our time are in the habit of laying it down as the selfevident proposition that no people ought to be free until they are fit to use their freedom. The maxim is worthy of the fool in the old story who resolved not to go into the water until he had learned to swim. If men are to *wait for liberty till they become wise and good in slavery, they may indeed wait for ever."*
(Essay on Milton).

Was not Macauley right ?

John Morley wrote the Life of Gladstone. In that work (Volume 1, p. 360) he says :

"Gladstone was never weary of protesting against the fallacy of what was called 'preparing' these new communities for freedom : teaching a colony, like an infant, by slow degrees to walk, first putting it in long clothes, then in short clothes. . . . . . In point of fact, every year and every month during which they are retained under the administration of a despotic government, renders them less fit for free institutions. . . . . It is liberty alone which fits men for liberty."

Let me quote two or three eminent Americans. There is no American scholar who is a higher authority regarding the peoples of the Orient, their governments and present condition, than Frederick Starr. Says Professor Starr :

"A government adapted to the economic development of a people and working up from within, is better than the most perfect government forced from above. The Americans are doing far more for the Philippines than Britain is for India ; yet it is my opinion that every day we remain in the islands, the Filipinos are less capable of self-government. They have all the while been better fit to rule themselves than we or any other foreigners are to rule them. The only way America can benefit them is by giving them independence at once."

I wish to cite a very instructive passage from the eminent German-American statesman, Carl Schurz. Mr. Schurz was general in the Union Army during the American Civil War, a member of the Cabinet of President Hayes, and for many years one of the nation's most honored and influential public leaders. In connection with his office of Secretary of the Interior he had large experience with the immigrants who at that time were coming to America in great numbers from lands of the Old World where they had been given no opportunities for self-government. How could they be made valuable citizens in a democracy—a nation where there was self-rule? In his "Reminiscences" (Vol. II, pp. 77-80) he says:

"One of the most interesting experiences of my life was the observation of the educational influence exercised upon men by the actual practice of self-government."

Persons attempting to exercise self-government for the first time, he declares,

"may do it somewhat clumsily in the beginning and make grievous mistakes, but these very mistakes, with their disagreeable consequences, will serve to sharpen the wits of those who desire to learn. Practice upon one's own responsibility is the best if not the only school of self-government. What is sometimes called the art of self-government is not learned by the mere presentation of other people's experiences by way of instructive example. Practice is the only really effective teacher. Other methods of instruction will rather retard, if not altogether prevent, the development of the self-governing capacity, because they will serve to weaken the sense of responsibility, and self-reliance. This is why *there is not any instance in history of a people's having been successfully taught to govern themselves by a tutelary power acting upon the principle that its wards should not be given the power of self-government until they had shown themselves fit for it.*"

This may well have been written with India directly in mind.

I quote another utterance, if possible still

more weighty, which was spoken with India directly in view. It is from the American historian and scholar, Charles Francis Adams. Speaking before the American Historical Association in 1901, this man of candor and of large learning said, (confirming in every respect the testimony of General Schurz, Professor Starr, Macauley and Gladstone):

I submit that *there is not an instance in all recorded history, from the earliest times until now, where a so called inferior race or community has been elevated in its character, or made self-sustaining or self-governing, or even put on the way to that result through a condition of dependency or tutelage.* I might, without much danger, assert that the *condition of dependency,* even for communities of the same race and blood, always *exercises an emasculating and deteriorating influence.* I would undertake, if called upon, to show that *this rule is invariable*—that from the inherent and fundamental conditions of human nature, *it has known, and can know, no exceptions.* This truth I could demonstrate from almost innumerable examples.

And Mr. Adams proceeded to make the direct application of this truth to India and declared in the most unequivocal terms that notwithstanding any or all material or other improvements made in the country by the British during the three hundred years and more since the East India Company began its exploitation and conquest of the land, British rule had been an absolute failure as a means for increasing the capacity or fitness of the Indian people for self-government,—it had not increased that capacity or that fitness in the slightest degree; but on the contrary, it had actually lessened it. And he held that there was no ground for believing that it would or could ever have any other effect. It was not by subjection or tutelage to another nation—no matter what that nation might be,—but by the very opposite, by *freedom,* by *actual practice of self-government,* by *experience,* by *making mistakes and learning wisdom from the same*—it was by this method and no other that *all capacity for self-government has been obtained in the past and must be obtained for ever.* It was by this method that India learned 3,000 years ago to rule herself, and had continued one of the great self-ruling nations of the world until Great Britain robbed her of nationhood. And *what she needs now is simply "hands off"* on the part of her foreign conqueror, so that her native capacity for self-rule, which Mr. Adams held has been weakened by British dominance, but by no means destroyed, may again, as in the past, come into activity and therefore into growth, normal development and permanent strength.

All these eminent scholars and statesmen simply confirm what all history affirms, that no people can teach another freedom: each people must learn it for itself. No nation can teach another how to rule itself. Each nation must find out by experience.

To say that India should be trained, educated, fitted for freedom and self-rule by Britain or any other nation before she is given freedom and self-rule is simply to fly in the face of all the best educational philosophy and practice of the modern world. The old method of teaching by theory without practice, teaching before practice, or even teaching in preparation for practice, is fast giving way to the far better method of teaching through and by practice. This is known as the "practice method" or the "laboratory method" or in law the "case method," and it has been adopted, or is being adopted, in schools and educational institutions of every grade and every kind. Geology and botany are taught by taking students into the fields, the woods and the mountains, to study the flower, the shrubs, the trees and the rocks, themselves. Mechanics is studied in the presence of and by the constant use of hammer, saw, square, anvil and lathe. Chemistry is learned almost wholly in laboratories. Languages are taught by actually speaking and writing the languages. Students of medicine go for study to laboratories, clinics, and hospitals. Our best law schools rely more and more on practice courts and case work.

Nations and peoples must acquire the art of government in the same way, by the practice method. They must learn self-rule by actually undertaking self-rule,—by trial, by experiment, by making mistakes and correcting them. There is no other way.

It is the judgment of the wisest thinkers of the ages that holding men in bondage instead of fitting them for freedom, has the exact opposite effect; it tends to spoil them for freedom; it is most likely to create in them the "inferiority complex," the slave mind; or if it does not do that, it is liable to produce in them the mind of the anarchist, of the revolter against all law and order. On the other hand, give men freedom, and they tend to grow thoughtful and serious under it, and to gird themselves to meet its responsibilities with intelligence and strength.

Says David Starr Jordan:

> "Good government means giving the people an opportunity to practice, to rule themselves. That is the basis of all possible good government."

Said Senator George F. Hoar (in an address in the United States Senate, in 1899):

> "I believe that the God who has created this world has ordained that his children shall work out their own salvation, and that nations should work out their own salvation. I believe that liberty, good government, free institutions, cannot be given by any people to another, but must be wrought out by each for and by itself."

Immanuel Kant put the same thought in a more philosophic way:

"If we were not designed to exert our powers till we were assured of our ability to attain our object, those powers would remain unused. It is only by trying that we learn what our powers are."

Sir Henry Cotton, the eminent British administrator in India, declares:

"No system of government can be beneficial which does not foster the self-reliance of the people, and encourage their aspirations to realize their destiny through their own exertions. It was one of Mr. Gladstone's most famous sayings (cited above) that it is liberty alone that fits men for liberty." *

Mr. John M. Robertson, one of England's ablest thinkers, argues that not alone civilized peoples, like those of India, should be permitted to rule themselves, but that all peoples, whether civilized or not, ought to be allowed to do so; that absolutely none should be forced under the rule of others. In his work on "International Problems"† he declares:

"There ought to be a general recognition of the fundamental fitness of self-government for all races. It is good for all men to be intelligent agents instead of recalcitrant machines. All countries should walk on their own feet. In short, no argument ever educed against autonomy or self-rule for any race has any scientific value. As a matter of fact self-rule exists at this moment among the lowest and most retrograde races of the earth; and probably no experienced European administrator who has ever carried his thinking above the level of a frontier trader, will confidently say that any one of those races would be improved by setting over them any system of white man's rule that has yet been tried."

Mr. Robertson does not by any means stand alone among scientific investigators in holding these views.

Think of the farce of trying to educate a nation

---

* "New India," p. 145.

† See pp. 41-45.

to recover from the evil effects of bondage, by prolonging its bondage. That is exactly what Britain's "educating India for self-rule" means. The only thing that training in slavery or under slave conditions can fit any people for, is more slavery. The only way any people can be trained for freedom is by their own efforts and under conditions of freedom. The Indian leaders regard this whole claim that India needs to be educated by Britain for self-government as not only a farce, but an insult. Who is Britain that she should make such a claim ? Did not the Indian people govern themselves for thousands of years before she reduced them to bondage ? The truth is, if India is not able to rule herself, the reason, and the only reason is, that Britain is on top of her, holding her down, with a sword at her throat. Let Britain get off her. Let her be given freedom, and time to recover from the financial impoverishment, the want of schools for her children, the deprivation of political experience, the slave mind, and the other evil effects of the slave treatment which has been inflicted upon her during her century and a half of bondage, and no future thing is more certain than that in due time she will again become one of the leading nations of the world.*

* Is it objected that the people of India are not fit to rule themselves because so many of them are illiterate ? There are two answers to this objection. The first is involved in the questions : Who are responsible for their illiteracy but the British ? Where is there any hope of its removal so long as the British remain ? The second answer is the fact that even if the Indian *masses are* ignorant, *their leaders are not*. As shown in another chapter, there are in India fully twenty-four or twenty-five million literates, besides a very much larger number still of men scattered, all through the land who, though not literates, are possessed of large practical intelligence, and a far greater knowledge of India's needs

How long would it take a child, kept on crutches, to learn to walk, run and perform with vigor on its legs? How long would it take a person kept out of the water to learn to swim? Of what value is training received from haughty masters who look down upon those being trained as inferiors and virtual serfs because their color is brown? Instead of the people of India needing more training from the British, the fact is, they have had far too much already of the kind of thing the British give. What they need is to get away from it and to be allowed to stand on their own feet like men and train themselves. Is there any reason to believe that Britain's so-called training or education of the Indian people for self-rule, conducted as it is now being conducted under virtual slavery and by virtually slave masters, that is, under the absolute dominance of the British bureaucracy,—is their any reason to believe that if it went on for a hundred years, it would fit them any better than they are fitted now by their own native intelligence, their own natural instincts for law and order, and their experience of three thousand years of actual practice of self-rule?

I repeat, England's whole manner of dealing with India in withholding self-rule from her until she is first "educated" and made "fit" for it, is contrary to the best modern psychology and the best modern systems of education. If there is anything that our best psychologists and educators unite on, and declare to be settled and certain,

---

than the British can possibly possess. Surely these are the men who should rule India. These men would rule with real intelligence. Furthermore, they would rule in the interest of the Indian people, and not in the interest of a far-off nation.

it is that the only way in which individuals or groups of individuals can be effectually trained or made really fit for anything practical, is by the method of actual doing, of experiment, of practice, of "trial and error" or trial under the possibilities of success and possibilities of failure. The child has to learn to walk by walking, to speak by speaking, to write by writing, to think by thinking, to use all his faculties and powers by using them, to do everything he has to do in life by doing. Every step forward in civilization has been attained by experiment, and experiment always involving the possibility of mistakes. It is by their mistakes as well as by their successes that men and nations always have to learn and to advance. There is no other way.

It is a calamity to India, of the first magnitude, that throughout all the dealings of the British with her this principle has been ignored. And it is ignored still. If England herself had been kept by some outside dominating power from self-rule until she was educated for it and in the judgment of that power she was "fit," she would to-day be in political slavery, as India is. The same is true of the United States. The same is true of every nation. Every nation in the world that rules itself has learned to do so by actual experience, and never by being taught by a foreign control. They have all learned to swim by going into the water. India simply demands the right to go into the water. One year of actually governing themselves making mistakes and correcting them, would do more to train the Indian people for self-rule than a millenium of the sham training which they are now getting from their British masters. Dare any Englishman deny that Gladstone was right in declaring that

"Every year and every month that a subject people

are kept under the administration of a despotic government, renders them less fit for free institutions ?"

For seventy years, ever since the Mutiny, Britain has been promising, promising self-rule to the Indian people. The Indian leaders are more and more asking. Will she go on promising for ever and really doing nothing ? Does she intend to do nothing ? Her so-called Reform Scheme seems to India only the last and most pretentious of these futile and irritating promises.

The poison element, the fatal element, the devil element, in this whole business, is that the Indian people are to receive self-rule *only when she (Britain) thinks them fit.* Ah, yes ! Will she *ever* think them fit ? Does she *intend* ever to think them fit ? India is asking these questions with constantly deepening earnestness. More and more she is *suspecting* that she is being intentionally and persistently *deceived.* She sees that these seventy years since the British Government took over India from the East India Company, have brought to the Indian people a few more privileges, a few more offices, but have they brought any *relaxation whatever of Britain's iron grip ?* Have they these seventy years brought to India any evidence that Britain *intends ever* to give her *real* self-rule—that is, *freedom to conduct her affairs as a nation otherwise than under the absolute, supreme control and domination of Great Britain ?* I say these are the *vital questions* which India is asking with *ever-increasing seriousness and persistence.*

If the British continue their present policy—if India is not given self-rule, and given it soon, in some real form—"dominion status" in association with Britain or full independence—will she not be driven to *desperation ?* Gandhi's influence for non-violence will not last for ever if the provocation continues. Is it said that Indians will not fight? Let Britain not be deceived. Let her call to mind India's fighting regiments that turned the tide in the first battle of the Marne and saved Paris. Let her remember the desperate fighting she herself had to do to conquer India. Let her remember the Mutiny, and the fact that only because the heroic Sikhs fought on her side was she saved from defeat and from being driven out of the land. If India is driven to revolution, it will not be a small part, as in the Mutiny; it will be all India. Dr. Rutherford tells us that on his recent visit to India he found absolutely all parties, races, religions and classes, however divided in other matters, united in their common desire and demand for self-rule.

In conclusion, and in a sense summing up all that this chapter has aimed to say: The whole dream of "educating a nation for freedom" by *outsiders* and *masters*, while at the same time *keeping the nation in bondage*, is a *delusion* or *worse*. The whole history of mankind has shown it to be such. The best informed and most authoritative students of the subject condemn it. Modern education and modern psychology declare its folly. It never has been successfully done in the whole history of the world. In the very nature of the case it never can be. "Nations by themselves are made." They cannot be manufactured by foreigners and set up like statues. If the British could teach the Indian people to create a government as like that of England as two peas in a pod, and to carry it on as perfectly as possible after the English model, it would not meet India's needs. The whole thing would be artificial, and therefore perishable. British ways are not India's ways nor British needs India's needs. The Indian people would have to change their government radically, after the British were gone, to suit it to their own ideals and to answer their own wants. Why cannot the British see this, and, without further foolish and hurtful delay, turn over the country to its rightful owners, for them to build up a government suited to their customs, their civilization and their needs, and therefore really useful and permanent ?

CHAPTER XXXIII

THE GREAT FARCE : BRITAIN'S CLAIM THAT INDIA IS HER "SACRED TRUST"

Whenever anything is said to Englishmen about giving self-rule to India, nearly always they raise the objection of what they call their "trusteeship," their "guardianship," of the country, which they declare compels them to stay there. India is their "sacred trust," which has been "committed" to them (not a few add "by Divine Providence"); and they dare not "abandon their solemn responsibility." This has an assuring, even a religious, sound. Unquestionably it causes many Englishmen of high character to support British rule in India who otherwise would not do so.

Is it a fact that Britain is in any true sense whatever India's trustee or guardian? Who appointed her such? Did India? Who else could do it? Can trustees or guardians be self-appointed? May I take possession of my neighbor's house, or estate, or property, or business, by force; may I occupy it, claim to own it, manage it for my own purposes, appropriate its revenues for my own use; and having done so, can I justify myself by the claim that I have appointed myself my neighbor's trustee, or guardian? Would my appointing myself his guardian or trustee make me such?

Then does Great Britain's conquering the Indian people, and taking possession of their territory and their revenues, constitute her their trustee and guardian, when they have never appointed her such, and indignantly deny that she is such ?

These are serious and wholly legitimate questions, which Englishmen are under the weightiest possible obligation to answer to India and to the world.

A few Englishmen of the nobler sort have answered them, not only intelligently but honestly, justly, in a way that no sophistry can refute.

Such an answer lies before me. It is from Mr. Bernard Houghton, a Member of Parliament, an eminent Englishman who long held a high position in the British Civil Service in India, and who, because he is an Englishman, is not likely to be biassed against his own country.

Mr. Houghton says :

"Wherever there is a trust some one with authority must have made the trust. Who was it in the case of India? Where and when was the deed consummated? As history tells us, England acquired India by the sword ; in parts, indeed, by means even more questionable than the sword. It will hardly do, then, to say that Providence has entrusted England with India for that would be to impute to Providence methods which all humane men must look on with abhorrence and which flout alike the dictates of justice and the principles of liberty. The people of India no more handed themselves over to English rule than did the Alsatians in 1871 give themselves to Germany or the Poles of the 18th century to the Czar. Whence then does the supposed trust arise? Contract explicit or implied there is none.

" 'Conquest' no doubt in these days has an ugly sound. If President Wilson achieved nothing else he at least compelled the robber Powers to hide their naked annexations or conquests under the fig-leaf of 'mandates,' a fig-leaf however which hides nothing.

"May it not be that this talk of 'trust' and 'trustee' is of the same order of words ? It is very comforting to regard India as a sacred trust. It entirely blots out the unseemly notion of England as a free-booter, dealing with other countries as Drake and Hawkins dealt with the Spanish treasureships. It substitutes the image of a charitable old gentleman undertaking from strictly benevolent reasons all the worry and trouble of looking after a minor's affair and ordering his education. It postulates a kind of guardianship on the one hand and a tender and respectful confidence on the other. Guardian and ward, teacher and pupil, what delightful pictures these conjured up! What kindly relations, what years of familiar and beneficial intercourse!

"Such deception is what comes of substituting dreams for reality. We know well that the East India Company conquered India for its own profit. We know how in the 18th century hundreds and hundreds of its servants returned to England loaded with the loot of the annexed territories. We know further that when this shameless confiscation was ended, it was replaced by a system which, though legal, places an intolerable burden in the shape of high salaries on the neck of India; which subordinate her trade to the interests of England; which sequestrates the major portion of her revenues to maintain an army to hold India in subjection and to fight the battles of the British Empire in other lands.

"A trusteeship is an honorary post, an often thankless task, involving much labour and not a little anxiety, with no monetary reward. But India has been to England from the first a matter of profit. It was conquered by the East India Company for the sake of profit. It was held on to by England for profit, profit in trade, in prestige, in military force and in the great number of careers it offers to sons of the governing class. It is in fact what business men call a 'paying proposition.'

"There is no more truth in talking of England holding India in trust than there would be in talking of the Romans holding Britain in trust, or the Germans holding Alsace-Lorraine in trust, or Austria holding Italy in trust. It is all sheer hypocrisy. If hypocrisy is the homage which vice pays to virtue, then the use of fair words to cover up ugly facts, indicates that, although much of modern civilization is still at heart barbarian, it is becoming ashamed of its kinship with the caveman; hence it talks of 'mandates' and 'trusteeship' and 'training peoples for self-government.'

"But does this hypocrisy really help matters? Is the covering up of selfishness and greed with soft words, an advance? Is it not better to say honestly, as we may suppose the caveman did, 'I want this or that, and I propose to have it because it profits me to have it.' England is not the trustee of India in any sense except one that is absolutely a fiction, and every Englishman knows it. The only trustee of India is the Indian people."

So much for Mr. Houghton. Who can answer the facts and the reasoning of this eminent and just Englishman ?

Englishmen give three or four reasons (or excuses) for what they call their right and duty to stay in India and govern it as its trustee. Let us see what they are.

1. They tell us they *have done it so long, therefore they must continue. Time gives justification.*

Is this claim sound ? Certainly not. The fact that a great wrong has lasted a long time, instead of being a just reason for its continuance, is an added reason why it should be removed without further delay. The delay has been too great already. Any further delay only makes the wrong the greater.

If long continuation of a wrong justifies it, then slavery, and the slave trade, and duelling, and the putting to death of supposed witches, and religious persecution, and war, and a hundred other evils that have come down from a long past, should continue right on throughout the future, and there should be no effort to remove them. But all such reasoning is false.

This applies exactly to India. The fact that Great Britain has been acting as a fraudulent guardian of India for more than a century and a half, instead of palliating her crime and giving her the right to continue it, only swells it as a crime to vaster proportions and makes its cessation only the more imperative. The longer I have held possession of property which I have stolen, from my neighbor, the greater is the wrong that I have done him, and the greater is my responsibility to return his property to him without further delay.

2. The British government often bases its claim to be India's trustee and to rule the country

on the ground of the *good* it has done to India, the *great service*, the *benefits* it has rendered the Indian people. In the discussion in Parliament in November, 1927, in connection with sending the Statutory Commission to India this claim was made over and over by Lord Birkenhead, Lord Winterton, and other speakers. Without a blush they asserted that the "immense benefits" rendered to India by the British gives them the "right" to claim the country as "their Indian Empire," and to rule and manage it as they please.

To which the Indian people reply: "Since when does conferring on one's neighbor 'benefits' which he does not ask for and does not want, entitle one to claim that neighbor's property as his own, or to seize it, manage it, and appropriate to his own use the income from it, under the fiction of having appointed himself his neighbor's 'guardian' or trustee?

As to the so-called "benefits" which the British claim to have conferred upon India, the Indian people make to the world essentially the following declarations:

(a). We did not ask for their benefits, and a large part of them we did not want, because we did not regard them as benefits at all.

(b). Everything that the British have done for us, whether beneficial to us or not, absolutely everything, we have we have paid for, in full, and much more than paid for. We even paid Britain's whole expense in *conquering us*. The British have *given* us *nothing*.

(c). We contend that whatever things of any value the British have done for us (done with *our money)* such as building railroads, telegraphs, irrigation systems, etc. (these are the things they *boast* of), could and would all have been done in due time *by ourselves*; and in ways that would have served us *better*, and at a *cost* to us *very much less*; just as Japan did all these things for herself, in ways far more serviceable to her, and at a cost far lower than any foreign rulers would have supplied them to her.

(d). The Indian people say further: Even if the British have benefited us in some ways, they have deeply injured us in others.*

On the whole, we believe British rule has been a calamity, not a benefit. The stealing of our wealth, the exploitation of our country, the reducing of us from the richest nation in the world to the poorest, and, above all, the robbing us of our freedom and independence, and the reducing of us from our proud position as one of the leading nations of mankind to that of a mere "possession" of foreigners, a mere "appendage" of an alien power—all these colossal wrongs which we have received at the hands of the British, we believe have far outweighed any and all the "benefits" which they have rendered us.

After a speech in the British House of Commons by Earl Winterton, the Under-Secretary of State for India (on July 8, 1927), in which that official had praised to the skies the numerous blessings which he alleged British rule had given and is giving to India—enumerating railways, telegraphs, irrigation, cotton raising, cotton mills, exports,

---

* The Indian people gladly acknowledge that they have received many kindnesses and benefits from individual Englishmen. For these they hold many Englishmen in honor and affection. It is the Government as a Government, the imperialistic foreign Rule, which robs them of their freedom and tyrannizes over them in a hundred ways, that they do not hold in affection or honor, but the contrary. The kindness and helpfulness of some individual English men and English women, does not change the nature of the alien Government, or cause the Indian people to regard its presence in the country as other than a humiliation and an evil.

imports, financial legislation, coinage, the army, etc. etc., Colonel Wedgwood followed with a rejoinder, pointing out that the noble Lord had not even mentioned the one blessing worth more *than all the rest put together*—the one blessing which the Indian people *desired, prayed for, demanded above everything else*—namely *freedom*. All these material things were good; of course, the Indian people wanted them; they themselves *could, and would have, obtained them*, as Japan did, *without any help from the British*; but all these together did not compensate, or *begin to compensate*, for *their loss of liberty and their degradation as a nation* from their proud place among the great nations of the world to their present *despised condition of subjection to a foreign power*.

Another Member of Parliament, following Colonel Wedgwood, characterized the eternal attempt of Britain to satisfy India by giving her these things instead of freedom, as "feeding her on lollypops when she wants bread." Would not the British themselves, he demanded, regard railroads, telegraphs, increased exports and imports and the like as mere lollypops if *they* were offered *these* in place of *freedom*? Why could not the British understand that freedom is the most precious thing on earth to the Indian as well as to the Englishman, and that to offer the Indian people anything else in place of it is an insult to them exactly as it would be to an Englishman?

Both those Members of Parliament were right. Liberty is as dear to the people of India as to the people of Great Britain.

Said an eminent Indian leader in Calcutta to the British who were complaining of the ingratitude of the Indian people for the things the British were "doing for them," and the "benefits they were receiving" from the British: "A curse on your so-called benefits; what we want is justice. A curse on the things you do for us; we want freedom to do for ourselves. If you did ten times more for us than you do, would that compensate for your robbing us of our liberty, and keeping us children, weaklings, slaves?"

3. Not a few Englishmen declare that Britain is justly a trustee of the Indian people and has a right to rule them as long as she pleases, for the "pious" reason that "*Divine Providence*" *has placed the country in her hands.*

Think what that means. Great Britain, a Christian nation, committing one of the greatest of possible *crimes against humanity*—the conquering and enslaving of a sister nation—and *attributing it to Divine Providence*!

John Bright said:

"We conquered India by breaking all the Ten Commandments."

Should a Government based on such a conquest be attributed to Divine Providence?

Mr. H. G. Wells says the conquest of India was a "tremendous piracy." Does Divine Providence inspire nations to piracy?

Dr. H. V. Rutherford, M. P., says:

"We, British, claim to be 'trustees' of India. We forgot to add that Indians denounce us as *self-appointed* trustees, *fraudulent* trustees."

Does Divine Providence inspire nations to become self-appointed, fraudulent trustees?

Says Sir Frank Beaman: "We stole India." Does Divine Providence cause nations to become robbers and to refuse to return their loot to the party from whom they have stolen it?

In one breath British imperialists call India Britain's "trust," and often in the very next breath they show that they mean nothing of the kind by declaring that they *intend never to return it to the Indian people,* its rightful owners. The following is an illustration—one of many.

On the 7th of July, 1925, Lord Birkenhead, Secretary of State for India, said:

"I am not able in any foreseeable future to discern a moment when we (the British) may safely either to ourselves or India abandon our trust."

Think what that means. Everywhere else in the civilized world, except in connection with Britain's "trusteeship of India" a "trust" is supposed to be limited in time, is to come to an end; and at a due date the property is to be turned over to the heirs or proper owners. But not so in connection with India. According to Lord Birkenhead it means their permanent possession. Their property held by Britain in so-called "trust" is never to be surrendered "within any foreseeable future." That is, it belongs to England. It is a part of King George's "My Indian Empire."

Of course, this is pure theft, pure embezzlement, pure robbery. The word "trust" is employed in no other possible sense than as a smoke screen, a deception, an exhibition of hypocrisy. This is the way the highest authority on India deceives the nations of the world by making them believe that India is Britain's real trust when he means that it is nothing of the kind!

What a brilliant example for all other robbers this is—stealing and covering up our theft by the benevolent word "trust"!

Let us see how it would look if applied else where say in my own case. Suppose I steal, not indeed a great country like India, but an estate, or a bank, or a great mercantile business, or a valuable diamond, or a million dollars. And then suppose I piously declare to the world that it is my "trust," placed in my hands by Divine Providence, and I "cannot imagine any time in the future when

I can with safety either to myself or to the party robbed abandon my trust." How shrewd I am! How wise! How far sighted! How grateful ought all robbers to be to me and to Lord Birkenhead for showing them how to steal and at the same time make people believe that they are doing a benevolent deed, by piously calling the property which they have stolen (and never intend to return) a "trust"!

Long ago, Machiavelli taught the lesson that the most effective of all ways to cover up an ugly deed is to give it a good, if possible a pious, name. Lord Birkenhead and some other British statesmen seem to have become adepts in practising this lesson in connection with India.

It brings to our recollection the old lines:

"And the devil went back to his study;
Said he, with a wink and a nod,
'Sure the true way still
To work my will,
Is to call it, *the work of God*'."

But alas! There is another side to the matter. The old Hebrew Prophet thundered in the ears of ancient Israel:

"*Woe* to them that *call evil good and good evil*; that *put darkness for light and light for darkness! As the fire devoureth the stubble, so their root shall rot.*"

The truth is, this whole claim of Britain that India is her "sacred trust," and that she (Britain) is India's "trustee" or "guardian" in any just sense whatever, is pure *fiction*. The claim is either *based on ignorance* or it is an attempt of men *conscious of doing great wrong, to ease their consciences by calling their wrong deed a virtue* or, it is *pure hypocrisy*, an *unblushing attempt to deceive the world.* Let the men who make the claim answer which.

In conclusion :

It is no pleasure to the present writer to use such severe words as "theft," "loot," "robbery" "hypocrisy," "crime." But how can he avoid it and be honest? It *is* hypocrisy if you deceive and know that you are deceiving, It *is* a crime against humanity when any nation deprives another nation of its freedom. It *is* theft, it *is* robbery, it *is* looting on an enormous scale and of the worst kind known in the world, whenever any nation conquers another, takes forcible possession of its territory and its revenues and rules and exploits it for the benefit of the conquering power.

The fact that many nations have done these things in the past does not justify them to-day. They have always been wrong ; but in the light of the twentieth century they are a far greater wrong than ever before. Done by a nation calling itself Christian, they are a ten-fold wrong. We shall never get rid of great black crimes against humanity, such as *war conquest* and the *forcible holding of nations in bondage,* so long as we deceive ourselves and the world by calling them by *gentle and innocent names.*

> "Let us speak *plain* : there is more force in names
> Than most men dream of ; and a lie may keep
> Its throne a whole age longer, if it skulk
> Behind the shield of some fair-seeming name.
> Let us call tyrants tyrants.
> Men in earnest have no time to waste
> In patching fig-leaves for the naked truth."

CHAPTER XXXIV

HOW INDIA IN BONDAGE INJURES ENGLAND

PART I.

In preceding chapters of this book we have seen in how many ways the Indian people are injured by British rule,—by being deprived of their freedom and their proper place among the great nations. In this concluding chapter we wish to reverse the mirror and look at Britain herself, inquiring whether she also is not very seriously injured by the wrongs which she inflicts upon India, and in just what ways she suffers.

The injury which England receives from her domination of India is of two kinds, namely, *moral* (that which comes to *individuals*), and *political* (that which comes to the *nation*). Let us look first at the moral harm—the dulling of the finer sentiments, manners and ideals of life, and the lowering of moral character, which comes—not to all persons who return from service in India, but to very large numbers, it is believed to a large majority.

In the very nature of things, any man who wrongs another man, or any nation that wrongs another nation inevitably suffers a lowering of its or his moral standards, and consequently a greater or less degree of moral impairment. This is a law of the moral universe which can no more be escaped than can the law of gravitation.

The moral hardening, the moral degeneration, which Englishmen suffer from the despotic rule which they practise in India, of course, manifests itself first in India itself.* But it does not stop there. The Englishmen return home to England as soon as their terms of Indian service expire, and of necessity bring with them the lowered moral standards and the autocratic, imperialistic spirit which have been bred in them.

This is a moral poison of a very serious nature, which is being introduced constantly into England with the return both of the civil service men and of the military service men. And there is no possibility of England getting rid of it so long as she holds India in forced subjection.

Many Englishmen themselves recognize and deplore this moral injury which their country not only suffers now, but has suffered ever since its domination of India began.

Macaulay, in his Essay on Lord Clive, gives us a graphic picture which makes clear the early part of the story. He tells us that the life lived by Englishmen in India and the enormous wealth which they acquired there, mainly by extortion and robbery, filled England with hundreds of "nabobs," men who returned from a few years in India, rich and proud, to strut, and parade their ill-gotten riches, to exhibit toward their fellows the same domineering spirit which they had shown to their subjects and virtual slaves in the East, and to corrupt and deprave the English society in which they moved. Says Macaulay,

"Many of them had sprung from obscurity; they had acquired great wealth in India, and returning home they exhibited it insolently and spent it extravagantly; they had crowds of menials, gold and silver plate, Dresden china, venison and Burgundy wine; but they were still low men."

The "nabobs" who come back from India now

* See previous chapters.

(if we may still call them by that significant name) are of a somewhat different kind. They are not generally so rich; some of them are not of so humble origin, though not a few are of an origin quite as humble. But no one who is acquainted with the social England of to-day can deny that many, even if not all, bring back from their years of "looking down" on everybody possessed of a "dark skin," and of "domineering" over the "natives," essentially the same autocratic, undemocratic, sometimes brutal and always dangerous spirit which characterized the earlier nabobs, although it is generally shown in less obtrusive and vulgar ways now than in the earlier days.

Let me cite some testimonies from Englishmen themselves regarding this matter.

Dr. V. H. Rutherford, M. P., after a tour of investigation in India in 1926, embodied the results of his observations and experiences in a book in which he says:

"Our forefathers took India for the purpose of exploiting its resources, and we hold it to-day for the same immoral purpose. Our Indian Empire has poisoned us with the virus of Imperialism, has lowered our standard of moral values at home and abroad, and fostered in us the spirit of arrogance, intolerance, greed and dishonesty, degrading our national life."*

Another testimony. In his book "Gordon at Khartoum" Mr. Wilfred Scawen Blunt says:

"It is impossible to exercise tyrannical authority abroad and retain a proper regard for liberty at home."

In another connection he adds:

"The two things are not compatible. My reading of history has taught and practical experience has confirmed to me, the fact that the task undertaken by a nation of ruling other nations against their will, is the most certain

---

* "Modern India: Its Problems and Their Solution." Introduction, p. x. London. British Labor Publishing Co.

step upon the road to national ruin. The virus of autocratic rule in foreign lands infects the body politic at home by a gradual process of contempt for human brotherhood and equal rights, which are the basis of all just law and the only guarantee of freedom in free nations."

Still another testimony from an eminent Englishman, Mr. J. B. Hobson writes :

"Our despotically ruled dependencies have ever served to damage the character of our English people by feeding the habits of snobbish subservience, the admiration of wealth and rank, the corrupt survivals of the inequalities of feudalism......Cobden, writing in 1860 of our Indian Empire; put this pithy question : 'Is it not just possible that we may become corrupted at home by the reaction of arbitrary political maxims in the East upon our domestic politics, just as Greece and Rome were demoralized by their contact with Asia ?' Not merely is the reaction possible, it is inevitable. As the despotic portion of our Empire has grown in area, a larger number, trained in the temper and methods of autocracy as soldiers and civil officials in our Crown Colonies, Protectorates and Indian Empire, reinforced by numbers of merchants, planters, engineers and overseers, whose lives have been those of a superior caste living an artificial life removed from all the healthy restraints of ordinary Europen society, have returned to this country, bringing back the characters, sentiments and ideas imposed by this bad foreign environment.?"*

---

* If any one would understand fully how imperialism, not only that of Britain in India, but the domination of one people by another everywhere, in all lands and in the very nature of things injures and degrades both rulers and ruled, and the rulers quite as much as the ruled, let him read M. Gaston Boissier's two books, "The Opposition Under the Caesars" and "Cicero and His friends," and there see how Rome's rule of her Provinces (comparatively enlightened as that rule was, gradually destroyed the higher and finer nature of the Roman people themselves, undermined their moral character and brutalized them, while at the same time it operated everywhere to destroy the self-respect, the manliness, the power of initiative, the intellectual and moral worth of the various peoples held in subjection.

Nor are the evil social effects of the aristocratic and irresponsible domination of India by Great Britain confined to English *men*. The poison extends also to English *women*, and often in a magnified form. This fact should not be overlooked. Indeed the change for the worse which I myself have seen in Englishwomen in India—a change which I knew had taken place as the result of their life there—is one of the things which first opened my eyes to the necessarily coarsening effect of British rule upon the British themselves. English writers have often called attention to the same.

Among others, Miss Margaret Noble (Sister Nivedita), an eminent English woman who lived many years in India and wrote some of the best books on Indian life that we possess, frequently mentioned and deplored this deterioration of English women as the result of the dominance of their race over a subject people. She pointed out that however kind, courteous and lady-like they are when they leave England, and however perfectly they manifest these high characteristics to their European associates in India, with far too few exceptions they soon come to treat their servants, and indeed all Indians, with a disdain harshness and often real cruelty that would have shocked them if they had seen anything of the kind in England. Living more secluded lives than their husbands and coming less in contact in large ways with the Indian people, their prejudices against them are often even stronger than that of their husbands, and their treatment of them more unreasonable and heartless. *

* This coarsening influence of British rule applies not only to English women, but to others—to all indeed who arrogate to themselves the "superiority" of being "white." A striking illustration which comes to my mind

Has Great Britain reason to be proud of a system of foreign rule the influence of which is thus to harden so many of its women? And when these English women in India at the end of their "banishment" return to live once more in England, they bring with them of necessity the virus that has gotten into their blood. They can never again be quite what they were before. They are always thereafter more domineering in their nature, less kindly; less sympathetic with any class except the aristocracy, less interested in the welfare of the people, than they would have been if they had not for years breathed the poison air of autocratic and irresponsible rule in India.

So much for the *moral* and *social* injuries which ruling India against her will brings to the

---

is that of an *American* woman, the wife of an English banker in one of the large Indian cities, in whose elegant home I was a guest for some days. We had been acquainted in America, and I had held her in the highest esteem as one of the most cultured and refined ladies within my acquaintance. Her husband was the son of an English clergyman and was generally looked upon as a gentleman of the finest type. But as I witnessed the treatment extended by both of them to their servants, of whom they had some fifteen or twenty, I was amazed. It was quite as unsympathetic, harsh and abusive as was ever seen among the Georgia and Louisiana planters in the old days of American slavery. And some of these servants were persons of intelligence and real refinement. I could hardly believe it possible that the woman whom I found treating her Indian servants in such a manner (and her treatment of other Indians, not her servants, was not much different) was the same lady who was entertaining me with such courtesy and whose life in America had always been marked by such refinement and such kindness to everybody.

There is something of this race prejudice and consequent unjust treatment of the Indian people seen among the missionaries; but not much. I noticed it clearly in only a few cases.

English people as *individuals*. Let us now consider the *political* injuries which come to the British *nation*, and see whether these are any less serious.

The recruitment in England of large numbers of men for civil and military service in India, with the high salaries and large pensions connected with the same, results in filling England with thousands of men who after the short period of twenty-four years in India return "home" to spend the last half of their lives in comfort and ease, often in wealth and luxury, supported by the poverty-stricken Indian people. What do these men, thus living in England upon the money which they have saved from their high salaries in India, and upon their fat pensions paid by India—what do these men do during these years of freedom and leisure at home—practically one-third or one-half of their lives? Do they devote their time, strength and money to advancing the interests of the Indian people from whom they are getting their living, and to whom they owe so much? That is, are they giving their influence in every way possible to create a public sentiment in England in favor of reforms in India, in favor of giving to India more and better education, better sanitation, better medical service, lighter taxes, more freedom, such treatment as will advance her toward the place she ought to occupy among the great nations of the world?

A few of them are; a few come home from India to spend their years as real friends of the Indian people and to do for them all they can. But the number of such is sadly small. The very large majority, poisoned and morally hardened by the imperialistic spirit, the autocratic and domineering spirit, the race and class pride and arrogance which ruling the people without their consent inevitably breeds, settle down in England to manifest essentially the same spirit still, and therefore to be political enemies of India, and at the same time (what is very serious for England) to be political opponents of progress and reforms in England. *

Historians of the period of Clive and Warren Hastings and the generation immediately following tell us that when the British conquerors, rulers and adventurers of that time returned from India with their enormous wealth, obtained by every kind of oppression and injustice, one of their favorite ways of spending their ill-gotten riches was that of buying up "rotten boroughs" and thus securing seats in Parliament. This was a stream of poison which began pouring itself into the legislation of England; for it was very

* The baneful influence which British rule in India exerts upon the political life of England is clearly recognized and often commented upon in India. Says *The Mahratta*, of Poona (January 16, 1910): "The autocratic and irresponsible system of British rule is not only largely responsible for the backward condition and the discontent here (in India), but it also makes its evil effects felt seriously in the home life and politics of England. The high officials who reign as veritable autocrats in India, seek to perpetuate their despotism also in England. The evil effects of this have often attracted the attention of British statesmen, who have more than once declared that the English Constitution is constantly threatened by these 'proconsuls' trained in the school of alien despotism. It was the nabobs, the men who had made money in India by means chiefly foul, who returned to England, bought up pocket boroughs, and were the ready tools of George III in his campaign against representative government, in the American Colonies. The 'prancing pro-consuls' returning from their autocratic rule in India to-day are the twentieth century representatives of the eighteenth century nabobs. They are more respectable, but they are all the more insidious. They have inoculated the whole British Tory party with their principles. Indeed these pro-consuls from India are the leaders of a plutocratic oligarchy in England."

soon discovered that these "nabobs" corrupted and morally hardened by their years of tyranny and extortion in India, could be counted on almost to a man to exert their influence in Parliament on the side of extreme conservatism and reaction, and against all measures looking toward enlightenment, reform and progress.

During the last more than one hundred years practically every reform and every progressive political, industrial or educational measure introduced into Parliament has had to calculate on the almost solid opposition of the men returned from service in India. No matter how broad-minded, liberal, progressive or freedom-loving they were when they went out, they came back with very few exceptions, conservative, backward looking, narrowed and hardened, imperialistic and militaristic in spirit, in sympathy with the privileged classes, in sympathy with conquest abroad and autocracy at home, giving their influence for an ever bigger army and navy, and, throughout their lives, active opponents not only of all legislation favorable to the progress and freedom of India, but equally opponents of all movements to advance the interests, whether political, social, educational or industrial, of the people of England.*

To be specific. The various immensely import-

---

* England's experience with India is simply one more demonstration in the world's long history of the truth of Lincoln's declaration: "This is a world of compensations; and he who would be no slave must have no slave. Those who deny freedom to others deserve it not themselves, and under a just God cannot long retain it."

Said the great Frenchman, Lamennais, in his work, "Le Livre de Peuple": "A people allowing itself to oppress another, digs the grave in which shall be buried its own liberty."

ant legislative movements which have arisen in England, particularly since the early thirties of last century,—to extend the franchise, first to men and later to women; to do away with political corruption, in many long-existing forms; to reform the barbarous criminal laws; to create juster taxation; to improve agriculture; to protect women and children in factories and elsewere; to protect minors; to advance popular education; to create better conditions for labor, and so on,—those progressive movements, as has been said, have had to face the pretty nearly solid opposition of the India pensioners—the men who in India became autocrats, and who came home bringing with them of course, their autocratic ideas, impulses and habits. This poisoning influence of India on British legislation has continued right on down to the present time. Thus to-day, the Liberal party in England, and the Labor party, and every party, under whatever name, that aims to promote progress and improve the condition of the masses of the people as distinguished from the privileged classes, has to fight the poison influence of India.

And what else can any reasonable man expect? "Can the leopard change his spots, or the Ethiopian his skin?" If a man with a slave-driver psychology comes from India to England, does the change of place change his psychology? Men whose business in India has been oppression, why should they favor liberty in England? Men who have opposed giving education to the people of India, why should they not oppose giving any more than the very minimum of education to English "common people?" Men who, with all power in their hands, have done practically nothing to elevate labor in India, why should they be expected to be interested in movements to elevate labor in England? Men who have spent all their years in India trampling on the rights of the people there, why should they be expected to care much for the rights of the people at home?

It was the autocratic and imperialistic Englishmen who were living in England on fat pensions paid by the poverty-stricken people of India, who were largely the leaders in keeping Ireland so long in bondage.

What was it that overthrew the Ramsay MacDonald Labor Party in England in 1924, and at the same time struck such a blow to the Liberal Party? Primarily it was India. All the erstwhile Indian officials living as nabobs in England, all the militarists and imperialists whose main reason for existence was to hold on to India, and all India bondholders, Lancashire cotton-manufacturers and men who had financial interests in India, all these were afraid that the Labor Party, or even the Liberal Party, might give the Indian people too much freedom, and thus hurt some British pocket-books. So they turned MacDonald and his following out, gave the Liberal Party a stinging blow, and set up an ultra conservative Bourbon Government which would be sure to keep a firm grip on India (together with Egypt, Mesopotamia, and the rest of the dependencies and mandates), and which at the same time would hold down at home all the too liberty-loving men and women, whether in the Labor Party or elsewhere.

It is noticeable that in the long struggle of the women of England to obtain the franchise, three of the men most prominent in opposing the movement, were Curzon, Cromer and Milner; all of them were schooled in the ruling of foreign peoples without their consent. As a matter of course men accustomed to tyrannizing over the people of India and Egypt would not be likely to see any good reason why English women should not always continue to be tyrannized over by British law and custom.

As is well known, India is the greatest of all the Bulwarks of the British House of Lords. Except for India that anachronism, that survival from an undemocratic and tyrannical past, that expensive remnant of Feudalism, that perpetual foe to British freedom and progress, would long ago have been swept away. But so long as Great Britain holds India, the House of Lords will remain, and remain essentially unaltered. The reasons are two. First, because it is a tradition which seemingly cannot be broken that all men who win distinction in India must be raised to the peerage (if they do not already possess that distinction); and second, because the inevitable effect of ruling a people without their consent is to create an aristocratic, imperialistic spirit, the necessary result of which is a ruling body based not upon the choice of the people, but upon privilege, upon birth, upon wealth, upon considerations wholly autocratic and feudal.

But not only is India a chief bulwark of the House of Lords, it is also the strongest bulwark of British aristocracy, of the whole semi-feudalistic system which divides the nation into two classes—one, the people, unprivileged, who pay their own way in the world, living by their own exertions, often unemployed, and too many of them in poverty; and the other, an aristocracy, privileged, living in luxury, and often in idleness, possessing titles which they did not earn, and many of them holding as their private preserves large and valuable areas of land inherited from feudal or semi-feudal times, which of right belong to the nation, and which ought in some way or other to be in the possession of the people, to give them employment and better homes, and to help feed the nation.

The framers of the Constitution of the United States expressly decreed that this country shall never have a hereditary and privileged aristocracy. No provision of that Constitution has more thoroughly proved its wisdom.

No other country is burdened with so extensive and expensive an aristocratic class, privileged class, or "caste," largely hereditary, made up of "sirs" ("knights"), "barons," "earls," "marquises," "lords," "dukes," "princes" and the rest, as is England. Will she ever get rid of it? Never, until she ceases sending thousands and thousands of her sons to India, to spend half their lives as an aristocratic, privileged, all powerful foreign caste, to domineer over a fifth of the human race, and thus fill their whole nature with the very worst spirit of privilege, of aristocracy, of autocracy, of caste, and of course to bring back the same to England when they return.

Lloyd George, in an address delivered at Shrewsbury on January 30, 1926, pointed out the terrible evils which England has long been suffering from the fact that the land of the country is so largely in the possession of the aristocracy who use it primarily for selfish ends,—for private parks, hunting preserves and the like, and only in a very limited extent to produce food for the nation or in any way to benefit the people. He declared that this condition of things is actually growing worse; that there are fewer owners of land and more tenant farmers now than there were half a century ago; that there is no hope for real prosperity in England until a very much larger proportion of the soil is owned by the agricultural laborers and is used to produce food for the people. He asserted that, with a proper distribution and employment of the land, the home production of food in Great Britain might easily be increased to the enormous extent and value of £ 250,000,000 ($ 750,000,000) each year.

Of course, British rule in India is not wholly to blame for this situation. But it is a prime factor in creating it, because as already said, it is the most powerful single bulwark of the whole British aristocratic system, a system which in its very nature keeps the land so largely in the hands of the few, and therefore cripples agriculture, drives to the cities millions of men who ought to be tilling the soil, and forces on the nation the expense and peril of bringing the larger part of its food from over-seas ; when the nation might and should produce at home each year this seven hundred fifty million dollars worth, and thus add an important sum to the public revenue, save the cost of the navy required to guard the food that comes from abroad, give prosperity to British agriculture, and, what is sorely needed, furnish permanent employment to several millions of the British people.

Another way in which India has been bitterly injuring Great Britain for more than a century and a half is by robbing her of so many of her young men, who were sorely needed home. No other so great and irreparable loss ever comes to any country as that of its manhood, especially its young manhood. This is why war is so terrible to victors as well as to vanquished.

From the first, Britain has sent to India a never-ceasing stream of her sons, of two classes, one, as soldiers, to conquer the land and forcibly hold it in subjection, the other, as civilians, to adminster its government. Let us first consider the *soldiers*.

For nearly all of Britain's first hundred years in India there were wars, wars, wars, of conquest, most of them bloody, some of them very bloody. Then came the sanguinary "Sepoy War," or "Mutiny," which India likes best to call "The War for Indian Independence." After that there were no more wars in India, but many on her borders, generally to extend her area, and many in distant countries of Asia, Africa and even Europe, fought against nations that were supposed to covet India, or to keep Britain's passage clear and safe to India, or an account of international complications growing out of Britain's possession of India.

Englishmen to-day little realize how numerous and serious these wars have been, and therefore what a vast amount of blood was shed and what an enormous number of British young lives were sacrificed.

Mr, James Macdonald, Editor of the Toronto *Globe*,' in an address in Carnegie Hall, New York, April 21, 1912, drew the following picture :

"Every part of the United Kingdom tells the same story. From every parish the choicest sons, generation after generation, went out to wars (a large proportion of them fought in India or on account of India.) Sons of the palace and sons of the manse, sons of the castle and sons of the cottage, out they went, the best nation bred, and only the shattered remnants came back. Every village has its monument. In every great cathedral and in every parish church you may read in marble and brass the tell-tale lists of officers and men. Worse it was than the Egyptian sacrifice of the first-born, for war is no respector of persons. What wonder that Britain's city slums are filled with human dregs, and that throughout her villages disease brought from the barracks and camp life of India leaves behind it the white-faced, the hopeless, the unfit!

The toll taken from Ireland, Wales, and Scotland has not been less wasting than from England. Every valley, every moor, every hamlet, every mountain glen—they all have sent their best, and their best have never come back....The tragedy of the Celts is in the sentence: "Forever they went out to battle, and forever they fell." The Grants stained the marble palaces of India vermilion with their blood; few of their clan are left in their "ain dear glen."

The cost (of our Indian Empire) has been not alone the death of so many brave men who fell, but that those heroes in their youth and prime have *left no breed behind*. The heroic sires died with heroic sons unbred in their lives. It is the countless heroes that *ought* to *have been* but are *not*,—that neverending phantom host who had no chance at life, had they taken the places left empty by the fall of their sires, the loss had not been so fearful, so far beyond repair."

Such is a part, only a part, of the terrible price Britain has paid, and is paying still with no surcease,—for what? For her crime (yes, *crime*) of conquering a great civilized people that had done her no wrong, robbing them of their freedom and nationhood and ruling and exploiting them. Think of it! Actually hundreds of thousands of lives of British young men lost! Actually hundreds of thousands of graves over every one of which the line of Gray's "Elegy" might well have been placed:

"Some mute inglorious Milton here may rest."

Yes, or some mute inglorious Watt, or Stephenson, or Harvey, or Lister, or Ruskin, or Arnold, or Joshua Reynolds, or Wesley, or Wilberforce, or Robert Burns, or Newton, or Darwin, or even Shakespeare! Who knows!

Has Britain received from her "slave India" any adequate return for the loss of all those young lives?*

---

* In another chapter of this book it has been shown that it was Britain's possession of India that really sowed the seed of the Great War of 1914-1918. That is to say, it was Britain's Indian Empire that aroused Germany's jealousy and inflamed her with an ambition to obtain for herself an equal "place in the

But we have not done yet with the young men whom she sends to India as soldiers. There is more to be said. A part of the heavy price which England pays for her Indian Empire,—a part which the world knows little or nothing about, and which England herself only very imperfectly understands (else a shock of surprise and horror would run through the land, and millions of Englishmen and especially women would cry out as they have never done against the whole evil (India business), is the introduction into England and the wide dissemination among the people, of venereal diseases, caused by the return from India of infected British soldiers.

The fact that India is a subject country, held by the power of the sword, makes it necessary to keep a large army there. The young men composing that army, living an unnatural life, in a foreign land, far removed from the moral restraints of home, are subject to severe temptations to which it is easy to yield, with the result that large numbers become seriously infected with sexual diseases, which, of course, they bring back with them when they return home to England, and there spread them abroad. As already said, only a very few Englishmen understand how serious this condition of things is ; and, of those who do, fewer still have the courage to let it be

---

sun." Out of this grew her determination to build her Berlin to Bagdad railway, her creation of a great navy and great army, and finally, as an inevitable result—the collision, the great conflict. Thus to the price which Britain has really paid for her possession of India must be added the 807,451 men of the British Empire killed in the Great War, the 64,907 missing and never found, the 2,059,134 wounded; besides all the war widows and orphans, and the enormous national debt and crushing taxation from which she cannot recover in a generation, if ever.

known, and to protest against a foreign policy of the government which requires such a sacrifice of the country's young men and of the nation's health.

Mr. John M. Robertson is one who knows and dares to tell the facts. He writes :

"India as we govern it, is not only poisoning the higher Englishman, and through him poisoning England ; but it is also poisoning the lower Englishman, 'Tommy,' the soldier, and through him poisoning England no less. The British soldiers who serve in India are recruited from our best English yeomanry. But no Englishman can contemplate the life which large numbers of them live in India, without being deeply pained. Naturally they are good, jolly fellows who, if they had remained at home as husbands and parents would have been able to retain the fine qualities which heaven had bestowed upon them. But in India they are confined in barracks like so many bulldogs, and fed and nourished upon meat and rum which brutalizes all their higher sentiments. Ponder for a moment the depraved condition of those wretched men. Not a few of them would brutally murder innocent Indians, were they to fail to supply them with wine and women. Many of them, on returning home, are poisoning the lower classes in England by the loathsome diseases which they have contracted—diseases whereby not only do they ruin themselves physically and morally but also their own innocent countrymen and country-women at home. Englishmen in England, as a rule, know nothing of the way in which tens of thousands of their fellow-countrymen,—fine specimens of humanity,—are enlisted as soldiers, deported to India, converted into something like brutes, later to return to England to bring and spread their brutalism and their diseases here."*

---

* It must not be understood that venereal diseases are more prevalent among the Indian people themselves than among the people of other lands. As a fact, syphilis, the worst of these diseases, does not seem to be really Indian at all, but foreign, brought into the land by foreigners. Says Frederick Tice, M. D., in his "Practice of Medicine," (Vol. III, p. 442) : "The researches of Okemura and Sesuki for Japan and China and Jolly and others for India, showed that syphilis did not exist in

No Englishman or Englishwoman should for a moment forget that this too is a part of the terrible price which Britain pays for India; a part of the deep and irreparable injury—injury of many kinds and in many forms—which comes to her as the inevitable result of her crime of robbing a great nation of its freedom and holding it in forced subjection.

PART II

Let us turn now from soldiers to civilians.

The men whom Britain sends to India to carry on the civil government there, of course, are generally educated, and for the most part of a

---

any of these countries until it was introduced from Europe." Indeed, in the Indian system of medicine this disease is called *Pheranga Roga*, Feringhee disease, which means European disease.

Soldiers are in danger of contracting venereal diseases in all lands. This is one of the evils universally connected with armies and wars. If the evil is particulary grave in connection with the British army in India, it is not at all because Indian women are of lower character than other women. It is because the British army there is large, it stays a long time, and, the fact that the country is not free, but is a subject land, causes the British soldiers to look down on the Indian people and take liberties with their women which they would not do with the women of a free nation.

That British soldiers in India contract venereal diseases is not primarily the fault of India, but of the soldiers themselves or of the British government that sends them there is shown by the fact that the Indian people deplore the presence of these soldiers among them. In my own travels in India I found that all communities in or near which soldiers were stationed, particulary foreign (British) soldiers, regarded their presence as a danger to their women, and always felt greatly relieved when the soldiers were ordered away.

higher class than the soldiers who are sent to hold the country in subjection. As has been said, these civilians are expected to remain there twenty-four years, minus four years allowed for furloughs. Thus they spend away from home, in a foreign land where they should not be, the best half, and generally a little more than half of their adult lives. This means that Britain herself (Britain at home, the real Britain), is robbed of their lives and their service to that extent. This privation, this loss, this injury, which she suffers, is very, very serious; the British nation has no more pressing need than to get its eyes open to a realization of how very serious it is. It has meant in the past, and it means to-day, nothing less than the drawing away of a steady stream of the nation's *intellect*, *intelligence*, *energy*, *efficiency*, *spiritual life-blood*, during all these years, and *with no adequate return*.

Notice how England has suffered educationally, by the draining away to India of the men needed at home to build up her schools—primary, secondary, and high, her colleges and universities, her scientific and technical institutions, her schools to teach every kind of practical knowledge necessary to keep her abreast of the scientific and industrial progress of the age. For thirty or forty years it has been recognized by intelligent foreigners, and known and deplored by all enlightened Englishmen, that as compared with some of her neighbor nations on the Continent, and also as compared with the United States. England has been backward in nearly every kind of education. These other nations mentioned did not throw away their men of education and brains, but kept them at home doing constructive and vital work for the advancement of their people. Therefore these nations forged ahead.

In the *New York Times* of June 16, 1915, Mr. H. G. Wells said :

"We in Great Britain are intensely jealous of Germany, because in the last hundred years while we have fed on vanities the Germans have had the energy to develop a splendid system of national education, to toil at science and art and literature, to develop social organisation, to master and better our British methods of business and industry, and to clamber above us in the scale of civilization. Unfortunately this has humiliated and irritated rather than chastened us."

In the same issue of *The Times*, Mr. Arnold Bennett confirmed the testimony of Mr. Wells, saying :

"There can be no doubt that Germany has surpassed us in education, the organization of knowledge, social organization and at least two arts. There can be no doubt that she has been more industrious and more serious than we."

It is easy to see how and why the sending away of so many of England's young men to India, as soldiers, to be killed or physically wrecked, and, in addition to this, the even more disastrous banishing of so many of her educated men and so much of her brain power, have necessarily resulted not only in impeding her educational progress, but also in causing a decline of her industrial efficiency as compared with several other nations, in a general lowering of the English physique, and in a wide-spread impoverishment of the masses of the English people.

In a lecture delivered by Dean Inge before the British Science Guild, London, November 21, 1927, that eminent churchman is reported as declaring that

"With the exception of the upper class Englishman who is a fine animal, the whole British nation is physically inferior to the French and the Germans, and the miserable physique of England's town population is without parallel in Europe."

The scientific investigators of the physique of the British people during the war of 1914-1918 were appalled by what they discovered. Men undersized, their muscles undeveloped and flabby, their hearts weak, their lungs showing signs of tuberculosis, with "rotten flesh and bones of chalk" is the phrase of one investigator. In Manchester of eleven hundred young men examined for the army, nearly nine hundred were found unfit, and it must not be forgotten that these unfit men were the ones who were left behind to become the fathers of the next generation, while the best, who were too precious to be lost, were sent away to the battlefields to be killed.

Said a bishop of the Church of England in a recent public address in London:

"The slums of England's cities are a disgrace and a peril. The conditions under which millions of Englishmen, women and children labor are inhuman. The inequality in the distribution of wealth is shocking, and it grows worse. Poverty, want, ignorance, destitution, physical and mental degeneracy abound. Fourfifths of the soil of the nation is in the hands of the favoured class. At one end of our great cities wealth literally festers; at the other end ill-clad, hopeless women work fifteen hours a day to keep soul and body together. And for the worker there is always the fear of unemployment, which when it comes means suffering and often actual starvation, and for children conditions too terrible for description. Meanwhile vice and disease are everywhere."

Mr. G. K. Chesterton has written a poem entitled "The Lords of England," which contains the following terrible lines:

"Lo! my Lords, we gave you England—and
you gave us back a waste,
Hamlets breaking, homesteads drifting,
peasants tramping, towns erased;
Yea, a desert labeled England, where you
know (and well you know)
That the village Hampden's wither and the
village idiots grow."

Turn to British agriculture. We have already quoted from Lloyd George, showing its deplorable condition, largely because so much of the soil of Britain is in the hands of the aristocracy and is used by them for their own selfish pleasure instead of being employed to feed the nation. But more should be said on this subject.

Says a writer in the *New York Times* of August 8, 1926:

"England, naturally a rich agricultural country, is cursed by the herding of people in the industrial centers, in the space of thirty years (from 1891 to 1921) the number of souls in Britain (England, Scotland and Wales) rose from 33,000,000 to 42,750,000, an increase of 9,750,000 inhabitants. While this enormous increase in the number of human beings to be fed was going on (can it be believed?) the number of persons engaged in agriculture actually and seriously declined.

There was a time when native-grown grain fed 24,000,000 of the population; now it provides for less than 8,000,000. Britain's food import bill has risen about $50,000,000 in the last two years, with an annual outlay of something like $600,000,000. It is one of the ironies of the situation that in a country of fertile soil and plentiful labor, where grain-growing was once the premier industry, to-day the people are the most vulnerable to starvation of any considerable people in the world."

Turn to British manufactures. Says a writer in the *New York Times* of August 8, 1926:

"Men now living can easily remember when Great Britain was the premier steel-producing country in the world. Now America, France and Germany, are well on the lead, with the output in the United States five or six times that of Britain.

When it comes to competition, the British are falling farther and farther behind America in applying to manufacturing the principles of scientific mass production. The British have been slow to adopt labor-saving appliances in the mining of coal and in the weaving of cloth. Not less than two-thirds of American looms are automatic, as compared with 10 per cent. in the British Isles."

What does all this mean ? Why is it that in so many ways Great Britain has thus fallen behind other nations, when she ought to be at the front ?

Her soil is rich ; her climate is good ; she has abundance of coal and iron, which are the most important natural elements in modern industry ; her situation is one of the best in the world for commerce and trade ; her people are descendants of a hardy ancestry, and ought to-day to possess vigor and energy second to none.

One other element of distinct advantage should be noticed. For two centuries after the Reformation, the population of England as a whole was recruited and greatly invigorated by the immigration of Protestant refugees from Continental European countries where religious persecution had made life unbearable. Large numbers of French Huguenots, Germans and others, generation after generation, found refuge in England, and brought with them an enormous accession of intelligence, economic power and industrial efficiency. Among these independent thinkers were the most skilled artizans of the Continent, who introduced into England trades and arts previously unknown there. It may even be said that they laid the foundation of the country's at least temporary industrial greatness. For a considerable time she was distinctly the industrial leader of Europe. Why her decline ? Why is she not leading Europe to-day, not only in industries but in education, in science, in freedom, in every kind of progress ?

Doubtless the explanation is not simple. There are more elements than one entering into it.

But can any intelligent and unprejudiced Englishman doubt, and especially can any intelligent student of the situation looking on from the outside doubt for a moment, that it is essentially and centrally what has been intimated and urged above ? It is Britain's *wars and conquests* ; it is her *aristocracy* ; above all it is *India.*

It is widely believed by Englishmen that the possession of India has greatly increased England's wealth. Even if this were true, would it compensate for the moral loss which England has suffered in so many ways from that possession ?

In what way has it increased her wealth ? Has such wealth as has come into the hands of a few, reached the real people of England ? Has it been a benefit to anybody in England, except the very small minority—the money lords who have used it to increase their own riches and power ; the great manufacturers, who have used it to build great factories, in so many of which men, women and children have toiled cruelly long hours on cruelly low wages ; the aristocratic class who have employed it to enlarge their parks and hunting preserves, to build fine mansions and to increase their personal luxury ; the militarists and imperialists who have used it in propaganda to get larger armies and especially bigger and ever bigger navies, which the people have had to pay for, and which have led the country into ever more and more wars ? How much of it has gone for education or for anything calculated to lift up or in any way benefit the masses of the English peole ?

Mr. J. K. Turner, in his book "Shall It Be Again ?" says (p. 226) :

"Britain has a larger leisure class, in proportion to her population, than any other nation, and at the bottom of its social scale a most pronounced destitution. By virtue of her "glorious empire" (Primarily *India*) England lives more largely on forced tribute ? The British *people* ? By no means. The great body of the population that constitute the British nation do not share in any degree in British Imperial prosperity. The standard of living of the masses of England is no higher than that in neighboring countries that possess no "subject empire"... The British common laborer is no better paid than the Dutch, the Belgian, the Norwegian, the Dane. The British slums are the most notorious in Europe. All this is because the "Empire" and all it means is for the *upper classes.*"

More and more the British Labor Party see this, and therefore are demanding India's freedom, and a radical reform of Britain's whole evil imperialistic and militaristic policy which centers in her domination of subject India.

Said Richard Cobden in the House of Commons :—

"I do not think, for the interest of the English people any more than for the interest of the Indian people, that we should continue to govern India......I see no benefit which can arise to the mass of the people of England from connection with India, except that which may arise from honest trade."

This statement of Cobden's is as true now as when it was uttered, seventy years ago ; and British rule in India is maintained now, as it was then, not because it profits the English people as a whole, but because it profits those British classes and interest which ever seek to dominate and use the English people.

It is the unqualified verdict of history that the vast treasures which Spain obtained from her conquest and plunder of Mexico and Peru, brought no permanent benefit either to the Spanish people, or to the nation as a nation. On the contrary, it corrupted her whole national life and hastened her decay. Moreover, the wealth itself was soon gone, because it had not been used for the enlightenment, elevation and betterment of the people.

The iniquitous slave trade which was carried

on so long under the British flag, did not benefit the British people, but only certain British ship-owners and capitalists. Slavery, which so long disgraced the Southern States of the American Union, did not benefit the people as a whole, or those States as states. It enriched only a small class. The country and the people generally were injured. The Northern States, where there was no slavery, far surpassed the South in education and in everything pertaining to the general welfare, and it is only of late years, since the curse of slavery has been removed, that the Southern States are beginning really to prosper.

During the fifty years preceding the Great War, Germany, without any India and without colonies worth mentioning, increased in trade, commerce, manufactures, industries of all things, and wealth much more than did Great Britain. The same was true of several of the smaller nations of Europe that were without colonies. These facts alone show that colonies and dependencies are not necessary in order to secure trade—trade of the most profitable kinds trade to the fullest degree.

One reason why the industrial prosperity of a nation does not require the owning of colonies and dependencies, is the fact that armies and navies and police and vast imperialist machinery which such ownership involves more than consume the profits. It has been proved a hundred times over that the motto, "Trade follows the flag" is not necessarily true at all. What trade follows is friendship, intelligence, enterprise, absolutely honest and fair dealing. A large part of the best trade of every nation is with peoples not under its flag. This is true of America. It is true of every nation of Continental Europe, it is true of Great Britain herself. The United States did not require to "possess" the Philippines in order to reap most profit from their trade. Since she conquered them they have been an actual expense to her. What she needed, to promote her trade, was the friendship of the Filipino people. Great Britain covets the rich trade of China. What she must have in order to secure it is the friendship and thorough confidence of the Chinese people,—these, and not British gunboats on their rivers, British battleships in their harbors, British police in their cities, tyrannical exterritoriality, unjust customs exactions, and concession obtained by force. Friendship, enterprise, absolutely fair and just dealing will bring to Britain and every other commercial nation far more and better trade with every part of the world than all their armies and navies can possibly extort.

This is the lesson that Great Britain needs to learn concerning China, and still more concerning India.

Many Englishmen claim that Britain by her possession of India has gained protection and safety, because she has been able to draw upon the Indian people for recruits for her armies.

Nothing could be farther from the truth than this claim. From the very first day of Britain's possession of India, India has been Britain's danger point, her weakness, her peril,—the part of her empire most liable to flame into revolution; the part most coveted by other nations and therefore which has had to be most constantly protected against other nations; the part of her empire to guard which she has had to maintain an army much larger and more expensive than otherwise she would have needed, and a navy several times as costly as otherwise she would have required. This shows how very great a danger and how very great an expense the possession of India has been, and all the while is, to Great Britain.

Many Englishmen justify their domination of India on the ground that it gives their nation prestige. Yes ! unquestionably it does, of the kind that comes from conquering nations and ruling them without their consent ; prestige based upon brute military power—"devil prestige" ! Does Britain want such ? If so, her religious teachers, if she has any who really believe in justice and moral law and God, may well sound in her ears the solemn lines of her Kipling :

"Far-called, our navies melt away;
On dune and headland sinks the fire ;
Lo, all our pomp of yesterday
Is one with Nineveh and Tyre !"

And also the following lines, not less applicable to her case :

"The ruins of dynasties passed away
In eloquent silence lie ;
And the despot's fate is the same to-day
That it was in the days gone by.
Against all wrong and injustice done
A rigid account is set,
For the God who reigned in Babylon
Is the God who is reigning yet."

One further very important thought, in conclusion :

If Great Britain can spare her best young men from the great task of building up her important interests at home, and can afford to send them away to a foreign land, why does she send them to India, a full land, a crowded land, where they are not wanted, where they have no right to be, where their task is that of perpetuating human bondage ? Instead, why does she not send them to her *own dominions, Canada, Australia, and the rest,* where they have a right to be, where they are wanted,—her own spledid lands of vast, unpopulated spaces, rich in every kind of material wealth,—lands which have long been calling them, calling them, to come, and build up new homes, new communities, new cities, new states, new civilizations, for the enlargement of the bounds of human freedom, for the strengthening and glory of Britain, and for the benefit of the world ?

Canada and Australia are vast areas, almost continental in extent, possessing unlimited material resources,—one containing only about nine millions of inhabitants and the other less than six millions, yet each capable of sustaining in comfort and prosperity a population of fifty, or seventy-five, or a hundred millions. Both countries have begged incessantly for population, and none would have been so welcome or so valuable as immigrants from the home land. Both have sorely needed capital, and have been full of opportunities for its investment where it would not only have brought ample returns but also would have served the immensely important purpose of developing free countries and building up strong nations.

Here, in creating in these lands great and rich civilizations—other and greater Englands—was a career for Great Britain worthy of her best sons, worthy of her most ardent and sustained energies and of her highest ambitions. Why has she turned aside from, neglected, rejected, such glorious and unprecedented opportunities to serve both herself and the world, and instead, has thrust herself, forced herself, into a land, fully populated, where her sons have had to spend their years in the un-British task of ruling men against their will and gaining wealth and power by injustice and tyranny ?

Looking at the matter from any side, considering the case on any ground even the lowest, has India been an advantage to Great Britain ? Has Britain been wise in pursuing her career of conquest, oppression, exploitation and robbery (in the later years legal robbery) in India, and at the same time neglecting her dominions, her free colonies ?

General Gordon, who had an intimate knowledge of both England and India, wrote in his Journal (1st Ed. p. 133):

> "India to me is not an advantage. It accustoms our men to a style of life not fit for England It deteriorates our women. If our energy expended there were expended *elsewhere*, it would *produce ten-fold*. India sways our policy not to our advantage but *to our detriment*."

Many other British men express in private conversation, and not unfrequently make bold to say in print, the same word as that of General Gordon. In the *Glasgow Herald*, I find a letter written by a Glasgow gentleman, saying:

> "Let us suppose, for the sake of argument, that British rule in India has proved to be a benefit to the Indian people—which to say the least is very questionable,—does it follow that Britain should continue to rule India? Assuredly not, since there is strong reason to believe that the British talent, energy and capital which have been absorbed in that far away land where we can stay only by forcing ourselves upon an unwilling people, would have been very much *more productive of solid benefit to ourselves and to the world* if this *talent*, *energy* and *capital* had been used to *develop the resources of the British Islands*, and of *those parts of the world where we are wanted*, where we have a *right to be*, and where people of British birth and descent can settle as permanent colonists and *build up great new British dominions*."

The present writer has lived some years in different cities of Canada, and he knows how many Canadian people feel that the "mother country" has been anything but wise or just in devoting so much of her thought, attention and capital, and sending out so many of her best men, to India, to the neglect of her own important dominions—Canada, Australia, and the rest. Many Canadians believe that several millions of emigrants intelligent, vigorous, enterprising people, who have come from the British Islands within the last half or three-quarters of a century to the United States, and who were exactly the kind of men and women that the British dominions needed to develop their new civilization, would have come to these British lands instead of to the United States if the mother country had shown half the interest in helping and developing these lands that she has shown in ruling and exploiting a country that did not belong to her and that brought her no strength and no real good.

To cite a sample Canadian utterance. In the London *Times* of Sunday, June, 6, 1926, appears a quotation from a prominent Toronto Editor, addressed to Great Britain, declaring that British neglect is being taken advantage of by the United States to draw Canada more and more under her influence. He says :

"We Canadians do not want to be tied up with these people south of us ; but what are we to do ? You British care nothing about Canada. Two per cent. of the capital invested in the Dominion is British ; more than seventy per cent is United States capital. Even when your big people—prominent authors and the like—come across the water, they choose the States, and seldom come to the border even to shake hands. Who are we ? God's lost sheep."

The people of Australia even more than the people of Canada feel the unwisdom and folly of Great Britain, and her injustice to her own children, in praying so little attention to them, and especially in devoting such an enormous amount of her capital and her man-power and brain-power to the altogether questionable enterprise of maintaining her "Indian Empire," when all this capital, man-power and brain-power are urgently needed in the great Australian Continent to develop there a rich and powerful daughter nation of infinitely more value to Britain than any slave Empire held in allegiance by bayonets can ever be.

Says an American Quaker, who has lived both in Canada and in India:

"Why does not England send her sons to Canada, instead of to India? Under Canadian conditions the best that is in them would be brought out. Pioneer life, the conquest of natural forces, the building up of free institutions in a free land make manly, strong, honorable and noble men. But under such conditions as exist in India, the worst that is in men is developed. The domination of a subject people destroys manhood, and degrades the character of all who have part in it. In Canada I have always been proud of Britain. In India I have always been ashamed of her. Why does she not have the wisdom to give up her slave empire, washing the stain of it from her hands, and put all her energies into building up her splendid *Free Commonwealths, Canada, Australia and the others*?"

In the story of Jesus we read:

"And the devil taketh him unto an exceeding high mountain and showeth him all the kingdoms of the world and the glory of them; and he said unto him, All these will I give thee if thou wilt fall down and worship me. Then said Jesus unto him, Get thee hence, Satan."

When Great Britain was taken up into a high mountain and shown the kingdoms of the world and the glory of them; and when the devil said unto her, All these will I give you if you will fall down and worship me, what answer did she make? Was it that of Jesus? Or was it the opposite—Give me the kingdoms; above all give me India; and I will fall down and worship thee?

As surely as day follows night, a future age, wiser than ours, will come, which will see and declare that Britain in conquering and maintaining her "Indian Empire," like Jacob of old "*sold her birthright*" (and a splendid birthright it was) "*for a mess of pottage*,"—nay for a *cup of poison for herself and for half the world.*

CHAPTER XXXV

HOW INDIA IN BONDAGE MENACES THE WORLD

Again and again it has been declared by statesmen in Europe that the real cause of the World War of 1914-1918 was India. The possession by Great Britain, for more than a century and a half, of so vast and rich an empire in Asia as India is, had been all the while kindling jealousy, envy and lust of conquest in the breasts of the other nations of Europe. All the other leading nations had looked on with envy, and said : If Great Britain holds her vast and rich Indian possessions as the result of conquest by the sword, why should not we also use the sword and conquer rich and lucrative possessions ? If by her navy and her army she has won for herself such a splendid 'place in the sun,' why should not we create armies and navies and win an equal place in the sun ? Says Herbert Adams Gibbons, in his book "The New Map of Asia :"

> "No one can understand the foreign policy of Great Britain, which has inspired military and diplomatic activities from the Napoleonic Wars to the present day, who does not interpret wars, diplomatic conflicts, treaties and alliances, territorial annexations, extensions of protectorates, all with the fact of India constantly in mind."

England has fought more wars during the last two centuries than any other nation, and the larger part of them have been directly or indirectly caused by India.

England's wars carried on against the tribes to the northwest of India, against Afghanistan and against Tibet, were ostensibly to give India a "scientific frontier". But that really meant, to enlarge the boundaries of India and to obtain possession of the passes and strong military positions to the north, northwest and west, and thus guard the land against a possible or imagined invasion from Russia.

England's conquest of Egypt in 1882 was primarily to get control of the nation in whose territory lay the Suez Canal, and thus protect her passage way to India ; and her refusal to grant freedom and independence to Egypt to-day has the same meaning.

It has been England's hold of India that has made her regard it as necessary not only to obtain possession of the Suez Canal and lands on the route to India, such as Egypt, Cyprus and areas on the Arabian Coast and the Persian Gulf, but also to possess and powerfully fortify such strongholds as Gibraltar (conquered from Spain), Malta (which properly belongs to Italy), and Aden at the entrance to the Red Sea (wrested from Arabia), and that has recently caused her to build her great naval base at Singapore.

England's great navy, the existence of which has created so much uneasiness among all other nations and which has been a constant incitement to them to increase their navies, owes its existence mainly to India—to England's felt necessity for keeping open her sea route to her distant possession and for defending that possession against any nation that might want to rob her of it.

As to England's army too, although it seldom has been as large as those of several of the other European powers yet it has been usually kept at fully double the strength (counting both British and

Indian troops) that would have been necessary except for India. Thus England's influence in stimulating the growth of modern armies has been greatly increased by her conquest and holding of India.

England's long enmity to Russia, shown in the Crimean War, in her siding with Turkey at the close of the war of 1877, and in many other ways, has been caused primarily by her fear of Russia's encroachment on India.

On the other hand, it has been Britain's great prestige, power and wealth gained through her possession of India that more than anything else has inflamed Russia with Asiatic ambitions, and caused her to push forward her own conquests with a view to obtaining a place in Asia as important as that of her British rival.

It has been largely envy of England's rich possession in India that has made all the great European powers eager to get slices of China. If England had India, why should not they have China? If the big rich Asiatic cake was to be cut and divided up, and if Great Britain had already secured such an enormous slice in India, why should not they bestir themselves and seize slices elsewhere?

All these ambitions of the other leading European powers to follow Britain's example and get slices of the Asiatic cake, of course, made her the more anxious to protect her slice.

Great Britain's diplomatic and military operations in Persia for some years before the war in Europe, and her co-operation with Russia in reducing Persia to the position of a dependency of Great Britain and Russia, had India in view. Great Britain wanted to get Persia under her control, and thus be able to use her as a barrier between Germany and India.

Britain's hostility to Germany, which had been growing for fifteen or twenty years, before the war of 1914, sprang largely from her fear that Germany's ambition to gain a foothold in Asia might limit her own influence there, and especially might endanger her hold on India. Particularly had she been alarmed over Germany's project of a railway from Berlin to Bagdad, because such a great highway would bring Germany so much nearer to England's great Indian possessions.

If twenty years ago Britain had admitted India to partnership within the British Empire, with home rule, Germany would never have dreamed of her Berlin to Bagdad railway project. Germany went into the Great War believing that India was Britain's weakness, and that the Indian people would take the war as an occasion to revolt against their British overlords. This mistake would not have been made by Germany if India had been a contented partner in the British Empire. Thus there would have been no war. This means that if Britain had been wise enough to extend to India, in time, the hand of justice, friendship and brotherhood, as noble Englishmen like John Bright and Herbert Spencer and John Stuart Mill and A. O. Hume and Sir Henry Cotton and Sir William Wedderburn and others urged her to do, instead of being guided by her blind imperialists and militarists the results would have been to-day an England leading the world in prosperity and peace, instead of a land mourning the loss of millions of its noblest young men, the widowing of millions of its wives and mothers, the unemployment of millions of its workers, the piling up of a crushing debt of billions of pounds, and the crippling of its industries to a degree never known before; and, what is even more important, the results on the

European Continent would have been, the nations there in prosperity and peace, instead of being, as most of them now are, in conditions of simply indescribable fear, hate, misery and hopelessness. Thus England has paid dear, and Europe has paid dear, for an India conquered, exploited and held down by the sword.

It is not only true that India has been the main cause of England's wars for two centuries, but it is also true that India has been a constantly inciting cause, even more so than the Balkans or Turkey (although not always realized), of Europe's political jealousies, ambitions, intrigues, rivalries, secret diplomacies and wars.

All this that I am saying and very much more on the same lines, is affirmed by the most trustworthy authorities in England, India and elsewhere. Let me cite some of their words which are well worth the thoughtful attention of all persons who care for the peace of the world and the future welfare of mankind.

Mr. Lajpat Rai, the eminent Indian publicist and leader, says in a personal letter to the present writer:

"The problem of India, that is, the problem whether great India is to be free or slave, is not only an important problem to Great Britain, but it is one of the gravest possible concern to the whole world. It is a question upon which, more perhaps than upon any other whatever, the future peace of Asia, Europe and the whole world depends.

"India is such a huge slice of the earth, and contains such an immense population, that no person interested in world-affairs can ignore its importance. India's human potentialities of all kinds are very great. Commercially it is strategic for nearly half the globe. It is the key to the Indian Ocean and the clearing house of the larger part of the Orient. This is why militarism and imperialism have always looked upon it with eyes of greed. This is why India has inspired Alexanders, Tamerlanes, Napoleons, Wellesleys, Czars and Kaisers with visions of world-empire. This is why for two centuries Great Britain has shaped her foreign diplomacy, her military plans and her imperial policy with a constant eye to strengthening her hold on India, her richest province, her greatest source of wealth and prestige. This is why she has carried on so many wars to guard the borders of India, to keep open her road to India, to weaken any nation that might endanger her possession of India.

"Nor will India in the future be any less an apple of discord among the nations, a source of endless plottings, jealousies, intrigues and wars, so long as she remains a subject people,—a rich prize to be coveted, sought for and fought for by rival nations. Her only safety and the only promise of peace and safety for the Orient or for Europe lie in her freedom; in her ceasing to be a pawn on the chessboard of the world's diplomatic, imperialistic and capitalistic plottings, and in her power to protect herself, a power which she would abundantly possess if free. In the very nature of the case no League of Nations and no other possible agency or power can ensure peace to the world so long as a great civilized nation, located in the very center of the world's greatest continent and possessing one-fifth of the entire population of the globe, is in bondage. We see, therefore, why the problem of India's freedom or bondage is not only a world problem, but a problem more fundamental to the world's peace and safety than any other whatever."

Professor Parker T. Moon, of Columbia University, says in his recent work, "Imperialism in World Politics" (p. 311):

"India occupies a most important place both in the British Empire and in world-politics...... India is the greatest of British possessions, and one of the least secure......Protection of India has been a motive in British aggression in Persia, in Mesopotamia, in Afghanistan, in Tibet, in Burma, in Egypt, in the Mediterranean. In the history of European diplomacy during the last century, India might well appear on every page, so far-reaching has been its influence."

Dr. V. H. Rutherford, M. P., in his recent book, "Modern India: Its Problems and Their Solution," says in unequivocal language (Introduction, pp. X and XII):

"In order to tighten our hold on India, we (British) have descended into barbarism, by seizing Egypt, Cyprus Aden, Somaliland, Mesopotamia, etc.: by partitioning Persia, which evil has been undone since the war; by consolidating our South African Empire by wars; by making a naval base at Singapore; by waging wars against Afghanistan; and by indulging in armaments on an enormous scale, with a view to making ourselves the greatest military and naval power in the world."

And again :

"India has been used as a pawn by Great Britain in her imperial designs on China, Afghanistan, Persia, Mesopotamia and Egypt, making Indians hated by Asiatics and Africans, and robbing them of self-respect by using the Indian army in attacks upon the liberty and independence of these countries."

The truth of these terrible statements has been strongly corroborated by professor Robert Moss Lovett, of the University of Chicago, in the following plain language :

"It is a fact of which all the nations of the world may well take notice, that the foreign policy of Great Britain has long been determined, is determined to-day and in the future must be determined, by her possession of India. This makes her relation to India not a domestic affair but a matter of world-concern. Ever since the end of the eighteenth century, when the immense Mogul Empire of India fell into her hands through a war of conquest, her heart has been increasingly with this treasure ; and her attitude with respect to her neighbor nations has varied from conciliation and friendship to suspicion and hostility according to the measure in which their looks toward this treasure have seemed to her covetous or otherwise. At the same time, the treasure has been a constant challenge and temptation to her rivals. Other nations notably France, Russia and Germany have believed that they had as good a right to its possession as had Great Britain. It is not too much to say that this rich treasure upon which she had got her grip in India has caused Great Britain, like the giant Fafner, to turn herself into a dragon, watchful, warlike, ready to rush from her cave breathing fire, upon any nation that she deemed covetous of her possession. Only this must be added, that instead of a mere mass of metal, of gold, the treasure in India over which Great Britain stands guard is composed of human beings and human destinies.......It is only by the acquiescence, the virtual consent, of the world, that Great Britain has been able to maintain herself in possession of her "Indian Empire," an acquiescesence secured by propaganda, intrigue, quid pro quo, alliance, intimidation and war......The freeing of India would go farther than any other conceivable action toward the settling of the imperial control of the nation by other nations throughout the world. And India would be set free if the world viewed with clear, truthful eyes the monstrous nature of her subjection and its menace to the world's peace. There can be no possibility of the world having permanent peace so long as a great civilized nation, containing one-fifth of the population of the globe, is held in political servitude."*

Writes a distinguished Englishman whose name I am not at liberty to give:

"The great War of 1914 to 1918, which ruined and drained Europe, of which few if any confess the true aims, was a war for the possession of the routes to Asia, for the possession of Asia, particularly India. Nothing can disarm the rival ambitions of the European powers so long as the prey they covet remains for them a possible prey. Peace will come to Europe from Asia when Asia becomes free, not before. It is not solely for the uplift of Asia, but in the interest of Europe herself, that one must wish for the end of her Asiatic domination. The time has come for her to loose her deadly grip on Asia, for her own sake. The sword with which she struck has turned back, dripping with blood, against herself. The hour has come for Europe to die to her old life of Asiatic conquest, greed, exploitation and domination, that she may be born again. The rebirth of Europe has for its condition the restoration, the restitution of Asia. Of Asia—yes! and first of all, India. For without India there is no real Asia. There is no Asia free without India free. For India is not simply a part of Asia; she is its living heart, the soul itself."

The conquest of India was the greatest theft

* Introduction to "India in World Politics," by Taraknath Das, New York, B. W. Huebsch, 1923.

in the history of the modern world. The exploitation of great India with its vast population and its enormous material resources, has been the modern world's richest loot. Is it any wonder that the other great nations have been envious of England, and have plotted and planned how they might either capture from her this richest of all her prizes, or, failing that, get possession of other territories in Asia or elsewhere, and thus obtain power, and prestige and wealth in some measure commensurate with England's ?

Thus it is that ever since the eighteenth century the conquest and exploitation of India have stirred up perpetual rivalries, jealousies, strifes, plots, hatreds and wars among the nations of Europe. And this is only another way of saying that India held in subjection—held as a rich prize by one European nation and coveted by the rest—has been the leading influence in turning all Europe into an armed camp, and thus, as already said, making inevitable the terrible conflict which began in 1914.

Nor can things be permanently better so long as India remains a subject land ; that is, so long as this prime cause of the plottings, jealousies and hostilities of nations continues.

All the peoples of the world want peace. But right-thinking men everywhere agree that permanent peace can be based only on justice and freedom. So long as nations are held in bondage by other nations there can be no peace that will last. On July 14th, 1917, Lloyd George, the British Premier, sent a telegram to the Prime Minister of Russia saying :

"There can be no lasting peace until the responsibility of Governments to their people is clearly established from one end of Europe to the other."

Why did he not add, what was quite as true and quite as important : "There can be no lasting peace until the responsibility of Governments to their people is clearly established *from one end of Asia to the other?"*

The Allies in the late war all saw plainly and declared that there could be no permanent peace in Europe unless Belgium and Serbia and Poland were given freedom. Why did they not all see the same with regard to Asia, especially great India? A few of them did see this, but were over-ruled. All of them ought to have realized that a peace settlement with India still in chains, would leave her, as in the past, the danger spot of the world. And even more than in the past, for India is fast rising to a new self-consciousness, to a new sense of her wrong, to a new determination to be free.

At present India is striving to gain her freedom by peaceful means. What if that kind of effort fails? If the liberty which she seeks (either the liberty of Home Rule like Canada's in connection with the British Empire, or, if England will not willingly grant that, then entire independence) is refused to her until her patience is worn out—then what? Who can say that there may not be a revolt, like that of the American Colonies against Great Britain in 1776?—and a revolt caused by grievances borne and wrongs suffered far greater than those which drove the American colonists to rebellion! And England should understand that if a revolt comes in India now, after the Great War in which a million Indians fought as bravely and effectively as any European soldiers, and after the infamous Rowlatt Acts, which outraged all India, and after the Amritsar massacre which shocked all India and destroyed her faith in British justice,—if after all these experiences a revolt comes, it will not be another Mutiny like that of 1857. That was terrible enough. It strained the British Empire to its utmost to quell it. But that was confined to the native army, and only a part of the army at that; for a considerable portion remained loyal to Great Britain. Indeed, it was only by the help of loyal India and loyal Indian troops that the mutiny was quelled and British rule in India survived.

But the next revolt, if it comes—if, India is driven to it—will not be a mere local affair; as pointed out in a previous chapter it will be the uprising of all India. In 1857, India was divided. In many superficial matters it is divided now, but not in its desire and demand for self-government. In this demand and determination, fundamental to all others, there is now essential unity among absolutely all classes, races and religions,—Hindus, Mohammedans, Jains, Sikhs and Christians; and among all political parties, of whatever names, whether "nationalists," "swarajists," "liberals," "moderates," or others. Within the last half-century and especially within the last fifteen years, a New India has come into existence, which is feeling its power; which remembers that it has been a great nation among the nations of the world, and is determined to be the same again,—an India in whose heart burns a mighty flame of patriotism, of love for the Motherland and of determination that she shall be free! It is this India that must be reckoned with, if a revolt comes now.

If such a revolt—such a revolution—springs up India will be certain to have the sympathy of all Asia. Will she not have Asia's help, as the British Colonies in America had the help of France in their revolution and struggle for freedom? Will not Asia feel that India, in fighting her own battle for liberty, is also fighting the battle of all Asia? If such a struggle comes, will it not be likely to arouse all Asia, with the danger of arraying that great continent against Europe—the darker races against the white—in a struggle of inconceivable magnitude and horror?

Asia has a population of more than 900 millions, Europe of 450 millions.

More than half of Asia is now under the dominance of Europe. Think of the crime of it! This condition of things cannot always last. Most of the Asiatic peoples are as virile as Europeans. They only need to be aroused from their long slumber by the new spirit of the modern world (as they are fast being aroused), when they will be certain to revolt against their oppressors and set themselves up as free and independent nations.

Already Japan has arisen and taken her place beside the foremost nations of Europe. Turkey has followed. Persia and Afghanistan are following. Great China is coming forward slowly but surely into strength and influence. Great India's turn cannot be long delayed. It is incredible that a country like India, containing a population more than three-quarters as great as that of all Europe, with a civilization antedating that of Europe and with a great and proud history, should remain forever subject to a nation 6,000 miles away.

England by her present policy in India is creating for herself another Ireland, but on an immensely larger scale and involving vastly greater dangers to herself. More than that. By continuing her present Indian policy, England is creating in India another Balkan situation, only far more dangerous to Europe and to the whole world than the situation in the Balkans ever was. It will require only the igniting of a match in India, as little Serbia lighted a match in the Balkans, to start a conflagration which will be liable to become quite as terrible as that which was kindled in Europe. It will mean (if I may change my figure of speech) that the second most populus nation in the world has become transformed into a live volcano, planted in the very center of the greatest continent of the world, the eruption of which will be as certain to come as the tides, and the extent and devastation of which no man can measure.

Can the situation be saved ? Yes.

Great Britain can save it, in one way ; but only in one. That is, by granting to India the freedom which is her right ; and doing it without tantalizing, aggravating and fatal delays. It is this or Armageddon.

CHAPTER XXXVI

WHEN IS INDIA TO HAVE SELF-RULE ?

The Indian people believe they are fully capable of ruling themselves now. This means they believe they ought to have self-government granted them practically at once,—with no delay except what is necessary in order to set up an adequate Indian government, and to adjust matters so that no injustice shall be done to any parties, Indian or British.

The people of India believe their freedom ought never to have been taken from them; having been taken away, they believe it ought to have been restored long ago. Especially they believe it ought to have been restored at the end of the World War of 1914-1918, which was fought, India was told, and the world was told, "to make the world safe for democracy," and "to give freedom and self-determination" to all oppressed nations and peoples. If self-rule was granted to Poland, Czecho-Slovakia and other smaller, less important and less oppressed nations, why was it not granted to great, civilized, historic India ?

There is difference of judgment among the Indian people as to what form they desire self-rule to take,—whether that of absolute independence, with no relation to Britain except that of friendship ; or that of "Dominion Status" within the British Empire, like that of Canada, Australia and South Africa.

Up to the end of the Great War and a few

months after, the feeling of a large majority was in favor of the latter. As a result of events which have occurred since, there has been a change, and the change is still going on. It would not be easy to say what is the prevailing feeling in India at the present time. It was significant that the Indian National Congress at its session in Madras in December, 1927, voted almost unanimously that its goal was entire independence of Great Britain.

It is believed that the Government of India made the greatest possible mistake in not availing itself of the enthusiasm for England engenderd in India by the Great War, to extend to the Indian people at that time, in recognition of their self-sacrifice, their loyalty and the splendid service they had rendered in men and in money, the great boon which they so much desired and which they expected, namely, freedom and home rule, in the form of Dominion Status in the Empire. That would have allayed at once India's discontent, settled the dark problems that now loom so threateningly in her sky, fastened the Indian people to Britain with hooks stronger than steel, and saved the terrible blunders and disasters of the Rowlatt Acts, the Amritsar Massacre, and all the other Punjab atrocities and horrors. It is believed that then was the "psychological moment" when Britain, instead of acting the part of a suspicious, imperialistic oppressor, ought to have treated India in the same generous, noble, large-minded way that she treated South Africa. Will she not long have reason to lament that she did not possess, in that critical time, a Campbell-Bannerman, to lead her in the path of true statesmanship ?

But the past is gone. What now of the future? Will the British, learning nothing from their past mistakes, continue to treat India in the same old imperialistic way; dominating her by force; fastening upon her for a still longer term of years either Dyarchy or something worse; granting her the least liberty possible without danger of revolt; professing to be educating her for self-rule without giving her any assurance that she will ever be allowed self-rule at all?

Or will some real statesman arise in England, some new Campbell-Bannerman, some man large enough to see, and to make the British Government see, that just as South Africa could be saved to the British Empire only by freedom, so India can be saved only in the same way,—by a big, generous, impressive, dramatic act of granting her real home rule, and doing it without aggravating delay—of extending to her promptly the hand of frank, sincere, honest welcome to the place in the Empire (in the "Commonwealth of Free Nations") by the side of South Africa, Canada and the other Dominions? Will such a happy event occur? Let every lover of India and of England hope and pray that it may.

As to just when India ought to be given self-government, let us seek the judgment of some Englishmen well qualified to speak.

No Englishman knows India better than Rev. C. F. Andrews, who went there more than a quarter of a century ago, was for a time a missionary of the Church of England and a college professor, and who for some years past has travelled all over India devoting himself to work of social reform. Mr. Andrews tells us unhesitatingly that, in his judgment, the Indian people should have self-rule at once, that is, as soon as proper adjustments for it can be made, and that delay in order to carry on what is mistakenly called "educating them for freedom" is folly, and only makes conditions worse. Here are his words:

"A few days ago a professor from America asked me the question, whether India would prefer Swaraj (self-government) to-morrow, or wait for twenty years, when it might be had with less danger of confusion and disaster in the process. I said to him that the real danger was not that of the confusion which might take place if Swaraj came to India to-morrow, but rather the *danger* of *delay*; because every year that Swaraj was not obtained was another year of *foreign institutions, foreign government*, and *foreign trampling upon India's rights*. I asked him, as an American, what he would think if foreign institutions were imposed upon his own country. Would he wish to get rid of them immediately, even if there was some disturbance in the process? Or would he be willing to wait for twenty or any other number of years, during which those very foreign institutions would become *still more hard to get rid of*? He replied immediately, 'We would *never allow foreign institutions to be imposed upon America even for a moment*, much less a term of years.' I said to him. '*Then you see the whole Indian situation* at one glance, and you can understand why Indians are impatient, and cannot bear even a single year to be passed under the foreign yoke.' He confessed to me, 'I have asked Indians from one end of India to the other the same question that I asked you, and they have all given me the same answer. They have all said, '*We want self-government now. We protest against Britain's utterly unnecessary and exasperating delay.*' "

The following is what Mr. Bernard Houghton, long a distinguished member of the British-Indian Civil Service, says about delay:

"Why shall political freedom come to India slowly? It is ready for freedom to-day. It is not a barbarous country. It possesses a civilization far older than ours (that of Britain). In some respects, particularly in its village organizations, its civilization is more democratic and better than ours. Indians are peaceable, intelligent, quick to unite in group action. The writings and speeches of their leaders and the tone of their newspapers strike a higher note than in England. Indians really strive after ideals, they really believe in moral principles. Is not such a country ready for self-rule? It is no argument to say that because Britain has taken 800 years to attain democracy, therefore India too must advance at tortoise pace. Britain was not ruled by foreigners while she was attaining democracy. Events and ideas move a hundred times more swiftly now than of old. Look at the United States of America. At a leap they obtained freedom, and a constitution which after 150 years is still ahead of Britain. Look at Japan. Look at Turkey. India aspires to govern herself. For this she is ready. It will be a crime against humanity if she is prevented."

A number of times within the last half a dozen years the British Labour Party has declared itself unequivocally in favor of self-rule for India and not in some far-off future but immediately, as soon as proper arrangements can be made. One of its most recent declarations is the following :

"We believe that the time has come when our brothers in all parts of India are capable (not will be some time but are now) of controlling their own affairs equally along with South Africa and other British Dominions and we hereby pledge ourselves to assist in every way possible to bring about this much desired reform."

In the India debate in the House of Commons on July 8, 1927, Mr. Ben Spoor is reported as declaring that the fixed demand of the British Labor Party is that "India must be recognized without unnecessary delay as a free, equal and unfettered partner in the British Commonwealth of Nations, which is her inalienable right." Colonel Wedgwood emphatically confirmed the declaration.

In the London *Daily Herald* of October 17, 1927, Mr. Ramsay MacDonald declared that further so-called "tutelage" of India for self-rule is useless. She should have self-government at once. Here are his words :

"The moral justification that has always been made for the existence of our empire amongst subject peoples has been that we are training them for self-government. The most typical of that is our Indian Empire. A thousand and one reasons are given for a little more tutelge.....Now plain practical common sense should come to our rescue. Nobody can imagine that any harm will come from independence. Let independence be granted."

In a later article in the same paper (October 27, 1927) Mr. MacDonald declares unequivocally that the British idea of putting off and putting off India's independence in order that she may be trained for it by her British masters is folly. He affirms that she is ready for self-government now, and that the only training she needs is that of her own experience.

Still further. In a message purporting to come from Mr. MacDonald, cabled from London and published in *The Hindu* (Madras) May 24, 1928, it is declared that if the Labor Party comes to power one of its early acts will be "to put India on a footing of Dominion Status."

Later and more decisive still. Speaking at the British Commonwealth Labor Conference only July 9, 1928, he is reported as saying :

"I hope that *within the period of a few months, rather than years* there will be a New Dominion added to the Commonwealth of our nations, a Dominion of another race, a Dominion that will find self-respect as an equal within the Commonwealth."*

The Boers were not required to wait twenty years, or ten, or five, or two, for self-government. As soon as a constitution could be framed and proper governmental machinery could be set up, home rule was given them. And it has worked well. The Indian people see no reason why self-government should not be given to them as promptly as to the Boers.

What the Indian people demand is to have

---

* Cable published in *The Hindu*, Madras, July 12, 1928.

the useless crutch, the galling crutch, the weakening and injurious crutch of government by foreigners taken away without further annoying postponement, and to be allowed to use and develop their own legs.

No one has expressed this better than Mrs. Annie Besant, the eminent Englishwoman who knows India so well :

"Indians are tired of Britain's grandmotherly legislation which always treats them as babes. If the British think them babes, very well, let the babes crawl by themselves, get up and try to walk and then tumble down until by tumbles they learn equilibrium. If they learn to walk in leading strings they will always develop bowlegs. But as a fact wherever the Indians have been tried fairly in the matter of self-government they have always succeeded." *

It is no wonder that many of the Indian people feel themselves stung, insulted, outraged by the insistence of the British that they need to be *tutored* for self-rule, as if they were *children*, as if they had not ruled themselves for thousands of years,—tutored by a nation which is a *parvenu in self-rule compared with India,*

The plain truth is : There is to be found nowhere else on this planet such a stupendous farce as that of Great Britain claiming that India, the nation which has ruled itself longer than any other in the world, is not capable of ruling itself, and can be made capable only by years of training under foreigners. And what foreigners ? The very ones who destroyed her government and are holding her in bondage. The fact is, the men to whom Britain is committing the task of educating India for freedom and self-rule are the British bureaucracy in India, who, as everybody

---

* "The Case for India." p. 45. Theosophical Publishing Co. Madras.

knows, do not want her to have either one; who in the days when Lord Ripon was Viceroy were so enraged at him because he wanted to give India a small measure of freedom, that they nearly drove him out of the country. What kind of education for freedom and self-rule are such men as these likely to give India?

The case of Japan has been cited. Japan was capable of ruling herself from the beginning. She never required to be ruled a single year or a single day by a foreign power in order to become fit for self-government. The Indian people are in no way inferior to those of Japan. The British *do not need* to continue their rule in India, and they *ought not* to continue it, *a single day longer than is necessary to enable them to organize (or help the Indian people to organize) carefully planned Indian governments—national, provincial and local.*

How long does this mean? It is widely believed that one year is enough. Up to within a recent period the Indian people would have been willing to consent to five years, or even ten, if they could have been definitely and positively assured that at the end of that time self-government real self-government, and not a mere semblance, would be granted them. But there have been so many delays and so many disappointments, so many evaded or half-broken promises, that few now are willing to consider a time anywhere near so long.

To-day nearly all the most eminent and trusted leaders, and also not a few Englishmen, believe that *in a single year, or certainly in two*, the British government in India *can, if it will, set up as its successor, an Indian government, with every official position in it, from Viceroy to police man, filled by fully competent Indians (quite as competent as the men who fill the positions now), and do it with no confusion or disorder attending the going out of the old and the coming in of the new, and with no injustice to any interest. The Indian people are more peaceable and more law-abiding and naturally more orderly than the English,* and if in England the government of the country can pass from one political party to another, or if one King can die and a successor assume the crown with no disturbance of the peace, surely we have a right to believe that the British masters of India can arrange for proper elections there, national, provincial and local, and after the results of the voting are known, can turn over the government to the Indian officials chosen, and accomplish it all *as quitely, in as orderly a manner and with as much safety as one political administration succeeds another in England after an election. or as one King follows another. And why should they not be able to do it all within a single year's time?*

Such an Indian Government, while *doing no injustice to Britain* would *serve India incomparably better than the present Government does,* because it would be in the hands of men who *know India so much better than the British do* (or than any transient foreigners possibly can), who *sympathize with India's ideals and civilization* as the British do not, and whose *supreme interests are in India and not in a foreign land.*

Of course, whether India is fit for self-government or not depends upon what kind of a government we have in mind, and what we mean by fitness. If, as many seem to do, we entertain the ignorant and foolish thought that everything Indian is bad and that only things European or Western are good, and therefore that the Indian people will not be fit to rule themselves until they are made over into *imitators of Englishmen*, turning their back upon their own culture and ideals of thousands of years and adopting the language, customs, fashions, habits, education, religion and all the rest of *an alien and far-off land*; and if the kind of government which we insist that they must be fit for, is a kind not of their own, not what they want but what foreigners ignorantly and egotistically want them to have—an entirely European kind, and entirely British kind, a kind strange to India's ways, thoughts and ideals,—if this is what we mean by fit for self-government, then unquestionably the Indian people are not fit, and what is more, there seems no reason to believe that they ever will be.

But if India is to be allowed to *remain her own true self*, instead of trying to become a feeble and foolish *imitation of Europe*; if she is to be permitted to retain and develop her own unique and important civilization, instead of abandoning it for that of foreign masters; if she is to be permitted to have and develop a kind of government in harmony with her own experience and culture, and answering to her own ideals and needs, instead of a kind that came into existence under other skies and to serve other wants, then, as already has been urged, *she is unquestionably ready for self-government now*.

If it is objected that Indians competent to carry on the government cannot be found, the answer is, they can be found if sought for. As pointed out elsewhere, the Government of India, in nearly all its departments, is actually being carried on now mainly by Indians. And for two reasons: first, because there are not enough Englishmen to carry it on; and secondly, because in many respects the English are not competent,—

they are so ignorant of the languages of the country, of its history, institutions, customs, ideals, needs, and a thousand things which are necessary to be known to keep the government from making fatal mistakes. A large part of the most difficult, important and vital work of carrying on the Government in all its departments and branches simply *has* to be entrusted to competent Indians, or else everything would break down. The British occupy the high places, do the directing or "bossing", wear the honors and draw the high salaries. But they can all be spared. As has been said, there is no lack of Indians capable of filling and filling well absolutely every place of official responsibility from lowest to highest.

At this point let one thing be clearly understood ; and that is, that turning over the Government of India to the Indian people does not necessarily mean any such thing at all as that all Englishmen would be required to leave India, at once or ever. Businesss men, engaged in business that is legitimate, business not dependent upon unjust concessions to them as Englishmen, would not be disturbed. Beyond question the Indian government would do exactly as the government of Japan has done,—employ, at least for a time, not a few highly qualified foreigners, Germans, Frenchmen, Americans, and especially Englishmen, as professors in universities and technical schools, as managers and experts in developing the resources of the country and organizing its industries; and naturally this would continue (as in Japan) as long as there was need,—that is, until India felt herself abreast of the best science and other important knowledge of the West.

With regard to this whole matter of the relation of a self-ruling India to foreigners there seems to be a widespread misunderstanding. The impression has been created, and given out to the world, that the Indian people want to drive out "bag and baggage" not only the British Government but all Englishmen, if not all foreigners. No mistake could be greater. India has never demanded that Englishmen as individuals should leave, but only that they should no longer remain as rulers and lords of the country. Mahatma Gandhi has more than once taken pains to say, as have many other leaders of the highest influence, that Englishmen would be welcome to stay as citizens, as traders, and businessmen, as educators, and even as officials in cases where the Indian Government might see fit to appoint them as such. But they cannot stay as self-appointed rulers, masters and privileged exploiters of the land. They must take their places by the side of the Indian people, not above them.

Supplement :

DOES BRITAIN INTEND EVER TO GRANT INDIA SELF-RULE ?

I regret the need to dwell further upon the fact to which attention has been called above, that notwithstanding the constant assertions of the British that they are educating India for self-rule and intend to grant it as soon as she is fit, there is a growing feeling in India that they do not really intend anything of the kind, and that they will never pronounce her fit.

This feeling has two causes. One (already mentioned) is the constant and seemingly settled government policy of trying to allay popular discontent in India and lure the people on by promises so vague as to mean nothing. The other is definite statements made by men high in the government to the effect that Britain intends to possess and rule India permanently. Many such statements might be cited. I give here three—from Lloyd George, Lord Curzon and Lord Birkenhead, than whom there are no higher authorities.

(1) During the latter part of his term as Premier, Lloyd George made an address bearing on the Government of India Reform Scheme, in which he declared that Britain intends always to rule India, that there must always be in India's government a "steel frame" of British power, British authority, British dominance.

(2) Some years after the end of his term of service as Viceroy of India, Lord Curzon published two articles in the *North American Review* (June and August, 1910) on "British Rule in India," making it clear beyond a question that in his judgment Great Britain never should, never intends to, and never will give up her domination of India, closing his last article with the words:

"British rule of the Indian people is England's present and future task: it will occupy her energies for as long a span of the future as it is humanly possible to forecast."

(3) On the 7th of July, 1925, Lord Birkenhead, Secretary of State for India, said in the House of Lords:

"I am not able in any foreseeable future to discern a moment when we may safely either to ourselves or India, abandon our trust." (that is, the rule of India).

In these statements we have these three men, the highest authorities on the subject, declaring that in their judgment it is the *settled purpose* of the *British Government to hold India in its grip permanently*. Some of the words used are soft, calling Britain's relation to India a "trust," etc., but they all mean the same thing that Great Britain intends *absolutely to dominate India*, with or without its consent, (and of course it will be without it), *throughout a future as long as she can discern.*

To all this, what is to be said? There are two things to be said. One is that such a purpose, such an intention, on the part of Great Britain, *if it exists*, gives the lie to all her thousand times reiterated statements that she is educating India for *self-rule*; it shows that she intends nothing of the kind, and that her statements are made simply *to deceive India and the world.*

The second thing to be said is, that such a deliberate purpose on her part, *if it exists*, is *simply inhuman.* There is not a shadow of right or justice in it. It is neither Christian nor civilized; it is barbarian. It is nothing less than *outrageous.* Put in plain words it means that Great Britain *acknowledges no law higher than might.*

For myself I repudiate the utterances of these men—high officials though they are. I cannot and will not believe that they state truly the purpose of the British nation. If they do, it means that Britain intends to *hold in subjection permanently one-fifth of the human race by the power of the sword,* for she knows she can do it in no other way. In other words, it means that she deliberately plans to be, for all time so far as she can see, the greatest *aggressor nation*, the greatest *tyrant nation,* the greatest *leech nation,* the greatest *robber nation,* the greatest *slave-holding nation in the world,*—that she actually intends her future Empire to be one of *sixty millions or more of freemen and more than three hundred millions of thralls.* What a future for British men to look forward to!

Let those believe it who can. As for myself, I simply will not believe anything so MONSTROUS of the *nation of Hampden* and *Milton,* of *Burke* and *Wilberforce* and *John Bright.*

CHAPTER XXXVII

CONCLUSION

I began this book with three terrible statements and interrogations. In the light of the mountains of facts piled up in these chapters, am I not more than justified in ending it with the same?

1. A great civilized nation—the oldest and second most populous in the world, containing more than one-sixth of the entire human race, possessing a high and rich culture, for three thousand years free, self-ruling and filling a renowned place in history—is robbed of its freedom and nationhood, and held in forced bondage by foreign bayonets and bomb-dropping aeroplanes.

Is there anywhere in the world a greater crime?

2. If some European nation should conquer great civilized China and hold in forced subjection that historic people, would not the whole world declare it a monstrous wrong?

Is holding great civilized India in bondage a lighter wrong?

3. America was once guilty of holding in bondage three millions of human beings. We look back upon it with shame. To-day in India, three hundred millions of human beings are held in bondage, one hundred millions of whom, after a century and a half of British rule, are worse housed, worse clothed and worse fed than the slaves of America ever were.

Should this unparalleled crime continue? Should not the whole civilized world with one voice condemn it? Should not the British people themselves desire to end it? Will they not end it without unnecessary and dangerous delay?

BOOKS ON INDIA RECOMMENDED FOR FURTHER READING

A Short List. With Brief Descriptions and Comments

India as a whole, or in all its aspects, is a subject so vast that a list of books aiming to deal with it all would, of course, be out of place here. But it is believed that many readers may be glad to have their attention called to a reasonable number of the best and most trustworthy works giving further information on the important subjects treated in these pages, and portraying in a reliable way the real India of to-day, particularly in its higher and cultural aspects.

In making up the following list I have chosen for the most part books interesting to general readers; although a few are designed more especially for scholars and careful students. Also the list is restricted mainly to works published in America or England, because these are most accessible to American and English readers. However, a few of importance published in India are included; and more would be except for the fact that our public libraries and book stores are not as well provided as they ought to be with works issued in the orient.

I add brief descriptions of and comments on most of the books, with the hope that these may be of practical use to persons desiring to make selections for reading or purchase.

The List is arranged alphabetically, and not according to the relative importance of the books.

ANDREWS. C. F.

"*India's Claim for Independence.*"
"*Non-Co-operation in India: Why and How?*"
"*Indians in South Africa: Helots within the British Empire.*"
"*The Drink and Opium Evil.*"

No one is writing about India to-day with greater insight, courage and fairness than this eminent English missionary, college professor and helper of Tagore and Gandhi. The small popular books mentioned above (published by Ganesh and Co., Madras), are all written with the earnest practical aim of helping in the social and religious uplift and the political emancipation of the Indian people.

ART IN INDIA

For persons seeking information about Indian Art, no works are more valuable than those of E. B. Havell and A. K. Coomaraswami: which should be in all important libraries.

BANNERJEA, D. N.

"*India's Nation Builders.*" New York, Brentano.

Interesting Character-Sketches of fifteen of the most eminent and representative of the "Makers of Modern India,"—several of them being distinguished living educational and political leaders.

BANNERJEE, SURENDRANATH

"*A Nation in Making.*" The Oxford Press. 1925.

Fifty Years of Reminiscences of a great Indian Political and Educational Leader. Rich in information concerning India's struggle for freedom and the men and forces at work creating a New Nation.

BASU, MAJOR B. D.

"*Rise of the Christian Power in India.*" Five volumes, Calcutta, Modern Review Office.

"*The Colonization of India.*" Same publisher.

"*Ruin of Indian Trade and Industries.*" Same publisher.

"*Consolidation of the Christian Power in India.*" Same publisher.

"*Education in India Under the East India Company.*" Same publisher.

The first of these works (the five volume history) is indispensable for all persons making a careful study of British rule in India. It contains documentary material of Importance which can be obtained elsewhere only with great difficulty. The other works named are supplementary and valuable.

BESANT, ANNIE

"*India: Bound or Free.*" New York. Putnams.

"*India a Nation.*" London. T. C. and E. C. Jack.

"*The Future of Indian Politics.*" Adyar, India. Theosophical Publishing House.

"*The Case for India.*" Same publisher.

Mrs. Besant, who has lived more than a quarter of a century in India, is perhaps best known as President of the Theosophical Society. But she is also an ardent and able leader in political and social reforms. In 1917, she was President of the Indian National Congress. All the books mentioned above are arguments in support of India's fitness and right to freedom and self-rule.

BURKE, EDMUND

"*Speeches at the Trial of Warren Hastings.*" "Burke's Works." Vols. VIII, IX and X. Boston. Little and Brown.

These speeches of this great Englishman are

a classic, setting forth with great power the injustices, tryannies, duplicities, wholesale lootings and cruelties connected with the British conquest and early rule of India.

CASE, CLARENCE M.

"*Non-Violent Coercion.*" New York. Century Co. 1923.

A scholarly discussion of the philosophy of "Passive Resistance" and a history of its practical applications in religion, industries, politics, war, etc. It contains two chapters on Gandhi and his Non-Co-operation movements in Africa and India.

CLOSE, UPTON (JOSEF WASHINGTON HALL).

"*The Revolt of Asia.*" New York. Putnams. 1927.

This is a book of great significance. The author has been ten years in Asia, travelling extensively and holding responsible positions in China. In his chapters he gives us a startling array of facts showing that "Western control of Asia for profit, political and commercial, is discredited and in collapse"; that the Asiatic nations "have lost their fear of the white man; and are carrying forward resolutely their program of regaining control of their own governments and their own affairs." He argues forcibly that Great Britain must change her old policy of military imperialism—the policy of force to the new policy of friendship and service, or forfeit her leadership in the rest of Asia and lose India. The facts cited are of a nature to make the Western World do some very serious thinking.

CONGRESS, THE INDIAN NATIONAL

A large volume published by G. A. Natesan. Madras. Contains the Presidential Addresses,

Principal Resolutions and other historic material concerning the Congress from its organization in 1885.

COTTON, SIR HENRY

"*New India.*" London. Kegan Paul. 1907.

The author of this interesting book was more than thirty years a high official in India, and later a member of the British Parliament. He discusses Indian political conditions in the light of the largest knowledge, and confirms the contentions of Mr. Digby, Mr. Dutt, Major Basu and the Indian Nationalists in almost every particular.

DAS, TARAKNATH

"*India in World-Politics.*" New York. Huebsch (The Viking Press). 1924.

"*Sovereign Rights of Indian Princes.*" Madras. Ganesh & Co. 1925.

The first of these books is a clear and able treatment of the important subject of India in its international relations, and the far-reaching evil influence which its conquest and possession by Great Britain has had in creating the imperialistic spirit in the modern world and in promoting wars. During the past two centuries, Britain has fought more wars than any other nation, and fully two-thirds of them have been caused by the possession of India.

The second book is a brief and trustworthy account of the status and powers of the Indian Princes (and Native States) and their relation to the British Government.

DIGBY, SIR WILLIAM

"*'Prosperous' India: A Revelation from Official Records.*" London, 1900.

Mr. Digby was for a considerable time a

British official in India. This large volume contains a startling array of facts and figures obtained from the most trustworthy sources in support of the affirmation that British rule in India, throughout its entire history has been in effect a vast organized exploitation of the country, which has resulted in reducing the Indian people from their former industrial prosperity and wealth to a condition of more abject poverty than is to be found in connection with any other civilized nation.

DUTT, RAMESH C.

"*The Economic History of India*"—from the Rise of the British Power in 1757 to the Accession of Queen Victoria, in 1837. London, Kegan Paul, 1902.

"*India in the Victorian Age*"—from Economic History continuing the above. Same publisher, 1904.

"*Famines in India.*" Same publisher.

"*England and India.*" A History of India during a hundred years, from 1785 to 1885. London Chatto and Windus.

"*The Civilization of India.*" London. Dent & Co. (The Temple Primers).

Mr. Dutt was an eminent Indian scholar and statesman; member of the Legislative Council of Bengal, Finance Minister of the State of Baroda. Lecturer of University College, London. The first three works named have no superiors as histories of India from the beginning of British rule to the end of the reign of Victoria. They are luminous studies of the effects of British rule, in ruining India's finances and industries, in destroying her manufactures in the interest of those of England, and in causing her famines and present poverty. The fourth work is probably the best short history of India during the period that it covers. The last named work gives a brief and graphic history of Indian Civilization for 3,000 years (an abridgment of a valuable large work in two volumes, published by the Elm Press, Calcutta).

FISHER, REV. FRED B.

"*India's Silent Revolution.*" New York. Macmillan. 1919. This book by the American Methodist Bishop in Calcutta is an eminently fair and intelligent portrayal of social, political and religious conditions in India. While friendly to England, he is warmly sympathetic toward the aspirations of the people for freedom and self-rule.

GANDHI, M. K. (MAHATMA)

"*Mahatma Gandhi.*" By Romain Rolland. New York. Century Co. 1924. There is no better "Life" than this.

"*Gandhi the Apostle: His trial and His Message.*" H. T. Muzumdar.

Chicago. Universal Publishing Co. 1923 Contains much valuable information about Gandhi and also about India.

"*Young India.*" New York, Huebsch (The Viking Press). This is not a book about Gandhi: it is Gandhi himself. It is a compilation (in a volume of 1,200 pages) of all his most important speeches and writings during the three crucial years in which he was organizing his Non-Co-operation Movement in India. No other volume gives so complete a portrayal of his aims, his methods his religious, social and political philosophy.

Miss Blanche Watson of New York, has compiled a book of interesting gleanings from the American press, of opinions and miscellaneous information about Gandhi. It is published by Ganesh and Co., Madras.

It ought to be added, that Gandhi's Autobiography, under the title, "The Story of My Experiments with Truth." is being published serially in *Unity*, the Chicago weekly. The series began April 5, 1926.

GOKHALE, G. K.

"*Gokhale's Speeches,*" Madras. Natesan.

A volume of more than a thousand pages of discussions of all the leading political questions agitating India from 1880 to 1915. Mr. Gokhale was a Professor in Furguson College and a member of the Viceroy's Council. Mr. H. W. Nevinson declares that no abler or more statesmanlike addresses have been delivered in any country within the past forty years than these of this great Indian scholar and national leader.

HASAN, BADRUL

"*The Drink and Drug Evil in India.*" Foreword by Mahatma Gandhi. Madras. Ganesh and Co. 1922.

An excellent brief history of the use of intoxicating drink and opium in India in the past. Describes conditions to-day. Shows the responsibility of the Government.

HYNDMAN, H. M.

"*The Awakening of Asia.*" New York. Boni and Liveright. Mr. Hyndman was an eminent English publicist, who, througout his life, was an uncompromising advocate of justice and freedom to the Indian people. The chapters on India in this book are of much interest and value.

HARDIE, J KEIR. M. P.

"*India.*" New York. Huebsch (The Viking Prsss).

This bright plain-speaking book, by Britain's eminent Labor Leader, is a vigorous protest against the tyrannies which he found in India during a winter visit made there.

IYER, S. C. RANGA

"*Father India: A Reply to Miss Mayo's Mother India.*" London. Selwyn and Blount.

Mr. Iyer is a member of the Indian National Legislative Assembly. In his book we have a description of social conditions in India by a scholar and high government official who has spent his life in the country, as contrasted with that of a transient visitor from a foreign land. His condemnation of Miss Mayo's book is unqualified.

JONES, REV. E. STANLEY

"*The Christ of the Indian Road.*" New York. The Abingdon Press. 1927.

This is a book which portrays for us the new and very best type of Christian missions:—missions carried on by intelligent and broad-minded missionaries, who appreciate the Indian people, their civilization and their culture, look for the good in their religion and seek to build on it. The book should be read widely in America and England. It would tend to create broader and better home Christianity.

LA MOTTE, ELLEN N.

"*The Opium Monopoly.*" New York. The Century Co.

"*The Ethics of Opium.*" Same publishers.

These two small popular books give the exact facts and figures of the opium situation in India, the Orient and the world generally.

MACAULAY, THOMAS B.

The two Essays on "Clive" and "Warren Hastings" are classics, which should be read by everybody who would understand the real nature of the British conquest and early rule of India. They may be found in all editions of Macaulay's Works and collection of his Essays.

MACDONALD, J. RAMSAY

"*The Government of India.*" New York. Huebsch (The Viking Press). 1920,

"*The Awakening of India.*" London. Hodder and Stoughton. 1910. These books are important in themselves, and are particularly so as coming from the leader of the Labor Party in England and a former Premier. They advocate giving India "Dominion Status" in the British Empire, like that of Canada.

MACDONELL, A. A.

"*India's Past.*" Oxford University Press. 1927.

In this book an eminent Sanskrit scholar gives us what he calls "a summary of India's intellectual history;" in other words, a survey of India's races, languages, literatures, religions, philosophies, arts, sciences and cultures. Persons desiring to know the history and development of Indian civilization cannot do better than read this work.

MAX-MULLER, FRIEDRICH

This eminent orientalist wrote many valuable works on India and translated much important Indian literature. One of his books should be mentioned here—his popular volume, "*What Can India Teach Us?*" All students of India should read it. It can be found in most libraries.

MOHAMMEDANISM IN INDIA

India contains more than sixty million Mohammedans; and for some centuries before the coming of the British the rulers of the land were of that faith. Therefore, to know India one must have an adequate understanding of Mohammedanism. There is no more trustworthy work on the subject than "*The Spirit of Islam.*" by the Right Honorable Ameer Ali. New York. Doran and Co.

MOOKHERJI, RADHAKUMUD

"*The Fundamental Unity of India.*" London. Longmans. 1913. A short, learned, interesting work, substantiating the claim that India is essentially One—a Unity—not only geographically, but also in its history, civilization and permanent interests.

MOON, PARKER J.

"*Imperialism and World Politics.*" New York. Macmillian. 1926. A comprehensive and admirable survey of Imperialism as it exists in the world to-day,—it causes, methods and results as a foe to democracy and human freedom. Throws much light upon British rule in India.

MUKERJI, DHAN GOPAL

"*My Brother's Face.*" New York. E. P. Dutton.
"*A Son of Mother India Answers.*" Same publisher.

Mr. Mukerji is the author of a number of attractive books on India, all of which are to be commended as true pictures of Indian life. The The first of the two mentioned above is among the best of these. The second is a brief, bright and admirable reply to Miss Katherine Mayo.

NEVINSON, H. W.

"*The New Spirit in India.*" London. Harpers.

Although this book by one of England's ablest writers is now out of print, I give it a place here because it is to be found in many first class libraries, and because it is a work of extraordinary insight and charm as a portrayal of both external and internal India—the land, its places and objects of greatest interest, and the life, spirit and ideals of its people.

NOBLE, MARGARET E. ("SISTER NIVEDITA,").

"*The Web of Indian Life.*" London. Longmans.

Persons who would really understand Indian homes, Indian domestic life, Indian womanhood, and also the Hindu religion as it enters into the whole daily experience of the people, cannot do better than read this unique and interesting book. This gifted English-woman spent many years in India as a teacher, helper of the poor, and writer, entered into intimate and sympathetic relations with the people and won their affection to a degree perhaps unequalled by any other foreign woman.

PRATT, JAMES BISSELL

"*India and its Faiths,*" Boston. Houghton and Mifflin.

In the judgment of the present writer this book, by Professor Pratt of Williams College, is the most illuminating and on the whole the best work we possess, on the Religions of India, Past and Present. It is intelligent and comprehensive; critical, yet sympathetic; unafraid to recognize and reject the superstitious, the fanatical, and the morally evil, and at the same time keenly and warmly appreciative of the high, the pure and the good. With all the rest, it is charmingly written. Its interest is increased by the fact that it contains an excellent account of those two important religions and social reform movements, the Brahmo Samaj and the Arya Samaj, and a chapter on the Theosophists.

RAI, LAJPAT

"*Young India.*" New York. Huebsch (The Viking Press).

"*England's Debt to India.*" Same publishers.

"*The future of India.*" Same publishers.

"*Unhappy India.*" Calcutta. Banna Publishing Co.

Mr. Lajpat Rai is one of the most eminent living Indian publicists and national leaders. He spent five years, from 1914 to 1919, in America, during which he wrote the first three of these books, all of which throw great light upon the India of the past twenty years, and upon present conditions. The fourth book (written in 1928) is a thorough, complete, documented, crushing reply to Katherine Mayo's "Mother India."

RUTHERFORD, DR. V. H.

"*Modern India: Its Problems and Their Solution.*" London. Labor Publishing Co. 1927.

Dr. Rutherford, an eminent Labor Leader and Member of Parliament, went to India in 1926 to study conditions on the ground. The result was this clear and courageous exposure of tyrannies and shams, and unanswerable argument for self-determination.

SARKAR, B. K.

"*Hindu Achievements in Science.*" London. Longmans.

This book will greatly surprise many readers in the Western World by its revelations of the numerous important scientific discoveries made in India much earlier than in Europe.

SMITH, VINCENT A.

"*The Oxford History of India, from the Earliest Times to 1911*" (Second Edition, Cotinued to 1921, by S. M. Edwards). Oxford. Clarendon Press.

This is probably the best single-volume history of India (814 pages), written from the British standpoint. But it is not free from British bias.

SPENDER, J. A.

"*The Changing East.*" New York. Frederick A. Stokes Co. 1928. This eminent English publicist revisits the East, after fourteen years, and in this interesting book gives us his impressions of the marked changes that have taken place in Turkey, Egypt and India. His attitude toward India is that of a sincere well-wisher, and one who in a general way believes in self-determination for all peoples; and yet who can't quite bring himself to be willing to apply his belief, frankly to India. India must somehow be an exception! She is so valuable to Britain! He sees in the Indian people great qualities, and he wants them to be free, but, but -- under his beloved Britain: self-ruling, but—with the British Parliament over them, of course "for their good"! With this serious limitation, the book is one of our best on India.

TAGORE, RABINDRANATH

All persons who would know the real India should read Tagore.

His publishers are the Macmillan Company, London and New York. Since receiving the Nobel Prize for Literature, in 1913, he has been a world character. He is not only a poet, but also a publisher, a novelist and an educator, and has written extensively in all these directions, his published works including eleven volumes of Poetry, six volumes of Plays, five volumes of Essays, and five of Novels and Short Stories. Fortunately his fame is so great that the more important of his works may be found in nearly all libraries and in many book-stores. (Send to his publishers for full list). Several books have been written about him, among which may be mentioned "Rabindranath Tagore: a Biographical Study," by Earnest Rhys (Macmillan). "Santiniketan," his Bolpur School, by W. W. Pearson (Macmillan), and "Rabindranath Tagore: the "Man and His Poetry," by B. K. Roy (New York, Dodd and Mead).

WILLOUGHBY, W. W.

"*Opium as an International Problem, The Geneva Conferences.*"

Baltimore. Johns Hopkins Press. 1925.

In this large work, Professor Willoughby gives us a careful survey of the opium situation in the world and a full account of the imporant Opium Conferernces held in Geneva in 1923 and 1924.

INDEX

8 888000 584278